Faithful Renderings

Jewish–Christian Difference and the Politics of Translation

NAOMI SEIDMAN

The University of Chicago Press

CHICAGO AND LONDON

NAOMI SEIDMAN is the Koret Professor of Jewish Culture and director of the Richard S. Dinner Center for Jewish Studies at the Graduate Theological Union in Berkeley, California.

The University of Chicago Press, Chicago 60637
The University of Chicago Press, Ltd., London
© 2006 by The University of Chicago
All rights reserved. Published 2006
Printed in the United States of America

15 14 13 12 11 10 09 08 07 06   5 4 3 2 1

ISBN-13 (cloth): 978-0-226-74505-3
ISBN-13 (paper): 978-0-226-74506-0
ISBN-10 (cloth): 0-226-74505-8
ISBN-10 (paper): 0-226-74506-6

Library of Congress Cataloging-in-Publication Data

Seidman, Naomi.
    Faithful renderings : Jewish–Christian differences and the politics of translation / Naomi Seidman.
        p. cm. — (Afterlives of the Bible)
    Includes bibliographical references and index.
    ISBN-13: 978-0-226-74505-3 (cloth : alk. paper)
    ISBN-13: 978-0-226-74506-0 (pbk. : alk. paper)
    ISBN-10: 0-226-74505-8 (cloth : alk. paper)
    ISBN-10: 0-226-74506-6 (pbk. : alk. paper)
    1. Jews—Languages—Translating. 2. Hebrew language—Translating. 3. Bible. O.T.—Translating. 4. Bible. O.T. Greek—Versions. 5. Jewish literature—Translations—History and criticism. 6. Judaism—Relations—Christianity. 7. Christianity and other religions—Judaism. 8. Translating and interpreting—Political aspects. I. Title. II. Series.
PJ5067.S45 2006
418'02089924—dc22

2006010237

Contents

Acknowledgments

IN 1998, after an essay I had written on the Yiddish version of Elie Wiesel's *Night* (now part of chapter 5) received some attention, Pamela Ween Brumberg, of blessed memory, of the Lucius N. Littauer Foundation invited me to apply for a grant to expand the essay into a book. The grant, which the Littauer Foundation allowed me to use for babysitting, both sparked and funded the beginnings of this book. An American Council of Learned Societies sabbatical grant supported the work I did in 2001-2. A summer research grant from the Association of Theological Seminaries Lilly Theological Grants Program helped me to the finish line.

This book covers a multitude of fields and periods, into which I ventured with the encouragement of colleagues and friends at the Graduate Theological Union, the University of California, Berkeley, and beyond. Some of them read drafts; others supplied me with references, or lent me books, or talked me through impasses. I am amazed at their generosity—at their willingness to share my nearly decade-long obsession, if only to allow me the floor at a party for longer than was strictly mannerly. (If I have nevertheless made terrible mistakes, I know they will also be kind enough to take the blame.) Among those I remember (and I'm sure there were more) are Robert Alter, Tom Bates, Daniel Boyarin, Sergey Dolgoposky, Rena Fischer, Miki Gluzman, Peter Gordon, Marion Grau, Fred Greenspahn, Bluma Goldstein, Ron Hendel, Susannah Heschel (who invited me to present to the Dartmouth Feminist Theory Group), Arthur Holder, Josh Holo, Martin Jay, Ami Kronfeld (*z"l*), Richard Menkis, Margaret Miles, Chris Ocker, Ilana Pardes, Kim Novak, Lawrence Rosenwald, David Roskies, Marty Stortz, and Azzan Yadin. Doug

Robinson responded to an email inquiry with enough ideas and encouragement to last me for another project or two. Sarah Bailey, Devorah Schoenfeld, Jason Van Boom, and Lisa Webster provided me with exceptional research help. Paul Hamburg at the University of California Doe Library and Ann Hotta, Rachel Minkin, and Kris Vedheer at the GTU Library and Patricia Malmstrom at the Richard S. Dinner Center for Jewish Studies were the patron saints of this journey. At the University of Chicago Press, Alan Thomas, Claudia Rex, and Peter T. Daniels gave my manuscript extraordinary attention. Special thanks, for help and friendship both, to David Biale, Chana Kronfeld, and Dina Stein.

Aimie Jory-Hile watched my son so well that I could turn my attention elsewhere. My father-in-law, Ernest Schott, sent me books and references and, along with my mother-in-law Beatrice Schott, shared his love for Isaac Bashevis Singer with me. My mother, Sara Seidman, was my Yiddish expert and a guide throughout. Ezra Hillel Seidman-Schott, my son, who grew with this book and now loves reading as much as I do, kept me company in cafés as I was finishing it.

This book is dedicated with love and appreciation to my husband, John Schott, who makes the music in my life.

✳

The Translator as Double Agent

Probably [all] would agree that the 'translator's first duty is to be faithful'; but the question at issue is, in what faithfulness consists.
MATTHEW ARNOLD, *On Translating Homer*

It was found highly dangerous to employ the natives as interpreters, upon whose fidelity [the colonial administrators] could not depend.
WILLIAM JONES, *A Grammar of the Persian Language*

MY FATHER, Hillel Seidman, arrived in Paris shortly after Liberation along with a flood of East European Jewish refugees. Like many of these refugees, my father was a Yiddish-speaker; unlike most of them, he also spoke French (with a thick accent—my father joked that he spoke Yiddish in seven languages). Unusually, he had been raised in a Hasidic household wealthy enough to provide him with a French governess and enlightened enough to allow him to attend the Jozef Pilsudski University in Warsaw (now Warsaw University), where he had studied French history in the course of his Ph.D. work. For all these reasons, and because he had a background in communal service, my father was uniquely suited to take on the role of unofficial liaison between the French authorities and the Jewish refugee community in postwar Paris.

One morning, my father was called to the Gare de l'Est, where the police were holding a group of Jewish refugees who had managed to cross three or four borders without proper documents. The scene in the train station was chaotic, the refugees were upset and exhausted, and my father asked the police if he could speak with the group. "Yidn, hot nisht keyn moyre" (Jews, don't be afraid), he reassured them. While the French were certainly *goyim*, they weren't Nazis; nobody would be mistreated. My father explained to the group that he would keep track of where they were taken and the Jewish community of Paris would arrange for their release as soon as possible.

One of the police officers, curious about my father's rapid-fire Yiddish exchange with the crowd, asked him what he had said to calm them. Thinking fast, and thinking in French, my father "translated" his Yiddish words for the policemen: "I quoted to them the words of a great Frenchman: 'Every free man has two homelands—his own, and France.'[1] I assured them that they, who had suffered so much, had arrived at a safe haven, the birthplace of human liberty." As my father told it, the *gendarmes* wiped away patriotic tears at his speech.

I heard this story more than once from my father when I was growing up. For a child, the story reversed the usual exclusions of adult communication, allowing me to hear what others (policemen!) were kept from understanding. That thrill may alone explain the genesis of this book, which explores translation as a border zone, a transit station, in which what does not succeed in crossing the border is at least as interesting as what makes it across. This book situates translation between Jewish and non-Jewish languages (and particularly between Jews and Christians) not in the abstractions of linguistic theory but squarely in the contingent political situations in which translation and, inevitably, mistranslation arise. As banal as this insistence might seem, the historical and political dimensions of translation have often remained unacknowledged. In Western translation discourse, narrative—as history or as literature—has taken a secondary role to theory. There may be reasons for this that inhere in the conceptualization of translation in Western thought. Because translation is conceived as the production of a linguistic equivalent that will substitute for an "original" text, and because the dominant method for rendering such apparent equivalents has been the production of a fluent text that "reads like the original," the very figure of the translator, as a historical figure exercising creative agency, has been an encumbrance. As Lawrence Venuti argues in *The Translator's Invisibility*, the figure of the translator has been elided by the normative logic of translation.[2] And it is not only the translator who has been forgotten in Western translation. History, too, as the temporal horizon within which translations emerge and acquire their meaning, is collapsed and neutralized in a discourse that imagines translation as the "recovery" of an original meaning, or, in Eugene Nida's influential approach, as a technique that aims at restaging the effect of the source text on its first readers.[3] Translation, in these discourses, becomes the very erasure of time and difference from the scene of writing. Translation narrative, read not as transparent truth but rather as ideologically marked "emplotment," is the privileged means by which I will attempt to read the movement of history on the stage of Jewish–Christian translation; my father's story is the first of the narratives I will discuss.

Suspending for a moment the central question of whether the story can be described as a *translation* narrative, I would like to focus on my father's Yiddish words (in my English rendering) to the refugees. Ashkenazic Jewishness, Max Weinreich writes in his *History of the Yiddish Language,* "was not 'general' German life plus a number of specific supplementary traits, but a distinct sphere of life, a culture system."[4] The psychic separation of Jews from non-Jews expressed itself in many linguistic features, most manifestly in that category of vocabulary called *lehavdl loshn,* or "differentiation language": "There are words applied to Jews (or even neutrally, when no differentiation is intended), and these have a parallel series that has to begin with a derogatory connotation or one of disgust." Chief in this parallel series is the word *goy,* its derivations, and its semantic relatives—*shkotzim, shikses,* and so on. My father, then, in using the word *goyim,* was invoking the entire culture system Weinreich describes, one which sharply distinguishes between the realm that is "ours" and the realm that belongs to "them."

To his discussion of *lehavdl loshn,* Weinreich appends a remark of some relevance to my father's story:

> Since the rise of the secular sector the function of the differentiation language became even more variable, more dependent on the situation and the linguistic context. All in all, among very large segments of the community the entire category of differentiation language is now no longer in vogue, except for special purposes of stylization.[5]

A man capable of producing the French speech that followed was certainly also capable of drawing on a neutral vocabulary for referring to non-Jews— Weinreich mentions *nit-yidn* as one nonderogatory alternative; no doubt my father took advantage of these alternatives in other contexts. It is significant, then, that in speaking to the refugee group, he *chose* the traditional *lehavdl loshn* over a neutral secular code. Weinreich's suggestion that a secularized or modern Jew might have recourse to Yiddish's *lehavdl loshn* for purposes of stylization is not entirely illuminating here; nor does the story give us reason to suppose that my father particularly meant to denigrate the French policemen. Any disparagement implied by his language must have been secondary to his main purpose, which was to reassure the group of refugees that his intentions toward them were entirely friendly. If my father mobilized the differentiation resources of Yiddish, it was to signal to the group that he was a real Jew, one of "us" rather than a neutral player on the deracinated urban field. My father's words were thus a speech act, *doing* something with words rather than merely communicating information. Indeed, the performative quality of my father's Yiddish speech transcends his use of the word to which I have directed attention. Beyond the content of what he was saying, beyond the choice of the word *goyim*, and before the vocative *"Yidn,"* my father's Galicianer Yiddish was itself performing his Jewish affiliations, announcing where he came from and where his sympathies could be assumed to lie. Speaking Yiddish has been described as inhabiting a portable Yiddishland, and my father could be said to be clearing a shared Jewish space—indeed, given the dialectal variation among Yiddish-speakers, *constructing* a shared space—within the public arena of the European metropolis.[6] Yiddish, in such speech acts, has a metavalue, signifying in itself—in its distinctive sounds rather than in its communicable content. The implications of such an understanding of language are considerable: If the very use of Yiddish is a form of signification, translation becomes manifestly impossible.

The untranslatability of languages insofar as they are ethnic codes does not, however, entirely exhaust the meaning of the translation narrative I am presenting here. My father's Yiddish speech is not simply difficult or impossible to translate into other languages; he clearly didn't *want* to translate it, whether or not he could have. My father's translation performance, his refusal to translate, must be understood in the context of the scene at the train station: he spoke in the presence of the very embodiment of state authority (a state that, in the not too distant past, had collaborated in sending Jews to death camps), the French police. Against the "merely" semiotic differentiation enacted by Yiddish we must range the political power of the French state apparatus to differentiate between refugees and citizens, foreign aliens and new immigrants. It is within this power structure that my father's Yiddish remarks should be calibrated. From this point of view, his words comprise what James C. Scott calls a "hidden transcript," the secret communication of a subjugated group in contrast with the public transcript, that is, official history as the record of what can be said in the presence of power.[7] Sander Gilman has written of the view among Gentiles that Yiddish is the "hidden language" of the Jews, and Elisheva Carlebach documents the "attributions of secrecy" to Jews in Christendom.[8] Both of these studies demonstrate the extent to which these attributions are paranoid fantasies; it is my contention (and I don't think

Carlebach or Gilman would disagree) that Jews, like any other subjugated group, did in fact establish an intimate space in which the dominant culture could be discussed and strategies for survival developed. Scott argues that

> slaves, serfs, untouchables, the colonized and the subjugated ordinarily dare not contest the terms of their subordination openly. Behind the scenes, though, they are likely to create and defend a social space in which offstage dissent to the official transcript of power relations may be voiced.[9]

In the case we are studying here, my father's words to his fellow refugees are delivered not "behind the scenes" but rather in the very earshot of the authorities. As in other examples Scott cites, the hidden Jewish transcript here involves a direct, nonobsequious evaluation of the power structure on which the survival of the subjugated group depends. It is in the very nature of such communication that it not enter the public arena—French, in this case. Although Weinreich never states this explicitly, *lehavdl loshn* could be construed as necessarily such a hidden transcript, available to the Yiddish-speaking community if only for letting off steam, but never to be uttered before non-Jews who might understand it. The presence of Hebrew elements in *lehavdl loshn—beys hatifle* for church, *oysoy ha'ish* for Jesus—is further evidence that the language of differentiation was intended to be concealed; the major linguistic component of Yiddish, German, was more open to Gentile decoding. Mistranslation, then, is the crucial device that allows this transcript to remain hidden. My father's signaling of his Jewish affiliation in the Yiddish words, and his open evaluation of the dangers to the refugee group posed by their arrest by the French police, can hardly be separated from his refusal to render this speech transparent in translating it into French.

In speaking French to the police, my father was also performing, signaling a different set of affiliations: he was a foreigner, that much could hardly be denied, but an educated foreigner, whose knowledge of French extended to French history and who respected the ideals on which modern French society was based. This performance, unlike the Yiddish, built a bridge across ethnic lines, both in my father's very use of a language that was not his and in the words he spoke in it, which subtly recommended compassionate behavior by the police by flatteringly reminding them of French Enlightenment rhetoric. It is tempting to read my father's French remarks as a mere cover for the authentic speech he addressed to his fellow Jews, but I think that would negate the insight that his Yiddish remarks were *also* strategically chosen, and for the same ultimate ends as the French speech—to enable a calm encounter between frightened Jewish refugees and the French state. Moreover, my father's French was as unintelligible to the Yiddish-speakers he addressed as his Yiddish was to the French-speakers. It may also have been untranslatable into Yiddish. The words my father chose to express the role of France in bringing democracy to the world were precisely those that would have the least resonance in the experience of Yiddish-speakers: What could the sentence "Every free man has two homelands—his own, and France" possibly mean to someone who lacked even a single homeland? (The relevance of this "universal" discourse to other stateless people, and to women, is, of course, also an issue.)

The gap my father exposed as he concealed between Yiddish and French, and between French and Yiddish, is not one ordinary translation gap among others. What is inexpressible or irrelevant in Yiddish is the very philosophical and political grounds for translation itself. As Tejaswini Niranjana writes, "Translation has traditionally been viewed by literary critics in the West (at least since the Renaissance) as the noble task of bridging the gap between peoples, as the quintessential humanistic enterprise."[10] Aleida Assmann similarly views the modern impulse toward translation as emerging from the eighteenth-century "enlightened philosophers who invented universalistic concepts like 'natural law,' 'common notions,' 'lumen naturale,' or 'reason.'"[11] In suggesting by his translation performance that this universalist discourse was, in fact, properly French, my father implicitly exposed a chasm at the very heart of the enterprise of translation. Jewish experience serves here as the limiting case for the dream of the mutual transparency of cultures in the light of humanism and reason. Indeed, Jewish languages have historically played that role: Austria's 1781 Edict of Tolerance reversed the Jewish Regulations (*Judenordnungen*) and granted Jews "completely free choice of all non-civic branches of commerce . . . and wholesale trade" on the condition that they refrain from using Hebrew or Yiddish in the commercial sphere. Article 15 proclaims:

> Considering the numerous openings in trades and manifold contacts with Christians resulting therefrom, the care for maintaining common confidence requires that the Hebrew and the so called Jewish writing of Hebrew intermixed with German . . . shall be abolished.[12]

Toleration to Jews might be granted, but their languages could not be welcomed into the family of European languages as equals—or, to put it into translation terms, as "linguistic equivalents."

I have spoken of the Yiddish and French speech as two varieties of linguistic performance, but there is, of course, a third level of linguistic performativity implicit in this story, that of its retelling as a translation narrative in which both languages are rendered visible—either in the Yiddish version, as my father initially related the story to his family, or in its later (partially) English version, as I am rendering it here. These rewritings, or retranslations, belong to a number of genres: they serve as autobiographical allegory, stories that represent identity as split, multiple, or shifting. They are also trickster tales, boasting of the successful manipulation of a power with more official authority and fewer linguistic gifts (or at least a deficit in knowledge of Yiddish) at its disposal. My father's story is not only the tale of a trickster; it also draws the listener in on the joke, allowing her to share the narrator's privileged position above the unfortunate dupes who lacked Yiddish in the story. As a boast, we may fairly be skeptical of its faithfulness—did my father really call the French policemen *goyim*? Did he use the word Nazis, which they might have been able to pick out of the rush of Yiddish words? The medieval Jewish–Christian disputations in Paris, we might recall, produced two separate linguistic records, in Latin and in Hebrew, each declaring victory for its own side.[13] The Hebrew account in particular is full of devastatingly witty Jewish ripostes to the Christian disputants that would no doubt have brought grief to any disputant who had actually dared utter them.[14] In the safety of one's own language, and over one's own dining room table, history itself is translated as it is rewritten.

In focusing on translation performances that demonstrate the asymmetrical relations between cultures rather than essentially symmetrical relations between languages, I am indebted to the work of postcolonial translation studies. This subfield is often said to begin with the groundbreaking publication of Tejaswini Niranjana's *Siting Translation: History, Post-Structuralism and the Colonial Context* (1992). Exploring the Indian translational arena, Niranjana argues that translation cannot be understood outside of the trajectories of capitalism, Christian missionary movements, and European imperialism: a close reading of colonialist texts encourages us to recognize that translation "comes into being overdetermined by religious, racial, sexual, and economic discourses."[15] In particular, Niranjana is interested in "the question of the historical complicity in the growth and expansion of European colonialism in the nineteenth and twentieth centuries of those interested in translating non-Western texts (for example, missionaries engaged in spreading Christianity) and those involved in the study of 'man.'"[16] That such colonialist discourses are also operative in the heart of Europe, and long before the nineteenth century, is evident from a footnote in Niranjana's text, in which she warns us that "We must not forget . . . that the concept of the humanistic enterprise is enabled by the repression of heterogeneity *within* the 'West.' Imperialism allows the West to conceive of the other as *outside* it, to constitute itself as a unified subject."[17] If Niranjana is right about the utility of the repression of heterogeneity within the West precisely to the humanistic enterprise of translation, then Jews become paradoxically central to Western translation in and through the suppression of their difference. Jews are refigured in this conception not only as untranslatable figures—we might say, unconvertible to Christianity—but also as the very site of untranslatability.

Post-colonial scholarship has also provided the sharpest model for the trickster narrative I am viewing as (partially) emblematic of Jewish translation. Vicente L. Rafael demonstrates the transfiguration to which translation falls prey in the colonial encounter, in which the colonizers' texts may find themselves reproduced in a warped mirror. Exploring the ways in which Christianity was dependent, in the Philippines, on native vernaculars for its transmission, Rafael argues that "translation tended to cast intentions adrift, now laying, now subverting the ideological grounds of colonial hegemony."[18] In such a linguistic situation, submission and resistance were often impossible to distinguish.

Framing Jews as colonial subjects within Christendom only partly explains the position of Jews in Western translation. Jews are the target of Christian missionary hopes, but they are also the source of Christian genealogical anxieties—the reliance of Christianity on the texts, and indeed on the translations, of a rival religious group. The translational relationship that connects and separates Judaism and Christianity is a particularly rich and dense intersection: the asymmetries of Christian political power over Jews are complicated if not ameliorated by the Jewish possession of cultural capital in the form of Hebrew and Jewish-exegetical knowledge as well as symbolic capital in the shared Jewish-Christian belief that Judaism is the "original" of which Christianity is a "translation." Such a belief is not indisputable—Daniel Boyarin has been particularly deft as its deconstruction—but its ubiquity nonetheless has concrete political effects.[19] Moreover, the story of Jewish-Christian translation includes episodes (for instance, the composition of the Septuagint) that long predate the Christianization of Empire, indeed, that predate Christianity. Thus, a model of Jewish translation that focuses exclusively on the Jews as a dominated group or on Judaism as Christianity's other excludes a variety of other formations, including, in the case of Hellenistic Alexandria, a Jewish approach to translation that bears a distinct resemblance to the model of universal translatability of which Niranjana is so skeptical. In developing an approach to Jewish translation, or to translation in general, it is necessary to lay out the particular material, cultural, and discursive conditions of translation that Niranjana rightfully insists on and allow them to determine the shape of the story, whether as a narrative of negotiating power imbalances or as a dream of bridging human differences—or, as in the case of my father's story, as both at the same time. Such an approach would insist that translation stories are not merely epiphenomena to the true stuff of translation, the relationship between source and target texts, methods of achieving equivalence, obstacles to achieving equivalence, and so on. The narrative approach to translation would insist rather that translation cannot be separated from the material, political, cultural, or historical circumstances of its production, that it in fact represents an unfolding of those conditions.

Translation more particularly appears as a negotiation of an unavoidably asymmetrical *double*-situatedness. As such, it both complicates and is informed by issues of identity. Because translation is necessarily also a political negotiation, it appears not strictly as a linguistic exercise but also in a variety of relational modes: translation as colonialist, imperialist, or missionary appropriation but also translation as risk, as assimilation, as treason, as dislocation, as survival. Jewish translation history not only is a record of losses to the dominant language, it also includes moments in which translation is a coveted prize or a triumph over rivals. Nor is it always possible to separate gains from losses: The joke about the Yiddish theater troupe that presented "Hamlet, fartaytsht un farbesert" (Hamlet, translated and improved) rests precisely on an understanding of languages as unequal in status: on the one hand, the exalted language of Shakespeare; on the other, the *zhargon* of the unwashed Jewish masses. For Yiddish to presume to "improve" on "the greatest work in the English language" is laughable indeed. Nevertheless, such presumption apparently operates among even the most fallen of Jews, if only in the retelling of the joke, and translation is the privileged conduit for such acquisition of cultural capital. Whether we mobilize the rhetoric of colonialization and appropriation or that of chutzpah and upward mobility, it is clear that there are no absolutely neutral borders between languages, and certainly not between Jewish and non-Jewish languages. Traversing these borders, then, must involve the translator and the translated culture in the vicissitudes of history itself. Jewish translation is the history of Jewish bordercrossings, from the island of Pharos in Ptolemaic Alexandria (if not earlier) to the passportless refugees in post-Liberation Paris.

From this perspective, the Yiddish–French translation comes into focus as a translation when it is viewed not as a series of linguistic transfers but rather as a map of a particular set of intellectual influences (in this case, my father's Hasidic upbringing and his doctoral studies in French history), and as a strategy for a particular series of border crossings (from postwar Eastern or Central Europe, through Paris, to the United States). In this reading, what my father said in Yiddish and what he said in French are equally true, equally faithful to who he was, and equally illuminating of a journey he took, first in post-Liberation Paris and then again, in his subsequent retellings—"emplotments"—of this story and indeed in my own.

Translation narratives are thus temporal narratives, drawing our attention to the fact that translations unfold within time, paralleling and part of our mortal lives. In an otherwise famously difficult essay on translation, Walter Benjamin makes this much absolutely clear: Translations emerge from the life of an original text, or rather "from its 'afterlife'" (aus seinem "Überleben").[20] Benjamin writes: "In its afterlife—which could not be called that if it were not a transformation and a renewal of something living—the original undergoes a change."[21] The original changes not because of any necessary loss or deliberate concealment, but rather because it participates in the movement that is the necessary correlative of a text being alive. If we call this movement, in the case of Jews and their texts, diaspora, and resist as Benjamin does the rhetoric of loss, then Jewish culture, as other cultures, emerges as a continual translation and transformation, in different languages and at different moments in time.

The notion of translation as transformation steers clear of the assumption that translation must proceed through a strict equivalence, a fidelity to original sources, if it is not to risk their absolute betrayal; transformation assumes rather that translation, as André Lefevere argues, is one mode of "rewriting."[22] Jewish literature is everywhere a phenomenon of this sort of self-translation. And once one realizes that translation unsettles the distinction between Jewish and non-Jewish languages, such a process of self-transformation overflows the borders of Jewish life itself. Christianity is the name of one such overflow.

I have postponed asking the question of whether my father's story can be taken as exemplary of certain principles of Jewish translation—indeed, whether it counts as a translation narrative at all. Weinreich helps make the case that Yiddish discourse is centrally constituted by its capacities for differentiation—that is, by what might be seen as its untranslatablity. Such differentiation language, Weinreich implies, also characterizes Talmudic Aramaic, from which the Yiddish usage of *goy* derives (the biblical word means simply "nation" and applies to Israel as to her neighbors). In *The Periodic Table*, Primo

Levi describes a similar code for discussing the realm of Christianity in his own Jewish dialect of Italian. As Levi writes,

> In this case, the originally Hebraic form is corrupted much more profoundly [than in the case of codes used in commercial settings], and this for two reasons: in the first place, secrecy was rigorously necessary here because their comprehension by Gentiles could have entailed the danger of being charged with sacrilege; in the second place, the distortion in this case acquires the precise aim of denying, obliterating the sacral content of the word, and thus divesting it of all supernatural value. . . . *A-issá* is the Madonna (simply, that is, "the woman"). Completely cryptic and indecipherable—and that has to be foreseen—is the term *Odo*, with which, when it was absolutely unavoidable, one alluded to Christ, lowering one's voice and looking around with circumspection; it is best to speak of Christ as little as possible because the myth of the God-killing people dies hard.[23]

Such private languages or the attitudes they embody are not, of course, unique to Judaism. In a striking translation performance, Weinreich uses Tertullian's injunction that "Christians may live together with non-Christians, but it is not allowed to die together with them," precisely to illustrate Jewish cultural separatism.[24] The resistance to translation may in fact be a widespread phenomenon, an unavoidable byproduct of cultural identity in its differentiating mode. George Steiner suggests as much in *After Babel*, denying the commonsense notion that the function of language is primarily to communicate. Arguing that "mature speech begins in shared secrecy," Steiner hypothesizes the following narrative for the genesis of language:

> In the beginning the word was largely a pass-word, granting admission to a nucleus of like speakers. 'Linguistic exogamy' comes later, under compulsion of hostile or collaborative contact with other small groups. We speak first to ourselves, then to those nearest us in kinship and locale. We turn only gradually to the outsider.[25]

Whatever one makes of this as a history of the development of language, Steiner provides a useful corrective to the assumptions that cultures inevitably aspire to be translated and that translators aim to be accurate. Such an aim, universalist in its trajectory, is itself far from universal. It does, however, exist within Jewish culture, just as there are many instances of non-Jewish resistance to translation. The Jewish-Hellenistic philosopher Philo, for instance, writes of his satisfaction that the Septuagint had provided access to the Torah in the Greek tongue, so that "those admirable, and incomparable, and most desirable laws were made known to all people." Philo goes on to hope that if the reputation of the Jews continues to grow, "Every nation, abandoning all their own individual customs, and utterly disregarding their national laws, would change and come over to the honour of such a people only."[26] And although I have suggested that my father's Enlightenment speech was paradoxically untranslatable into Yiddish, I am reminded that he did translate it for the benefit, although perhaps not for the enlightenment, of his family. Evidence that Yiddish is perfectly capable of rendering a universalist, if not universal, message is very nearly coextensive with the history of modern Yiddish literature.

Nevertheless, I would argue that this story I have been studying stands well within the mainstream of Jewish translation discourse, even if does not pinpoint its essential nature. If rabbinic literature has a foundational narrative of Jewish translation, it would have to be the talmudic account—itself a reworking of earlier Hellenistic and patristic accounts—of the translation under Ptolemy of the Bible into Greek, an event perceived as world-altering both within and outside the Jewish community: while Philo as well as the Church Fathers had viewed this event as the providential beginning of God's communication with all of humankind, at least some rabbis considered the Septuagint both a lie and a sin, the substitution of an empty fetish for God's true word: "It happened that five elders wrote the Pentateuch in Greek for King Ptolemy, and that day was as hard for Israel as the day the [Golden] calf was made, because the Pentateuch could not be translated properly" (*Masekhet Soferim* 1:7).[27]

The rabbinic narratives of the translation itself, which appear in *Megilla* 9a and elsewhere, imagine the translation as having been forced upon an unwilling group of (most frequently seventy-two) Jewish elders who, although separated into individual cells, miraculously produce the same strategic mistranslations. (My father would joke that the real miracle would have been if seventy-two rabbis sitting in the *same* room had produced a single version.) God himself is invested in, indeed is a full participant in, the privacy of Jewish discourse, at least at a dozen or so strategic translation cruxes in the Hebrew Bible. The world, with Ptolemy's guidance, may have the Bible, but it does not have the Torah, and for Jews that has made all the difference.

The notion that not only the integrity of Jewish culture but also Jewish political survival somehow depends on strategic mistranslation continues to our own day. In the 1998 film *Life Is Beautiful,* Guido, the Italian-Jewish protagonist, mistranslates a concentration camp guard's German orders for the sake of his young son, who is hiding among the inmates; in the case of *Life Is Beautiful,* the mistranslation prevents a dehumanizing discourse from entering a Jewish realm rather than safeguarding Jewish secrets. In these three narratives—my father's, the Talmud's, and the scenario played out in *Life*

Is Beautiful—secrecy, linguistic opacity, double-talk, and mistranslation are linked with the integrity of the borders of the Jewish community in the face of external threat. As Matthew Arnold suggests in the epigraph to this chapter, faithful translation comes in more than one variety: Fidelity, in the sort of translation conducted under the watchful eye but uncomprehending ear of an Egyptian king, an SS guard, or even a benign *gendarme*, means faithfulness to one's embattled community rather than to any abstract ideal of linguistic equivalence.

My father's story also serves to introduce an additional area of inquiry of this book, that of the role of translation in Holocaust memory. For survivors like my father, the Holocaust initiated a series of linguistic as well as geographic displacements. (We might recall that a primary meaning of translation in the medieval period was movement, as in the translation of a bishop to a new see or relics to another reliquary.) Among the victims of Nazi genocide was the Yiddish culture of Eastern Europe—more specifically, the language of Ashkenazic Jewish intimacy as well as "secrecy." The loss of a large Yiddish-speaking community, through migration and acculturation as well as murder, necessitated the translation of Yiddish Holocaust testimony; the fact that this testimony found a large non-Jewish audience complicated the translation work. The literature of the Holocaust, I argue in chapter 5 of this book, is the first significant body of texts in Jewish languages since the Bible to "cross over" into non-Jewish territory and to do so through charged Jewish-Christian territory (the French Catholic writer François Mauriac found Elie Wiesel his first French publisher). Like the Bible, moreover, Holocaust discourse has acquired a penumbra of the sacred—that is, it is regarded as neither translated nor translatable; "the Holocaust" thus remains invisible as a product of translation (the term itself translates and recasts in a universal and theological register the Yiddish *der Khurbm* [sometimes written *ḥurban*], the destruction). Tracing the course of "the Holocaust" as a translation project can shed light on the boundaries between what Jews will say among themselves and what they will say in earshot, as it were, of non-Jews. Translation is the moment when Jewish culture reveals—as it conceals—its hand.

WHAT IS JEWISH TRANSLATION?

"For Europe," begins the opening essay in a recent collection entitled *Translating Religious Texts*, "the Bible has always been a translated book."[28] That Moses and Jesus did not speak King James's English is something the author of this essay assumes readers frequently need reminding. The author himself should be reminded that this is less true of Jewish readers, whether they read the Bible in Hebrew or another language. It has indeed been suggested, by those whose perspective on Europe is not limited to Christendom, that Jews have a uniquely strong connection to the original language of their sacred text and, concomitantly, an aversion to its translation. Solomon Grayzel, historian and editor-in-chief of the Jewish Publication Society, writes: "For us Jews, the sacred text is the Hebrew. No translation can replace it. If we do not try to study and read the Hebrew, we sin against our past and our future, against Israel and God."[29] Even the illustrious German-Jewish philosopher and Bible translator Franz Rosenzweig, who elsewhere defended translation, insists on the importance of Hebrew for Jewish readings of Scriptures: "The German, also the German in the Jew, can and will read the Bible in German—in Luther's, in Herder's or Mendelssohn's versions; the Jew can understand it only in Hebrew."[30]

There are signs, as well, that general studies of translation have begun to recognize the existence and distinctiveness of Jewish approaches to translation. The *Routledge Encyclopedia of Translation Studies* (1998) is the first anthology I know to acknowledge a Jewish alternative to the mainstream approach to translation in the West, including an entry for both Bible translation and Torah translation. Eugene Nida, the premier linguist and translation consultant of both the American and United Bible Societies, boldly begins his entry with the sentence "The Bible is the holy book of Christianity" and continues by celebrating Bible translating as "arguably the greatest undertaking in interlingual communication in the history of the world."[31] By contrast, Michael Alpert's entry for Torah translation suggests that translation among Jewish communities historically had a different function than in non-Jewish communities: "Generally speaking, translations of the Torah have traditionally been read not as texts in their own right but rather as aids to comprehension. . . . Jewish scriptural study is informed less by translation than by the running commentaries of the mediaeval scholars."[32]

Nevertheless, Jews could not and did not avoid translation; nor did they always see it as merely adjunct to the Hebrew text. Alpert himself writes that "the first historical report of translation is in the Bible itself," in the phrase in Nehemiah 8:8 that says that the Jewish exiles who returned from Babylon in the sixth century BCE "read from the book of the law of God clearly, made its sense plain and gave instruction in what was read" (NEB); he continues by citing the midrashic reading of this verse, "That is to say, they read the Torah with translation and commentary."[33] Whether or not we date Jewish translation as early as Alpert and the midrash do, Frederick Greenspahn points out that Jewish biblical translation certainly began even before the Bible had been completed and canonized—the Greek Septuagint, the first extant Bible translation (originally only of the Pentateuch), is dated to the third century BCE. In communities that had largely or entirely lost the ability to comprehend the Hebrew, for example Hellenistic Alexandria, Enlightenment Germany, or contemporary America, translation presumably functioned much as it does for Christians—as a replacement for the original Hebrew text and, at least for Alexandrian Jews, apparently as a sacred text in its own right. Even in Jewish communities in which Hebrew was retained by the intellectual elite, vernacular translations were produced, sometimes directed to women or children. Nor can such translations always be explained by their obvious utility—witness the copies of the Septuagint found among other biblical manuscripts at Qumran, where Greek was not the vernacular, or Martin Buber's completion of the Buber-Rosenzweig Bible translation in 1961, after its potential German-Jewish readership had been decimated.

Jews sometimes translated the Bible, Greenspahn reminds us, not to help their readers understand the Hebrew, but rather to help them learn the language into which it had been translated. Thus, Moses Mendelssohn explained his own German Bible as "the first step towards culture, from which my nation, class, is being kept in such a great distance."[34] The culture toward which Mendelssohn was striding was of course German culture—not Hebrew. Max Margolis similarly wrote that "We Jews of America—and of England—must study the Bible in English, read and reread it, that we may possess ourselves of an English style that may pass scrutiny on the part of those who know."[35] In this regard, there is some overlap between the colonial project of "civilizing" indigenous peoples through the English Bible and the various translation projects by which acculturating Jewish communities, in this sense the West's internal colonial subjects, worked on "self-improvement" by reading the Bible in translation.[36] In the case of Jewish readers of the Bible in English translation, the transformation of Hebrew into a proper English style served both as an educational tool and as a model of the transformation they were expected to undergo in their Americanization.

Not only have Jews often welcomed translation, translation has sometimes been seen as particularly characteristic of Jewish culture; this is not surprising, given the dispersion and mobility of Jews and their status as what Yuri Slezkine has recently called "service nomads" or "Mercurians."[37] In twelfth- and thirteenth-century Toledo, Jews and converts from Judaism played the key role of scholar-translators of Greek thought into Latin (often via Arabic and Hebrew translations), thus helping to revive and disseminate classical thought throughout medieval Europe.[38] Writing of the much different context of the Second World War, Primo Levi describes the linguistic facility of European Jews, himself included, as having contributed to their survival. Mobilizing the power of Jewish multilingualism, and transforming the antisemitic trope of Jews as mimics incapable of original production into a badge of honor, Levi's partisans in *If Not Now, When?* disrupt Nazi communication lines and mistranslate Nazi warning signs into partisan recruitment posters. In one memorable scene, a partisan entertains his comrades with a bilingual rendition of Hitler's speaking style:

> First he spoke in German with mounting anger: his speech was improvised, the tone counted more than the content, but they all laughed when they heard him address the German soldiers, urging them to fight to the last man and calling them, in turn, heroes of the Great Reich, bastards, flying hunters, defenders of our blood and land, and assholes. By degrees, his fury became more searing, until it choked his words in a canine snarl, broken by fits of convulsive coughing. All of a sudden, as if an abscess had burst, he dropped German and went on in Yiddish, and they were all writhing with laughter: it was extraordinary to hear Hitler, in the full flood of his delirium, speaking the pariah's language to urge somebody to slaughter somebody else, and it wasn't clear whether the Germans should slaughter the Jews or vice versa.[39]

As Sander Gilman comments on this passage, "The Jew is but the German disguised; the evil within the system, the shape shifter, the boundary crosser who, by his very nature, is the Other."[40] In other words, the Jew—almost by definition—is Europe's translator.

The status of the Jew as Europe's exemplary translator, however, does not correlate with the translatability of Jewish discourse. Slezkine describes the languages of "service nomads" (Jews but also Romani in Europe, as well as Chinese in Southeast Asia, Indians in West Africa, Lebanese in Latin America) as designed to protect the boundaries of the community:

> Their raison d'être is the maintenance of difference, the conscious preservation of the self and thus of strangeness. They are special secret languages in the service of Mercury's precarious artistry. For example, the argot of German Jewish cattle traders (like that of the rabbis) contained a much higher proportion of Hebrew words than the speech of their kinsmen whose communication needs were less esoteric. With considerable insight as well as irony, they called it Loshen-Koudesh, or "sacred language"/"cow language," and used it, as a kind of Yiddish in miniature, across large territories. . . . But mostly it was religion, which is to say "culture," which is to say service nomadism writ large, that made Mercurian languages special.[41]

Given this brief survey, can we speak of a Jewish approach to translation? Do Jews resist translation or are they exemplary translators? What might make a translation Jewish? Are Jewish translations simply those that are directed toward Jewish audiences, or which rely on Jewish sources, or which reflect Jewish exegesis? Alpert's article represents one among a growing number of critical essays that have argued that Jewish approaches to translation represent a radical alternative to those of the Christian West not only in audience or exegetical content but also in the assumptions about language, textuality, and religious truth encapsulated in these approaches. Edward Greenstein, for instance, claims that Jewish approaches to translation have been underwritten by a culture that insists on bringing readers to the sources rather than vice versa. For Greenstein, "Audience-oriented translation conforms to the evangelical thrust of Christianity as opposed to the covenant-centeredness of Judaism." Thus, while Christian translation reaches out to the world, "Jewish Bible translation ought to lead the audience to the Hebrew source."[42] Writing elsewhere, Greenstein contrasts "Hebrew-literal" translators of the Bible with those who value an idiomatic and fluent translational style, arguing that "it might not be too drastic a simplification to label the Hebrew-literal style of translation Jewish in contrast to the idiomatic, evangelical, Christian mode."[43] Such a Jewish approach to translation is distinctive as well in its underlying conceptualization of how language means. Greenstein thus links "the Hebrew-literal style" with the exegetical importance given in the Jewish tradition to the Bible's "configurations of Hebrew phrases, words, even letters."[44] Mainstream translation theory in the West rests on the separability of word and meaning, signifier and signified, enabling meaning to be transferred "whole" from one linguistic vessel to another. By contrast, midrashic hermeneutics views the signifier not as an empty container for meaning but as itself meaningful, a view that Greenstein sees as having produced not only a resistance to translation, but also a distinctive mode of translation; "The translations that were produced—and the Greek one by the proselyte Aquila in particular—endeavored to transfer word for word, particle for particle, each meaningful component of the original."[45]

Derrida makes a similar claim in a late lecture on the translation of *The Merchant of Venice*, linking Shylock's forced conversion and "the incalculable equivalence [of] the pound of flesh and money" with the traditional figuring of the Jew as

on the side of the body and the letter (from bodily circumcision or Pharisaism, from ritual compliance to literal exteriority), whereas after St. Paul the Christian is on the side of the spirit or sense, of spiritual circumcision. The relation of the letter to the spirit, of the body of literalness to the ideal interiority of sense is also the site of the passage of translation, of this conversion that is called translation.[46]

For Greenstein and Derrida, Jewish source-orientation or literalism contrasts with Christian evangelism; Christian translation embodies an attachment to the "spirit" rather than the Jewish "body" of the text; for Derrida, in addition, conversion from Judaism to Christianity recapitulates the translational passage from embodied to spiritual meaning. The history of translation and translation theory in the West, these studies imply, are intricately connected with the dialectical relationship between Judaism and Christianity.

A contrast between Jewish and Christian translation is much harder to draw, however, if one takes Sa'adia Gaon, or Maimonides and the Tibbonids, as exemplary of Jewish translation. Sa'adia's tenth-century Arabic Bible translation is a remarkably free version, even paraphrasing the text at times. A similarly sense-for-sense approach is defended quite straightforwardly in Maimonides' well-known epistle to Rabbi Samuel ibn Tibbon, translator of his *Guide for the Perplexed*, in which he lays out his philosophy of translation:

> Whoever wishes to translate [*leha'atiq melashon lelashon*], and tries to translate one word with another, and at the same time will keep to the order of words and sayings—will work very hard, and his rendering will be very doubtful and distorted [*mesuppeqet umeshubbeshet*]. . . . This is not the right way to do it; instead the translator should first try to grasp the subject, and then state the theme as he understood it in the other language. And this cannot be done without changing the order, putting a few words in place of one word, or one word instead of many words, adding or taking away words, so that the subject is arranged and understandable in the language in which he is writing.[47]

The Christian semiotics underlying the preference for sense-for-sense translation, which distinguishes between the corporeal word and spiritual meaning, can be heard even more clearly in the medieval exegete Abraham ibn Ezra:

> Words are like bodies and meanings are like souls, and the body is like a vessel for the soul. Accordingly, as a rule all scholars of any language will attend to the meanings and won't concern themselves with the differences between words when they are equivalent in meaning.[48]

It is surely significant that Sa'adia, Maimonides, and ibn Ezra are writing from within a Muslim context, while most of the other examples of Jewish translation mentioned so far arise within a Christian environment. Jewish translation, like so many other cultural formations, takes its shape within particular cultural settings, in conversation with others—indeed, it is an exemplary expression as well as the privileged conduit of these conversations.

If resistance to translation or translational literalism (the two, perhaps surprisingly, seem to be related phenomena) is characteristic of some Jewish cultural contexts, then how and why did such an approach arise? Should we read such resistance politically—the response of a minority community to a dominant culture?—or theologically—the expression of a philosophical tradition with distinct notions of language?

In an article entitled "Translating Gods: Religion as a Factor of Cultural Translatability," the Egyptologist Jan Assmann makes a powerful case that biblical Israel arose within an international Near Eastern culture in which it was commonly held that nationally specific gods were essentially identical to their foreign counterparts in function, rank, and so on. This general belief in the mutual translatability of local deities mirrored and enabled the "integrated networks of commercial, political and cultural communication" that characterized the milieu within which ancient Israel was to emerge.[49] By contrast with a more general international culture that promoted translation precisely through religion, religions of a new type arose; although Assmann takes Hellenistic Egypt as his own illustration, he considers "the Jewish paradigm the most ancient and the most typical" of these religions, and perhaps their model or origin as well. In minority conditions "where a hegemonic culture dominates and threatens to swallow up a culturally and ethnically distinct group," religious groups develop an "immune reaction" against the dominating system. "These religions," Assmann writes, "defy translatability. They are entered via conversion and left via apostasy."[50] Conversion is the mark of a religion that excludes translation, which insists on its incompatibility with, indeed superiority to other belief systems. Thus, while some gods easily transcend their local designations so that their adherents consider them to be known by different names in different regions, the Jewish God is not of that type. He appears on no international god-lists, recognizes no Greek or Egyptian relatives, is unknown outside the Jewish people:

> He does not say "I am everything" but "I am who I am," negating by this expression every referent, every *tertium comparationis*, and every translatability. He is not only above but displaces all the other gods. Here, the cosmotheistic link between god and the work, and god and gods, is categorically broken. . . . Varro (116–27 BCE), who knew about the Jews from Poseidonios, was unwilling to make any difference between Jove and Jahve. . . . But the Jews and the Christians insisted on the very name. For them, the name mattered. To translate Adonai into Zeus would have meant apostasy.[51]

Assmann pinpoints religion, in particular the conceptualization of the divinity and the construction of the religious rules by which entry and exit from the community are regulated, as providing the primary means by which groups either resist assimilation by a dominant culture or participate in transnational commerce and culture. Thus, the phenomena of conversion and apostasy are signifiers of Jewish resistance to translation, while the naming of God in Exodus 3:14 is evidence that the Jewish god is a tautological and thus untranslatable deity.

There is considerable evidence, however, that whatever Exodus 3:14 might "originally" mean—and this is far from clear—it was taken as the naming of precisely the cosmotheistic deity Assmann views as the eminently translatable God. Even Assmann, in a footnote to his discussion of the Jewish God, cites a quotation of Exodus in the Sybilline Oracles that interprets it cosmotheistically as "I am the Being One (*eimi d'ego-ge ho ōn*), recognize this in your mind: I put on the heaven as garment, I wrapped myself by the sea, the earth is the foundation of my feet, the air is around me as body and the stars encircle me."[52] Similarly, the *Letter of Aristeas,* generally believed to be of Jewish authorship, forthrightly declares (admittedly in the words of the Egyptian courtier Aristeas) that the Jewish God, "the overseer and creator of all things, whom [the Jews] worship, is He whom all men worship, and we too, Your Majesty, though we address Him differently, as Zeus and Dis."[53] As we shall see in chapter 4, Luther also claimed a universal translatability for the biblical God, resting his argument precisely on the verse in Exodus from which Assmann extrapolates divine untranslatability.

To further complicate any reading of the Bible as a manifesto of cultural untranslatability, there is very little evidence in biblical texts that the differentiation of Israel from the nations was ever conceptualized in terms of language. It is remarkable that, for all the importance of Hebrew in later Jewish consciousness, when it had ceased functioning as a vernacular, the Bible never thinks to name the language God spoke at creation, or the one in which the Pentateuch is inscribed, or the "one tongue" spoken before Babel. The Bible lacks not only a notion of a Holy Tongue, but even any sense of the special status of the Hebrew language. In 2 Kings 18:26, Hebrew (called *Yehudit,* or "Judean") is the language of the commoners "sitting on the wall," as opposed to the official Aramaic of the Assyrian empire, which the Judeans do not widely understand; as interesting as the episode is for thinking about imperial and local languages, insider and outsider speech, nothing in 2 Kings suggests the religious importance of the language of the Jews. The Hebrew Bible, in its various constructions of the difference between

Israel and its neighbors, may well have set the stage for Jewish approaches to translation, but these found articulation only later, alongside the growing religious and national value of Hebrew itself. Similarly, while biblical texts reveal their share of anxiety about the borders of the Israelite community, the phenomena of conversion and apostasy—central to Assmann's analysis of religious untranslatability—emerge only in the postbiblical period. If Assmann is right, it may be significant that the notion of a holy tongue and the phenomenon of conversion emerged in roughly the same intertestamental period. Thus, while Assmann's approach provides us with a model for thinking the connections between identity and translation, he paints too broad a picture. A politics of Jewish translation would have to account not only for the resistance to translation in Judaism but also for its embrace, for Philo's Septuagint dream as well as the rabbis' Septuagint nightmare, my father's French and Yiddish both—and all the meaning that accrues between them.

In an essay that stands in some (marital?) tension with Jan Assmann's, Aleida Assmann reviews the patristic literature that sets Jewish untranslatability against the Christian embrace of translation. Thus, while Jan Assmann takes Judaism and Christianity as related examples of cultural untranslatability in opposition to "pagan" translatability, Aleida Assmann focuses on the rhetoric that set Judaism and Christianity at translational poles. Many scholars have noticed that the emergence of Christianity is intimately tied with translation, and some have gone further to describe the religion itself as the expression of a translational impulse.[54] As Aleida Assmann puts it: "The spiritual status of the gospel was the gold standard that permitted the use of native tongues as convertible currencies. . . . From the very start, Christianity defined itself as a message rather than a medium."[55]

Assmann traces the drive to translation to the New Testament itself, to Acts 2 as the first stage of apostolic activity—that is, translation. In the Pentecost event, Assmann points out, the apostles who assembled in Jerusalem after Jesus's death experience a theophany in the form of what could be called a miraculous translation performance. The Holy Spirit that descends in tongues of fire among the apostles in Jerusalem is heard and understood "each . . . in his own native language" by a rainbow coalition of pilgrims to the Temple: "Parthians and Medes and Elamites and residents of Mesopotamia, Judea and Cappadocia, Pontus and Asia, Phrygia and Pamphylia, residents of Egypt and the parts of Libya belonging to Cyrene, and visitors from Rome, both Jews and proselytes, Cretans and Arabians, we hear them telling in our tongues the mighty works of God" (Acts 2:10). At Pentecost, Aleida Assmann writes, a new dimension opened in which unity, oneness, is miraculously achieved, this time not materially from below but pneumatically from above: the realm of the spirit. With the introduction of the concept of the Holy Spirit, Christian semiotics has changed fundamentally; a dividing line was drawn, separating the material word and letter from the immaterial meaning. This change in the sign system which occurred in the name of the Holy Spirit promoted transcendence of the written law and its letter, translation of the holy Scripture, transformation in history. In affirming the Holy Spirit as an immaterial energy, Christianity cut off its links with the letter of the law—that is, with its Jewish roots.[56]

As Assmann herself notes, however, this reading of the Pentecost event is a retroactive one, from a period when such linguistic and ethnic transcendence indeed marked a real departure from Judaism. Origen and Augustine read Acts 2 typologically, as recovering through Christ what had been sundered at Babel. In the first century, by contrast, the Pentecost event would have been recognized as a thoroughly Jewish narrative, with striking similarities to midrashic descriptions of God's theophanies to Israel as experiences of *ruaḥ haqodesh* (the Holy Spirit) manifesting itself as collective speech or song.

Assmann's juxtaposition of the Pentecost event with midrashic narratives describing the descent of the Holy Spirit upon the Jewish people in the desert underscores the double-edged potential of translation. On the one hand, the Holy Spirit (*pneumatos hagiou*) in Acts 2.4 is a precise gloss of the Hebrew *ruaḥ haqodesh* that undoubtedly underlay the Greek. On the other hand, the Greek rendition marks an absolute departure; where mutual incomprehension had once divided the Jerusalem pilgrims, divine harmony and mutual intelligibility now reign. The result achieved by this Hebrew–Greek translation is a new religion, if only in a retroactive patristic reading. The interpretation of Acts 2 as a foundational text for Christianity precisely in its drive for translational transparency thus itself depends on the opacity of this text as a translation of Jewish sources.

Willis Barnstone has made a similar argument that Christian difference is produced precisely through Hebrew–Greek translation. In an essay entitled "How through False Translation into and from the Bible Jesus Ceased to Be a Jew," Barnstone conjectures that the New Testament was redacted in the Greek with a deliberate aim of distancing Jesus from his Jewish identity, a goal reinforced in translation into other languages. "By sleight-of-hand editing and translating, only certain figures of the Christian Scriptures remain clearly identifiable as Jews—not John the Baptist, not Mary, not Jesus, nor James and Paul: even their names are not biblically Jewish."[57] Comparing parallel versions of Jesus's transfiguration episode in the three Synoptic Gospels, Barnstone concludes that

> whenever Jesus is addressed is Greek as "kyrie" (Lord), "epistata" (teacher), "didaskale" (teacher), or "despote" (master), the word in Hebrew and Aramaic was normally *rabbi*. If my assumption is correct, then for the English translation to be faithful Jesus would have been addressed as "Rabbi" on almost every page of the Gospels, and there would have been no possibility of forgetting that he was a Jewish rabbi. Had this one single politico-religious subversion of the text not occurred, the deracination of Jesus and his followers as Jews in the Scriptures would not have been plausible. Clearly, to address Jesus as "Rabbi" identifies him as a religious teacher of the Jews. To call him "Master" averts this unpleasant designation.[58]

What makes Christianity different, then, cannot be its Lord and master, or even the Holy Spirit. These are familiar enough from the Jewish world. Christian difference arises only once these terms find their Greek expression. Buber makes a somewhat similar argument, though he traces a crucial aspect of Christian difference not to the New Testament but rather to the Septuagint, in particular to the Greek "mistranslation" of Torah into *nomos*. It is this Greek narrowing of the concept of Torah into law that makes possible Paul's opposition of law and faith. "Without the change of meaning in the Greek, objective sense," Buber writes, "the Pauline dualism of law and faith, life from works and life from grace, would miss its most important conceptual presupposition."[59]

What is clear from these analyses is that Judaism and Christianity are both sharply divided and deeply connected by the vagaries of language. Even those texts that are read as asserting Christian difference turn out to be, on closer examination, profoundly shaped by Jewish sources. Aleida Assmann cites pneumatic rabbinic texts as the overlooked Jewish source for the Pentecost story, but there are also parallels in the Hebrew Bible for Acts 2: the Pitt Minion Reference Edition of the King James Version (published by Cambridge University Press) cross-references a number of biblical prophets who imagined the messianic age as a time when all peoples would speak one tongue. Zephaniah 3:9, for instance, similarly reverses the Babel story in a divine prophecy: "For then I will make the peoples pure of speech, So that they invoke the Lord by name, and serve Him with one accord." From this perspective, Acts is a messianic and perhaps even proto-rabbinic text. What Assmann does not mention is that Acts 2 is also an artifact of the Jewish Hellenism of its period, a milieu in which the translational impulse behind the

Pentecost story was familiar if not ubiquitous. Philo, writing in a similar Hellenistic milieu a few decades earlier, spoke openly of his aspiration to see the Torah translated for all humankind. More specifically, he imagined the composition of the Septuagint as a miraculous event accomplished by a mystical power that, as at Pentecost, descended from above. Philo's may in some sense be the more universal narrative, since he speaks of the Septuagint as the spread of God's word to the entire world; by contrast, the Pentecost miracle is experienced primarily by Jews and fellow-travelers, if a multicultural assortment of them. For both Philo and the author of Acts, the spiritual source and meaning of their religious proclamations is ultimately both the universal deity and the Jewish God. Philo's hope that, through the Septuagint, "Every nation, abandoning all their own individual customs, and utterly disregarding their national laws, would change and come over to the honour of such a people only," is cousin though perhaps not sister to Paul's Mission to the Gentiles (it is, after all, Jewish law that Paul insists Gentiles need not and must not observe). Philo's Judaism is a universal religion, though, like Christianity, of a particular and particularist variety. Christian universalism, from this perspective, can hardly be separated from its Jewish variety, and certainly not in the first century. It is perhaps only the working of translation that allows such a distinction to emerge. The evidence of Hellenistic Judaism, in which the Greek Bible had canonical status and laid hopeful claim to a worldwide readership, would necessarily qualify the arguments of Jan Assmann, who sees Judaism as espousing untranslatability in contrast with paganism, and Aleida Assmann and Edward Greenstein, who view Judaism as espousing untranslatability in contrast with Christianity.

If there is a Jewish resistance to translation that is not solely an invention of patristic consciousness, can it be traced to the rabbinic period? Given the evidence of the books of Maccabees and Jubilees and of the Qumran scrolls, the fundamental distinctiveness of Hebrew—as a holy tongue, as the language of creation, as the original language of humankind, as the messianic language, as an emblem of national identification—is already in place by the beginnings of the rabbinic period. Such a conception of Hebrew, though, could apparently coexist with Jewish universalist impulses: the early midrashic collection *Sifre Deuteronomy*, for instance, suggests that the revelation of the Torah took place in four languages simultaneously:

> "The Lord came from Sinai, etc." (Deut. 33.2). When the Holy One revealed himself to give the Torah to Israel, he revealed himself not in one language but in four languages, as it says, "The Lord came from Sinai," that is the Hebrew lan-

guage; "and rose from Seir [Edom] toward them," that is the Roman language [Latin]; "he appeared from Mount Paran," that is the Arabic language; "and He came from Merivevoth Kadesh," that is the Aramaic language.[60]

Moreover, the rabbis were generally surprisingly permissive in the use of translated Bibles and vernacular liturgy. Exemptions, for example in the inscriptions of such ritual objects as *tefillin* and *mezuzot,* are rare. Even the description of the Septuagint in *Megilla* 9 as a product of deliberate Jewish mistranslation under Ptolemy is related within a pericope that uses the story to authorize the translation—at least of the Pentateuch—into Greek. A scholarly consensus nevertheless holds that, despite this legitimizing of the Septuagint, the rabbis in fact unofficially rejected this version after it became the Bible of the early Church (and with the final canonization of a Hebrew Bible), turning to a number of Jewish retranslations in its stead.[61] As Markus Friedländer described this development,

> In Alexandria the day the Bible first showed itself to the world in Greek vestments is celebrated as a festival [*als eine Festtag*], in Palestine it is observed as a fast day [*als einen Fasttag*], as when the Golden Calf was built.[62]

By contrast, the rabbis praised and celebrated the translations produced under their own aegis, especially the Targum of Onkelos and the second-century Greek version of Aquila.

A number of scholars have recognized in rabbinic literature an evolution from an early embrace of universalism and translation to a later distancing not only from the Septuagint but from translation in general; the underlying assumption is that these rabbinic attitudes took shape against the background of Christianity—in this case, both the Christian adoption of the Septuagint and the translational ideology of the early Church. Central to this school of thought is the notion that early rabbinic culture was universalist, though certainly not in a manner to be confused with tolerance or pluralism. The notion of a lost rabbinic universalism is summed up in the title of Marc Hirshman's 1999 book, *Torah for all Humankind* (Torah lekhol ba'ei olam).[63] Hirshman argues that, although rabbinic literature hardly formulates doctrine or speaks in one single voice, it is possible to trace "the existence of a school of thought in the early rabbinic period that held that its book, the Torah, was indeed intended for all people."[64] Hirshman accounts for the dissolution of rabbinic universalism by suggesting that

> the unique fusion of empire and religion tilted the scales in favor of Christian universalism. Rabbinic Judaism eventually moved more and more to a strain of

particularism of the sort that may be observed in Akiva's school, banning the Gentile from the study of Torah. In the first centuries, however, the Rabbis were divided, with at least one school vigorously advocating a universalist approach— the path not taken in the coming generations.[65]

Azzan Yadin has drawn the argument in Hirshman's work more closely around the question of Bible translation, demonstrating how early rabbinic universalism was explicitly linked with a translational impulse and tracing the gradual obscuring of this strand of early rabbinic thought in its later redaction. Carefully studying the development of the motif of "the Torah in seventy tongues," Yadin shows the metamorphosis of an early rabbinic embrace of translation into more familiar expressions of rabbinic self-understanding. Crucial to Yadin's reading is a fragment of *Mekhilta Deuteronomy* found in the Cairo Genizah that reads Deuteronomy 27:8, in which the Israelites write "all the words of this teaching most distinctly," as referring to a universal translation of the Bible. "Rabbi Ishmael says: they wrote in seventy languages."[66]

In Yadin's reconstruction, the famous rabbinic dictum "the Torah has seventy faces" obscures an earlier rabbinic dictum that God gave the Torah in seventy languages. Scriptural polysemy, then, is a rewriting of what Yadin calls "scriptural polyglossia." Rabbinic literature not only gradually retreated from its earlier openness to translation, it also buried the traces of this retreat: "What started out in the tannaitic stratum of rabbinic literature as a very clearly defined statement by Rabbi Ishmael regarding the writing at the altar after the crossing of the Jordan was ultimately transformed into a polysemic manifesto."[67]

The analyses of Hirshman and Yadin can serve as evidence for rabbinic translational impulses directed to "the seventy nations." But rabbinic literature knows at least two varieties of translation: the first of these is emblematized by the Septuagint, with its ostensible Ptolemaic origins and its dispersion beyond the Jewish world; the second, which include the Aramaic Targums and Aquila's Greek "retranslation," are connected liturgically with the synagogue and exegetically with rabbinic methods. The rabbinic move from translation to midrash outlined in Yadin's article—that is, from a polyglossic to a polysemic Torah—marks not simply a growing resistance to translation, as is often assumed, but rather a move from one type of translation to another, one intercultural and the other intracultural.[68] What mattered to the rabbis about translating the Torah was as much audience as content.

A talmudic lecture by Emanuel Levinas on the the dense passage in tractate *Megilla* that is perhaps the most extended rabbinic discussion of translation is remarkably sensitive to the degree to which translation, for the rabbis, involved the negotiation of cultural boundaries. The Mishnah with which Levinas opens his analysis distinguishes between two varieties of Hebrew texts, one for which translation is permitted and another for which it is not:

> MISHNAH: Between the [holy] books on the one hand and the *tefillin* and *mezuzot* on the other, there is only one difference: the books are written in all languages, whereas the *tefillin* and the *mezuzot* only in "Assyrian" [Hebrew].

In Levinas's reading of the Mishnah, translations of the Bible "retain their dignity of Holy Scriptures. . . . Unlimited universality of the Bible and Judaism."[69] In contrast, those texts that are consecrated by ritual usage and inserted into religious objects—*tefillin* and *mezuzot*—must remain in Hebrew. "In addition to the universal Jewish spirit," Levinas writes, "the Hebrew 'materiality' is needed here. The Hebrew 'body' would appear to be indispensable in this case."[70] The Gemara, however, cites a *baraita*—an "external" rabbinic saying attributed to the Mishnaic period—that appears to contradict the Mishnah: the sacred status of the Bible persists only in books written in Hebrew characters. Levinas parses this as an alternative rabbinic view not only of translation but also of Jewish distinctiveness:

> There is a particularism in the *baraita*, according to which there is no universal meaning of Judaism separable from the traditional forms. An untranslatable Judaism. It is indissolubly bound to the letter of the text and the most literal meaning; not only to the singular genius of the original Hebrew and Aramaic that appears in its books, but also to the materiality of the letter. . . . Is Judaism, viewed in this manner, as a unique humanity, a humanity above humanity, open to conversion to it? Yes, but to a conversion of the whole soul—that is, to its entire culture, ways and customs.[71]

As with Jan Assmann, conversion is the symptom that expresses an underlying Jewish untranslatability. But Levinas makes a finer distinction than Assmann: in the universal view represented in the Mishnah, the Jewish "message" can freely pass to the world; in the *baraita*, this message cannot transcend its medium, just as non-Jews cannot come over to Judaism unless they accept its form, "its entire culture, ways and customs."

Among a series of attempts in the Gemara to resolve the contradiction between the Mishnah, with its openness to translation, and the *baraita*, with its wariness of translation, is this one:

> There is no problem: [in the *baraita*] it is a question of the Scroll of Esther, and in the Mishnah it is a question of the [other] books. For what reason [is] the Scroll

of Esther [not allowed to be translated]? Because it is written therein (chapter 8.9): "to the Jews, according to their writing, and according to their language."

Levinas seems skeptical of this "forced" talmudic explanation, "based on bits of verses and words." There are other problems with the Talmud's logic here: the biblical prooftext, which describes the royal letters to be sent to Jews throughout the Persian provinces "according to their language" permitting their self-defense against Haman, can as easily suggest a Jewish vernacular as the sacred tongue—why, then, should this constitute a prooftext for writing Esther only in Hebrew? That Esther should be the sole Hebrew book for which translation is not permitted is also curious. Esther is one of the two biblical books that do not mention God; moreover, as a late addition to the Hebrew canon, it might have a marginal status. Searching for his own understanding of why Esther should be uniquely untranslatable, Levinas writes:

> The Scroll of Esther, a book about persecution, a book on anti-Semitism, is intelligible only to Jews in their language and their writing! The suffering of anti-Semitic persecution can only be told in the language of the victim. It is conveyed through signs that are not interchangeable. It is not, whatever the sociologists may say, a particular case of a general phenomenon, even if the other problems taken up in the Scriptures are inter-human and can be translated into all languages. This text on the anti-Semitism of Haman and Amalek can only have meaning in a Jewish "body" and in its original tongue. . . . Is the word "holocaust" not too Greek to express the Passion?[72]

Levinas's reasoning here seems to stray from the immediate logic of the passage: what does the language in which the king transmits his edict have to do with the language in which Jews relate their own stories of persecution? But Levinas's thought is not, I think, utterly foreign to the Talmud's. Linking the untranslatability of the book of Esther to King Ahasuerus's (Hebrew?) letter to the Jews, as the Talmud does, suggests that the translational status of Esther should be discerned in the workings of communication between Jews and non-Jews rather than in the relative sacredness or profanity of the book. Nevertheless, Levinas seems to be sidestepping the issue: the talmudic justification for the opinion that views Esther as untranslatable depends on a passage in Esther that involves not only Jewish persecution but also Jewish self-defense and ultimately vengeance. As Levinas certainly knows, Esther is read at least as much as a carnivalesque celebration of Jewish victory (three days of pillaging and ravaging! All ten sons of Haman on the gallows!) as it is as a memorial to "the anti-Semitism of Haman and Amalek." Esther's untranslatability may be a reflection of its status as "Holocaust literature," but it is also an acknowledgment of the Scroll's function as a Jewish "hidden transcript." The Hebrew of Esther is not the untranslatable holy tongue but rather the untranslatable (for a different reason) Jewish discourse on persecution. The citation from Esther is thus shorthand for a charged translational circumstance: on the one hand, the Bible presents this marvelous moment (royal permission for Jewish aggression!) as a communication across ethnic and linguistic borders, from the Persian throne to the Jews dispersed through the kingdom; on the other, the later recitation of the Scroll throughout a range of Jewish diasporas represents a public reading of vengeful Jewish fantasies perhaps better performed within a strictly Jewish language. Levinas almost arrives at this conclusion, but stops halfway. The strictures of Jewish untranslatability may be operative even in this lecture.

Any reading of the lecture would have to allow itself to confront Levinas's own translation practice in the face of "the suffering of anti-Semitic persecution." Levinas opens *Otherwise than Being* (1974), the second of his two major philosophical works, with two dedications, one at the top of the page in French and the other below in Hebrew. The French dedication reads:

> To the memory of those who were closest among the six million assassinated by the National Socialists, and of the millions on millions of all confessions and all nations, victims of the same hatred of the other man, the same anti-semitism.[73]

The Hebrew reads:

> To the memory of my father and teacher R. Yehiel, son of R. Abraham the Levite,
> My mother and teacher Devorah, daughter of R. Moshe,
> My brother Dov son of R. Yehiel the Levite, and Aminadav son of R. Yehiel the Levite,
> My brother-in-law R. Samuel son of R. Gershon the Levite, and my sister-in-law Malkah daughter of R. Hayim.
> May their souls be bound in the bonds of eternal life. [*TNZB"H*][74]

What is clear enough is that the Hebrew and French dedications can hardly be called translations of each other, although a reader without Hebrew (presumably the majority of Levinas's philosophical readers, as opposed to those of his lectures on the Talmud) might easily assume otherwise. The Hebrew dedication is formulaic and conventional in the extreme, signifying not only Levinas's memories of those family members who died in the Holocaust (how they died need hardly be said) but also his fidelity to the liturgical norms of Jewish commemoration. Such formulas, absolutely familiar—although no less poignant for that—to the Hebrew reader, signify entirely differently in another language. The French (here rendered in Alphonso Lingis's English) makes a completely different set of gestures, linking the broadest themes of Levinas's philosophical work—"the same hatred of the other man"—with the most personal if obliquely rendered of the philosopher's concerns—"those who were closest among the six million." Read against the background of Levinas's lecture on translation, what is most jarring is the contradiction between this French dedication and Levinas's claim in the Talmud lecture that antisemitism is not "a particular case of a general phenomenon." Levinas thus both insists on the untranslatability of the experience of Jewish persecution and then nevertheless translates it in precisely the universalizing language he ruled out in the talmudic lecture; that this Hebrew–"Greek" translation is a mistranslation may indeed be the very sign of the untranslatability of Jewish suffering.

My own approach has certainly been signaled by now: I reject any model that views Jewish translation as an essential phenomenon, whether it distinguishes it from Christianity or earlier Near Eastern religions. Jewish approaches to translation are, I believe, best understood not as purely philosophical or religious stances but rather as an expression of how the translators saw themselves vis-à-vis various "others." Finally, I rely on what could be called a Derridean insight, that Jewish translation may be hard to categorize not only because it takes shape in a variety of contexts and periods, but also because translation is a term for doubleness and difference, the very site of undecidability and ambivalence. The Septuagint legends, which include claims of both translational perfection and mistranslation, descriptions of lavish patronage and miserable enslavement, can stand in here for this complexity. The Septuagint, too, is the site where Judaism and Christianity meet, before they can be named as distinct religions. From the earliest translation project to the "Holocaust" and beyond (the term "holocaust" is, of course, taken from the Septuagint), the rich details of translation can serve as a map of Jewish–Christian identity, that is, of Jewish–Christian difference.

PLAN OF BOOK

Faithful Renderings explores translation as a site for Jewish–Christian encounter and uses Jewish–Christian relations as a lens to study translation. Translation discourse has long been haunted by theological-political specters; among the aims of this book is to read the recurring controversies of translation discourse—the question of translatability, the choice of word-for-word versus sense-for-sense translation, or of "fidelity" versus "treason," or of the "invisibility" of the translator—as religious and political rather than "purely" linguistic questions. For reasons I discuss in this book, translation discourse has often served as barely concealed Jewish-Christian polemic, with Christian approaches forming the "common sense" mainstream of a discourse in which Jewish alternatives rarely come into view. The wordplay of my title is meant to suggest that the very phantasm of the faithful translator both obscures and hints at the degree to which the equivalence of a source text and its translation is a matter of faith rather than evidence, ideology rather than technique—inevitably, given the aporia that structures translation.

This aporia can also be said to structure the relationship between Judaism and Christianity, a connection that might be termed in some sense translational. At the least, translation provides a model for theorizing "Judeo-Christianity," since translation assumes connection but also difference, equivalence as well as transmutation. In his introduction to *The Medieval Translator*, Roger Ellis puts this ambivalence very elegantly, recognizing translation as both an act of "growing out of" an original and an act of "outgrowing" this original. Playing as well with the notions of "bearing over" and "overbearing," Ellis takes as his parade case of this ambiguity the "complex, frequently contentious, sometimes accommodating, relations of Christianity and Judaism with one another." Ellis writes:

> From the very beginning a vital ambiguity existed about the extent to which the new religion had grown out of, or outgrown, the old. Sometimes, for example, Jesus declared an intention to fulfill the Mosaic Law, at others he saw himself doing away with it entirely (e.g. Matthew 5:17ff). Similarly, a crucial passage in Hebrews 7 uses the term 'translation' to describe a new priesthood, Christ's. This new priesthood marks Christ's simultaneous continuity with, and break with, the traditions of the past. Continuity, in that it was prefigured by one Old Testament priest, Melchisedek; breach, in that it abolished the Levitical priesthood embodied in another, Aaron. Translation, that is, marks both continuity and rupture. The translator as scribe . . . cannot be understood without reference to the translator as author/interpreter.[75]

Ellis's view of Jewish-Christian relations is suggestive, and his point deserves underscoring. The kinship models that have governed both translation studies and conceptualizations of Jewish-Christian relations still structure the discussion of translation as a kind of "bearing," in which a source and its offspring can be clearly differentiated and the legitimacy of their connection "contractually" established. In other words, the traditional view of Mother Synagogue and Daughter Church (or even of "sister" religions) and the related notion of original and translation thus assume the very relations they should be explicating. By contrast, the flexible model of translation-as-juncture I mobilize in this book can alert us to the ways that these linguistic and religious relations are textually constructed rather than genetically guaranteed. Whether one sees Judeo-Christianity as the term for a rupture or a continuity depends *only* on language.

There is another point worth stressing in this connection. Although Ellis challenges the kinship model of Jewish–Christian development, he continues to assume that Judaism is "first," whether or not Christianity is a true or false offspring, fulfiller or usurper of Israel's promise. Throughout this book, I try to resist the triumphalist notion that Judaism is an original of which Christianity is a (mis)translation, although such notions are of course part of the history I explore. In the translational history of Judaism and Christianity, insofar as Christianity is viewed as "growing out" of Judaism (rather than only outgrowing it), Jewish texts and translators have possessed a form of symbolic capital—the term is Pierre Bourdieu's—that has complicated if not ameliorated the position of Jews in Christendom. Nevertheless, this book is an examination of this form of Jewish symbolic capital, not its assertion: it is no longer possible to ignore the poststructuralist insight that the original is always already a translation, or that—as Ellis rightly implies—a translation is itself another original.

Faithful Renderings is not a historical survey of translation as a site of Jewish–Christian encounter. It makes no attempt to be comprehensive, preferring the local to the global, the illuminating anecdote to the broader historical sweep. Nor do I see myself as tackling the field of translation studies as a whole; my work engages only a small number of themes emerging from this rapidly expanding field, and only those of some bearing on my subject. The chapters typically introduce a particular theme in translation studies—translational "fidelity," literalism, the figure of the translator, translation and conversion—using this theme to illuminate some aspect of Jewish–Christian translation history. The conceptualization of translation as a performance taking shape within a field of asymmetrical power relations is not a theme but the implied background of the book as a whole.

The first chapter of this book, "Immaculate Translation: Sexual Fidelity, Textual Transmission, and the Virgin Birth," analyzes two primary Jewish–Christian debates in late antiquity, the first over the accuracy and canonicity of the Septuagint, the Jewish Bible translation that became the Bible of the early Church, and the second over the virginity of Mary, a theme tied to the Septuagint through Matthew's citation of the Greek for Isaiah 7:14 as prophecy of the virgin birth. I argue that these themes are not only linked, they are in fact parallel, producing a conception of the perfect reproduction of God's word in both the Septuagint and the figure of Jesus Christ.

The second chapter, "'The Beauty of Greece in the Tents of Shem': Aquila between the Camps," studies the figure of Aquila, whose word-for-word Greek renderings of the Bible in his second-century retranslation "toward" the Hebrew produced what is considered an unreadable text and earned him a place in standard evaluations as perhaps the worst translator ever to practice. My own analysis focuses on the Christian stakes in the preference for sense-for-sense translation and reviews the rabbinic literature on Aquila as a culture hero, bringing Greek "spoils" into Hebrew tents.

The third chapter, "False Friends: Conversion and Translation from Jerome to Luther," argues that the ideological stakes for what has been called "the invisible theory of translation," the assumption that languages are neutral media for a separable "content," can be read in the controversy that pitted the Christian Hebraist and New Humanist Johannes Reuchlin against the Jewish apostate Johannes Pfefferkorn at the dawn of the Reformation. In taking the side of Reuchlin over Pfefferkorn and in recommending that translators "go to the Jews for the Hebrew grammar and to the [Christian] theologians for the sense," Martin Luther separated the (Jewish) body of the Hebrew letter from its (Christian) spirit and laid the groundwork for a Protestant approach to the Hebrew Bible unmediated either by the Jews or by Rome. The invisibility of the translator, from this perspective, is no historical accident—it is a politically and religiously overdetermined erasure. The absence of the Jew, as both privileged and suspect interpreter of Hebrew sources, not only is necessary for the Christian appropriation and German domestication of the Bible, it is also paradoxically central to the development of modern translation in the West.

The fourth chapter, "A Translator Culture," examines German-Jewish culture through the lens of translation, beginning with Moses Mendelssohn's Bible translation and ending with the translation theory of Walter Benjamin. While previous scholarship has tended to conceptualize German-Jewish translation in the light of cultural integration or symbiosis, I argue that the formulation of translation as a variety of cultural encounter (itself a German-Jewish notion) has served to conceal a variety of tensions and asymmetries in the German-Jewish translation project. Benjamin's model of an interlinear Bible translation, along with Buber and Rosenzweig's attempt at creating a German Bible in which the Hebrew original would somehow be visible, can be traced to philosophical and political circumstances comparable to those that shaped Aquila's work. The "translator cultures" of Hellenism and German-Jewish modernism, I argue, divested the sacred tongue of what had been its correlate: untranslatability. In this cultural context, translating the sacred necessarily produces a difficult or incomprehensible text as guarantee that translation has not succumbed to the chimera of linguistic transparency or the demands of cultural assimilation.

The fifth chapter, "The Holocaust in Every Tongue," studies the significance of translation in Holocaust discourse, arguing for the connection between survival and translation in both Jewish experiences during the war and the transmission of this Jewish experience "in every tongue." The "Holocaust," as a discourse, emerges through this translation, as a result of a careful negotiation between Jewish writers and their larger audience. Close readings of the production and reception of such central texts as *The Diary of Anne Frank* and *Night* demonstrate the paradoxes and limits of Jewish–Christian post-Holocaust conversation—the divide between Jews and Christians has narrowed, but partly because a certain discretion is exercised.

The sixth chapter, "Translation and Assimilation: Singer in America," examines the English translations of Singer's work, focusing particularly on "Gimpel the Fool," Singer's first short story to be translated, and "Zeidlus the Pope." The English versions of both stories censor "anti-Christian" sentiments in the Yiddish; in the case of "Gimpel," this censorship obscures the story as a modernist rewriting of the Gospels that sees Joseph as the hero of Christianity.

An epilogue explores the ethics of one aspect of the project I have undertaken in this book, the exposure of the Jewish "hidden transcript." Among the arguments I make for my project is this one: what has been hidden from those in power is now concealed from my own generation of American Jews. American Jews, who are no longer kept from exercising other forms of power, are now in the position of outsiders to their own history.

Because I began this book with few presuppositions about what constituted Jewish translation, I made no attempt to pursue a single narrative line. Rather, I explored what seemed to be a promising variety of translational sites in which Jewish–Christian tensions could be discerned. It was with some gratification, then, that I discovered that themes and *topoi* central to the early chapters of the book recurred, sometimes in surprisingly transformed ways, in the chapters that analyzed translation and Jewish modernity. The Septuagint, apparently rejected by the Jewish community sometime in the second century and replaced for Western Christianity by Jerome's Vulgate (it is still the Bible of Greek Orthodoxy), nevertheless managed to contribute, through the King James Version, a crucial term to twentieth-century Jewish experience—the "Holocaust." Aquila, the second-century Hebrew–Greek translator, turns up again (at least to my eyes) in Benjamin's "Task of the Translator"; the *ruaḥ* he argues over with Hadrian breathes as well in the Buber-Rosenzweig Bible. The virgin birth, central to early Jewish–Christian translation debate, reappears as crucial intertext to the Yiddish version of Singer's "Gimpel the Fool." And the convert-translator of the Middle Ages has pride of place in the other Singer story I discuss, "Zeidlus the Pope." That the Bible has had a fascinating life in translation was among the hunches that propelled this project. That this life has itself given rise to a rich array of afterlives was the discovery that accompanied its completion.

CHAPTER ONE

✳

Immaculate Translation

Sexual Fidelity, Textual Transmission, and the Virgin Birth

> *Many a man has made his way into an honest girl's bedroom by calling himself a god.*
>
> OVID, *Metamorphoses*

IT IS A founding insight of feminist translation theory that translation discourse in the West has been profoundly sexualized, drawing on a web of erotic folk wisdom, misogynistic epigrams, and ribald innuendo. The Hebrew poet Haim Nahman Bialik reputedly declared that reading a poem in translation was like "kissing the bride through her veil"; Gilles Ménage coined the phrase "les belles infidèles" to describe a "free" translation; and a familiar witticism holds that, like women, translations may be either faithful or beautiful but never both. Following Barbara Johnson's pioneering analysis of the analogy between translation and matrimony, Lori Chamberlain writes:

> Fidelity is defined by an implicit contract between translation (as woman) and original (as husband, father, or author). However, the infamous "double standard" operates here as it might have in traditional marriages: the "unfaithful" wife/translation is publicly tried for crimes the husband/original is incapable of committing. This contract, in short, makes it impossible for the original to be guilty of infidelity. Such an attitude betrays real anxiety about the problem of paternity and translation; it mimics the patrilineal kinship system where paternity—not maternity—legitimizes an offspring.[1]

That this sexualized rhetoric is more than a little slippery can be gleaned even from Chamberlain's summary. While she begins by asserting the femininity—and potential infidelity—of the translation as wife, the passage slides, propelled by its own allegorical logic, into the problem of the translation as (potentially illegitimate) child, whose relationship to the original/father is called into question by the translator's infidelity. Once one recognizes that not only infidelity but also kinship itself is at stake, the implicit threat to the very meaning of translation encoded in this rhetoric becomes clear. Translation and paternity announce a relation, between source and target texts, between father and child, that is open to disruption by the very conduit—the translator/mother—through which this relationship is established. The legal and contractual apparatus that hedges kinship and translation can never hope to control the mysterious gestational process at their center.

This sexual semantics of translation is often accompanied by a religious rhetoric. *Translatio* has a long and various theological history: to be translated is to ascend to heaven without dying; the Nicene Fathers discuss the translation of bishops from one see to another; and, for the medievals, sacred relics are translated in being moved. The rhetoric of "faithful" translation further suggests the influence of the religious as well as marital (and political) spheres. Unfaithful translations sin against originals, while faithful translations acquire their sacred aura. But just as the marital analysis of faithful translation calls into question the relationship between original and translation, reading faithful translation through a theological lens threatens to expose the faithfulness of a translation as a religious rather than an ostensibly neutral linguistic judgment. As with the laws of paternity, the idealized and disembodied model of semantic equivalence acts as a cover for the ideologies and loyalties of particular translators, stifling the recognition that the equivalence-value of a particular translation is a matter of faith (in both senses) rather than verification. In the case of translations that cross religious boundaries, where translators render texts of another religion or where one "faith community" adopts a translation composed by translators affiliated with a rival group, the stakes multiply.

It is just such a fraught contest that stands behind the Septuagint, the Greek translation of the Hebrew Bible, which has often been described as the first great translation project in the West. The Septuagint (or Seventy, abbreviated as LXX) was originally composed by Alexandrian Jews, by most accounts for their own use. The Septuagint was later adopted as the Bible of the early Church (it remains so for the Greek Orthodox Church) and rejected as inaccurate by the Greek-speaking Jewish community that had been its first readership.[2] The curious controversy that resulted, in which it was the Christian community that, until Jerome's fateful return to the *hebraica veritas*, insisted on the fidelity of the Alexandrian Jewish translators while Jews of the same period cast doubt on this faithfulness, poses the problem of faithful translation both at its origin and at its most intricate.

The Septuagint opens the problem of faithful translation in its sexual as well as religious dimensions. Nowhere, in fact, does the overdetermined significance of faithful translation—as linguistic accuracy, sexual fidelity, and religious orthodoxy—come closer to the surface than in the Hebrew-Greek translation crux in Matthew 1:23. It is in this famous verse that Matthew cites the Septuagint version of Isaiah 7:14. In 7:14, Isaiah gives Ahaz a sign that his salvation is soon to come. Isaiah promises: *"Hiney ha'almah harah veyoledet ben veqarat shemo 'imanu'el"* (Behold, the young woman [*ha'almah*] is with child and about to bear a son and she will call him Immanuel).[3] Matthew, rendering Isaiah's Hebrew word *'almah* as *parthenos* in accordance with the Seventy, cites Isaiah as saying that a virgin (*parthenos*) will give birth, thus casting Isaiah as the Hebrew prophet of Jesus's virgin birth. At stake in the Jewish-Christian interpretations of this crucial passage is not only the reliability of the translation Matthew was using, which would have been the Septuagint, the Bible of Greek-speaking Jews and Christians of the first century.[4] In the arguments over this passage in Matthew, no less is at issue than the legitimacy of Jesus, the virginity of Mary, the relationship between the Hebrew Bible and the New Testament, and, ultimately, between Judaism and Christianity. To rephrase this complex hermeneutic knot in terms of Chamberlain's feminist analysis, the difference between the Hebrew *'almah* and the Greek *parthenos* simultaneously throws religious authority, textual reliability, and the paternal line into anxious question.

To outline the problem, Matthew 1:20 describes the angel coming to Joseph to urge him to take Mary into his home, "for what is conceived in her is from the Holy Spirit" (NIV). In 1:22–23, the narrator continues:

> All this took place to fulfill what the Lord had said through the prophet: The virgin will be with child and she will give birth to a son, and they will call him Immanuel, which means "God with us." (NIV)

A fierce controversy over this passage erupted almost immediately. The debate between Justin Martyr and his fictionally constructed Jewish interlocutor, described as a philosopher and Jewish leader, in *Dialogue with Trypho the Jew* (ca. 150 CE), centers largely around a double issue: the virginity of Mary (to which Justin is one of the first post-Matthean witnesses) and the reliability of the Septuagint as prophetic testimony to this virginity. While Justin is generally willing to dispute using Trypho's own Hebrew texts, on this crucial point he insists on citing the Greek. Trypho's rejoinder sets the stage, at this early point, for what would become the standard Jewish response to Matthew:

> And Trypho answered, "The Scripture has not, 'Behold, the virgin shall conceive, and bear a son,' but, 'Behold, the young woman (*nēanis*) shall conceive, and bear a son,' and so on, as you quoted. But the whole prophecy refers to Hezekiah, and it is proved that it was fulfilled in him, according to the terms of this prophecy."[5]

Trypho, claiming privileged access to Hebrew sources and Jewish readings, rejects both Matthew's messianic typology and his use of the LXX. In Trypho's view, the prophetic line that, for Justin, connects Isaiah's prophecy with the birth of Jesus is interrupted by two mistranslations: one restores a Greek hymen to a young Hebrew girl, and the other postpones the fulfillment of Isaiah's pregnant prophecy for seven hundred years after its proclamation— a long gestation indeed!

Controversy over this crux has not abated even in our own time. The Revised Standard Version of the Bible (completed 1952) was burned by some American fundamentalists because it had "young woman" rather than "virgin" in Isaiah 7:14, thus opening an awkward gap between Matthew and his prophetic proof text.[6] Two decades later, "the reading 'virgin' in Isaiah was imposed by a decision of the American bishops on the reluctant Catholic translators of the [New American Bible, 1970]."[7] Until the RSV's "heresy," the translation of *'almah* had served as a dividing line separating Jewish and Christian translations, with Christian translations rendering the word as "virgin" while Jewish translations unfailingly had the prophet make reference to a girl or young woman.

The narrowest discussions of the issue are philological: what are the precise meanings of *'almah, parthenos,* and the Vulgate's *virgo* (the term from which our English discussion most closely derives), and what is the relationship among these terms?[8] Does *parthenos,* as some scholars claim, mean either a young girl or a virgin (perhaps having different meanings at different periods or different locales), which allowed it to serve as a bridge or pivot between the less ambiguous Hebrew and Latin terms?[9] The discussion was not clarified even with the third-century "Jewish" (or Jewish–Christian) translations of Aquila, Symmachus, and Theodotion that attempted to "correct" the Greek Bible toward the Hebrew: these three translations have *nēanis* rather than *parthenos* in Isaiah 7:14. While Jewish readers took for granted that *nēanis* meant a girl or young woman, the third-century Father Origen argued that *nēanis* also signified a virgin![10] Nor does Jerome's turn to the Hebrew sources in the 390s simplify the discussion, as Adam Kamesar has shown; conceding the Jewish point that 'almah is not the usual Hebrew term for virgin, Jerome combines Christian theological aims and rabbinic midrashic technique to derive the hyper-virginity of Isaiah's 'almah from the Hebrew root signifying "concealment."[11] As in the description of Rebecca in Genesis 24:42, Jerome argues, the Hebrew word 'almah means "a virgin secluded, and guarded by her parents with extreme care."[12] Kamesar points out that Jerome here transforms the patristic discourse of "double virginity," which normally signifies a spiritual virginity beyond the merely corporeal, into a "super-guaranteed *physical* virginity."[13]

These philological questions are, moreover, complicated by textual problems. Matthew 1:23 differs from extant LXX versions of Isaiah in a number of details (though not in the word *parthenos*), making his citation simultaneously an interlingual and an intralingual translation—that is, the citation involves both a crossing of the Hebrew–Greek linguistic border and a rewriting of the Septuagint in slightly different Greek words.[14] That the Hebrew *Vorlage* of the LXX is no longer extant, and represents a different textual tradition from the ones manifest in the Masoretic or the Qumran textual traditions, renders problematic the very notion of source and target text. Finally, both Jewish and Christian copyists and translators were (and are) suspected not only of the usual scribal errors and textual misunderstandings, but also of deliberate interpolations, censoring, and alterations guided by ideological, religious, and political *Tendenzen*.[15]

Given these textual issues, is it possible that the Hebrew *Vorlage* used by the Seventy originally had the word *betulah*, which some commentators suppose more unequivocally means virgin (though that is far from a unanimous view)? If so, does that *Vorlage* represent a Jewish tradition alternative to the Masoretic one that is now reflected only in translation, or did the Jews later create this difference by deliberately falsifying their Hebrew manuscripts to avoid bearing witness to the divinity of Jesus, as more than one Father suspected?[16] Is *parthenos* simply one problematic translation among many in the Septuagint, as the many pre-Christian Jewish revisions of the LXX itself, and the retranslations of Aquila, Symmachus, and Theodotion, seem to imply? If *parthenos* does indeed normally mean virgin, then did the LXX translators intend to suggest by the phrase "the virgin will conceive" that "a woman who is now a virgin will (by natural means, once she is united to her husband) conceive the child Emmanuel," as Raymond Brown postulates?[17] Or does Matthew simply have it wrong, reading *parthenos* as testimony to the virginity of the young girl in Isaiah's prophecy when no such claim was intended by the Seventy, as a long Jewish tradition has insisted? Amidst this discussion, one thing is undeniable: while Christian biblical interpretation has often had recourse to Jewish exegesis, and Jewish translation has been influenced, perhaps less consciously, by Christian interpretation (Orlinsky's example is the "spiritualizing" of Hebrew *ruaḥ* in many Jewish translations of Genesis 1:3), in the case of Isaiah's *'almah*, Jewish and Christian interpretive communities have, until very recently, gone their radically separate ways.

The driest philology, in exploring these questions, is forced to acknowledge the indeterminacy, even the patriarchal violence, that renders the signification of these Hebrew, Greek, Latin, and English words so difficult to establish. Implied here, after all, are the legal categories, religious meanings, and physical determinations that govern the status of a woman within a patriarchal system and that rest on the notion of her "possession," legal or sexual, by a man. This possession, moreover, is charged with a range of uncertainties both reflected in and constructed by language. Are the terms *'almah* or *parthenos* legal or clinical categories? Do they signify age, marital status, or sexual condition? Within what regime does virginity function, and by whose testimony is it established? Does it signify a presence—an intact hymen—or the absence of a husband or lover? Is it guaranteed by the *veritas* of a Hebrew root, or the walls of a cloister? That patriarchal marriage and the patrilineal line have often hinged on female virginity is evident from the Bible itself, not least from Matthew's infancy narrative—even if it is not entirely clear what is socially or legally at stake in Joseph's hesitation about accepting the pregnant Mary into his house. That virginity is sometimes difficult to prove is at the root of a rich and various body of folklore and ritual practice; as we shall see, internal Christian as well as Jewish-Christian discussion of the birth of Jesus revolve around this uncertainty. Indeed, for Derrida, the word "hymen" becomes the very site of the undecidable.[18] The concept of virginity, then, disorders meaning *within* a language as well as destabilizing the fixed relations between languages. Pregnancy and virginity, and *a fortiori* the paradoxical sign of the pregnant virgin, suggest the workings of difference in language, the unstable borders between appearance and reality, between lack and supplement, and between self and other.

M Y intention in this chapter is to enter into neither the textual nor the theological details of the *'almah-parthenos* debate—and certainly not to attempt to settle it! As Daniel Boyarin has argued, insistence on the *hebraica veritas*, for contemporary scholars as for Jerome, slights the integrity and legitimacy of the Christian exegetical traditions—Origen and Augustine, in Boyarin's view, were right to hold fast to the Septuagint.[19] My aim here is to leave the "substance" of the *'almah–parthenos* crux and turn, rather, to its "form," illuminating the architecture of the debate in its two primary and, I will argue, interconnected aspects: the sexual and the translational. Because Matthew's narrative consists of both a sexual and an intertextual claim, Christian and Jewish responses to it encompass both the textual arguments sketched above and sexual/genetic arguments—the questions of whether a virgin can conceive, whether Mary was in fact a virgin, the Davidic ancestry of Jesus, the status of Jesus as son of God, and the cultural meaning of virginity. It is certainly significant that the *'almah–parthenos* debate brings together two relational processes, translation and gestation, whose workings and provenance are shrouded in obscurity and open to accusations of infidelity. I will argue here not only that these two aspects of the debate are isomorphic, but also that this sexual-textual knot forms the very center of what came to constitute Jewish–Christian difference. From the perspective of translation studies, an analysis of the *'almah–parthenos* crux promises to ground the feminist discussion of fidelity in translation within a more particular historical context than it has so far discovered, that of the Jewish–Christian polemic over the perfection of the Septuagint. As a contribution to the study of Jewish–Christian relations, the paired analysis of translation and kinship aims to bring into focus not so much the separate terms "Judaism" and "Christianity" as the dash that connects them—that is, the notion of relationality as such.

To reduce the argument about Matthew's citation of Isaiah to its simplest formulation, the position that retrospectively came to be associated with Christian orthodoxy increasingly insisted on the virgin birth and the perfection of the Septuagint translation. Jews, in contrast, denied both Mary's virginity and, after it was adopted as the Christian Old Testament, the accuracy and canonicity of the Septuagint. Such a dichotomizing of Jews and Christians in antiquity, though, strips the discussion of all nuance: the various beliefs about Mary's virginity and Jesus's parentage, and the value of the Septuagint, were fairly fluid among the populations from which rabbinic Judaism and orthodox Christianity emerged, a population that we can now see included, *inter alia*, Jewish Christians, Judaizing Christians of Gentile origin as well as Judaizers of non-Christian affiliation, and Jews attracted to various aspects of Christian belief or practice. As numerous scholars have pointed out, the terms "Christian" and "Jew" cannot do justice to such a motley demography. Nevertheless, what does seem to emerge clearly in this sketch is the *link* between the beliefs in the virgin birth and the reliability of the Septuagint from the mid second through the fourth centuries; the Christian veneration of the Septuagint finally began to erode with Jerome's return to the Hebrew truth.

For the first few centuries of the Common Era, then, the sacredness of the Septuagint and the virginity of Mary went hand in hand, constituting a dividing line by which Jewish and Christian identities could be constituted. In Justin Martyr, the first writer to deal extensively with either of these themes, the claims of virginity and translational perfection are so interdependent as to form a single argument; Martin Hengel remarks that although the Septuagint is at issue throughout Justin's *Dialogue with Trypho the Jew,* the LXX wording of Isaiah 7:14 is "the only fully articulated controversy between Justin and Trypho concerning a concrete translation question."[20] That belief in the virgin birth and the reliability of the Septuagint are related is evidenced perhaps most starkly by the "middle positions," particularly that of the Ebionites, who are characterized as having rejected both Mary's virginity and the LXX. Marcel Simon writes:

> All the heresiologists are agreed on the Ebionite's rejection of the virgin birth. *Neque intelligere volentes quoniam Spiritus Sanctus advenit in Mariam, et virtus Altissimi obumbravit eam* [Not wishing to understand that the Holy Spirit came upon Mary, and the power of the Most High overshadowed her], Irenaeus 5,1,3; Jesus is therefore the son of Joseph. Irenaeus says that, in order to support their opinion, the Ebionites followed Theodotion and Aquila in their translation of Isaiah 7:14, *idou hē nēanis en gastri hexei kai texetai huion* [Behold, a young girl will conceive and bear a son], rejecting the *parthenos* of the Septuagint, which was the official translation of Orthodox Christianity.[21]

The debate within Christian circles about the virginity of Mary rests on factors beyond just Matthew's use of a possibly unreliable translation of Isaiah. Matthew's infancy narrative and Luke's parallel account are ambiguous—possibly even self-contradictory—on the crucial point of who, exactly, Jesus's father was. Scholars are agreed that Matthew's narrative impulse (or, as Raymond Brown posits, a "Davidic strand" of the Matthean narrative) was directed at least in part toward demonstrating the descent of Jesus from the royal House of David, a descent important to the Jewish Christians who were among Matthew's first readers; the lengthy genealogy tracing Jesus's ancestry through David that opens Matthew is sufficient testimony to this impulse. Foregrounding the virgin birth would have had the effect of at least complicating this genealogy, since Jesus's Davidic descent is traced, in both Matthew and Luke, through Joseph (though somewhat differently in each case).[22] The problem of Jesus's double paternity, as it were, has left its traces on the tradi-

tion: the famous insertion of Luke—or his redactor—into the Lucan genealogy of Jesus provides an early model for the approach that views Joseph as
Jesus's father solely in a legal and social sense: "Now Jesus himself was about
thirty years old when he began his ministry. He was the son, *so it was thought*
[*hos enomidzeto*], of Joseph, the son of Heli, the son of Matthat," etc. (Luke
3:23). A number of versions and translations of Luke, sensitive to the apparent contradictions between the narrative of the virgin birth and Joseph's status as Jesus's father, similarly replace Jesus's "father and mother" in Luke
2:33 with the less problematic "Joseph and Mary."[23] Exegetical traditions
have sometimes taken another tack, supporting Jesus's genetic claim to Davidic ancestry by describing Mary as Joseph's cousin, and thus a descendant
of the royal house in her own right.[24]

Some early Christians, not all of them Jewish Christians, perceived no
paradox in the double truths of Mary's pregnancy by the Holy Spirit and
Joseph's paternity.[25] Aphraates, the fourth-century Syrian Father, believed
that divine and human paternity stood in no necessary contradiction, while
Diodore, Bishop of Tarsus (also of the fourth century), apparently also disputed the literalist view that Jesus could have been the son of God only if he
had no human father.[26] Jane Schaberg has recently and controversially argued that Matthew in fact made no claim at all that Mary was a virgin at
Jesus's conception (although, unlike the Ebionites, Schaberg is inclined to
view not Joseph but rather an unknown "seducer" as the father). Matthew
1:20, on her reading, describes Mary as pregnant not *by* the Holy Spirit, but
rather with the blessing of or in accordance with [*ek pneumatos estin hagiou*]
"a spirit that is holy."[27]

> [Matthew 1:20] is about a creative act of God that does not replace human pa-
> ternity. Sexual and divine begetting are integrated. Jesus is begotten through the
> Holy Spirit in spite of—or better, because of—his human paternity. . . . This
> child's existence is not an unpremeditated accident, and it is not cursed.[28]

By most scholarly accounts, either the emphasis on the virgin birth or indeed the very belief in it originates in the first communities of Gentile Christians, though we should not assume that the belief was universal, or universally had the same meaning, even within these communities. Geza Vermes
puts it perhaps too schematically: "Whereas in Palestinian and Hellenistic
Judeo-Christianity the colorful narrative of the birth of Jesus in Matthew
1–2 and in Luke 1–2 was read as evidence of his Messiahship and proof of his
Davidic lineage, in the Gentile Christian world it was understood to prove the
divine nature of the son born miraculously to a virgin."[29]

Belief in the virgin birth, then, solidified only gradually in the first few centuries of the Common Era, with a changing interpretive community and under the pressure of anti-Christian debate. Similarly, arguments for the perfection of the Septuagint, linked to the doctrine of Mary's virginity through Matthew's citation of the Septuagint in his infancy narrative, evolved over the course of a few centuries. With the adoption of the Septuagint as the Christian Bible, this belief in its perfection also developed in dialectic response to the rejection of the Septuagint by the Jewish community. But while the virgin birth is arguably a Christian *novum* (in relation to Jewish if not pagan thought), the belief in the perfection of the Septuagint was firmly rooted in the Hellenistic context that is the backdrop to the emergence of both Christianity and rabbinic Judaism.[30] The legends about the origins of the Greek Bible are emblematic of the Alexandrian Jewish cultural project, which has been widely characterized as a marriage of Hebraic monotheism and Greek philosophical universalism. In Paula Fredriksen's view, the Septuagint embodied this fusion in its very language:

> This translation of the Hebrew scriptures into Greek both echoed and facilitated a transfer of ideas from one cultural system to the other. With the Greek language came *paideia*. When, for example, the Jewish God revealed his name to Moses at the burning bush (Ex. 3:14), the Hebrew *ehyeh* (I am) became in the LXX *ho on* (the Being): anyone with an even rudimentary Hellenistic education would recognize in this designation the High God of philosophy. Similarly, when the Lord established the heavens "by a word" (Psalm 33:6), the Hebrew *davar* became the Greek *logos:* the Creator had suddenly acquired a very Hellenistic factotum. Greek concepts, in brief, did not need to be read into scripture. They were already there, by virtue of the new language of the text.[31]

According to a long-held scholarly consensus, the Septuagint is an internal Jewish translation, designed for a diaspora readership that could no longer understand the Hebrew text. By rendering the Bible accessible in Greek and, Fredriksen argues, by *Hellenizing* the Bible, the Septuagint also paved the way for Christianity. As Adolf Deissmann memorably put it at the beginning of the last century, "the Bible whose God is Yahweh is a national Bible, the Bible whose God is *kurios* [LORD] is a universal Bible."[32] From Deissmann it is only a small step to the recognition that the Christian God and Christianity are not only dependent on translation but also a product or effect of translation—more strikingly, of *Jewish* self-translation.

Analyses like Fredriksen's and Deissmann's foreground the philosophical *Tendenz* that shapes the Septuagint as a distinctly Hellenistic artifact. It is the same Hellenism that forms the cultural background for the widespread denial of any difference between the Hebrew and Greek Bibles; most emblematic, in this context, is the "romance" that circulated in antiquity of the Septuagint as a perfect translation, a miraculously precise replica of the Hebrew Bible.[33] This judgment was only rarely based on linguistic argument: a critical comparison of the Hebrew and Greek Bibles would await the facing columns, obelisks, and asterisks of Origen's *Hexapla,* which demonstrated just how far apart, for anyone paying attention, the Greek and Hebrew Bibles actually were (in fact, they represent two divergent textual traditions). It is not until the talmudic versions of the legend that the narrative actually incorporated passages from the Hebrew and Greek (in Hebrew retroversion) by way of making its claim—not of perfection, but rather of perfect mistranslation. Outside these texts, the claim for the accuracy of the Septuagint is advanced through translation narrative, a genre inaugurated in the *Letter of Aristeas* (ca. 130 BCE).

The *Letter,* narrated ostensibly (though hardly believably) by a Gentile courtier in Ptolemy's service who was also an admirer of the Jews, recounts the commissioning of the Septuagint by Ptolemy II Philadelphius (r. 285–247 BCE) for his royal library. The historicity of Aristeas's account has been doubted since at least 1684, when Humphrey Hody, Professor of Greek at Oxford, published a detailed critique positing that the *Letter* was a "forgery" composed by a Jewish pseudepigrapher that constituted an apologia for Judaism. Suspicion was aroused by, among other details, the seventy-two "elders, good and true, six from each tribe"—centuries after the ten northern tribes had been "lost"! In another detail not attested in other sources, Aristeas describes Ptolemy's goodwill gesture to the Jewish translators: the monetary redemption of 100,000 Jewish captives, trained soldiers among them. Erich Gruen writes:

> The tale, of course, should not be confused with history. How likely is it that Ptolemy II marshaled royal resources, commissioned a large number of Palestinian scholars, and financed an elaborate translation of the Books of Moses just to add some volumes to the Alexandrian library? . . . The yarn spun by the *Letter of Aristeas* is largely creative fiction.[34]

If the *Letter* does not describe the origin of the Septuagint, then what cultural circumstance does it reflect? On most readings, the *Letter* records the desire for if not the reality of Jewish–Greek coexistence in the first centuries before the Common Era. Victor Tcherikover characterizes Aristeas as trying to impress upon his readers that "no abyss separates Judaism from Hellenism.

With some good will on both sides, it would be easy to bridge the two worlds."[35] Aristeas's celebration of the Greek Bible, combined with his allegorical readings of Jewish law in a moral-religious language "open to any man who strives to acquire a profound philosophical knowledge," create a space in which neither their distinct languages nor the laws of the Bible can separate Greek and Jew.[36] It seems to me significant that this cultural interaction is expressed through translation narrative—more specifically, through the claim that a *perfect* translation resulted from Jewish–Greek collaboration.[37] From Aristeas through Augustine and beyond, the claim for the equivalence of the Hebrew and Greek is refracted through narrative, mobilizing character, plot, and setting as the necessary background for both producing and evaluating translation. In the *Letter*, for instance, only four or five lines of the more than three hundred describe the translation work itself, although these few lines provide the core of the legend: the seventy-two Jewish elders who come together at the end of each day to agree on a single version, completing their work in exactly seventy-two days "as though this coincidence had been intended."[38] By contrast, the narrative lavishes attention on the commissioning of the translation, the negotiations between Ptolemy and the High Priest Eleazar, the journey of the translators and their sacred scrolls from Palestine to Egypt, the philosophical discussions between the translators and the King, the accommodations made for the translators, and, finally, the celebrations that mark the completion of their work.

Aristeas, then, constructs the perfection of the Septuagint by translating its semiotic operations into cultural and philosophical converse. King Ptolemy and Eleazar the High Priest not only grant retrospective approbation to the LXX translation that had been circulating in Alexandria, they also function as embodiments both of the Egyptian-Greek and Jewish communities and of the Greek and Hebrew languages; and they do so, moreover, with a purity and stature unavailable to the anonymous bilingual Alexandrian Jews whose identities have been lost to history. In these exalted and unadulterated forms, Hebrew and Greek could "meet" to negotiate their political, theological, and cultural equivalence. Not only does political "goodwill" stand in for linguistic translatability; translatability serves the end of political cooperation. In petitioning the King to release Jewish captives taken by his father as a goodwill gesture to the Jews, Aristeas argues for the humanity of these captives through the Hellenistic prism of *theokrasia*, the identification of different national deities as a single, universal God: "Release those who are afflicted in wretchedness," Aristeas urges, "for the same God who has given them their law guides your kingdom also, as I have learned in my researches. God, the overseer and creator of all things, whom they worship, is He whom all men worship, and we too, Your Majesty, though we address him differently, as Zeus and Dis."[39] In the elaborate negotiations between Ptolemy Philadelphus and the High Priest in Jerusalem lies the assurance that this translation will rests on an economy of roughly equivalent gains and losses. The bounteous feasts with which the translators are feted counter any rhetoric that might view translation as a sign of cultural impoverishment, for instance the "diasporic embarrassment" David Gooding postulates was present in Jewish Alexandria.[40] The King treats the translators to the intellectual and sensual riches of a Greek symposium; the translators wash their hands according to Jewish ritual before they partake. The wedding of Greek and Hebrew, cast here as the mutual embrace of philosophy and Torah, could hardly be more vividly celebrated. In the consensus arrived at by the end of each day's work and, most explicitly, in the "coincidence" of the numbers of translators and days in which they complete their work, Aristeas signifies the unity that lies behind the apparent diversity of gods, peoples and sign systems, thus presenting a series of metonymic arguments for translatability.

The reading advanced here, which views translation and cultural encounter as mutual figurations, rests on long-held assumptions about the *Letter of Aristeas* (and, by implication, Jewish Hellenism) that have recently come under critical scrutiny. In Gruen's view, "the idea, prevalent in modern scholarship, that [the *Letter*] promoted a synthesis between Judaism and Hellenism is inadequate." "Aristeas," the fictional narrator who is a courtier in Ptolemy's court, may democratically assert the interchangeability of the gods, but the High Priest Eleazar is of quite a different opinion, one that presumably corresponds more closely with the Jewish author's: "Eleazar affirms the uniqueness of Jewish practices and principles, Jewish sages surpass Greek philosophers, and the Torah receives obeisance from the king of Egypt."[41] For Gruen, the *Letter* is not only a work of fiction, it is a transparent and extravagant fantasy that does not "refrain even from a few sly pleasantries at the expense of the king and his ministers." Gruen concludes: "Jewish readers would have found it immensely gratifying."[42] Aristeas in his *Letter* thus rewrites the Exodus story for a new era, imagining a Torah so attractive to Greek-speaking Egyptians and so ripe with divine wisdom that it neatly springs the lock on Jewish captivity.[43] On the other hand, the narrative makes clear that, even for Aristeas, translation remains a fraught enterprise, just as Egypt remains the house of bondage for the twelve tribes and their seventy(-two) descendants. That Pharos in its sublime seclusion may also become a prison, a new Goshen for the laboring translators—the subtext only fully realized in the separate paranoia of the Fathers and the Rabbis—is the threat that troubles even Aristeas's irenic tableau.

THE legend of the composition of the Septuagint is attested in roughly seventy ancient versions (might there be exactly 72?!), but Philo's, which can be retroactively read as the "pivot" between Jewish and Christian versions, holds a particularly consequential place. Philo, like Aristeas, translates textual equivalence into narrative terms, mobilizing setting and plot to illustrate the perfection of the Septuagint. But while Aristeas lovingly details the social intricacies, the hesitations and flirtations of the Septuagint romance, Philo is barely interested in the encounter between Greek and Jew, only roughly sketching Ptolemy's dealings with the High Priest and the translators and eliminating the character of Demetrius the librarian altogether.[44] Even communication among the translators has been stilled. In Aristeas's account, the translators perfect their work through dialogue and, at the end of each day, arrive at consensus through a comparison of drafts. For Philo, who broadens and generalizes the peaceful quiet of Pharos's bedchambers, it is in sublime and absolute solitude that "every one of them employed the self-same nouns and verbs."[45] Aristeas's encounter of Greek and Jew is cast in Philo (or in the tradition from which Philo draws) as a harmony between nature and text, and between God and humanity. Aristeas suggests the divine provenance of the translation through an unexpected, even arbitrary coincidence of the number of translators and the number of days they worked. Philo, in contrast, bolsters his explicit claim of the Septuagint's divine equivalence to the Hebrew Bible through the non-arbitrary correspondences of Creator and creation, nature and Torah.[46]

> Having taken the sacred scriptures, they lifted them up and their hands also to heaven, entreating of God that they might not fail in their object. And he assented to their prayers, that the greater part, or indeed the universal race of mankind might be benefited, by using these philosophical and entirely beautiful commandments for the correction of their lives.
>
> Therefore, being settled in a secret place, and nothing even being present with them except the elements of nature, the earth, the water, the air, and the heaven, concerning the creation of which they were going in the first place to explain the sacred account; for the account of the creation of the world is the beginning of the law; they, like men inspired, prophesied, not one saying one thing and another another, but every one of them employed the self-same nouns and verbs, as if some unseen prompter had suggested all their language to them. And yet who is there who does not know that every language, and the Greek language

above all others, is rich in a variety of words, and that it is possible to vary a sentence and to paraphrase the same idea, so as to set it forth in a great variety of manners, adapting many different forms of expression to it a different times.

But this, they say, did not happen at all in the case of this translation of the law, but that, in every case, exactly corresponding Greek words were employed to translate literally the appropriate Chaldaic words, being adapted with exceeding propriety to the matters which were to be explained; for just as I suppose the things that are proved in geometry and logic do not admit any variety of explanation, but the proposition which was set forth from the beginning remains unaltered, in like manner I conceive did these men find words precisely and literally corresponding to the things, which words were alone, or in the greatest possible degree, destined to explain with clearness and force the matters which it was desired to reveal.[47]

Philo here finds a stunning way around the age-old problem of establishing the equivalence of a source text and its translation, displacing the site of equivalence from an interlingual aporia to the verifiable correspondence among independently produced versions: that the translation must be accurate—even divinely inspired—is proven by the fact that numerous translators, working in isolation, produce identical versions. The unanimity of the translation is a mystical achievement, a form of spirit-channeling.[48] Although Philo appreciates the idiomatic quality of language and thus the difficulty of precise translation, the Septuagint stands in a unique correspondence with its divine referent that approaches the signifying clarity and univocality of "geometry and logic." The passage continues: "If Chaldaeans were to learn the Greek language, and if Greeks were to learn Chaldaean [Hebrew], and if each were to meet with those scriptures in both languages, namely the Chaldaic and the translated version, they would admire and reverence them both as sisters, or rather as one and the same both in their facts and in their language; considering these translators not mere interpreters but hierophants and prophets to whom it had been granted in their honest and guileless minds to go along with the most pure spirit of Moses."[49]

Francesca Calabi points out that Philo's term here for the translation "is not, as might be expected, *metagraphein*, but *hermeneuein* [interpretation]."[50] (Aristeas's *Letter*, by contrast, introduces the translation project toward the opening of his narrative with the first verb, "translation," and only uses the second, "interpretation," in describing the perfect finished project.) While *hermeneuein* might imply a (loose) "exegetical" translation, Philo uses the term to signify the uniquely precise relationship between the *Logos* and its expression—but only in rare instances, most emblematically in Moses' "translation" of God's thought into the "mathematically" perfect transcription of the Torah.[51] Philo's *Logos*, Ronald Williamson stresses, has many meanings, but "the one that it definitely should not have—despite the Vulgate's *verbum* and some English translations of the Prologue to John's Gospel—is the meaning 'word.'"[52] *Logos* is rather "the spiritual Mind of the transcendent God" and its manifestations "in the natural world and within man himself."[53] Thus, *hermeneuein*, as Calabi makes clear, refers not to the transfer of meaning from one language to another, but rather to the translation of divine thought into human language.[54] The Septuagint is a perfect translation not because the Hebrew and Greek match each other but because both the Greek and the Hebrew perfectly "translate" the *Logos;* that Philo refers to both Moses and the translators as *prophetēs* and *hierophantēs* suggests the identity of their activities. Scholars who take Philo's assertion of the equivalence of Hebrew and Greek Bibles as evidence that he knew no Hebrew misunderstand his linguistic theory, according to David Winston:

> If the original Hebrew text and its Greek version did not, to say the least, appear to be all that close, Philo could readily attribute this discrepancy to the narrowly limited perspective that guides the superficial reader, who is unable to plumb the deeper significations of either text. Philo evidently assumed that every divergence of the Greek version, when properly understood, reveals the true meaning of the Hebrew biblical text.[55]

The superficial similarities between Aristeas's and Philo's versions of the Septuagint legend—the commission of the work by Ptolemy, the importation of translators from Judea, the setting of the work on Pharos, the celebration upon completion—should not obscure the radical reorientation of the very conception of translation that occurs in Philo. Where Aristeas employs what could be called a primarily horizontal theory of translation, Philo's imagination is captured rather by what could be constructed as the *vertical* axis of translation, the relationship between a transcendental signified and its human signifiers, neutralizing or reducing the horizontal play of meaning between languages.[56] Aristeas figures the translational meeting of Hebrew and Greek through a series of paired encounters, most emblematically the translators working toward consensus, but also the King and the High Priest, the librarian and the translators, and so on, arriving at a version through cooperation and exchange. Philo envisions translation, of the Bible at least, as a relationship that connects the individual translator with a single "invisible prompter" in the heavens toward which the translators prayerfully raise their (closed?) books. Translation is no longer about the space where languages meet, a politically, socially, and religiously charged frontier; translation, at least of the Bible, occurs rather in the ether *above* all languages, through the one source of truth and meaning connecting transcendence and immanence that, for Philo, is the *Logos*. The *Logos* (re)produces not merely close relations—sisters—below, but its own univocal reflection: two languages, perfect twin offspring of the *Logos*, become one.

NOT surprisingly, it was primarily Philo's version of the Septuagint legend that was adopted and elaborated by the early Church. As others have argued, however, Philo's Platonic dualism and allegorical hermeneutics undergo a dramatic shift in the Fathers, with the oppositions soul/body, signified/signifier, *inter alia*, viewed not as complementary if hierarchical pairs but rather as antagonistic rivals. That Philo distanced himself from what he considered the extremism of the Allegorists, who rejected the literal observance of Jewish law in favor of its spiritual significance, while Pauline Christianity arguably begins with such a rejection (at least for Gentiles), can serve as an exemplum of this shift. In Rosemary Radford Ruether's words, Philo knew of Hellenistic Jews "who would take the relationship between outer law and inner meaning as accidental and discardable," but "it remained for Christianity to take [Philo's] spiritualizing midrash and to interpret the relation of spirit and law as antithetical, and even as divinely abrogated by the 'coming' of the inner spiritual meaning of that which was 'foreshadowed' in the outer law and history."[57] The stricter policing of Philo's dualist borders must surely be linked to the fact that the root opposition body/spirit and its corollaries were increasingly mapped onto Jewish–Christian difference, with Jews representing Israel "according to the flesh" (*kata sarka*) and Christians taking the superior role of Israel "according to the spirit" (*kata pneuma*). Paul's usage of *in the flesh* and *in the spirit*[58] is elaborated in patristic thought into a taxonomy of Jewish and Christian interpretation, in which the Jew is aligned with the "body" of language and the Christian with its "spirit."

By Augustine's time, however, this distinction is well in place as a myth of Christian origins. Augustine's privileging of *cognitio* (thought) over *locutio* (spoken words) derives its basic structure from Philo's *Logos* theory, which viewed mind as the divine aspect of human existence and speech as its fallen, corporeal dimension. Nevertheless, the "political economy" of Augustine's thought is propelled as least partially by the supplementary associations of Christianity with thought and Judaism as the husk and shell that is speech— associations Philo would obviously not have endorsed. It is in patristic thought that what could be called a Christian translation theory is systematically constructed, promoting, in Aleida Assmann's words, "transcendence of the written law and its letter, translation of the Holy Scripture [or *Logos*], transformation in history. In affirming the Holy Spirit as an immaterial energy, Christianity cut off its links with the letter of the law—that is, with its Jewish roots."[59]

The evolution of the Septuagint legend is only one lens among many for tracking the crucial shift from Philonic to patristic semiotics. Precisely because it describes translation through ethnically encoded narrative, though, the legend provides a uniquely transparent view into the ideology underlying this philosophical process. The Christian sign theory that emerged in close conjunction with the patristic development of the Septuagint legend eventually achieved a dominance that rendered its political subtext nearly invisible. In the analysis of the Christian Septuagint legend, where characters and plot take the place of a universalizing and ethnically neutral symbology, the Jewish–Christian stakes in Western sign theory rise tantalizingly close to the surface.

In moving from Philo to the Fathers, the account of the composition of the Septuagint undergoes both a political and a semiotic shift. Most strikingly, the translators are explicitly viewed not as Ptolemy's honored guests but rather as his untrustworthy prisoners. The hero of the Christian tales is Ptolemy, who wrests the true Word of God from the cunning and reluctant Jews by ingeniously devising a plan that will prevent them from colluding. The logic behind this translation-as-incarceration method is clear enough: while for Philo, the Septuagint is perfect because the translators are pious prophets, for the Fathers, the Septuagint is a perfect document *despite* its having been composed by Jews. The authority of the Septuagint, as the Bible of the early Church, needed to be defended not only against the Hebrew texts of Jewish interlocutors but also against the second-century Jewish (or Jewish–Christian) retranslations of Aquila, Symmachus, and Theodotion, which presented themselves as corrections of LXX inaccuracies. The legend in Aristeas and Philo that spoke to the hopes for Jewish–Greek cooperation turned out to have legs in the service of Jewish–Christian difference: if the Septuagint is a perfect rendering, then the Hebrew sources of the Jews are irrelevant. For early Christians dependent on the translations of rival groups, the existence of a tradition guaranteeing the sacredness, accuracy, and divine inspiration of this translation was itself literally heaven-sent. That the translation was completed before the birth of Jesus meant that these Jews could be trusted not to have deliberately obscured the Christological dimension of the texts; on the other hand, it could also never be claimed that they had appended the messianic prophecies Christians saw so clearly in their texts. Irenaeus, defending the Septuagint as free of either anti-Christian animus or Jewish pandering, emphasizes that the translation

> was interpreted into Greek by the Jews themselves, much before the Lord's advent, that there might be no suspicion that the Jews, perhaps complying with our humor, did put this [messianic] interpretation on [Isaiah's] words. These translators indeed, had they been cognizant of our future existence, and that we should use these Scriptures, would themselves have never hesitated to burn their own Scriptures.[60]

For Aristeas and Philo, the perfection of the Septuagint is a tribute to the learning and wisdom of the translators. In Irenaeus, the perfection hinges rather on their *blindness* to the significance of their own words. This blindness, expressible as the difference that inheres between the Christological signified and Jewish signifier, is mobilized in Irenaeus to quell anxieties about deliberate Jewish mistranslation.

Philo had already put in place most of the elements necessary for a Christian appropriation of the legend. The equivalence of the translations in Philo guaranteed that the translators were divine prophets—Christians needed only to add that God, foreseeing a world of Christian readers, had graciously provided, centuries in advance, a Bible in their own tongue.[61] Such an argument could also explain apparent discrepancies between the Septuagint and Hebrew manuscripts, since the LXX constituted the Christian Bible: Augustine, for one, conceded that even if the Septuagint was not a perfect replica of the Hebrew Bible it was nevertheless divinely ordained, since the Seventy "translated in the manner in which the Holy Spirit, who guided them and gave one voice to them all, judged to be appropriate for Gentiles."[62] It was Philo, too, who introduced the element of the isolation of the translators, though primarily to underscore the dominance of the vertical, *Logos*-oriented mode of translation over Aristeas's horizontal, interlinguistic structure. For the Christian versions from Justin on, Philo's vertical model serves as well to rule out the very possibility of horizontal translation. Thus, Pseudo-Justin expresses the isolation of the translators not through Philo's "contemplative" discourse but rather through an elaborated architecture of translation:

> Ptolemy ordered the construction of as many cottages as there were translators, not in the city itself, but seven stadia distant. . . . He ordered the officers to prevent any communication with one another. This is so the accuracy of the translation could be verified by their agreement. When Ptolemy discovered that the seventy men not only had all given the same meanings but had even used the same words . . . he believed that the translation had been written by divine power. . . . I myself have seen the remains of the little cottages at the Pharos.[63]

The translators who in Aristeas and Philo work in the hope of granting the nations access to the Torah are viewed as unwilling—if perfect—conduits of the *Logos* whose reliability is imposed by the administrative genius of a gentile king and, as is characteristic of etiological legends, verified by a reliable eyewitness—Saint Justin himself. The translation is a triumph of Greek wisdom and Christian providence over Jewish obduracy; biblical secrets were wrested from the Jews. In Christianity, Philo's vision was both frustrated and fulfilled: the Torah, spiritualized in its Greek translation, had crossed over to humanity, but the Jews, unwilling transmitters and literalist misreaders of their texts, were deterred from following. The Augustinian and Saussurian bar between signified and signifier, between divine message and Jewish medium, is itself literalized in the patristic Septuagint tradition, becoming the barred cells that immobilize the translators while setting free the works— the works are unlocked to all with precisely the key that is turned against their translators.

For Philo, as we have seen, translatability rests on the uniquely perfect correspondence of the *Logos* as transcendental signified and its human "translation" by such prophets as Moses and the Septuagint translators; more accurately, Philo's *Logos* serves as the mediator between transcendent and immanent meaning. Philo's sign-system is not entirely coherent, however. David Winston claims, in fact, that Philo describes two sign-systems: one that imagines the perfect and non-arbitrary relation of divine thought and human language in certain special circumstances, for instance Mosaic naming; and another, more general, sign-system that characterizes human language as the fallen and arbitrary vessel of exalted thought. The name, writes Philo, "is always subsequent in order to the subject of which it is the name; being like the shadow which follows the body."[64] As Winston characterizes it, in the great majority of his writings Philo expresses a "virtual revulsion from the spoken word" as belonging to "the sense-perceptible realm of duality and infirmity, whereas [the mind] as based on the indivisible Monad is characterized by perfect stability and resembles the pure and unalloyed speech of God."[65] In Winston's account, Philo's "exaggerated attempt" to emphasize the "absolute precision of Mosaic name-making" (and, I would add, the perfection of the Septuagint) "clearly transgressed the bounds of his own epistemological principles."[66]

Philo distinguished the perfect correspondence of *Logos* and signifier in the writings of Moses and the Septuagint translators from all other imperfect signifying practices because of his "irrepressible urge to [Jewish] one-upmanship," in Winston's phrase. The patristic adoption of Philo's more general theory of signification, in which the spiritual meaning is valorized over its embodiment in human language, might be credited to *Christian* one-upmanship. With the patristic development of the Septuagint legend, we arrive at a theory of translation that rehearses the distinction between signifier and signified, encoding this distinction through Jewish–Christian difference—in striking contrast to Philo's figuring of the *union* of signified and signifier through the perfect Jewish prophet, whether Moses or the anonymous Septuagint translator. According to Derrida, the distinction between signifier and signified that grounds Western linguistic theory cannot be ultimately upheld; that this distinction is never absolute, Derrida writes, does not

> prevent it from functioning, and even from being indispensable within certain limits—very wide limits. For example, no translation would be possible without it. And in fact the theme of a transcendental signified was constituted within the horizon of an absolutely pure, transparent and unequivocal translatability. Within the limits to which it is possible, or at least *appears* possible, translation practices the difference between signified and signifier.[67]

Although the difference between signified and signifier is implied, according to Derrida, in all translation, patristic translation theory puts a particularly persistent pressure on this difference, separating signified and signifier by fiat according to what could be called an incarceral logic that prevents their interaction. Nowhere is this logic more fully elaborated than in the account of Epiphanius of Constantia (392 CE), who introduces the notion of thirty-six pairs of translators only to raise the walls higher against their tricks. (The thirty-six translator-pairs in Epiphanius are sometimes explained as arising by association with Luke 10:1, in which the seventy disciples go out to the world in pairs.) As in Aristeas, Philo, and Justin, the Jewish elders are lodged on Pharos, but Epiphanius adds a number of telling details:

> The [thirty-six] cells were erected by the aforementioned Ptolemy on the island across the water. He made them in two compartments and shut in the men two and two, as I said; and he shut in with them two ministering attendants to cook and to wait upon them, and they had two shorthand writers in addition. He did not so much as make windows in the walls of those cells, but had what are called "skylights" opened in the roofs above their heads. So they lived from morn until eve under lock and key and so they translated. . . . When the work was completed, the king took his seat on a lofty throne, and thirty-six readers sat at his feet having the thirty-six reproductions of each book, while one held a copy of the Hebrew volume. Then one reader recited and the rest diligently attended; and there was found no discrepancy.[68]

As in Philo's version, Epiphanius figures translation as the flow of a spiritual message from a higher to a lower region. But while Philo's translators receive the divine *Logos* through mystical identification, Epiphanius insists on the subordination of the translators, whose obedience to the message they transmit is assured solely by the walls that compel this relation. When the translation is complete, the translators mimic their subordination to God's word in sitting at the king's feet; Epiphanius's articulation of the perfect consonance of religious and imperial authority may indeed reflect the recent triumph of Christianity as the religion of the empire. The "skylights," apparently Epiphanius's personal contribution to the tradition, are a syncretistic architectural feature, combining the vertical axis of Philo's translation theory with Justin's restraint of internal Jewish conversation. The high walls may have come from Philo, too, though not from the *Life of Moses,* where the Septuagint is discussed, but rather from his lovingly detailed portrait of the Therapeutae; it is surely not irrelevant, in this context, to mention that Philo's description was taken by Eusebius for a depiction of the early Christian community in Alexandria:[69]

> And this common holy place to which they all come together on the seventh day is a twofold circuit, being separated partly into the apartment of the men, and partly into a chamber for the women . . . and the wall which is between the houses rises from the ground three or four cubits upwards, like a battlement, and the upper portion rises upwards to the roof without any opening. . . .
>
> Then, when each chorus of the men and each chorus of the women has feasted separately by itself, like persons in the bacchanalian revels, drinking the pure wine of the love of God, they join together, and the two become one chorus.[70]

Philo's description of the choruses of male and female ascetics joining together above their separate enclosures echoes his celebration of the harmony and unity of the Greek and Hebrew Bibles as more than sisters. On the spiritual plane, above the walls that "preserve the modesty which is so becoming to the female sex," the erotic union of masculine and feminine may occur, as a symbol of the union of the soul with the One. Epiphanius preserves the high walls, but to other ends: the "purity" of the translators, the restrictions against their intercourse, are for the spiritual benefit not of themselves but of the Christian text they produce. In the solitary confinement of the Jewish translators, Epiphanius imagines a translation degree zero, with the translator reduced to the status not of the *perfect* channel of the *Logos* (as in Philo), but rather of an *empty* channel, the medium or vehicle for a message that not only transcends its signifiers but also travels cleanly through them, without contamination by these conduits. For the Fathers, Douglas Robinson writes, "the only way the Hebrew Bible can lay claim to being God's word is if its translators wrote not as their human selves but as the channels of God's spirit; and the only way the Septuagint can lay claim to being God's Word is if its translators channeled that same spirit also."[71]

Epiphanius and Augustine, then, not only imprison the Jewish translators, they also convert them into (involuntary) monks.[72] Augustine, who composed a monastic Rule, and Epiphanius, Bishop of Salamis, who founded monasteries throughout Cyprus, were both major figures of the fourth-century monastic revolution, which elaborated and institutionalized the earlier Christian fascination with (primarily female) virginity. Gregory of Nyssa, in his discourse *On Virginity* (ca. 375 CE), explains the value of celibate life, in Mark Hart's summary, "with a metaphor, comparing it to a canal that prevents water—our erotic inclinations—from spreading out all over in disorderly streams and thus being unable to reach the appropriate goal—the 'truly good.'"[73] Monastic architecture from Philo on literalized and materialized this metaphor, guiding the suppression of the body through the impenetrable and controlling walls that also figured the suppressed body itself. The walls signified as they compelled virtue: the Desert Mother Amma Sara took pride in never once having seen the Nile flowing beneath her cell, and surely her worldly neighbors pointed with pride at the walls that enclosed her.[74] Drawing on the second-century *Protevangelium of James*, fourth-century writers also found a model for female seclusion in the dedication of the Virgin Mary, at the age of three, to the Temple.[75] Pharos, the site of the Septuagint translation in every account beginning with Aristeas, was close to the epicenter of the ascetic imagination: the hermits' cells and fortress monasteries outside Alexandria or clinging to cliffs in the Egyptian desert had provided images of the monastic life, if not since Philo's *Therapeutae*, then certainly beginning with Athanasius's wildly popular *Life of Anthony*.

In Epiphanius's elaboration of the Septuagint legend, then, there is a contagion between the two great patristic subjects of the fourth century, translation and virginity. That the Jewish elders, mistrusted opponents, are turned into monks, the century's culture heroes and representatives of heaven on earth, is less of a paradox than might first appear. The cell imprisons the monk's body the better to free his eternal soul; by patristic analogy, (the body of) the Jewish translator is put behind bars the better to free the eternal *Logos*. Monks might, it was fervently hoped, perfect a spiritual as well as physical virginity; for the Jewish translators (as for Isaiah's *'almah*), only their physical "continence" mattered, and that was taken care of by the cell walls that enclosed them.

In a book-length meditation on the "discipline" of translation, Douglas Robinson describes Augustine's translation theory as an *askesis*, a "'subtraction' of the self" in which the translator is taught "piety toward the source text and submission toward the institution that maintains it (controls its interpretation, commissions its translation)."[76] From Augustine on, Robinson argues, Christianity has idealized translation as a form of self-erasure, and this ascetic imperative continues to shape (to *oppress*, in Robinson's view) translation in the West.[77] The severity of this disciplinary regimen, I would add, is overdetermined at its patristic inception. If the monks' cells are also prison cells, it is because the translators are also Jews.

VIRGINITY AND (PERFECT) TRANSLATION

In the monk's cell, as in the *'almah–parthenos* crux, the parallel discourses of translation and virginity very nearly meet. But the discourses of translation and virginity are related metaphorically as well as metonymically. The perfection of the LXX translation, in early Christian thought, develops according to a hydraulic logic that also appears in Christian conceptions of the Virgin Mary. In both cases, the divine *Logos* flows without impediment into the human realm. The identical translations of the Seventy connect the *Logos* with its textual manifestation in the Septuagint; in structurally similar ways, Mary's virginity connects Father and Son, *Logos* with its embodiment in Jesus Christ.

Mary's virginity has been interpreted (especially recently) as a symbol of her freedom not only from sin but also from possession by and subjugation to men. Certainly, as Raymond Brown eloquently puts it, "The virginal conception has given a *woman* a central role in Christianity. . . . When no woman could stand publicly in the sanctuary of churches, it was symbolically significant that a statue of the Virgin stood there."[78] But, as many Christian feminists have argued, the doctrine of Mary's virginity has also functioned to control female sexuality and eventually—in the Nicene Trinitarianism (325) that underscored the paternal relationship—to appropriate her role in bringing Jesus into history. Increasingly throughout the patristic period, Mary is figured as God's perfectly passive instrument, the passageway between Christ's heavenly and earthly abodes rather than his sole procreator. Christian writers echoed the Stoic view of conception, in which the man's seed, divided into body and soul, joins with a part of the woman's *pneuma* to form the embryo. In the most radical of these accounts, the homunculus enters a woman's womb "whole," with the mother merely providing the environment for its growth; Tertullian (d. ca. 230), for instance, writes that "the whole fruit is already present in the semen."[79] To illustrate Mary's role, Christian art sometimes depicted Mary holding a baker's tray, to symbolize her role as the oven in which Jesus, the bread of life, was baked.[80] The Apostles' Creed (early fourth century) affirms that Jesus Christ was "conceived of the Holy Spirit, born of the Virgin Mary" (conceptus est de Spirito Sancto, ex Maria Virgine). Jerome, countering Jovinianus's belief that the birth of Jesus was "a true parturition," insists rather that the miracle in Isaiah's prophecy is "that a woman should compass a man, and that the Father of all things should be contained in a virgin's womb."[81]

With the move to a religious community comprising primarily Gentiles, the early Christian reduction of first Joseph's and then even Mary's role in the conception of Jesus served the purpose, among others, of constructing Jesus as the child not of Jewish parents, but of a universal God. It is just such a sexual manipulation that can be glimpsed in the writing of Gustav Volkmar, a theologian who participated in the nineteenth-century Protestant project of distancing Jesus from his Jewish environment: "The Judaism that formed the religious background to Jesus and Christianity was not the Pharisaic Judaism dominant during the Second Temple era, but the 'virgin womb' of the God of Judaism."[82] Volkmar presents us with a modern revision of the medieval depictions of a perfect, fully formed infant Jesus in his mother's womb. In these and other images of the Virgin Mary, the uncomfortable dependence of Christianity on Jewish texts and Jewish women's bodies—on *any* body—is reduced to the barest minimum.

JEWISH counterarguments to the patristic beliefs in Mary's virginity and the perfection of the Septuagint are either absent or difficult to discern, in part because of a history of censorship and self-censorship. We can often best reconstruct such arguments from their citation in Christian sources. Summarizing this evidence, Marina Warner writes that "the doctrine of the virgin birth was attacked far more frequently because it was common in pagan belief than because it was unlikely in nature. Its resemblance to the metamorphoses of the gods of antiquity exposed a Christian nerve."[83] In his *Dialogue with Trypho,* for example, Justin expends considerable effort rejecting Trypho's claim that the Christian belief in Jesus's virgin birth is an obvious borrowing from pagan religions, and thus as unsuitable for a Christian as for a Jew. As Justin quotes Trypho,

> In the fables of those who are called Greeks, it is written that Perseus was begotten of Danae, who was a virgin; he who was called among them Zeus having descended on her in the form of a golden shower. And you ought to feel ashamed

when you make assertions similar to theirs, and rather [should] say that this Jesus was born man of men.[84]

Justin's *Apology* makes clear his indignation at such suggestions, distinguishing sharply between the erotic encounters between mortals and gods in pagan religion and the sexless conception of Jesus Christ:

> Lest some, not understanding the prophecy which has been referred to [in Matthew], should bring against us the reproach that we bring against the poets who say that Zeus came upon women for the sake of sexual pleasure, we will try to explain these words clearly. For "Behold, the Virgin shall conceive" means that the Virgin would conceive without intercourse. For if she had had intercourse with anyone, she would not have been a virgin; but God's power, coming upon the Virgin, overshadowed her, and caused her to conceive while still remaining a virgin.[85]

The claim that the virgin-birth motif was borrowed from pagan myth was accompanied by charges that Mary had been seduced by a Roman soldier named Panthera or Pandera. From Origen's *Against Celsus* (ca. 248), historians have tentatively reconstructed a Jewish counternarrative to the New Testament through what constitutes third-hand evidence (Origen quotes the pagan philosopher Celsus who recounts a Jewish rumor); Origen writes, "Let us return, however, to the words put into the mouth of the Jew [by Celsus], where the mother of Jesus is described as having been turned out by the carpenter who was betrothed to her, as she had been convicted of adultery and had a child by a certain soldier named Panthera."[86]

Some corroboration of Celsus's rumor may be provided by a number of oblique talmudic references, some to Jesus as Yeshu ben Pandera.[87] The sole passage in the Mishnah that has sometimes been read as referring to Jesus (though this is very far from a consensus view) describes Rabbi Simeon ben Azzai responding to the question "Who is a bastard?" by saying, "I found a family register [*megillat yoḥsin*] in Jerusalem and in it was written so-and-so [*ploni*] is a bastard [*mamzer*] through [a transgression of the law against having sex with] a married woman."[88] Taken together, the charge that virgin conception is a pagan notion and the charge that Mary had relations with a Roman soldier serve to deny Jesus a Jewish father and Christianity a Jewish cultural patrimony. In describing Jesus's father as a Roman soldier, the mission to the Gentiles is recast as sexual collaboration, as "sleeping with the enemy." In this discourse, Jesus's father is not the universal God but rather an earthly parody of divinity in the form of a strutting Roman soldier; that some of these Jewish texts date from the period following the conversion of the Empire should come as no surprise. The God of Christianity is implicitly exposed, in both versions, as a pagan; it is not the Jewish message that reached a Gentile world in Christianity but rather Gentile beliefs—and soldiers—that corrupted the integrity of Hebraic monotheism and the purity of Jewish bloodlines.

If evidence for an early Jewish counterhistory of Christianity is slim, the Talmud does present an extraordinary Jewish counternarrative to the patristic Septuagint legends (which themselves, of course, are variations on the Jewish Septuagint romances of Aristeas and Philo).[89] The tale is recounted in numerous versions; here is the best known:

> It has been taught, the story goes that King Ptolemy assembled seventy-two elders and lodged them in seventy-two rooms without disclosing to them the reason for assembling them, and he went in to each and ordered them, "write me the Torah of Moses your master." The Holy One, blessed be He, put wisdom in the heart of each one so that they agreed with one accord and wrote for him . . . [here follows the list of LXX alterations—N.S.]. (b. Megilla 9a)

The basic elements of the patristic legend are in place, most importantly Ptolemy's cells. And not surprisingly. Although the initial rabbinic view of the Septuagint seems to have been positive, the translation was apparently viewed with increasing ambivalence in the course of the rabbinic period, as I discussed in the introduction to this book. A translation this lamentable, with its dismal afterlife as the Christian "Old Testament," *must* have been initiated by a non-Jew and could *only* have been produced under compulsion. Where the rabbinic story differs sharply from the patristic versions is in implying that the elders deliberately altered the Greek Bible—the very charge the patristic legend is aimed at refuting.[90] In Philo and Justin, divine inspiration guarantees the accuracy, indeed the perfection, of the translation. Here God's invisible prompting produces, in crucial passages, identical *mistranslations* (though presumably the rest of the Greek Bible constitutes a perfectly accurate translation in the rabbinic as in the patristic versions). Irenaeus defends the Septuagint as untouched by Jewish tampering; the Talmud boasts that even Ptolemy's cell walls could not stop Jewish collusion. The Fathers imagine the Jewish translators as passive channels of God's message to the world; in the talmudic account God works to keep certain things between the Jews and himself, not only sanctioning Jewish conspiracy but taking the role of conspirator-in-chief. In this regard, the talmudic rewriting of the patristic Septuagint legend is a trickster text: the translator is a trickster, who in folklore "represents the weak, whose wit can at times achieve ambiguous victories against the powers of the strong."[91] Not only does the Talmud present the composition of the Septuagint as an elaborate Jewish trick, it also describes those passages in the Hebrew Bible itself as a "hidden transcript," the private discourse of a minority culture.

As Scott writes in another context, "What may look from above like the extraction of required performance can easily look from below like the artful manipulation of deference and flattery to achieve its own ends."[92] The talmudic list of alterations suggest that the Septuagint is both a "required performance" and one that manipulates, at least in part, through "deference and flattery." *Megilla* records fifteen changes, five of which correspond with the LXX as we have it (another is close); other passage have longer or shorter lists (of course, there are not fifteen differences between the Septuagint and the Hebrew Bible the rabbis had, sometimes referred to as the proto-Masoretic text, but rather hundreds, including entire books—the texts belong to different manuscript families).[93] The alterations are a varied group, ranging from apparently "theological" revisions—the alteration of those verses in the Hebrew that speak of God in the plural, for instance—to the last and most curious revision, which the Talmud forthrightly describes as political. The Talmud tells us that the translators wrote *tse'irat raglayim* ("young-footed")[94] in the verse in Leviticus 11:6 that describes the hare as un-kosher: "and they did not write *arnevet* ("hare," or Greek *lagos*) since Ptolemy's wife's name was 'hare,' that he might not say 'the Jews have mocked me by putting my wife's name in the Torah.'" This last alteration, with its radical drop in register, has the effect of retroactively suggesting a political reading of the entire list, including the "theological" changes (in fact, Jerome advances such a political reading of the alterations in his own discussion of the Septuagint). From this perspective, the "union" of Greek philosophy and Hebraic religion is revealed not as a noble attempt to strip the Bible of anthropomorphism and the remnants of its attachment to "pagan" myth, but rather as a series of obsequies, strategic gestures for the survival of a people in the face of the overwhelming culture that surrounded it. Reversing the patristic plot, the translators are released from their cells, while the Hebrew Bible remains enclosed behind the high walls of the Hebrew language; what the Gentiles get is something else altogether. Submission and subversion here turn out to be simultaneous strategies: the Septuagint, as an imperfect translation, is also a perfect mistranslation. In this account, the translators' infidelity interrupts the perfect communication between Hebrew and Greek, God and Gentiles, in the name of linguistic difference, ethnic survival, and the privacy of Jewish discourse.

The hermeneutic that underlies the patristic legend assumes a transcendental signified "above" all languages and peoples that functions as the guarantor of perfect translatability; that the translators are Jews is thus rendered irrelevant to the transcription of this universal meaning. In the hermeneutic at play in the rabbinic Septuagint legend, "the Holy One, blessed be He" is in close alliance with the Jews; rendering the divine message for any people, in any other language, produces a new message. The patristic distinction between signified and signifier reappears in the Talmud as a distinction between signifier and signifier. The movement I am tracing here, from patristic to rabbinic sign theories, has an echo as well in the passage from Derrida that I quoted above. Having argued that translation depends on the difference between signifier and signified, and that this difference relies in turn on the notion of translatability, Derrida goes on to complicate this syllogism:

> But if this difference [between signifier and signified] is never pure, translation is no more so; and for the notion of translation we would have to substitute a notion of transformation: a regulated transformation of one language by another, of one text by another. We will never have, and in fact have never had, any "transfer" of pure signifieds—from one language to another, or within one language— *which would be left virgin and intact* by the signifying instrument or "vehicle."⁹⁵

Derrida, in this passage, argues against virginity and perfect translation simultaneously. But while Derrida denies the *possibility* of such a "virginal" translation, the rabbis rather implicitly deny its value. For a virginal translation, the rabbis substitute a divinely "regulated transformation of one language by another." The transformation recorded in the Talmud, though, is less a translation theory than an assertion of the unique relations between "the Holy One, Blessed be He," the "Holy Tongue," and the Jewish people; the Bible, in any other language, for any other people, is a different Bible altogether.

THE literature on both sides, read as a generalized play of discourses and counterdiscourses, can sometimes appear as a series of stubbornly opposing truth claims: Jesus is the only-begotten son of God, or, on the other hand, Jesus is the illegitimate son of a Roman soldier. But not only is there internal variation within these discourses, as I have tried to show; even the most polemical or straightforward of Jewish or Christian claims about translation or conception reveal the shakiness of the ground on which they stand. The most graphic descriptions of Jesus's conception and birth that we can find in Jewish or Christian texts, for instance, implicitly acknowledge the difficulty of knowing with utter certainty, about anyone at all, the circumstances of their coming into being.⁹⁶ Pushed to the wall of narrative realism, the stories of Jesus's birth testify that the truth claims made about the father and the son,

in any patriarchal culture, nevertheless rest uncomfortably on the reliability
of a woman's word and the faithfulness of a woman's body.

Sefer Toldot Yeshu, a Jewish version of the life of Jesus that exists in numerous versions and which circulated widely but clandestinely from perhaps the
fifth century on, makes the unequivocal claim that Miriam, while betrothed
or married to a man named Yohanan, was seduced by a Jewish man named
Joseph ben Pandera (some versions reverse the names of her betrothed
and seducer):

> Now at the birth of Jesus his mother was Miriam, a Jewish woman betrothed
> to a man of royal lineage, from the house of David, named Yohanan, a Torah
> scholar and God-fearer, and she had a good-looking neighbor named Joseph ben
> Pandera, who had his eye on her, and one Saturday night, he passed by her house
> while he was drunk and went into her room and she thought he was Yohanan
> her betrothed and she hid her face in shame. She told him not to touch her, since
> she was menstruating, but he paid no attention to her and lay with her and she
> conceived. And at midnight Rabbi Yohanan came in and she was surprised, say-
> ing to him that it had never been his custom to come to her twice in one night
> and he said to her that he had only come once, this time. She said, you came to
> me and I told you I was menstruating and you paid no attention and you did
> what you wanted. Immediately Yohanan realized that Joseph ben Pandera had
> set his eyes on her and done the deed.[97]

The *Toldot Yeshu* may "know" who the rough seducer was, but, at least
initially, Miriam does not. Clearly, this narrative draws upon the familiar biblical, midrashic, and international folk motifs of switched beds, demonic
lovers, and mistaken identities. In the Bible, this motif regularly provides
an ironic commentary on the Hebrew conflation—in the double meaning of
the verb "to know"—of sexual intercourse and knowledge. Sex, these stories
suggest, may indeed be a form not of knowledge but rather of ignorance.
"Lacking witnesses required for the punishment of Joseph Pantera," the
Toldot Yeshu continues, the couple leaves for Babylonia. (We may remember
that a woman may not be called to witness in biblical law and, in any case,
two witnesses are required to bring a criminal to trial.) Skepticism over the
claims of the virgin birth is an ongoing feature of Jewish responses to Christianity. In his twelfth-century polemic against Christianity, Joseph Kimhi responds with this skepticism to his fictional Christian interlocutor's argument
that Isaiah must have been speaking of a virgin birth because only such a
unique event would constitute a prophetic "sign." Kimhi argues:

> Even if a virgin were to give birth, how would people believe that was a sign?
> Wouldn't people rather think that she had been seduced and the child was ille-

gitimate? One cannot call something a miraculous sign if it arouses doubt in people, since we have seen many young girls (*'almot*) who were considered virgins (*betulot*) but we had incontrovertible evidence that they were not truly virgins.[98]

The *Toldot Yeshu* is bolder in its assertions that Jesus was not in fact born of a virgin. Nevertheless, it holds back from suggesting that Mary knowingly committed adultery and that Christianity is built on an intentional sin. The situation described in the *Toldot Yeshu,* ungenerous to Christian claims as it is, might rather stand as an allegory for the mysterious birth of religions, Judaism as well as Christianity, in moments composed equally of union and difference, "knowledge" and misrecognition, in which the principal actors may be missing or have only a glimmer of what actually took place. With origins in question, identity itself must be cast into radical doubt.

Early Christianity records a story that can serve a similar function. The *Protevangelium of James,* one of the earliest of the Christian Apocrypha (ca. 150), describes Joseph finding a midwife to attend to Mary's birth. Hearing that this woman is "pregnant by the Holy Spirit," and seeing "a cloud of light" fill the cave, the midwife proclaims the miracle. But when she tells another midwife, Salome, that "a virgin has bought forth, a thing which her condition does not allow," Salome expresses her skepticism: "Unless I insert my finger and test her condition, I will not believe that a virgin has given birth" (the presence of a hymen *post partu* obviously compounds the miracle). What follows is surely one of the most astonishing passages in religious literature:

> 20. 1. And the midwife went in and said to Mary, "Make yourself ready, for there is no small contention concerning you." And Salome inserted her finger to test her condition. And she cried out, saying, "Woe for my wickedness and unbelief; for I have tempted the living God; and behold, my hand falls away from me, consumed by fire!" 2. And she bowed her knees before the Lord saying, "O God of my fathers, remember me; for I am the seed of Abraham, Isaac and Jacob; do not make me pilloried for the children of Israel, but restore me to the poor. For you know, Lord, that in your name I perform my duties and from you I have received my hire." 3. And an angel of the Lord appeared and said to her, "Salome, Salome, the Lord God has heard your prayer. Bring your hand to the child and touch him and salvation and joy will be yours." 4. And Salome came near and touched him, saying, "I will worship him, for a great king has been born to Israel." And Salome was healed as she had requested, and she went out of the cave.[99]

The *Protevangelium* presents Salome as a literal-minded, female (and Jewish?) counterpart to the angels, evangelists, and Fathers, with their annunciations of and excurses on the virgin birth. Against their theology, she sets gynecology and is turned away—burned—at the very portals of the woman's body. (The withering of Salome's hand has generally been taken as incontrovertible evidence of Mary's virginity, but it is not entirely clear that it should.) The infant, divine and radiant, may be touched—in fact, the child heals Salome's burn; so may even the open wounds of the resurrected Christ be touched, as doubting Thomas does in John 20. But although the tradition forthrightly admits that "there is no small contention concerning" Mary, and invites us to picture the place from which her child emerged, it forbids us forever from wielding the speculum.

IN fact, patristic thought rapidly abandoned the speculum in favor of a different form of speculation. The shift in conceptualizations of the virgin birth from Matthew to Tertullian, from Palestine to Nicaea, follows something of the trajectory taken by the Septuagint narrative from Aristeas to Philo and the Fathers. The horizontal model, whereby translation and conception occur through a copula situated *between* languages, texts, translator-pairs, and bodies, is replaced by a vertical model, whereby meaning flows "down" into language and the *Logos* is fully embodied in human flesh. For Christian translation theory, the result is a perfect Bible; for Christian theology, the result is a clone of God. The architecture of translation and the anatomy of conception undergo a similar reorientation: Epiphanius's skylights, which guarantee the vertical flow of *Logos* to the translators, reappear in the "displacement upward" (to use Freud's phrase) of conception from Mary's vagina or womb to her mind and, more literally, her ear. Mary thus *translates* Jesus, and she does so according to Philo's rather than Aristeas's model. The theory of Mary's conception of Jesus through the words of the angel was literalized in the popular Christian belief that it was through her ear that Mary conceived. In a widespread related image, the *Logos* streamed down as light at Jesus's conception. As a thirteenth-century hymn describes it, "Just as the sun enters and passes back through a windowpane without breaking it, so were you an intact virgin when God, who came down from the heavens, made of you mother and lady."[100] Mary's body, like the translator's cell, is open above; below she is impenetrable and intact.

Ordinary human reproduction (to belabor the obvious) involves the joining of two individuals to produce a third; ordinary translation involves the encounter of a source text and a translator to produce a translation that, in some sense, is the product of both the original text and the translator. In the Greek translation of the Bible, and in the birth of Jesus, the differences that underlie ordinary translation and birth are nullified, first between the "parents" and ultimately between the "generations" as well. Jesus and the Septuagint are perfect replicas of the *Logos,* their sole procreator. The force of the Nicene phrase "begotten, not made" is precisely calibrated to cancel both the biological difference between father and son and the Jewish difference between Creator and creation.

Critics have described the evolution of Christian "orthodoxy" as a function of what Rebecca Lyman describes as "a reduced access to the divine," whereby "the fourth-century heavens remained open, but the process was now weighted through a corporate, ecclesiastical conduit, rather than a multiplicity of individual journeys."[101] Virginia Burrus has further argued that the Nicene doctrine that asserts that the Father and the Son are *homoousios,* of a single substance, arises alongside an ecclesial structure that reduces "the multiplicity of individual journeys." Thus, Burrus suggests, the assertion of the consubstantiality of Father and Son and the establishment of a patrilineal apostolic succession are mutually legitimating discourses. The legends that emerged about Nicaea claimed, as Philo had about the Septuagint translators, that the participants spoke as one; when the Council was concluded, the signatures of two participants who had died in the course of the proceedings appeared on the final document.[102] Athanasius, carrying the memory of Nicaea forward, composes a synodal *Letter to the African Bishops* (ca. 370) that rests its case entirely on the demand for and evidence of consensus. As Burrus summarizes, Athanasius insists that members of the synod, following the words of the Nicene Fathers, "do no more than retrace the letters already inscribed, writing with one pen—all 90 of them."[103]

Burrus's interest in Nicaea is directed toward its consolidation of a new model of Christian manhood that delivers men from "the material mess and ambiguity of the maternal realm" to "the certainties of an immutable patriliny."[104] She notes the links between legitimate episcopacy and "an orthodox sonship defined by loyalty to the Nicene Fathers and the willingness to sign on (quite literally) to the words inscribed by those Fathers at Nicaea." The Nicene insistence on the consubstantiality of Father and Son, Burrus writes, "both mirrors and further sublimates the patrilineal structures in which its authority is embedded."[105] But Christian unity (or univocality) and legitimacy depends on the paternal line as an exclusion not only of maternal but also of Jewish difference—the Arian distinction between Father and Son is conflated in Athanasius and elsewhere with the doctrines of the Jews. The discourse of unanimity developed by Philo and the Fathers to annul the difference between Hebrew and Greek reappears here as a genetic warranty guaranteeing the equivalence in substance of Father and Son. In the doctrine of consubstantiality and the legend of perfect translation, the Fathers asserted their vision of sacred history and established their own place in it against the "material mess" of both mothers and Jews.

JEROME IN THE COVER OF THE NIGHT

The fourth century saw the discourses of virginity and translation at their closest convergence; by the turn of the fifth, the two courses had dramatically diverged. In 392, Epiphanius—monastic leader and tireless pursuer of Arian heretics—constructed the most impermeable of the walls that had guaranteed the "slavish" faithfulness of the Septuagint. In the decade that followed, Jerome (Epiphanius's friend and translator)[106] struck the series of blows to those walls that first opened the gap between (Western) Christianity and its "perfect" Greek Bible. In 401 Jerome snorted that "I know not who was the first lying author to construct the seventy cells at Alexandria, in which [the translators] were all separated and yet all wrote the same words." Aristeas, Jerome reminds us, says that the translators "conferred together," not that they prophesied; rejecting Philo's equation of *hermeneia* and prophecy, Jerome insists that "it is one thing to be a prophet, another to be an interpreter."[107] The Septuagint legend from Philo through Epiphanius had denied that translation was a form of dialogue, of human relation. In Jerome this dialogue becomes newly apparent, in the highly charged form of Jewish–Christian converse and in the meeting between the classical tongues and the Hebrew language. Jerome complains about the "trouble and expense it cost me to get Baraninas [the Jew who taught him Hebrew] to teach me under cover of the night." About Hebrew itself, Jerome describes the misery, after studying "the fluency of Cicero, the seriousness of Fronto and the gentleness of Pliny," of having to begin to learn a new alphabet "and to study to pronounce words both harsh and guttural."[108] In the person of his secret tutor and in the rough gutturals of the language they study, Jerome rematerializes Hebrew, moving translation narrative inside both the translator's workshop and his body; translation rests for Jerome on the painful and frustrating acquisition of an utterly foreign tongue, and it is not the transcendent mind but rather a resistant throat that "channels" the Hebrew word.

In place of the cells of the "lying authors" where translators transmit the word of God in regulated isolation, Jerome's translation narrative presents us with a cell the walls of which keep out neither sinful thoughts nor a stream of visitors. In a letter to a young monk describing his early years in Egypt, "when the desert walled me in with its solitude," Jerome derides the efficacy of a monastic cell for the preservation of spiritual purity. Only hard work can keep sin away, Jerome warns: "Do not let your mind stray into harmful thoughts, or like Jerusalem in her whoredoms, open its legs to every chance comer." In search of a cure for his own mental turbulence, Jerome writes, "I betook myself to a brother who before his conversion had been a Jew and asked him to teach me Hebrew."[109] Jerome presents his course of study as a sexual prophylactic and views his knowledge of Hebrew as a triumph for Christian access to the biblical truth. But in the charges of Judaizing that accompanied his translation career, the translator's cell is figured as a place of unnatural converse between Christian and Jew, where the Christian scandalously "opens the legs" of his mind to the Jewish "comer" rather than penetrating (as is proper for a man as well as a Christian) into the secret space of the Jew. "Under cover of the night," outside of Ptolemy's strict supervision, the mysterious goings-on in the translator's cell shook the patristic translation paradigm to the very core.

That Jerome's cell was in fact the site of Jewish–Christian converse of the most profound sort is everywhere apparent, beginning with the Preface to *Hebrew Questions on Genesis* (393), the text that first introduces the term *hebraica veritas.* In justifying his rejection of the Septuagint, Jerome claims not only that the Septuagint is inaccurate, but that it was deliberately (though justifiably) altered by the Jews. Remarkably enough, Jerome knows—indeed he seems to be the *only* Father who knows—the (apparently still oral!) rabbinic LXX tradition. Jerome's adoption of the rabbinic Septuagint narrative puts him in direct opposition to at least two different patristic assumptions: that the Jews might have falsified their *Hebrew* manuscripts; and that the Septuagint, whether it was "accurate" or not, represented God's special message to the Gentiles.[110] Paying due respect to the Septuagint, Jerome asserts that he means

> neither to charge the Septuagint with errors, as jealous people slander us, nor do we regard our own work as a censure to them, since they were unwilling to make known to Ptolemy, king of Alexandria, mystical teachings in the Holy Scriptures, and especially those things which promised the coming of Christ, lest the Jews might appear to worship a second God also. For the king, being a follower of Plato, used to make much of the Jews, on the grounds that they were said to worship one God.[111]

The Preface to the *Hebrew Questions,* and the work as a whole, demonstrates Jerome's access to the "hidden transcript," in his accurate citation of the rabbinic tradition of the LXX alterations—although it is obviously Jerome's addition that the translators' bringing the Bible into line with strict monotheism (its greatest asset in the eyes of philosophical Greeks) also inadvertently effaced the Bible's prefigurations of Christ. In another sign that Jerome knew this tradition, Jerome's commentary on Genesis 2:2 reproduces the very charge— that God labored on the Sabbath, although the Jews "boast of the repose of the Sabbath"—that the LXX alteration of that verse, according to the rabbis, is designed to preclude.[112] The trickster text finds its match here in Jerome.

Against suspicions that his converse with Hebrew, Jewish exegesis, and Jews involved Jewish contamination, Jerome develops a translation theory that turned such encounter from the charged territory of interreligious, interethnic contact to the safer and more flattering ground of imperial conquest and transfer.[113] Adapting Cicero's imperial rhetoric, developed in the context of Roman appropriations of Greek sources, to Christian purposes, Jerome argues for the power and freedom of a translation over the original. In translating a number of Greek biblical homilies into Latin, Hilary the Confessor "has not bound himself to the drowsiness of the letter or fettered himself by the stale literalism of inadequate culture. Like a conqueror he has led away captive into his own tongue the meaning of his originals."[114] The converse in the translator's cell between Christian and Jew may look to prurient minds like a form of sex, but for Jerome it marches like war. From the long nights in unsavory company Jerome emerges not only with Hebrew, but also with the Christian truth it ultimately signifies.

Christian orthodoxy has maintained largely intact the virginity of Mary and the perfect divinity of the "only-begotten" Son. By contrast, the attempts at formulating a model of perfect translation from Aristeas to Jerome to Eugene Nida in our own time have not succeeded in quelling the discourse that suggests, at least as regularly, that translators are traitors and translation the art of adultery. The history of translation in the West, in its compulsive recourse to the rhetoric of infidelity, renders genealogy itself a transparent fiction, charting the birth of a succession of bastard children, products of uncertain parentage and unholy unions.

The rabbis, it has been argued, ultimately relinquished translation for midrash, trading in a Torah in seventy languages for a Torah with seventy faces—all of which were turned toward themselves. They embraced hermeneutics without, however, relinquishing the claims of a patrilineal transmission, from Moses to Joshua and on to their own time, that could legitimize their own connection with Sinai. That this hermeneutics, too, was open to disruptions and reversals, by women and by the vagaries of language itself, is a subject requiring a separate study.

———— ✳ ————

CHAPTER TWO

"The Beauty of Greece in the Tents of Shem"

Aquila between the Camps

Tell me what you think about translation and I will tell you who you are.
MARTIN HEIDEGGER, "Hölderlins Hymne 'Der Ister'"

IN WHAT IS frequently and justifiably referred to as his "monumental" history of translation, George Steiner judges that there have been no more than a handful of writers who have had "anything fundamental or new" to say on the subject.[1] What serves as translation theory for much of the history he documents is a "sterile debate" over "sense-for-sense" versus "word-for-word" (often called "free" versus "literalist") translation. This debate goes at least as far back as Cicero and Horace and includes as major manifestos the remarkably similar letters of Jerome and, eleven hundred years later, of Luther in heated defense of translating not the individual words of a text, but rather its general sense. The debate has been both repetitive and unbalanced: in the best-known writings on the issue, it is nearly always the champions of sense-for-sense translation who state their case (though there are also a fair number who urge translators to steer a judicious course between the two "extremes"). For Western translation theory if not practice, the result of this debate has been a consensus: sense-for-sense translation is just common sense, while word-for-word translators are either pious pedants or eccentric fools.[2]

The terms of the debate were fixed early on, in Cicero's introduction to his *Best Kind of Orator* (46 BCE). Comparing his own translations of two Greek orators to the literalism that characterizes the work of earlier interpreters, Cicero writes:

> I did not translate them as an interpreter, but as an orator [*non converti ut inter-*
> *pres sed ut orator*], keeping the same ideas and forms, or as one might say, the
> "figures" of thought, but in language which conforms to our usage. And in so
> doing, I did not hold it necessary to render word for word [*verbum pro verba*],
> but I preserved the general style and force of the language. For I did not think
> I ought to count them out to the reader like coins, but to pay them by weight,
> as it were.[3]

Cicero contrasts the creative art of his own translational work with what he
implies is the mechanical technique of the "interpreter," who renders the
source text word for word; indeed, what we know of the technique of the
interpreters that preceded Cicero seems to confirm his judgment. The able
translator of Greek oratory, in Cicero's view, should himself be an orator in
his own right rather than focusing on providing a precise equivalent for each
word of the original text. Horace similarly asserts that in translating he makes
no attempt to be a *fidus interpres*—Willis Barnstone's rendering of the phrase
as "obedient interpres" rather than the usual "faithful translator" captures
something of the distaste behind Horace's term.[4] The interpreters against
whom Horace and Cicero are inveighing left no manifestos, introductions, or
apologia; translation theory thus begins with their critics. The approach of
such Roman translators as Horace, Cicero, and Quintilian (and, indeed, often
their terminology) continues to dominate translation manuals and theoretical discussions to our own day. While Eugene Nida's enormously influential
distinction between "dynamic equivalence" and "formal correspondence"
widens the notion of word-for-word translation to include adherence to *any*
of the "formal" dimensions of the source text, Nida's thinking remains in
many respects no more than an updated reformulation of Cicero's principle.
Nida presents his typology as delineating two varieties of "correspondence,"
but it is clear from his definitions that not all equivalences are created equal:

> *Dynamic equivalence:* quality of a translation in which the message of the origi-
> nal text has been so transported into the receptor language that the response of
> the receptor is essentially like that of the original receptors. Frequently, the form
> of the original text is changed; but as long as the change follows the rules of back
> transformation in the source language, of contextual consistency in the transfer,
> and of transformation in the receptor language, the message is preserved and the
> translation is faithful. The opposite principle is FORMAL CORRESPONDENCE.[5]

> *Formal correspondence:* quality of a translation in which the features of the form
> of the source text have been mechanically reproduced in the receptor language.
> Typically, formal correspondence distorts the grammatical and stylistic patterns
> of the receptor language, and hence distorts the message, so as to cause the re-

ceptor to misunderstand or to labor unduly hard; opposed to dynamic equivalence; see also LITERALNESS.[6]

For Nida, it is dynamic equivalence that represents "faithful" translation (unlike Horace, Nida aspires to faithful translation), insofar as it generates a response that is "essentially like that of the original receptors." By contrast, formal correspondence is mechanical, distorts the message of a text, and requires that the reader work too hard. Nida's definitions are thus also prescriptions, selling dynamic equivalence not only as more equivalent, but also (as long as one follows Nida's transformational rules) as more human, even more alive.

While anthologies of translation theory often read as a series of manifestos for sense-for-sense translation, one would be hard put to name a major defense of word-for-word translation before the modern period. Word-for-word translation appears for the most part as the foil for the consensus view, an example of what to avoid and the occasion for yet another defense of "free" translation. Word-for-word translators are mindless technicians, ruled by ignorance, superstition, and submissiveness. Willis Barnstone, in an essay entitled "Fifteen Quick Looks at the Philosophy of Literalism," gives a summary of historical attitudes toward literalism that include such assessments as: "Literalism aspires to operate like a machine, an internal photocopier of meaning, giving automatic, predictable and repeatable versions"; "Literalism abuses literature pompously"; "The philosophy of literalism demands perfection, claims fidelity and virtue, and dresses itself in the authority of the dictionary"; and

> Literalism's servant-translator should be pitied, because, as George Chapman says in the preface to his complete *Iliad* of 1611, the pedantic translator must suffer a double loss: necessarily unable to capture the native "full soule" of the original in a new language, he also sacrifices the grace of his "naturall dialect" by his rude attempt.[7]

Dryden's simile for literalist translation may be best known: "'Tis much like dancing on ropes with fettered legs: one may shun a fall by using caution; but the gracefulness of motion is not to be expected."[8] From Cicero's declaration that "literalism is a feature of boorish translators" (*interpretes indiserti*) to Octavio Paz's contention that "servile translation [*traducción servile*] is a depository made of a string of words to help us read the text in its original language" and Nida's diagnosis of literalism as a cultural ailment in which "the heavy weight of tradition . . . stifles a translator's creativity,"[9] critics have spoken nearly in one voice in disparaging literalism.[10]

Among the bad translators who serve as cautionary figures in translation history, the absolute worst appears to be Aquila, who has served as least as far back as Jerome as prime evidence that literalism is an unworkable strategy. Aquila's Greek Bible version, produced in the first half of the second century for use in the synagogue and perhaps also in Jewish–Christian disputation, replaced the Septuagint in the Jewish community once the Septuagint had become the Bible of the Christian Church.[11] In attempting to bring his Greek text closer to the Hebrew source and its Jewish interpretations, Aquila fashioned what is generally considered an unreadable text (although it was used in Greek-speaking synagogues as late as the sixth century). Origen is perhaps the first to describe Aquila as "slavish to the Hebrew style" (*douleuōn tē Hebraikē lexei*), a characterization that would very nearly become Aquila's epithet in Christian circles.[12] In Jerome's letter to Pammachius on translation, it is the absurdities of Aquila's word-oriented technique that bolster Jerome's own argument for a sense-for-sense approach to translation: "Aquila must with unhappy pedantry (*kakozēlōs*) translate syllable by syllable and letter by letter thus—*sun ton ouranon kai sun tēn gēn*—a construction which neither Greek nor Latin admits of."[13] Jerome is quoting Aquila's rendering of Genesis 1:1, *et hashamayim ve'et ha'arets,* in which Aquila renders the Hebrew accusative particle *et*—a grammatical construction Greek lacks—with the Greek conjunction *sun*, which ordinarily means "with." In English, this would read nonsensically or blasphemously as "[In the beginning God created] *with* the heaven and *with* the earth."[14] Perhaps the clearest example of Aquila's attachment to the Hebrew formulation of the biblical text, as fragments found in the Cairo Genizah show, is Aquila's transcription of the Tetragrammaton in old Hebrew characters rather than in a Greek transliteration or translation of God's name. The Septuagint, by contrast, had rendered the Tetragrammaton as *Kurios,* Lord, in a double displacement from the Hebrew name; Jews traditionally pronounced and read the Tetragrammaton as the Hebrew word *Adonay,* Lord or my Lord, and the Seventy translated that intralingual "translation." More generally, Aquila attempted to reproduce as many features of the Hebrew text as he could, fusing a Greek vocabulary with Hebrew word order and other syntactic and stylistic features. In Jerome's view, the linguistic contortions that Aquila's attempt to render the Hebrew word for word inevitably led to provided the most powerful justification for his own sense-for-sense technique.

Aquila's version occupied a column alongside the versions of Symmachus and Theodotion (two other second-century retranslations of the Bible) in Origen's *Hexapla,* an invaluable resource for Jerome's work, but only fragments or citations of the *Hexapla* or Aquila's version in separate form have survived. Modern discussions of biblical history thus work on less evidence than the ancients had, but they generally echo the assessment of Origen and Jerome. The *Catholic Encyclopedia* of 1912 writes that Aquila was "a slave to the letter" of the Hebrew text, Henry St. John Thackeray characterizes his rendering as "barbarous," Sebastian Brock talks of the "mechanical character" of Aquila's translation, and the Bible translator and historian Bruce Metzger calls Aquila's version "severely literalistic."[15] In a more elaborate description, Julio Trebolle Barrera writes of "Aquila, who sacrifices Greek grammar and style on the altars of excessive fidelity to the 'sacred' Hebrew text."[16] Aquila is not the sole Jewish target of such rhetoric: Frederick E. Greenspahn remarks that "numerous Jewish renderings have been criticized for being overly literal and wooden."[17] Thus, the Ferrara Bible was called "barbaric and alien" (*barbaro y estraño*), and Zunz's version was criticized for being "sklavisch, wort getreue."[18]

In these judgments, Aquila is more than just a sadly inadequate translator. Aquila also provides translation history a portrait of the literalist as pedant and slave, a dark mirror with which to frighten budding translators. The tendentiousness of this representation is suggested by the fact that while Aquila is commonly described as a slave to the Hebrew, his liberties with Greek syntax are never treated as themselves a variety of creative freedom. (We might recall that Walter Benjamin rhetorically asks, "For what is meant by freedom but that the rendering of the sense is no longer to be regarded as all-important?")[19] It is enslavement to his Hebrew sources, combined with a lack of concern for the integrity of Greek, that distinguishes Aquila's approach. Put this way, it becomes clear that Aquila's *loyalties*—and not merely his technique—are at stake. E. A. Speiser thus pointedly remarks that Aquila's literalism can be traced to his conversion to Judaism rather than to any linguistic tics: "As a relative of Emperor Hadrian," Speiser writes, "Aquila knew his Greek very well. But subsequent to his conversion to Judaism, his fidelity to the Hebrew text became extreme, so much so that Aquila became known as 'a slave to the letter.'"[20] That we are dealing with cultural affiliations becomes evident as well in the odd assertion on the website of the Orthodox Bible Project, an organization dedicated to translating the Septuagint into English "for the twenty-first century," that Aquila's translation preferences are also characteristic of his Jewish readership. Aquila's version is thus described by the Project as "completely incomprehensible to non-Jews," although in earlier times "the Jews held this translation (if so it could even be called) in highest esteem."[21] That Jews are peculiarly capable of understanding and even

admiring a text unreadable by all others may be a mangled paraphrase of
H. B. Swete, who more reasonably writes:

> The version of Aquila emanated from a famous school of Jewish teachers; it was
> issued with the full approval of the Synagogue, and its affectation of preserving at
> all costs the idiom of the original recommended it to orthodox Jews whose loyalty
> to their faith was stronger than their sense of the niceties of the Greek tongue.[22]

As Swete makes clear, Jews had reasons for preferring Aquila's translation
that had little to do with his technique. Nevertheless, even Swete's distaste for
Aquila's "affectation" and the loyalties of his "orthodox" Jewish readers is
hard to miss.

The view that only Jews can appreciate Aquila exposes a certain political/
theological dimension in the recurrent debate over literalism and free translation. Literalism is not only the poor technique of certain translators, it is
also the poor taste of Jewish audiences. As George Campbell put it in the
translator's introduction to his 1789 version of the Gospels,

> A slavish attachment to the letter, in translating, is originally the offspring of the
> superstition, not of the Church, but of the synagogue, where it would have been
> more suitable in Christian interpreters, the ministers, not of the letter, but of the
> spirit, to have allowed it to remain.[23]

Christian interpreters must be ministers of the *spirit* of a text, free of the Jewish attachment to its word. In giving expression to a normally concealed sub-
current of Western translation history, Campbell provides us with the key to
reading the "sterile debate" at the heart of translation theory as a disguised
manifestation of Jewish–Christian polemic.

In exploring the historical assessments of Aquila and literalism, I am not
arguing that Aquila or other literalists are perfectly good translators. Nor am
I dismissing the debate on word-for-word versus sense-for-sense translation
by insisting at the outset, as theorists have increasingly begun to do, that the
distinction between the word and the sense of a text is not only "sterile" but
also incoherent and theoretically unsupportable (among Derrida's projects
in *Of Grammatology*, for example, is the undermining of just this distinction).[24] My aim in this section is rather to trace the theological subtext that
haunts the word versus sense debate and regularly demands the denigration
of the word. In reframing translation history as theological polemic rather
than methodological inquiry or linguistic theory, I also hope to clear space
for the expression of Jewish alternatives to the consensus that has shaped
translation in the West.

As the reference to Cicero and Horace at the opening of this chapter makes clear, the preference for sense-for-sense translation obviously cannot be said to emerge as a by-product of Christian thought, since it predates the formation of Christianity. Moreover, such a preference is abundantly attested not only in Islamic and Buddhist, but also in Jewish translation discourse: within the world of medieval Islam, for example, Jewish and Arab writers shared an Aristotelian translation theory that underwrote their advocacy of sense-for-sense translation.[25] Conversely, expressions of the necessity of literal translation, in particular of sacred Scripture, are common enough in Christian writings as well and become the (now largely forgotten) mainstream in medieval Christian translation.[26] Even Jerome's letter on translation, a prime manifesto for Christian sense-for-sense translation, includes an aside claiming that he makes an exception to the rule of translating the sense of a text: "in the case of the holy scriptures where even the order of the words is a mystery"; that the sincerity of Jerome's assertion has been justifiably doubted does not diminish the fact that he felt compelled to assert it.[27]

In short, I am not suggesting that Christian translators normally use and promote sense-for-sense techniques while Jews are word-for-word translators—although there are both Jewish and Christian writers who make precisely this claim. I am arguing, rather, that the debate over free versus literalist translation has been shaped by Christian theology for the greatest part of its history; within this sphere of influence, the literalist position has come to be *perceived* as Jewish, a perception that has had powerful ramifications for both Jewish and Christian translation history. I would further argue that the conflation of Judaism and literalism, as a stereotypical artifact of Christian polemic, has tended to obscure rather than illuminate Jewish translation theories and practices. For a variety of reasons, some of which I will be exploring here, Jewish writings on translation have largely remained outside the broader discourse on translation.[28] Returning Jewish discourse to the study of translation does not just add to the sum total of our knowledge of translation. Rather, such a project aims to transform how translation can and should be thought today.

OPENING THE LETTER: FREEING THE SPIRIT

The earliest of the programmatic statements advocating sense-for-sense techniques, as we have seen, were set forth by such Latin writers and translators as Cicero, Horace, and Quintilian. By contrast, Greek writers (with the significant exception of such Jewish Hellenists as Aristeas and Philo) were much less concerned with translation theory or practice than the Romans. Nevertheless, it is Greek philosophy that provided the building blocks from which Roman and later translation theory are constructed. Translation theory is indebted to Platonic notions of language, which differentiated between the "name" as "imitative sound" and the idealized form to which this name, or sign, only obliquely refers. Socrates famously argues with Cratylus that "He who follows names in the search after things, and analyzes their meaning, is in great danger of being deceived."[29] As Susan Handelman puts it, in Platonic ontology "language belongs to the realm of the imperfect and contingent, while true knowledge is possible only in the realm of the immutable forms."[30] Handelman links Plato's "conquest of language" in his theory of forms with "the Church's attempt to surpass the letter of the Biblical text for the spirit." More directly influential for the Church than Plato's idealism, though, was the later Hellenistic reconfiguration of Plato's theory of immutable forms into a philosophical and religious system that differentiated the outward form (thus radically shifting the value of the term "form") from the inward content, most emblematically in the material body and imperishable soul of a human being. Distinguishing between the inner and the outer, soul and body, and spirit and letter (a distinction first formulated by Protagoras [481–411 BCE]), Platonic Hellenism simultaneously laid the foundations of an ontology, anthropology, and linguistics. Daniel Boyarin summarizes:

> In the hermeneutics of a culture that operates in the Platonic mode of external and internal realities, language itself is understood as an outer, physical shell, and meaning is construed as the invisible, ideal, and spiritual reality that lies behind or is trapped within the body of the language.[31]

Boyarin suggests that meaning can be viewed in this system as "trapped within the body of language," but it is clear from writings on translation that linguistic theory in the West has also been able to imagine the body and soul of language as separable, in parallel with the soul's liberation after death or metempsychotic transfer to another body.[32] In the rhetoric that praises translations that "capture the spirit" of a text, translation discourse invokes the Hellenistic association of the meaning of language and its spirit or soul (sometimes these terms are near-synonyms, but the spirit is also at times conceptualized as the unity of body and soul, or the third element of breath). The body is also implicitly remembered in this discourse, though only in the negative sense of what is left behind or transcended in translation.

Translation signifies transcendence at least in part because the inner meaning that constitutes the spirit of language in Platonic thought represents a realm in which the diversity, contingency, and differences that characterize the outer level of language are overcome. Meaning is thus shared, although its particular representations are not. Such a claim is explicitly set forth in Aristotle's view of the relationship between language and its referents; Aristotle's insight here would become the basis of Augustine's linguistic (and theological) theory in *On Christian Doctrine*. Aristotle argues:

> Spoken words are the symbols of mental experience and written words are the symbols of spoken words. Just as all men have not the same writing, so all men have not the same speech sounds, but the mental experiences, which these directly symbolize, are the same for all, as also are those things of which our experiences are the images.[33]

The ramifications of this dualism for translation are evident: on the level of the sounds and letters that comprise the "body" of a language, languages indeed are self-evidently different. The level of the meaning, whether it is psychological and thus lies *within* the body or "real" and thus lies *beyond* the body, is one of shared truths. In differentiating between letter and spirit, or between contingent signifier and "transcendental signified" (to use Derrida's term), Greek philosophy not only constructed the foundations of Western linguistics but also implicitly offered a powerful argument for translatability.

The distinction between letter and spirit is crucial for the history of translation; the overlay of the distinction between Jew and Christian onto this more basic distinction is central to the present project. The imposition of the Jewish–Christian dualism onto that of the body (or letter) and spirit has sometimes been traced to Paul—the reading of gender into this distinction has, of course, earlier origins. Paul's letters place enormous weight on the difference between "Israel according to the flesh" (*kata sarka*) and "Israel according to the Spirit" (*kata pneuma*); these two categories have been taken for much of the history of Christian interpretation, it hardly needs saying, as referring to Jews and Christians respectively. Paul has also been credited with radicalizing the distinction between these terms, famously insisting that "the letter kills, but the Spirit gives life" (*to gar gramma apokteinei, to de pneuma zouopoiei*) (2 Corinthians 3:6).[34] In Christianity we have not merely the supremacy of the spirit over the letter—that is true of Greek philosophy as well—but increasingly the hostility of the spirit to the letter, a hostility evident in Campbell's rejection of "superstitions of the Synagogue" if not elsewhere.

As historians have pointed out with increasing frequency, however, it is anachronistic to assert that "Judaism" or "Christianity" as discrete religious entities have any place in Paul's thinking. Paul was rather imagining two different ways of conceptualizing "Israel," one dependent on kinship ties and one which understood this appellation as referring to "The People of God"— that is, all believers.[35] Jonathan Z. Smith, who views Paul as "preeminently a boundary-crossing figure," argues that what is at stake in Paul's allegoresis "is the attempt to establish a new taxon . . . no longer to be classified by the old divisions" of circumcision or uncircumcision.[36] Paul specifies to the Galatians that "neither circumcision nor uncircumcision counts for anything, but new creation" (6:15). In this reading, Paul's spiritual interpretation of "Israel" as an entity in which "There is neither Jew nor Greek . . . for you are all one in Christ Jesus" (Galatians 3:28) rejects "literal Israel" only because an adherence to kinship ties and religious practices threatens the formation of a single community of Jews and Gentiles in Jesus Christ. This, of course, describes the situation in the Galatian community, where the common fellowship of the circumcised believers and those who had only been baptized was under attack by emissaries of the Church in Jerusalem. Paul reminds the Romans as well that "he is not a Jew, who is one outwardly; nor is that circumcision, which is outward in the flesh: But he is a Jew, who is one inwardly; and circumcision is that of the heart, in the spirit, and not in the letter" (Romans 2:28–29 [after KJV]).

Paul's hermeneutic could gain support from the Bible, which had already implied the possibility of a "spiritual" interpretation of circumcision in declaring the importance of "circumcising" the heart (Deuteronomy 10:16; Leviticus 26:41), although, unlike Paul's, this interpretation did not thereby negate the importance of physical circumcision. But the allegorizing thrust in Paul is taken primarily from the Hellenistic Platonism of his day, which not only assumed the superiority of the spiritual over the fleshly dimensions of reality but also preferred a universalist to a particularist religious approach.

According to a growing scholarly consensus, then, allegory is Paul's tool rather than a motivation in itself: the ultimate goal of his letters to the Galatians and Romans is to prevent a rift in the new movement. And although Paul's view on the law and kinship sharply distinguishes the literal from the allegorical meaning, spiritual from fleshly circumcision, and "carnal" Israel from "spiritual" Israel, it certainly does not see these distinctions as Jewish versus Christian hermeneutical approaches. On the contrary, Paul's hermeneutic is in places thoroughly Jewish, insofar as his investment in allegory and privileging of the spiritual over the "carnal" meaning is shared by the Jewish Hellenism of his milieu.

The Church indeed depended for the richest and most systematic exposition of the allegorical method not on Paul but rather on Philo, whose tour-de-force biblical allegoresis uncovered the spiritual dimensions of the full range of Jewish laws—without, however, recommending their abrogation. Rosemary Radford Ruether writes that, unlike Paul's allegoresis, Philo's "Hellenistic midrash had no intention of abandoning the letter of the Law. It sought rather to invest the letter with spiritual and ethical significance that would make it meaningful to those who had learned to think of truth in philosophical terms."[37] Philo explicitly argued against the temptation to view the literal fulfillment of Jewish law as irrelevant once its spiritual meaning was understood (as indeed his radical Jewish contemporaries, the Allegorists, did). Mobilizing the trope of body and soul to make his point, Philo wrote: "Just as we take care of the body because it is the abode of the soul, so also must we take care of the laws that are enacted in plain terms."[38]

It is only in later Christian thought that Paul's two forms of Israel come to stand unequivocally for the Jews and Christians. For Origen, Nicholas de Lange has demonstrated, "'Jewish' can be used simply as a synonym for 'literal.'"[39] De Lange helpfully distinguishes the use of literalism by patristic writers from modern significations. Moderns take the literal meaning as something like the "plain sense" of a text, what the writer intended or what the words mean in their original context. For late-antique writers, literalism has a rather different range of connotations: Christian writers, according to de Lange, primarily associated the literal level of a text with the laws that Jews derived from it, whether these laws were derived from a "plain" or fanciful reading of the text; it was to this "literalist" reading that Paul opposed his doctrine of "faith" and "spirit." But literalism also signifies what the Fathers saw as the Jewish attention to the "body" of the text, the belief (exemplary of the school of R. Akiva, although far from universal in rabbinic literature) that "every word of the text, almost every letter, is capable of imparting some deeper meaning."[40] For Origen and Augustine, of course, rabbinic exegesis did not plumb the "deeper meaning" of Scriptures; it remained on the material surface of the text, blinded to more profound significations by a fixation on the text's "corporeality." "Behold Israel according to the flesh" (1 Corinthians 10:18), writes Augustine in his *Tractate against the Jews*. "This we know to be the carnal Israel: but the Jews do not grasp this meaning and as a result they proved themselves indisputably carnal."[41] Jews are "carnal Israel" not only because they define themselves as belonging to Israel through fleshly ties, but also because they do not grasp the possibility of defining Israel spiritually. In their notion of fleshly affiliation, in their observance of the law, and in their reading of texts, Jews are literalists, attached to the body of language rather than its spirit.

Christian attitudes toward Jewish literalism were not uniformly hostile: Origen and Jerome both conceded the usefulness of Aquila's approach for reconstructing his Hebrew *Vorlage*, however vociferously they condemned Jewish literalism in general.[42] And other patristic writers, too, had uses for Jewish literalism. Jeremy Cohen has shown that the Jews, as "living letters of the Law," functioned as placeholders in Christian theological thinking not only on biblical hermeneutics but also on such subjects as the function of terrestrial history and the relationship between body and soul.[43] So inseparably coupled in his thinking were the Jews and the letter/body, Cohen writes, that Augustine's attitude toward the Jews was eventually ameliorated by his "increasingly positive inclination to a literalist hermeneutic."[44] From Augustine to Aquinas, Jewish fortunes rose and fell on the shifting attitudes toward the body and/as the letter.

As Jewish scholars have not tired of pointing out, the patristic equation of Jews and the body fundamentally distorts rabbinic perspectives even as it captures something accurate about Jewish–Christian differences. Daniel Boyarin begins *Carnal Israel* by quoting Augustine on Jewish carnality and adding, "Augustine knew what he was talking about. There was a difference between Jews and Christians that had to do with the body."[45] This difference, however, should be put into a historical context the Fathers often ignored. Early Christianity and other Hellenistic Judaisms, along with early rabbinic Judaism, drew from the same Platonic notions of body and soul; and rabbinic Judaism and patristic Christianity only gradually differentiated themselves through their discourses of the body. Moreover, Augustine's depiction of the Jews as carnal hardly does justice to rabbinic conceptualizations of the relationship between body and soul, caricaturing Jews as interested only in the body in a perverse mirroring of the Christian valorization of the soul. Nor, of course, does patristic thought register the range of rabbinic views on signification and the body. Alongside R. Akiva's belief in the meaningfulness of "every jot and tittle" of Hebrew Scriptures one can place R. Ishmael, who proposed what one might call a "plain-sense" approach to exegesis under the slogan "The Torah speaks in human language" (*Sifre Numbers* 112); such a maxim would not be out of place in Augustine's work.[46]

The presence of Platonic elements in rabbinic thought as well as the distinctions between Christian and rabbinic dualisms are carefully traced by Ephraim Urbach in his book on the rabbinic sages. Urbach acknowledges that the rabbis distinguish between a body and a soul but stresses that they lack the sense "of an absolute dichotomy, 'body–soul,' which is characteristic of Platonic thought."[47] Thus, Urbach argues, "Despite all the elements in dualistic anthropology that are common to the teaching of the Sages and the Stoic-Platonic views, which were prevalent in the Hellenistic world, the conception of dualism and the antithesis between flesh and spirit in the Rabbinic dicta are less drastic."[48] As Urbach writes, the rabbis insisted that holiness was a property of the body as well as the soul. "Unlike Greek thought," he adds, "Rabbinic teaching does not speak of the immortality of the soul, but of the resurrection of the dead."[49] Urbach's writings on the body and soul are part of his exploration of rabbinic anthropology, but they clearly have ramifications for rabbinic linguistic philosophy: *nefesh* (soul), *guf* (body), and *ruaḥ* (breath or "spirit") form an indivisible entity, so that "man is a psycho-physical organism." Urbach continues: "This union finds expression in lack of differentiation between the word and the substance in the Hebrew tongue, and the relationship between the word and the substance is like that between *nefesh* and *guf*."[50]

In *Carnal Israel*, Boyarin presses this point further, agreeing that rabbinic Jews resisted the Platonic dualism that sharply distinguished between body and soul, but also insisting that "rabbinic Judaism invested significance in the body which in the other formations [Greek-speaking Jewish cultures, including Christianity] were invested in the soul." Thus, "for rabbinic Jews, the human being was defined as a body—animated, to be sure, by a soul—while for Hellenistic Jews (such as Philo) and (at least many Greek-speaking) Christians (such as Paul), the essence of a human being is a soul housed in a body."[51] Boyarin's interest in *Carnal Israel* is primarily in understanding what such a conceptualization of the human being meant for the rabbinic reading of gender and sexuality and in registering the value of rabbinic embodiment as a cultural practice that resists the "flight from the body to the spirit with the attendant deracination of historicity, physicality, and carnal filiation which characterizes Christianity." Nevertheless, he views rabbinic anthropology (with Urbach) as bearing with it a linguistic theory. The relation between person and language is no mere parallelism, as the midrashic text on circumcision that Boyarin cites amply demonstrates:

> All Israelites who are circumcised will come into Paradise, for the Holy Blessed One placed His name on Israel, in order that they might come into Paradise, and What is the name and seal which he placed upon them? It is SHaDaY. The Shin [the first letter of the root] He placed in the nose, the Dalet He placed in the hand, and the Yod in the circumcision. (*Tanhuma Tsav* 14)[52]

This midrash reinforces Urbach's point about the resurrection of the dead, in that it is the sanctified body that enters Paradise, not the immaterial soul; the sanctified rabbinic body is neither outward form nor (at least here) corrupt flesh. The circumcised—thus necessarily male—Israelite is "in the image" of God, not merely through the "natural" mimesis of (the shape of) the letters of God's Hebrew name in his nose and hand, but also in the "cultural" Hebraic inscription of the circumcision. The Jewish body is thus both a Hebrew text and a sacred text, one written by God as it is written by—and on—Jews, in their practice of circumcision. Boyarin lays out the implications of the midrash quoted above for rabbinic perspectives on language as well as the body:

> In contrast to Paul and his followers, for whom the interpretation of circumcision was a rejection of the body, for the Rabbis of the midrash, it is a sign of the sanctification of that very physical body; the cut in the penis completes the inscription of God's name on the (male, Jewish) body. The midrash speaks of circumcision as a transformation of the body into a holy object. It constitutes, moreover, an insistence (typical of midrash) on the meaning of the actual material form, the shapes of letters and sounds of language. It is this insistence—and not "playfulness," as in some currently fashionable accounts—that leads to midrashic punning and seeking of significance in such very concrete, physical, material features of the Hebrew language.[53]

The linguistic anthropology outlined here suggests both obstacles to and opportunities for translation, which any rabbinic theory of translation we might extrapolate from it would be compelled to negotiate. If the Jewish body and the Hebrew letter are not contingent "containers" of a separable soul or spirit, the metempsychotic transfer of the soul of Platonic and patristic thought cannot serve as an avenue for the transfer of meaning. The Hebrew language and its Jewish "carriers," who literally bear its signifiers on their bodies, cannot be easily divided. Translation, in such a linguistic anthropology or anthropological linguistics, would have to incorporate rather than transcend the corporeality of Hebrew and the Jewish body. In Aquila, the rabbis imagined they had found a translator who could do that. In what follows I will argue that the rabbinic notion of translation can productively be read through the lens of circumcision, in the sense of a transcription that signals affiliation in which the body of language—the letter—is marked as Jewish. Translation, in this mode, must be understood in terms of the signifier rather than the signified, and thus as transformation rather than equivalence. Aquila's literalism, so visible to patristic and Western translation discourse, is scarcely mentioned in the rabbinic literature. What comes in place of the discussions of his enslavement to the word, I will argue, is a narrative reading of the displacement and transfiguration of the translator's body.

THE CIRCUMCISED TRANSLATOR

That the rabbis connected Aquila's translation with circumcision is attested in a number of midrashic texts. While Aquila's status as proselyte is mentioned in the patristic as well as rabbinic sources, it is the rabbinic sources that repeatedly eye Aquila's body, arguing through the figure of the translator that only a circumcised man may study Torah. *Exodus Rabba*, expounding on the verse "He declares his word unto Jacob" (Psalm 147:19), relates:

> Akilas once said to Hadrian the King: I wish to convert and become a Jew.
>
> Hadrian said: Do you really want to join this people? How much have I humiliated it! How many of them I have killed! You would get mixed up with the very lowest of nations? What do you see in them that makes you wish to become a proselyte?
>
> He said: The least among them knows how the Holy One created the world, what was created on the first day and what was created on the second day, how long it is since the world was created and on what the world is founded. Besides, their Torah is the truth.
>
> He said: Go and study their Torah, but do not be circumcised.
>
> Akilas said to him: Unless he be circumcised, even the wisest man in your kingdom, even a venerable man who is a hundred years old, cannot study their Torah, because it is said: "He declares His word unto Jacob, His statutes and His ordinances unto Israel," and He did not do this for every nation. To what nation? To Israel.[54]

In explaining to Hadrian—described in various sources as a relative, usually his uncle—why he wishes to be a Jew, Aquila poses arguments for studying the Torah that might appeal to any human being: the Torah, after all, relates the order of Creation and the foundation of the world, indeed, "the truth." (The rabbis, we might recall in this connection, etymologically linked Torah and *theoria*.) Nevertheless, access to this apparently universal truth is available only through Israel, here explicitly understood as including circumcised converts.[55] Indeed, it is precisely the narrative of the proselyte that midrashically illustrates God's exclusive converse "unto Jacob."[56] Put otherwise, Judaism is a commodity of universal value but controlled access, the price of entry to which is a painful and transformative initiation. We might profitably contrast the correspondences drawn here between the Torah and the translator's body with those Philo traces between the Torah and (in the vista that lay before the translators on Pharos) the natural universe, "the earth, the water, the air, and the heaven, concerning the creation of which they were going in the first place to explain the sacred account."[57] If for Philo the natural world is the sharpest mirror of Scripture, for the rabbis the Torah is best reflected in the circumcised (Jewish male) body, in which the very shape of the Hebrew letters might be discerned.

The figure of Aquila embodies the perfect concordance between circumcision and access to Torah, dramatized in his move from Greek to Hebrew and from uncircumcision to circumcision. This perfect concordance, however, conceals its own philosophical and political tensions—between the Torah's universal message and its transmission to and through Israel, and between the claims of imperial power and religious truth. The danger of Aquila's position is compounded, in this tale, by the circumstance that Aquila is speaking with Hadrian, who is described throughout rabbinic literature as having outlawed circumcision among other Jewish practices, an edict that led to the Bar Kokhba revolt (132–35 CE). Whether Hadrian in fact banned circumcision, either before or in the wake of the revolt, and whether this prohibition—if indeed it was issued—was limited to prohibiting the practice among Jews in particular, is a bone of some scholarly contention.[58] What is important in this context, however, is that Hadrian is linked with the ban against circumcision in Jewish memory.[59] The story, then, records more than a difference of opinion between Aquila and an older relative; it also potentially constitutes an act of anti-imperial defiance.

There are philosophical as well as legal and national stakes in the contention around circumcision. According to Boaz Cohen, the notion that circumcision constitutes an unnatural act and that law should follow the principles of the natural order is already evident in Paul, who "justified the abolition of circumcision by the argument, first, that it is against nature."[60] Jonathan Z. Smith bolsters Cohen's argument by reading Paul's invective in Galatians 5:12 (rendered pungently in the NIV as "As for those agitators, I wish they would go the whole way and emasculate [apokopsantai] themselves"!) as an indirect reference to the Greco-Roman view that circumcision was "an act of bodily mutilation which takes its place in a series of such acts, from tattooing and branding to loss of limb and castration—a series seen as shameful operations performed on the body, most frequently on the body of a criminal and slave."[61] While no Roman record of Hadrian's view on circumcision is extant, we know that his immediate successor Antoninus Pius (138–61) prohibited Jews from circumcising non-Jews (including prospective proselytes), although they were permitted to circumcise their own sons. Both Smith and, more extensively, Ra'anan Abusch read Antoninus's legislation within the larger context of slave law reform and understand the ban against Jews circumcising non-Jews as an extension of the earlier prohibitions of

Sulla, Domitian, and Nerva against castrating slaves.[62] Circumcision apparently troubled Roman imperial culture not only as a marker of Jewish distinctiveness—indeed, Shaye Cohen reminds us that it hardly constituted an infallible sign of Jewishness.[63] From Paul's letter to the Philippians (3:2–3), which refers to those "that mutilate their flesh" (tēn katatomēn, rather than the proper word for circumcision, peritomē), to the Historia Augusta, which records—possibly satirically—that "the Jews went to war because they were forbidden to mutilate their genitals," circumcision was viewed as the degrading mutilation of the natural perfection of the male body.[64]

Boaz Cohen finds evidence that the rabbis directly engaged the charge that circumcision is unnatural, for instance in R. Judan's reading of Genesis 17:1, which relates Abraham's circumcision:

> R. Judan said: "just as the fig has no imperfection except for its stem, so remove it and nullify the blemish, so the Holy One, blessed be He, said to Abraham, you have no imperfection other than the foreskin; remove it and nullify the imperfection: 'walk before God and be whole [tamim, alternatively, innocent or perfect].'" (Genesis Rabbah 46.1)[65]

In passages like this one, the rabbis expressed their conviction that circumcision is an improvement over nature, the enhancement of an otherwise imperfect human form. The circumcised body is not mutilated in removing the foreskin, any more than the fig is rendered unnatural in the removal of its stem. Circumcision, then, has multiple significations beyond its biblical meaning of a covenant connecting the Jewish people with their God: it is a marker of Jewish affiliation for native Jews and proselytes, an act and symbol of resistance to imperial legislation, the final step toward aesthetic perfection, a bodily representation of Hebrew discourse, the access to Torah that constitutes a barrier for non-Jews and non-males, and perhaps also a sign of linguistic talent (remembering the biblical diagnosis of Moses' influent speech as "uncircumcised lips").[66]

The Aquila narratives emerge from a certain convergence of these significations of circumcision, particularly as they intersect with language and translation. While the literature attests to a rabbinic ambivalence about translation in general and the Septuagint in particular, in Aquila the rabbis find a translator whose work they can fully appreciate.[67] Highest praise comes in the context of exegetical commentary on Genesis 9:27, the verse from which the title of this chapter is borrowed. Where Western and, especially, Christian discourse has taken the Tower of Babel story as a primary text for theorizing biblical views of translation, rabbinic literature focuses its discussion of translation—primarily halakhic and narrative rather than theoretical—on a verse a chapter or so before the Babel story, Noah's blessing to his three sons:

> May God enlarge Japheth [*yaft elohim leyefet*]
> And may he dwell in the tents of Shem
> And may Canaan be a slave to them.

As this rabbinic prooftext attests, translation is of particular interest to the rabbis as an activity that traverses ethnoreligious borders, particularly those separating Jews and non-Jews. It is thus Noah's blessing, which the rabbis read as ethnic taxonomy and political prophecy, rather than God's curse at Babel, which concerns humankind *in toto*, that elicits their most pointed thinking on translation. An interpretation of Noah's blessing as prophesying the crossing of ethnic borders is by no means inevitable. Philo, for instance, takes the verse as the occasion for a characteristic meditation on the value of a rich man (the "enlarged" Japheth) seeking out the company of wise men—of any nation.[68] For rabbinic readings, however, it was precisely the image of Jewish–Gentile converse that demanded commentary: If Shem is taken to mean the Jews, and Japheth the Greeks or some larger ethnic-cultural grouping such as Hellenism, then what historical circumstances fulfill the conditions of Japheth's dwelling in the tents of Shem? This implicit question is answered most directly not in the midrashic literature but rather in *Targum Pseudo-Jonathan*, which renders Genesis 9:27 as

> May the Lord enlarge (or adorn) the borders of Japheth and their children will convert and dwell in the study houses of Shem.[69]

Referring to *Pseudo-Jonathan* as well as a number of similar targumic renderings, Steven Fine emphasizes that

> the sense of dwelling among the Jews means conversion to Judaism and in no sense refers to happy multicultural commingling. The reality envisioned by the biblical author was certainly far from that of late-antique Palestine, where the unconverted children of Japheth were certainly not welcome "dwelling" among the Jews of the Holy Land. . . . No rabbinic source of which I am aware interprets this verse to refer to the actual presence of Japheth's unconverted (and by Byzantine times, supersessionist) descendants living as accepted members of Jewish communities, even as "godfearers."[70]

Nor was Noah's blessing read as predicting harmonious coexistence by Christian interpreters: Jerome shared with the rabbis the understanding that "from Sem were born the Hebrews, from Japheth the people of the Gentiles," but glossed the reference to Japheth dwelling in the tents of Shem by commenting, in his *Hebrew Questions on Genesis:* "This is prophesied about us [i.e., Christians], who are engaged in the learning and knowledge of Scriptures after Israel has been cast forth."[71] By the rabbinic (and patristic) period, Noah's promise of harmony could no longer be taken at face value by the descendants of either Shem or Japheth. *Genesis Rabbah* on the passage provides at least two alternative readings of the blessing, the second of which directly concerns translation:

> "May God enlarge Japheth." This is Cyrus who decreed that the Temple be rebuilt, even so, "And he shall dwell in the tents of Shem," God does not dwell except in the tents of Shem.
>
> Bar Kappara said: May the words of the Torah be spoken in the language of Japheth in the tents of Shem. R. Judan said: From here we have a biblical source [allowing] for translation [of the Torah].[72]

Our midrashic passage responds to the implicit quandary of linking Japheth and Shem by splitting 9:27 into two sections, reading the *vav* in "and he shall dwell" adversively as "even so." Thus, while God's enlargement of Japheth is taken to refer to the Persian emperor Cyrus, who commissioned the rebuilding of the Temple, "He shall dwell" refers not to Cyrus or to Japheth but rather back to God, who dwells only among Shem. Noah's blessing, which seems to invite us to envision the two "good" sons (Kana'an, of course, is a different story) as destined to live together in peace, becomes in this rabbinic reading a reaffirmation of the chosen and unique status of the descendants of Shem. Midrashic exegesis is often described as arising from textual problems: gaps, ambiguities, "surface irregularities," as James Kugel calls the oddities of biblical usage that call for commentary the way a grain of sand "elicits" a pearl.[73] But it seems clear in this interpretation of our passage that the problem addressed in the midrash is not internal but external to the text, residing in the difficulty the rabbis had conceiving of a situation where Japheth or his descendants might take up residence in Semitic tents. Thus, the rabbis could be said to have *introduced* a gap where they might have easily discerned a bridge, constructing a midrashic barrier to set off the people with temporal power and the people among whom, *only* among whom, God will dwell.

Ben Kappara's commentary reverts to the understanding of "and he shall dwell in the tents of Shem" as referring to (the descendants of) Japheth. Here, too, however, it is possible to discern rabbinic ambivalence shaping the interpretation, since Japheth is no longer a Greek, nor even a Greek proselyte, but rather a personification of the Greek language, which metaphorically enters the tents of Shem when the Torah is discussed in the study hall in that language. Rabbi Judan infers from the discussion that the Torah may be translated, although it is not yet clear into which languages.

The halakhic discussion of the permissibility of translating the Torah is more extended in the Babylonian Talmud, but there, too, it revolves around Noah's blessing. On the issue of whether "the books" (rather than *tefillin* or *mezuzot*) may be translated, R. Shimon ben Gamliel finds textual warrant for their translation specifically into Greek:

> Rabban Shimeon ben Gamliel said: The books also may not be written [in any language] other than Greek. R. Abbahu said in the name of R. Yohanan: The law is according to Rabban Shimeon ben Gamliel. R. Yohanan said: What was Rabban Shimeon ben Gamliel's reasoning? It says, "May God enlarge Japheth and he shall dwell in the tents of Shem." The words of Japheth will be in the tents of Shem. But what of Gomer and Magog? R. Hiyya bar Abba said: This is the reason; it says: "May God enlarge Japheth," the beauty of Japheth will be in the tents of Shem.[74]

The question raised about Gomer and Magog, two children of Japheth other than Javan, who is traditionally seen as the ancestor of the Greeks, is a pertinent one: How do we know that, of all the children of Japheth, it is the Greeks that are the reference of Noah's blessing? The response takes its cue from an etymological reading of Japheth, and of *yaft*, the verb usually translated as "enlarge," as deriving from the Hebrew word for beauty. In this reading, Noah's punning blessing becomes: "May God beautify Japheth, the beautiful one." The name Japheth refers to the beauty that will emerge among his descendants, specifically through the Greek language. For the rabbis, in this passage and elsewhere, Greek is uniquely beautiful, indeed the embodiment of the aesthetic principle. Thus it is this beauty that will dwell in the tents of Shem.

The Palestinian Talmud, in discussing Rabban Shimeon ben Gamliel's ruling on the permissibility of Greek translation, comments: "They investigated and found that the Torah cannot be adequately translated [*lehitargem kol zorkha*] except in Greek." Apparent evidence for this translational adequacy is the version of Aquila:

> R. Yirmeyah in the name of R. Hiyya bar Abba said: Akylas the proselyte translated the Torah before R. Eliezer and R. Yehoshua, and they praised him, and said to him: You are more beautiful than (all) the children of men [*yafyit mebnay adam*].[75]

The Palestinian Talmud weaves together both themes of Noah's prophecy: that Greek proselytes will study in Jewish study halls—"before R. Eliezer and

R. Yehoshua" means also under their tutelage—and that the Torah will be expressed in the beautiful Greek tongue. Aquila's translation is beautiful, the passage implies, both because it is Greek and because it echoes Noah's Hebrew blessing, to which his teachers append their own. As their punning implies, Aquila is not only the most beautiful, he is also the most Japheth-like, as proselyte and translator, of all Adam's (and Noah's) descendants. That this pun is expressible only in Hebrew marks Greek beauty as a phenomenon of specifically *Jewish* significance. Among the pleasures of Aquila's beautiful version is that in him Noah's prophecy found its multiple fulfillments.

The intricacy of this talmudic exegesis might easily blind us to what is most striking about its thematic approach to translation. It is almost universally the case that translation is conceptualized as the exportation of a text from a "source" language or culture and its importation by a "target" language or culture. This movement is implied in the very terminology of translation: *Translatio* is a verbal noun deriving from the past participle, in Latin, of *transferre* (related to the Greek *metaphorein*), a transmission ordinarily imagined as moving from an original to its translation.[76] Sometimes, indeed, these transfers are seen in more aggressive terms, as the capture or appropriation of a text by a conquering culture. What has remained beyond the horizon of Western translation theory is the notion of translation as a cultural gain to the *source* rather than the target culture. In the rabbinic passages we have just read, Aquila's Greek version of the Torah is precisely such a gain, a coveted acquisition by the descendants of Shem of the beauty of Japheth.[77] The Bible does not, in being translated, go out to all nations as either captive or missionary but rather brings the choicest of them home to the rabbinic study hall, in fulfillment of its own Hebrew vision.

As a proselyte, Aquila can be clearly counted as symbolic capital transferred from the Greek to the Jewish community, and particularly valuable symbolic capital, since he is a member of the ruling class. But his translation may also be so calculated, and not only because Aquila's version is a "Jewish" rendering of the Bible. In Aquila's translation, the Greek is, as we have seen, radically Hebraized—we might almost say, "converted" to Judaism. The Hebraized Greek body of Aquila the proselyte is thus mirrored in the Hebraicized Greek text he produced. Patristic readers discerned what linguists might call Hebrew "interference" in Aquila's version, tracing his distortions of "natural" Greek syntax to an embrace of rabbinic exegetical techniques.[78] In his adherence to Akiva's hermeneutic principles and in his embedding of Hebrew words into his Greek text, Aquila thus constructs a Greek Bible in which the Hebrew is not transcended but reproduced. Hebrew is inscribed into the Greek, we

might almost say circumcised on it, as a mark that signals both Jewish affiliation and divine mimesis. In the proselyte and in his translation, the materiality of Hebrew is visible in—and on—the Greek; from the "Greek" perspective, this is a scandalous mutilation. Barrera's description of Aquila as having
"sacrificed Greek syntax" on the altar of Hebrew is apropos: the blood of circumcision, after all, is frequently associated with the blood of the sacrifice. In
the Christian critique of Aquila's work, disgust at Aquila's mutilated text, I
would suggest, is cousin to the horror of such a corporeal desecration. Aquila,
as translator and proselyte, is an unnatural and even uncanny figure.

The rabbis, in contrast to Aquila's numerous detractors, celebrate a Greek
Bible that bears the distinctive stamp of its Hebraic allegiances, the methods
of the rabbinic academy, the whiff of Semitic tents. Nor do they see this stamp
as a mutilation: the Greek retains its grace, even in Semitic garb and under
the Hebraic knife. Aquila's literalism is not the awkward fetters Dryden saw
in that method but rather a vehicle by which Greek beauty rides into the Hebrew sacred library. The rabbis, though, are less concerned with the details of
Aquila's work than with the ethnic and religious gestures that constitute for
them its true value. What emerges from their writings is a delight in Aquila's
text as a rich marker of identity, one that connects Greek and Jew, beauty and
truth, body and language, the human and the divine, contemporary reality
with biblical prophecy. From this perspective, Aquila's text communicates
multiple layers of meaning, we might say *performs* a dense and hybrid identity, even if it is—in the normative scheme of things—"unreadable." The rabbis are perhaps less literal in their reading of Aquila than those who dispar-
age Aquila's literalism. What they read in Aquila's version goes beyond the
individual letters that march across the page to the broad gesture of ironic
appropriation: they see the beauty of Japheth in the tents of Shem.

TRANSLATION AND LIBERATION

The denigrations of Aquila surveyed at the beginning of this chapter are bolstered with a highly charged rhetoric of enslavement and liberation. Thus, literalism is not only poor technique, but more damningly an expression of ser-
vility; by contrast, the sense-for-sense translator exhibits creativity, power,
and freedom. It is not, at first glance, evident why it should be the case that
fidelity to one dimension of a text should be considered a variety of freedom
while fidelity of another sort should be enslaving. We might also ask why the
liberation of meaning from the confines of the word should be so celebrated
if translation merely effects its renewed entrapment in another linguistic

prison. If the spirit, or Spirit, were not already the realm of freedom, and the letter a kind of prison or tomb, the rhetoric of sense-for-sense translation as the activity of free translators would be considerably harder to advance.

Paul is certainly not the first to imagine the letter as enslaving, but it is his disparaging of the letter of the law in favor of its spirit that propels this discourse in Christian Europe. Paul's writings, in particular to the Galatians warning them against circumcision, return repeatedly to the notion that the law (*nomos*, the Septuagint rendering of Torah) is a prison from which the spirit liberates. "Before this faith came, we were held prisoners by the law, locked up until faith should be revealed" (3:23). Paul implores those who would turn back to the law:

> It is for freedom that Christ has set us free. Stand firm, then, and do not let your-selves be burdened again by a yoke of slavery. Mark my words! I, Paul, tell you that if you let yourselves be circumcised, Christ will be of no value to you. . . . But by faith we eagerly await through the Spirit the righteousness for which we hope. (Galatians 5:1–5, NIV)

As part of his argument that those who are bound by the letter of the law— or the rules of the flesh—are slaves, Paul radically rereads the Genesis narrative of Abraham's two children; Paul's typological reading thus also works as a performance of the power and license of allegorical exegesis, measuring the reach of its spiritualizing method in its very distance from the traditional, literal, and "historical" Jewish interpretations:

> For it is written that Abraham had two sons, one by a slave and one by a free woman. But the son of the slave was born according to the flesh, the son of the free woman through a promise. Now this is an allegory: these women are two covenants. One is from Mt. Sinai bearing children for slavery; she is Hagar. Now Hagar is Mount Sinai in Arabia; she corresponds to the present Jerusalem, for she is in slavery with her children. But the Jerusalem above is free and she is our mother. . . . But what does the Scripture say? "Cast out the slave and her son; for the son of the slave shall not inherit with the son of the free woman." So, brethren, we are not children of the slave but of the free woman. (Galatians 4:21–31, NIV)

In this striking typology, Israel according to the flesh is Ishmael, the child of the slave woman, while Israel according to the promise is the community of Paul's fellow believers. It is precisely the power of allegory to reverse biological kinship ties (and traditional Jewish interpretation) in order to forge new spiritual communities, superior to those that propagate in the usual way. The free woman corresponds to "the Jerusalem above" (itself a familiar rabbinic trope, though one that in no way negates for the rabbis the Jerusalem "below") in Paul's curious admixture of Platonic idealism and rabbinic geography. Correspondingly, the children of the flesh are disinherited servants, serving the children of the promise who have inherited their portion and now rule them. By Augustine if not earlier, Paul was understood to be talking perfectly straightforwardly about Jews and Christians, and, moreover, as having predicted the political disempowerment of the Jews under Christian authority. In Augustine's rewriting of Paul's allegorical interpretation of Abraham's two sons, it is Noah's sons who play the roles of Christian(s) and Jew. While it is Shem, of course, who is traditionally seen as the ancestor of Israel, Augustine casts the Jews as descendants of Ham, who was cursed by Noah to be "the lowest of slaves . . . to his brothers" (Genesis 9:25):

> The middle son—that is, the people of the Jews . . .—saw the nakedness of their father, since he consented to the death of Christ and related it to his brothers outside. Through [the Jews'] agency, that which was hidden in prophecy was made evident and publicized; therefore it has been made the servant of its brethren. For what else is that nation today but the desks [scriniara] of the Christians, bearing the law and the prophets as testimony to the tenets of the church, so that we honor through the sacrament what it announces through the letter.[79]

In a powerful conceit, Augustine views Ham's uncovering the nakedness of his father as a prefiguration of the Jewish participation in the Crucifixion (and also of the sin of relating it to their "brothers outside," a probable reference to the Church tradition that, after the Crucifixion, the Jews sent messengers to every corner of the world to slander the Christians).[80] While the crime of the Jews seems to lie in their having publicly shamed Christ, Augustine also suggests that they served and continue to serve a valuable role in rendering visible what had been hidden in prophecy. In the Crucifixion, after all, God's plan is revealed on earth, in full view—this is a horrific but ultimately necessary, even salvific, accomplishment. Their enslavement, then, is not simply punishment for the crime of exposing God's nakedness; it also constitutes a useful service: the Jews as servants of their Christian brothers continue to unwittingly move the Christian agenda forward by bearing witness to the letter of the law and prophets, functioning as the desks on which Christian theology can rest its sacramental interpretations. Hegel's master-slave relationship is evident in Augustine's subtle ambivalence: the Jews may be enslaved by their literalism, but their effectiveness as servants of the letter enslaves Christian exegetes in turn, who are compelled to rest their spiritualizing interpretation on the solid, flat surfaces the Jews provide. Without these scriniara, Christian theology might be tracing its figures in the air.

Augustine's reading, of course, transcends the literal level of the text, which Christians as well as Jews have read as faithfully recording the genetic origins of the peoples of the world. As such, Augustine's exegesis can be contrasted with the rabbinical interpretation of Noah's blessing, which keeps more strictly to the kinship lines laid out in the Bible even as it reconfigures and expands these connections to include both proselytism and translation. But like the rabbinic understanding of Noah's blessing, Augustine's interpretation is not merely exegetical, an exercise in allegorical mastery or a clever manipulation of tropes; it also reflects as it shapes the political conditions under which Jews live in Christendom. It is no surprise, then, that Christian translation rhetoric increasingly rests as much on Roman imperial conceptions of translation as on Paul's Platonic conceptions of the law and the Spirit. When Paul described "Israel according to the Spirit" as free and "Israel according to the flesh" as enslaved, these distinctions had an existential and theological but not necessarily political resonance—both categories (they cannot be called groups yet) were in similarly subjugated circumstances. Roman translation rhetoric, by contrast, mobilized military and political realities to demarcate the relationship between translator and translated; with the Christianization of the Empire, these realities could also describe the relations between Christian and Jew. By the late fourth century, the Christian translator could well revel not only in spiritual freedom but also (more literally) in a sense of imperial power.

Elaborations of the Latin translation of Greek culture, a cultural project that formed the core of Roman imperial identity, forthrightly describe this cultural transfer in terms of an imperial right to conquer an outworn, if once-glorious, civilization.[81] Nietzsche famously celebrated the Roman urge to translate old Greek gods and histories into living Roman realities, to "breathe new life into a dead body." In Nietzsche's summary:

> These poet-translators did not know how to enjoy the historical disposition; anything past and alien was an irritant to them, and as Romans they considered it to be nothing but a stimulus for another Roman conquest. In those days, indeed, to translate meant to conquer. Not only did one omit what was historical, one also added allusions to the present and, above all, struck out the name of the poet and replaced it with one's own—not with any sense of theft but with the very best conscience of the *imperium Romanum*.[82]

Jerome's writings demonstrate just how easily certain dimensions of Roman imperial translation could survive the Christianization of the Roman Empire. This is not to say that Jerome's sense-for-sense translation theory was equivalent to Cicero's; Rita Copeland has cautioned that the "terminological continuity between Roman and early Christian theory actually disguises a dramatic difference between the two."[83] While Roman translators sought to displace Greek cultural meaning, Jerome's valuing of the Bible allowed no such agonistic substitution. Through Jerome, Copeland writes, "The Middle Ages inherits the formula 'non verbum pro verbo' as a model of textual fidelity rather than difference, as a theory of the direct conservation of textual meaning without the impediment of linguistic multiplicity."[84] It is my point, however, that the Christian overcoming of "the impediment of linguistic multiplicity," with its careful service to a signified retained in this multiplicity, represents not a rejection of the model of translation as conquest but a rewriting of it for new conditions. The revolutionary changes in the Empire notwithstanding, Roman models of translation did serve the Christian sphere and outlived even the collapse of the Empire.[85] The Roman translation of Greek wisdom provided a model for conceptualizing and neutralizing the relationship between Jewish sources and their translation, in which a "dead" or deficient culture—which yet contains some treasures worth plundering— must submit to the superior might of a conquering army of translators; and this displacement of one set of signifiers operates despite Jerome's fidelity to the transcendent content toward which it points (it is this fidelity that is missing, in Copeland's view, in Ciceronian translation). Christian translation, then, liberates the spiritual message enchained in the Jewish letter with a freedom and impunity that is a function not only of the theological superiority of spirit over letter but also of its new imperial clout. Both Pauline and Roman conceptualizations are apparent, it seems to me, in Jerome's approving words for the sense-for-sense translations of Hilary the Confessor (quoted in the previous chapter), who, in turning some homilies on Job and many commentaries on the psalms from Greek into Latin, "has not bound himself to the drowsiness of the letter or fettered himself by the stale literalism of inadequate culture. Like a conqueror he has led away captive into his own tongue the meaning of his originals" (sed quasi captives sensus in suam linguam victoris jure transposuit).[86] Whatever Jerome means by an "inadequate culture," what matters is that the rights of the Latin, and of the Christian, must triumph over the paltry claims the translated language may put forth. Sense-for-sense translation is the natural expression of the translator culture's thoroughgoing superiority—its liveliness and force—over that of the source text. As Hugo Friedrich writes, Jerome's defense of sense-for-sense translation sounds "like a declaration of power by a Roman emperor."[87]

Elsewhere, Jerome speaks of translation not through the semantic lens of military conquest but less dramatically as a form of international commerce—the target, often enough, of imperialist expansion. Thus, Jerome assures readers that they have no reason to fear his new translation, since they need consult it only if they wish to: "Let foreign merchandise come by boat only to those who desire it: peasants may not buy balsam, pepper, and the fruits of the palm tree."[88] Jerome's self-presentation as the purveyor of exotic goods invites us to read translation with the lens provided by Pierre Bourdieu, who describes language as shaped by the laws of the marketplace: competition, monopoly, manufactured scarcity, profit, capital, and so on. Bourdieu argues against the illusion of "linguistic communism which haunts all linguistic theory." Language, in Auguste Comte's "communist" formulation, is a "a kind of wealth, which all can make use of at once without causing any diminution of the store . . . a general treasure,"[89] while Saussure speaks of language as a "treasure deposited by the practice of speech in subjects belonging to the same community."[90] Comte and Saussure refer to the treasure shared by a single language community, while Jerome speaks of the transfer of cultural treasure across linguistic borders. Nevertheless, both the domestic market of a national language and the international market propelled by translation are illuminated by Bourdieu's insights into language as an arena for economic struggle. In the internationalization of the linguistic market, economic domination easily translates into plunder and dispossession.

The rhetoric of slavery versus freedom that propels the word–sense debate simultaneously draws on three semantic realms—those of Christian spiritual transcendence, Roman imperial conquest, and international trade. Sense-for-sense translation is thus "free" in two senses: The sense-for-sense translator is free because he allies himself with the realm of freedom, the spirit of language rather than its fleshly prison; and the translator is free in his power vis-à-vis the source text, which cannot resist its exportation, its transfer to enemy territory, or its being paraded before curious and unfriendly crowds. Herder describes the French translation-cum-conquest of Homer in just such graphic terms:

> Homer must enter France a captive, clad in the French fashion, lest he offend their eye; must let them shave off his venerable beard and strip off his simple attire; must learn French customs and, whenever his peasant dignity still shines through, be ridiculed as a barbarian.[91]

Homer is susceptible to such maltreatment by having the unfortunate disadvantage of being long dead. The vivid detail of Herder's translational parable, which raises him from the dead only to turn him into a prisoner of war, reminds us that the juxtaposition of liberation and translation in translation discourse is not just a metaphorical way of figuring the transposition of texts from one language to another in anthropomorphic terms. Historically, translation has also accompanied imperial conquest, enabling colonial control or channeling cultural spoils. It is not surprising, then, that translation discourse records a series of historical or quasi-historical narratives that juxtapose the movement of language with that of prisoners, in parallel or opposing trajectories. The narratives discussed in the previous chapter, which I discussed in terms of translational perfection, are also narratives of captivity and liberation, beginning with the *Letter of Aristeas*, which lists as the very first among the preliminary negotiations for the Bible translation the release of 100,000 Jews held captive in the kingdom since the previous regime (vv. 12–20). Aristeas takes the opportunity of the king's interest in the Bible to point out to him the *alogon*, the illogic, of translating the laws of the Jewish people while "a multitude [of Jews] subsists in slavery in your realm" (v. 15). Aristeas's own logic here is not crystal clear.[92] Nevertheless, that the ransom of captives could count on the royal ledger as payment for the translation of the Bible returns us to the overlap Bourdieu identifies between linguistic and economic/political capital: the Jews, by having a monopoly on this valued linguistic artifact and its language of composition (of course, this perspective is the Jewish one), command access to the royal treasury as well as the royal ear. The transfer-as-translation of Jewish symbolic capital in one direction must be balanced by the transfer-as-restitution of Jewish demographic capital in the other.

In the Hellenistic, patristic, and rabbinic tales of the composition of the Septuagint, it is clear that translation takes place within a marketplace of political and economic disparities, and that the circulation of texts and signification cannot be abstracted from the circulation of slaves, prisoners, and other valuable goods. These narratives represent this double economy in a variety of relationships: Aristeas imagines that translation might be read not only as plundering and conquest, but also as restitution, so that prisoners and texts might move in opposite directions, each serving as payment or ransom for the other.[93]

Scholars have recognized the degree to which, in Jerome's rhetoric, the "capture of the spirit" of a text roughly coincides with a series of imperial conquests, the historical subtext of his discourse. For Jerome, Robinson writes, translation "is not a simple technical process for achieving equivalence but a conflict or contest, a question of 'bind or be bound,' 'chain or be chained,' 'capture or be taken captive.'"[94] (Bourdieu, of course, would argue that such competition is inevitable, even if the slave market has largely given way to one focused on other forms of capital.) In the rabbinic discourse of translation-as-conquest, the battlefield or marketplace that governs translation is more visible to the naked eye: the Septuagint has been extracted by imperial force, and its translation occurs—is figured as—a tragic captivity. For the rabbis, however, the Septuagint narrative also supplies an occasion for a trickster tale, in which even the incarceration of the translators cannot guarantee the "capture" of an accurate translation. The Jews may be subject to state power, but their texts have not been entirely conquered.

The rabbinic narratives about the composition of the Septuagint stand in stark contrast with those that describe Aquila's translation. While the Septuagint is a treasure wrested from or tricked out of Jewish control, Aquila's version represents a cultural acquisition in the other direction, in which the Greek language itself is the trophy won by the Jewish community not by force or scheming but rather by the power of its religious message. Nevertheless, both translations are viewed against the backdrop of the radical asymmetry that governs the relations between the state authority and its Jewish (or any other subjugated) subjects. It is the figure of Aquila that provides the rabbis with the bridge, the mediating voice that can traverse the vast space separating them from the Emperor himself:

Aquilas, who was Hadrian's nephew, wished to become a proselyte but was afraid of his uncle Hadrian. So he said to him: I want to go into business.

Hadrian said: If you lack gold and silver, my treasure houses are open to you.

Aquilas said: I wish to do business and understand how people think, and I seek your council on how to go about that.

Hadrian said: Any merchandise whose price is depressed, go and deal with it, for in the end you will realize a profit.

Aquila intended to convert, so he went to Israel and studied Torah, and after some time, R. Eliezer and R. Yehoshua found him and his countenance had changed. And they said to one another: Aquilas is learning Torah. He asked them many questions and they answered.

Then he went to Hadrian, who asked: Why has your countenance changed?

Aquila said: I have studied Torah, and not only that, I have had myself circumcised.

Hadrian said: When?

Aquila said: When you told me to find merchandise whose price is depressed I went around among all the nations and found none less valued than Israel, but in the end they will be exalted, as Isaiah said: "Thus says the Lord, the Redeemer of Israel, his Holy One, to him who is despised, to him who is abhorred of nations, to a servant of rulers: Kings shall see him and rise, princes shall prostrate themselves" . . .

> Hadrian said: You should have learned Torah without being circumcised.
>
> Aquilas said: You would only give an officer a victory medal if he were carrying his weapon. So a man cannot study Torah if he is not circumcised, as it says, "He declares his word unto Jacob," to those who are circumcised as Jacob, and he did not do so to the uncircumcised nations.[95]

Aquila is figured here as a careful manipulator, resisting Hadrian only after first flattering him by asking his advice. In a daring ploy, Aquila couches his very conversion as obedience to his royal uncle, saying, in effect, that he was merely following Hadrian's sage counsel! If Aquila, as relative of the emperor, serves as the perfect vehicle for rabbinic fantasies of access to the imperial ear, as translator he fills an equally crucial role, of locating the point at which Greek and Hebrew discourse can be seen to converge. For all the time and space it covers, this rabbinic tale revolves around a single issue: the relative value and mutual exchangeability of Greek and Hebrew wisdom. Bourdieu focuses on language as symbolic power primarily within a single class-differentiated society, in which both dominant and dominated group essentially agree on what constitutes linguistic value even if they do not share equal access to this capital.[96] Greek certainly has a large measure of prestige in rabbinic literature, which functions to that extent as the expression of a linguistically dominated group; nevertheless, what primarily interests the rabbis in the literature on Aquila is the fluctuating status of *two* competing sign-systems, one of which lays claim to an undeniable store of political, cultural, and aesthetic power and another that holds exclusive title—not only in its own view but to some extent even in that of (some of) its religious and cultural rivals—to a literature with ultimate religious value. The economic rhetoric of the *Tanhuma* tale provides a unified marketplace for these apparently incommensurable commodities, an international stock exchange in which religion and politics are invited to stake their relative claims.

Attempts at such an exchange are common in translation narrative: Aristeas manages to secure an arena for Hebrew–Greek converse in the theological and philosophical symposium, at which the translators were feted and grilled at the end of each day's session. By the rabbinic period, such symposia were less easily imagined. In Aquila's dialogues with Hadrian, they calculated and recalculated how to wring a profit from the Hebrew–Greek market they could hardly avoid entering. It is surely reassuring that the capital gains accrued by Aquila's Greek-Hebrew translation are already implicit in Hadrian's advice to "buy cheap, sell dear"; that is, the value of the Jews is comprehensible from within a Greek frame of reference. The fulcrum Aquila discovers

in this tale, between commercial wisdom and religious truth, is a spectacu-
larly successful one, since investing in undervalued stock results not in
equivalence but rather in extravagant profit. And while religion and commerce operate in this story along similar universal principles, religious profit
is also translatable to political power—princes will bow before this underap-
preciated human merchandise. The dazzling series of linguistic transformations Aquila engineers thus produces the very opposite of the situation at
hand: kings paying tribute to Jews, not only in Isaiah's prophecy but already
in Aquila's achievement of obtaining an apparently respectful audience from
the very greatest of these kings.

That Aquila discovers this unforeseen value by amplifying rather than
contesting Hadrian's words suggests the transformative power of his translation, in which slaves are exalted to the highest rungs and sacred truths lurk
in the banalities of marketplace clichés. Aquila, in this narrative, is no slave,
either to the Hebrew or to the Emperor, just as the Jews only seem to be the
"servants of rulers." Aquila even succeeds in translating his circumcision, in
the Greco-Roman mind the mark of the slave, into a soldier's weapon, evidence of his worthiness to receive the king's medal. His circumcision may
have changed him, but not in the direction Hadrian imagined—as evidence
of a loss in his business dealings. Aquila's circumcision has given him access
to an exclusive market of the highest possible value, a value even the military
or commercial mind would have to appreciate.

Aquila's translation in this story is both skilled imperial mimicry and a
form of resistance, an overturning of the Greek values he also mirrors.
Aquila's Greek retranslation of the Bible, as an attempt to trace a Jewish-
Greek space separate from what had become the Christian Bible, can similarly be read as a resistant text, manipulating the "niceties" of Greek to
Jewish advantage. Tejaswini Niranjana describes retranslation as a prime
strategy for the post-colonial reconstruction of identity:

> The post-colonial desire to re-translate is linked to the desire to re-write his-
> tory. . . . To read existing translations against the grain is also to read colonial
> historiography from a post-colonial perspective, and a critic alert to the ruses of
> colonial discourse can help uncover what Walter Benjamin calls "the second tra-
> dition," the history of resistance.[97]

Niranjana associates postcolonial retranslation with literalist techniques,
particularly the literalist reworking of earlier "free" versions. The "deliberate
roughness" of Niranjana's own literal retranslation of a Sanskrit *vacana* "allows the text to 'affect,' as Benjamin would have it, the language into which

it is being translated, interrupting the 'transparency' and smoothness of a totalizing narrative like that of [the colonialist version she is retranslating]."[98] Niranjana insists on the political significance of maintaining the Sanskrit form of the proper names in her text, in particular of gods. "Given that colonialism's violence erases or distorts beyond recognition (as witness in innumerable colonial texts) the *names* of the colonized, it seems important *not* to translate proper names in a colonial or decolonizing practice."[99] The correspondences between Niranjana's retranslation and Aquila's are striking: Aquila's version, like Niranjana's, interrupts the smoothness of the earlier translation, "affects" the language into which it is being translated, and insists on transcribing rather than translating God's "proper name." In his nearly unreadable text, Aquila interrupts the communication of the biblical message beyond Jewish borders, just as Niranjana's version impedes the easy export of Sanskrit texts to the West. I have already argued, though, that Aquila's text does indeed communicate, though the gestures and codes it expresses lie on the plane of the signifier rather than the signified, as outward form and corporeal identification. This preference, as Niranjana helps us see, is already a form of resistance.

That rabbinic literature considers Aquila something of a rebel is readily apparent in the tales that render his conversations with Hadrian. But the dominant discourse on Aquila—that is, the discourse of the dominant group "betrayed" by Aquila—also hints that his very slavishness is a variety of defiance. Speiser reminds us that Aquila certainly knew Greek well enough to render the Bible in it according to the rules of Greek usage. That is, Aquila knowingly and voluntarily "abused" his native language. Once again, it is Bourdieu who sheds light on the phenomenon at issue: linguistic incorrectness as treason:

> All social destinies, positive and negative, by consecration and stigma, are equally *fatal*—by which I mean mortal—because they enclose those whom they characterize within the limits that are assigned to them and that they are made to recognize. The self-respecting heir will behave like an heir. . . . There are exceptions: the unworthy heir, the priest who abandons his calling, the nobleman who demeans himself and the bourgeois who turns common. . . . That is the function of all magical boundaries: to stop those who are inside, on the right side of the line, from leaving, demeaning, or down-grading themselves.[100]

The symbolic danger posed to the dominant group by those who scorn or squander their inheritance precisely glosses the paradox of Aquila's status as rebel-slave. Aquila is no Prince Hal, slumming for a season before he is called to take up again the royal mantle; he has gone native, even if he keeps in touch with his relatives in high places. In abandoning the symbolic capital of Greek eloquence—the mark of the educated male of his milieu—for the language of a despised people, Aquila not only degrades himself, he also devalues the stock of "correct" Greek. The literature that champions, for ostensibly neutral linguistic reasons, idiomatic Greek also polices the political boundaries that separate emperors from their slaves and Greeks from Jews. From this perspective, the rabbinic literature makes explicit what is elsewhere left unsaid, that Aquila only appears to be slavish. In his submission to the Hebrew letter, his outrageous identification with a subjugated people, he is also a grave threat to the very Empire.

THE TRANSLATOR'S BODY

With his late poem "Conferences, Conferences: Malignant Words, Benign Speech," the Israeli poet Yehuda Amichai paints a portrait of modern Jerusalem as a city full to the brim with pilgrims. These pilgrims have come, however, not to visit sacred sites but rather to attend international "conferences and symposia, too numerous to count." Among these are conferences "on the import and export"

> of one religion to another, exporting Torah from Zion and babies
> into the world, importing the dead. Or a major conference on Job:
> dermatologists on skin diseases, anthropologists
> on pain and suffering, legal scholars on justice and injustice,
> God on the nature of Satan, and Satan on the notion of the divine.[101]

That Amichai is staging a (Jewish) retelling of the Pentecost event narrated in Acts 2 is suggested not only in the omnipresence of translators and languages among these international conferees but more specifically in the appearance of "the spirit of God" as the force that circulates the words they speak and hear:

> The translators sit and recycle all to another
> recycling plan that has no end, and the spirit of God [*veruah elohim*]
> hovers above [*merahefet lema'alah*] with the whirring wing-blades of a giant fan
> whipping the air, the words whipped over and over like foam.[102]

In this passage, Amichai reactivates some of the material force of the phrase "spirit of God" (*ruah elohim*), bringing to bear in a startlingly literal fashion those associations of the term in Acts and Genesis that include both "breath" and "wind." What he suggests is that this *ruah* is no more than hot air, a groundless and eternal circulation of words without substance or fixed meaning. Nevertheless, Amichai's poem is no nihilist manifesto. However difficult it is to fix the meaning of these words, they are the expressions of a human pathos he does not deny. Describing the work of the translators at "the major conference on Job," Amichai writes:

> And the translators translate pain to another kind of pain,
> remembering to forgetting, forgetting to remembering,
> curse to blessing and blessing to curse.
> Sometimes they fall asleep in their cubicles like newborns
> in their bassinets in the maternity ward.[103]

In these last two lines, Amichai goes beyond the vision he has laid out, of Jerusalem as a world in which words circulate *ad infinitum* to no effect. Turning abruptly from the signifying activity of the translators in their cubicles, in which the translators function as mere vehicles of a perpetual-motion signifying machine, Amichai gives voice to the experience of the translator in a passive realm—"like newborns"—untouched by language. It is characteristic, perhaps, of Amichai's poetics of concreteness that he moves here from a declaration of the exhaustion of language to a recognition of a different kind of exhaustion, one of the body. In "Conferences, Conferences," the translators become the most vivid of Amichai's cast of characters, as if the poet were presenting their embodiment in deliberate defiance of the mere instrumentality of their role, refiguring the narrow cubicles they inhabit as cradling bassinets. The last of the fourteen short sections of the poem returns the translators to their role as agents of a linguistic transformation, but this transformation is now reimagined as a quasi-biological process—a double one, with an erotic as well as intellectual dimension:

> The translators, men and women, sit in their cells
> and make honey, like bees, from all the buzz and babble:
> a cultured honey behind their eyes,
> a wild honey under their pubic hair.[104]

What is most startling about this final image is that these varieties of honey, the cultured and the wild, are produced from the same "buzz and babble"—perhaps in some sense are the same. This vision of the translator, though, may emerge quite naturally from the first words in this stanza: "The translators, men and women." It is Amichai's gift to us simply to present this truth, that translators are, after all, men and women, with all the appurtenances of this embodied existence.

That the corporeal life of translators has been normatively seen as irrelevant to the work of translation is the claim at the heart of *The Translator's Turn*, Douglas Robinson's manifesto for the return of the body to translation studies. Robinson argues that Western translation theory from Augustine to Saussure has relied on the meaning of a word as "a transcendental label identifying and unifying the fleeting physical (graphological or phonological) sign."[105] And meaning "remains just as transcendental for Saussure as it was for Augustine, just as systematically abstracted out of the carnal messiness of actual speech."[106] What interests Robinson (as it does me) about this state of affairs is the extent to which this theory has rested on a denial of what he calls the "carnal messiness" of language, the connectedness of language to the physicality and specificity of human speech. Against this suppression of the "body" of language in linguistic theory, Robinson insists rather that words are understood through all our somatic faculties:

> We smell words, all of us, as well as see them; taste words as well as hear them. Because our culture discourages perception of language in terms of sensation, however, these somatic responses to words remain subconscious and therefore often dormant, unused, unacted-upon. . . . To situate meaning in feeling, as [William] James does, is to bring language back down to earth, into the realm of human subjectivity: precisely that realm consistently perceived as the root of all evil by scientistic thinkers from the early Middle Ages to the present.[107]

In the traditional distinction between the letter-as-body of language and the spirit-as-meaning, the letter, like a body, is a mere container for what is truly of value, a receptacle of glorious spirit; to cleave to the body is to remain a slave to all that is fallen and debased. In championing a corporeal conception of language and translation, Robinson also revalues the body: far from being a cave or crypt of language, the body is an arena for its play. Translation is an erotic discovery, the record of multiple aversions and pleasures and turns— in one of the multiple meanings of the title, Robinson plays on the translator's activity as a bodily "turn" from one language to another. Translators, of course, also turn things into other things, generating texts as Amichai's translators turn "buzz and babble" into honey behind their eyes and pubic hair. (At the most fundamental level, Robinson's title insists on reversing the invisibility of the translator, on her having a "turn" to speak.) Although Robinson does not address the denigration of word-for-word translation as an auxiliary symptom of the suppression of the body in translation theory, the implications of his reclamation effort for this denigration are clear: if the body of the translator is now to be readmitted to the arena of translation, attention to the "body" of language must no longer be considered a symptom of servile literalism but rather appreciated as an exploratory method of the sensually attuned translator.

Robinson's most extended description of the somatics of translation comes in his account of one of these "turns," his narrative of being won over by a group of his students in their unanimous repetition of what he knew full well to be a translation error:

> As the bombardment continued, as I reached the thirtieth and then the fortieth paper, the translation that I had begun by feeling "incorrect" now seemed like the only "natural" one. "North from Helsinki"—of course! How else could you say it? What alternatives were there? I was then ready to go back and accept all the "froms" I had marked wrong. My body had been brought around, persuaded, literally "swayed."[108]

In his attention to translation as suasion and persuasion—as the swaying of the translator from one sense of what "feels right" to another—Robinson has captured something of what fascinated the rabbis about translation, the overlap between linguistic transformation and religious conversion. Where Aquila figures in translation discourse largely through his translational techniques, rabbinic literature remembers him almost entirely as a proselyte, in the story of his turn from paganism to Judaism. Rabbinic literature records very few programmatic statements on translation that might be made to serve as proof texts for rabbinic theorizing about translation. (One exception seems to be the often-quoted dictum in *Tosefta Megillah*: "He who translates literally is a liar, while he who adds anything is a blasphemer.")[109] It is hard to discern even a clear preference for one sort of translation over another— that there seems to be a literary conflation of the figures of Aquila and Onkelos, two very different kinds of translators, is symptomatic of this relative unconcern for translation technique. The preference for narrative over theory, however, may itself have some theoretical justification. Once one relinquishes the transcendental route provided by an immutable signified, translation can indeed only unfold temporally, as a narrative succession: there is no arena above or beyond the flow of historical time in which to imagine its work. (In Robinson's anecdote, this temporality is represented in the tracing of the difference between the first and fortieth encounter with a particular "error"; in Steiner's scheme, it is expressed in the translator's durational "leaning towards" a text, and in the restitution that must follow upon the imbalance.)[110] In attending to the "spirit" of language, translation theory provides its own justification for a synchronic account of linguistic transfer.

Once it takes the body of language and of the translator seriously, translation discourse is compelled toward the diachronic pulse of narrative. It is in the twists and turns of a translation plot, therefore, that rabbinic thought on translation takes its characteristic shape.

The narratives about Aquila in rabbinic literature view him invariably as a proselyte as well as translator; moreover, he is presented as not having left his original community completely behind him upon his circumcision. Thus, Aquila is a liminal figure, moving between communities as well as between languages—even his conversion is seen, in one story, as not absolutely final.[111] Taken together, these narratives construct an arena for thinking through the connections between community and language, between the convert and the translator, and between the body of language and what Bourdieu would call the *habitus*—the corporeal-linguistic disposition—of the translator.[112] The translator-convert story revolves around a number of related motifs. The first is suasion, the "swaying" or "leaning" that marks a shift from one language community to another. Language, in this view, is no neutral medium of communication; meaning cannot be separated from the social relations it inhabits, indeed comprises.[113] What distinguishes the narrative tradition about Aquila is its particular attention to the crossing of linguistic borders as ethnic and religious transgressions; these stories take their shape not only within the dense materiality of a colonial scene, they also derive their interest from the overcrowded intersection of (the Hebrew) language and (the Jewish) body.

Although narrative is the distinctive translation genre of rabbinic literature, patristic literature also records stories about Aquila and other translators. Epiphanius recounts a popular Christian legend about Aquila—the first traces of which are to be found in Irenaeus[114]—that speaks of him as a pagan who converted to Christianity, impressed by the "great signs, healings and other miracles" he saw among the disciples of the disciples of the apostles. Nevertheless, he failed to give up his interest in astrology, "but every day made calculations on the horoscope of his birth" and, in disputations, "tried to establish things that have no existence, tales about fate." On his expulsion from the Christian community,

> he became a proselyte and was circumcised as a Jew. And being painfully ambitious [*epiponōs philotimēsamenos*], he dedicated himself to learning the language of the Hebrews and their writings. After he had first been thoroughly trained for it, he made his translation. He was moved not by the right motive, but by the desire to distort certain of the words occurring in the translation of the Seventy-Two.[115]

According the Epiphanius, Aquila is a rebuffed Christian whose translations are motivated by anti-Christian resentment. Such accounts by religious communities of why an individual might have left the fold are formulaic; the Talmud, for instance, speaks similarly of Jesus as a rebuffed Pharisee, in a tale that also involves the interpretation and misinterpretation of signs.[116] In providing an explanation for the absurdity of rejecting Christianity, the narrative imagines Aquila as fascinated with language, the "great signs" of Christianity but also the empty signs of astrology and the corrupt signs of Judaism: Aquila is someone who exhibits a talent for languages and other sign-systems, without being able to distinguish the ultimate truth within them. The phrase "painfully ambitious" makes it clear that Aquila acquires linguistic competence the way others accumulate material possessions, rising through the ranks of various religious groups through the symbolic capital of language. That language can provide such social power (and that social power governs what constitutes linguistic competence) is precisely Bourdieu's argument; what is noteworthy here is that so "secular" a perspective on language should express itself so clearly in this patristic account. The metaphysical "content" of these religious sign-systems recedes in the face of Aquila's movement among sign-systems, uncovering their structural characteristics: their mechanisms of exclusion (Christianity will not tolerate astrology alongside its own "signs and wonders"), their modes of differentiation and promotion (knowing Hebrew is Aquila's pathway to social advancement), and their competition (Aquila produces a new Bible version as ammunition against the one used by his former coreligionists). In such a religious marketplace, Aquila moves from one community to another not because he has discovered any permanent truths, but rather because he is won over by various semantic demonstrations, or rebuffed by symbolic rules, or attracted by the possibility of himself wielding linguistic power. It is just this "suasion" that Epiphanius's Septuagint narrative—which fixes the translators in separate cells—is designed to combat. In Epiphanius and other versions of the Septuagint narrative, a perfect translation is achieved outside the push and pull of human commerce; Aquila, by contrast, is enmeshed in—one might say, contaminated by—the circulation of the religious signs of his day, the inescapable lure of other people's words. Those who traffic in language-shift are themselves shifty characters, the legend seems to imply. By placing Christian signs at the center of his narrative, between astrological signs and the Hebrew language, Epiphanius ends up casting doubt on the reliability not only of this particular reader of signs but also of any sign system, including his own Christian one.

Although there is evidence that Aquila's version was used in Jewish–Christian disputation—most directly, his substitution of *nēanis* for LXX *parthenos* in Isaiah 7:14—rabbinic literature imagines Aquila most often in conversation with the pagan Hadrian rather than with representatives of Christianity. As Daniel Boyarin writes,

> Rabbinic literature strikingly, stunningly, seems to ignore the presence and eventual world-shaping growth of Christianity, the Christianization of the Empire. This has been called "the most thunderous silence in Jewish history." Here and there, however, there are texts that construct the reaction of the Rabbis to the enormous religious events that were taking place around them.[117]

A note on this passage continues the thought by remarking that "the presence of pagan Rome is everywhere felt in [rabbinic texts], and often, I think, disguises through anachronism the Christian Rome that is both context and referent."[118] Boyarin's notion, that pagan Rome is often a stand-in for Christian Rome in the Amoraic literature, provides us some traction for understanding what is perhaps the most puzzling of the Aquila narratives, his conversation with Hadrian about *ruaḥ* (or, in the Aramaic, *ruḥa*). The story appears in *y. Ḥagiga*, immediately following the famous passage that restricts the public study of mystical subjects, including the esoteric teachings on Creation:

> R. Judah bar Pazzi in the name of R. Yose b. R. Judah: Hadrian asked the proselyte Aquila: Is it true that you [Jews] say that the world depends on *ruḥa* (or is suspended on air)?
> Yes, said Aquila.
> Hadrian said: How will you prove it to me?
> Aquila said to him: Bring me young camels.
> He brought him young camels. He loaded and raised them up. He made them sink down, took them and strangled them.
> He said to Hadrian: See your camels, raise them up!
> Hadrian said: After you have strangled them!
> Aquila said to him: What is it except that the *ruḥa* has gone out of them?[119]

A longer version in *Tanḥuma*, in a commentary on the first verses in Genesis, makes explicit the connection between the camel's *ruaḥ*, which allows him to bear his load, and God's *ruaḥ* in Genesis, on which the world depends:

> [Aquila] said to Hadrian: Tell the camel to stand.
> Hadrian said: You choked him and he should stand?!
> Aquila said: Have I killed him or is he missing a limb?
> Hadrian said: You took his *ruaḥ* away!

Aquila said: And if it wasn't the camel that suffered and bore his load but rather the *ruaḥ* that was in him, how much more so does God's *ruaḥ* carry the entire world.

Hadrian was silent.[120]

Aquila, according to a pattern we can already discern in this family of tales, begins as an obedient submissive subject who complies with Hadrian's desire for theological discussion. Hadrian, also according to a pattern that goes far beyond the Aquila-Hadrian tales, is made to acknowledge, if not speak, Jewish truths.[121] The story, though, does not entirely add up. Unlike the Hadrian-Aquila stories discussed earlier, the theological topic at hand is not circumcision or the value of the Jewish people—topics of obvious relevance to Aquila and his uncle, and in which each of the participants take the expected position. The discussion in this narrative revolves around *ruaḥ*, a more abstract topic than they had previous engaged, and one in which the positions taken by the disputants—especially Aquila's defense of the view that Jews believe the world depends on *ruaḥ*—are harder to pin down. Why would it matter to Hadrian whether the Jews think the world stands on *ruaḥ*? Why would Aquila defend a position that has so little rabbinic warrant? What, in short, is this dispute really about?

We might begin to unpack this puzzle by noticing the untranslatability of the word *ruaḥ* in this story. *Ruaḥ*, as is well known, has a range of meanings, from wind to its metaphorical extensions as breath and, at a greater distance, spirit. Translation into Greek would not be difficult, since *pneuma* has a similar range of meanings; *spiritus*, however, reverses the primary and secondary significations to foreground the abstract, immaterial, and theological meanings of the terms. Although the tale does not directly thematize translation, the problem of understanding *ruaḥ* "literally" or "spiritually"—as breath/wind or as spirit—is the crux of the conversation between Hadrian and Aquila; the word *ruḥa* poses a telling problem for the English translator, since the story hinges on the semantic vacillation between breath and spirit, and translating *ruaḥ* as one or the other would render the story's wordplay incomprehensible. Hadrian assumes at the outset that *ruaḥ* means spirit, while Aquila's victory rides on his demonstration to Hadrian that it (also) means breath; the tale thus works as a violently physical sort of pun, in which Aquila pulls the rug from under Hadrian's "spiritual" usage, grotesquely proving that the world depends on *ruaḥ* by squeezing the breath from a hapless beast.

The discussion between Hadrian and Aquila, I would argue, makes sense only as a displaced form of Jewish–Christian polemic, the theological arena in which the signification of the word *ruaḥ* was and is a live issue. Harry Orlinsky writes, "The two major passages that involved and divided the two communities theologically were Genesis 1:2 and Isaiah 7:14."[122] It is precisely this difference in understanding Genesis 1:2 that is at stake in our narrative. Although the verse is not quoted, it is in the background of the narrative: The *Tanhuma* is explicitly a commentary on Genesis 1:2, and the talmudic version occurs in the context of a discussion of Creation, in which Genesis 1:2 is mentioned as evidence not that the world stands on *ruaḥ* but rather that *ruaḥ* stands on water, as the Hebrew would seem to imply.[123] By contrast, Genesis 1:2 is the locus classicus of Christian readings of *ruaḥ elohim* as the spirit of God, evidence, in later periods, that the "Holy Spirit" was present at Creation. Jerome insists that the phrase refers to the Holy Spirit (*Hebrew Questions* 1.2); Augustine's meditation on Creation in the last book of his *Confessions* similarly describes how he discerned the entire Trinity in Genesis 1:1–2:

> By the name of God, who made these things, I now understood the Father, and by the name of Beginning, the Son, in whom he made them. And believing my God to be the Trinity, as I did believe, I searched into his holy words, and behold, your "Spirit was borne above the waters." Behold the Trinity, my God, Father, and Son, and Holy Spirit, creator of all creation.[124]

Aquila's discussion with Hadrian, in this context, comes into focus not as the occasion for Aquila to prove that the world depends on *ruaḥ*, but rather as an irrefutable argument that *ruaḥ* must be understood as the Jews do, as spirit but *primarily* as wind and breath, its "corporeal" significations. These significations, moreover, are not separable theological entities, even if they are invisible and immaterial. They are fundamentally interconnected in and as the spiritual/physical being of the world, in its gross as well as lofty permutations. It is at least partly the point of Aquila's violence that the spirit may be abstracted from the body only at mortal peril. The division of *ruaḥ* and body—that is, the Platonic-Christian exegesis of *ruaḥ* as spirit—produces a corpse, not "pure" spirituality.

Aquila's insistence on the inseparability of body and spirit is not only semantic or theological; it is also political. The spirit and the body, the "higher" and "lower" functions, are ranked hierarchically, a ranking that has genuine consequences for those groups (women, Jews, peasants, animals) that are culturally associated with the body rather than the spirit. Aquila's move, then, is radically democratizing, deflating as it does the spiritual pretensions on which the exercise of power rests. The body demystifies this pretension, equalizing the relations between ruler and ruled, spirit and flesh. Bakhtin's analysis of the "grotesque realism" that is the backdrop to Rabelais's art may also apply to the Aquila tale: "The essential principle of grotesque realism is degradation, that is, the lowering of all that is high, spiritual, ideal, abstract; it is a transfer to the material level, to the sphere of earth and body in their indissoluble unity."[125] Rabelais indeed lends a grotesque materialization to the very term at issue in the Aquila story, describing Pantagruel's journey to the Island of Ruach, populated by windbags and flatulents who live on wind and, tragically, often die of it as well: "They all fart as they die, the men loudly, the women soundlessly, and in this way their souls depart by the back passage."[126]

Aquila's savagery goes beyond Rabelais's comic deflation of the spiritual pretensions of Christendom (including its spiritualizing reading of the Bible). The camel is not only a coarse body, reminder of the carnal existence no creature can transcend; he is also the Emperor's property and servant. In the political theater of their theological debate, Aquila both proves his point and kills the Emperor's beast of burden: the rebellion here is double, since the dead camel is also a disobedient camel, refusing to rise and kneel at the royal command. Semantic argument is brought back here to the political realm, operating within the workings of competition and domination. Semantics, that is, is never *merely* semantics. To be a literalist is not just to adopt one technique among others. As this tale suggests, literalism is a method of marshalling resources within a power structure, a weapon mobilized against both linguistic abstraction and imperial rule. The narrative of Aquila further suggests that these are variations of a single principle.

Taken together, the portraits of Aquila the literalist in the patristic and rabbinic literature form a strange, asymmetrical diptych: on the one side, the opaque figure of the servile translator, his fetters clanking dispiritingly, his character as unreadable as the Bible version he laboriously produced; on the other side, we can set the translator-proselyte of rabbinic literature, whose outlines are also opaque but only strategically so, and only to those in power. To those whose ranks he has joined, Aquila's actions and translations speak loud and clear: He is a rebel hero, a creature of rare beauty, cunning, and defiance. The arena that is opened for Aquila in the rabbinic literature, in which the proselyte-translator has his say to the very emblem of power, could hardly be further from the "sterile debate" Steiner saw in translation discourse, in which sense-for-sense translators triumph again and again over their servile counterparts.

※

CHAPTER THREE

False Friends

Conversion and Translation from Jerome to Luther

FALSE FRIENDS (or FAUX AMIS) A standard term used to describe SL and TL items which have the same or very similar forms but different meanings, and which consequently give rise to difficulties in translation (and indeed interlingual communication in general).
MARK SHUTTLEWORTH and MOIRA COWIE,
Dictionary of Translation Studies

Gerade durch diese gemeinsame Sprache, durch diese Hebraica veritas, *waren die Juden und die Christen getrennt.*
JAROSLAV PELIKAN, "Hebraica Veritas"

THE IMPORTANCE OF Martin Luther to translation history does not rest primarily in his having rendered the Bible into a modern European vernacular—other translators preceded him along that path. The decades between the 1455 Gutenberg Bible (in Latin) and the 1522 appearance of Luther's New Testament saw the publication of at least a dozen German Bibles, and others in Italian, Dutch, Catalan, French, Czech, and English.[1] What distinguished Luther's Bible from these precursors and prepared the ground for modern translation was the clarity and accessibility of Luther's German style. Where these earlier Bibles had kept close to the Vulgate, indeed were often designed as aids for understanding the Latin, Luther "strove to render his version in natural, idiomatic German, intending his version to serve as a substitute for the original text."[2] Commenting on his translation, a text that had given him no end of trouble, Luther records his satisfaction at having rendered the biblical book easily comprehensible: "Anyone can run their eyes over three, four pages without bumping up against anything once, and never becoming aware of the stumps and stones there used to be in what he goes over now as over a smooth board."[3]

Luther acknowledges here that, although the reader would never know it, his "smooth" prose was achieved only with difficulty, through a laborious plowing of what Luther perceived as rocky biblical soil. This was especially true of the Old Testament: while Luther breezed through the New Testament in a matter of months, he worked on the Old Testament translation for a full decade (1522–32). The problem was not only the predictable difficulty of learning and understanding the Hebrew, a language Luther never completely mastered, or of finding appropriate teachers or advisors; as Luther complained, the very voices of the Old Testament seemed to resist his approach. In the Preface to Job, Luther had compared the translator's labor to a farmer; elsewhere he spoke rather of the Bible as living speech, and the translator's work as compelling these foreigners to speak a tongue alien to their own— indeed, nearly to mutate into another species! Hard at work on Isaiah in 1528, Luther spoke of the prophet's recalcitrance, sighing, "Lord, what hard work it is to compel Hebrew prophets to speak German. They resist relinquishing Hebrew and imitating barbaric German."[4] The evolving shape of Luther's transmutation of Hebrew into German speech can be traced through his multiple revisions of already published translations, which reflect an increasing attention to the language of the reader. In a postscript to the 1534 reissue of the Psalms, Luther explained the need for a new translation by describing his still-evolving technique: "Our previous German Psalter is, in many places, closer to the Hebrew and further from the German; this one is closer to the German and further from the Hebrew."[5] Luther means by "genuinely German" the register of plain speech, the language of "the folk," as is evident from his famous "Open Letter on Translation" of 1530. As Jerome's letter on translating had been, Luther's *Sendbrief* is a defense of what his critics viewed as his overly "loose" translation practice; as had Jerome, Luther argues that he follows a sense-for-sense technique rather than being held captive to the word. Both the critique and the defense of the translator's freedom are familiar enough, then. Where Luther's innovation arises is in the sharpness and commitment of what Douglas Robinson calls his "reader-orientation."[6] Luther's attention to target-language norms goes beyond the tired question of whether one should translate the Bible word-for-word or sense-for-sense, or even his articulation of the principle that a translation should be rendered in proper target-language idiom; Luther's formulation of his approach could serve as a manifesto for the importance of rendering the Bible in the language of the people, in living German speech:

> You have to ask the mother in her house, the children in the street, the ordinary man at the market and look at their mouths as they talk, and translate that way so they'll understand you and realize that you're speaking German to them.[7]

As critics have long acknowledged, Luther's role was not in *reflecting* idiomatic German speech, but in fact in imagining and *forging* a German that transcended the existing patchwork of dialects and that could serve as a German *lingua franca*. As Franz Rosenzweig put it, Luther's Bible "became the fundamental book not only of a particular church but of the national language itself."[8] To take his own example, Luther moved the angel Gabriel's words "Hail Mary, full of Grace" (Luke 1:28) closer to the simple cadences of German love-talk (even if he stopped short of that goal). Ridiculing the long-established tradition of translating the phrase word-for-word, Luther asks:

> And what German understands what that means, "*voll Gnaden*"? He would think of a barrel full of beer or a purse full of money. That's why I translated it "*Du holdselige*" [you charming one] so that a German can realize more quickly what the angel meant with his greeting.[9]

In moving away from the Vulgate and translations that cleaved to it, Luther also rejected the heavy sedimentation of theological commentary that had accrued to the Latin. To illustrate, the words Luther was translating in Luke, "*Ave Maria gratia plena*," were the subject of a lengthy scholastic commentary by Gabriel Biel, "the last of the Schoolmen" (d. ca. 1495). Biel had much to say, as might be expected, on the theory of grace, but he also expounded on the Latin word *plena*. I will cite here only a brief excerpt of Werner Schwarz's summary:

> Biel distinguished four kinds of fullness of which the first, "fullness of sufficiency" (*plenitudo sufficientiae*), has four subdivisions: it suffices either for the acquisition of eternal life, from which fullness every mortal being is excluded, or it suffices for a task to which man is ordained, or thirdly for the grace to which man is preordained from God, or fourthly for having the nimbus or aureole. Here "nimbus" means the essential reward while "aureole" is accidental only since it adds nothing essential to the nimbus.[10]

Schwarz goes on for another few pages, but the point, I think, is clear enough. It was precisely this exegetical tradition, with its unreflective reliance on the particular wording of the Vulgate, that Luther dismissed, first in going back to the Hebrew and Greek and secondly in imagining the angel

Gabriel speaking simple German to the lovely young Mary. In rendering biblical speech into nontheological German, Luther exalted German and its speakers by the same stroke that humanized—and Germanized—biblical characters. "And I don't know," Luther writes, "if you can say the word 'liebe' so lovingly and contentedly in Latin or in any other language, so that it burrows and resounds in your heart and through all of your senses as it does in our language."[11] The cultural distinctiveness of German, rather than acting as a barrier to translation, becomes the very pivot that enables Luther to naturalize the Bible as a German text.

In *The Translator's Invisibility*, Lawrence Venuti makes the case that translation has been governed for the last few centuries by the unspoken expectation that a translation should be like "a pane of glass," not calling attention to its own status as translation or to the operations of the translator. In Venuti's words, a translation is acceptable only

> when it reads fluently, when the absence of any linguistic or stylistic peculiarities makes it seem transparent, giving the appearance that it reflects the foreign writer's personality or intention or the essential meaning of the foreign text—the appearance, in other words, that the translation is not in fact a translation, but the "original."[12]

Against what he sees as this normative idiomatic or "domesticating" model, Venuti champions a "foreignizing" model of translation. As Friedrich Schleiermacher famously put it, translation could be conceived as working in two possible directions: "Either the translator leaves the writer alone as much as possible and moves the reader toward the writer, or he leaves the reader alone as much as possible, and moves the writer toward the reader."[13] Venuti, echoing Antoine Berman's influential reading of Schleiermacher, views these as *ethical* choices: a translation that "leaves the reader in peace" is complicit in the evils and complacency of ethnocentrism; in "moving the reader" to a foreign-language author, though, a translation may become "a site where a cultural other is manifested."[14] Venuti goes on to identify modern English-translation practice as a seldom interrupted series of British imperial conquests of foreign texts, in which "the illusion of transparency concealed the process of naturalizing the foreign text in an English cultural and social situation."[15] As one seventeenth-century translator proudly claimed for his "Englishing" of Virgil, what "was borne a Forraigner" was in translation "esteemed as a Native."[16]

While acknowledging that "domesticating" translation has a history as long as translation itself, Venuti dates the modern invisibility of the translator to seventeenth-century England, in which an aristocratic and monarchist literary culture underwrote the Anglicizing of the classics. The fluent translation norms of modern Europe are at least as profitably traced, however, to Martin Luther's Bible translation a century earlier. Once one takes Luther's Bible and other Reformation Bibles as a starting point for modern translation history (as indeed Berman and others do), it becomes clear that domesticating translations cannot be seen categorically as instruments of hegemonic nationalism.[17] On the contrary, the vernacular Bibles of the sixteenth century—Luther's and William Tyndale's most prominently—were perceived as undermining both ecclesiastical authority and the institutions of the State; thus, a 1530 royal proclamation of Henry VIII prohibited the possession of any copy of "the New Testament or the Old translated into English," because such translations were propagated "to stir and incense [the people] to sedition and disobedience against their princes, sovereigns, and heads."[18] Luther's principle of *sola scriptura*, from this point of view, was a challenge not only to Rome, but indeed potentially to any authority external to an individual reader—that Luther himself repeatedly denied that he was encouraging political foment hardly alters the subversive power of this principle.

The explicit and potential threats that Luther's translation project posed to various ecclesiastical and secular authorities have been well explored. What I will argue in this chapter is that Luther's project also constituted a response to Jewish biblical authority, which retained a significant claim on Christian readings of the Bible despite the political powerlessness of the Jews themselves. From this perspective, Luther's domesticating translations functioned much as Venuti argues English-language translations did, to neutralize what Berman calls "the experience of the foreign." As the early-twentieth-century classicist Albert Schaeffer described Luther's Old Testament, Luther "recreated the Book of the Jewish People as a Book of the Germans."[19] But Luther's aim was not only to recast biblical characters as Germans; it was also to construct an understanding of the Bible independently of the Jewish exegetical traditions on which previous Christian scholarship had so heavily relied. Such a departure from translational norms was not to be taken lightly: Luther's 1532 "Defense of the Translation of Psalms" is a response to those who take exception not only to his having "departed so freely in many places from the letter of the originals" but also to his having "followed an interpretation different from that taught by the Jewish rabbis and grammarians" (zuweilen auch anderem Verstand gefolget, denn der Jüden Rabbini und Grammatici lehren).[20] No matter that Luther does in fact follow various Jewish manuscripts and interpretations in his renderings of the Psalms, or that, as Harry Orlinsky pointedly remarks, Luther's reliance on Nicholas of Lyra is also a reliance on Nicholas's primary source for "the plain meaning" of the Hebrew text, the "Jewish rabbi and grammarian," Rashi.[21] For all Luther's dependence on Jewish sources (evidence, perhaps, that even the most determined of Christian Hebraists could hardly escape such influence), Luther measured the distinctiveness of his own translation by its distance both from the Hebrew style of the Bible and the Jewish exegetical tradition by which the Bible had been read. Luther frequently expressed his conviction that neither Hebrew grammar nor Jewish exegesis could be the ultimate guide for a Christian translation. In a 1542 conversation with the Hebraists Ziegler and Forster, Luther criticized Sebastian Münster's Latin Bible as making "too many concessions to the rabbis" and described his own approach as avoiding such concessions. Luther records that on one occasion when his Hebrew advisors informed him of the rabbinic interpretation of a certain passage, he asked them: "Could your grammar and points allow you to render the sentence so that it rhymes with the New Testament?" When his advisors agreed, Luther went ahead with his interpretation, with the result that "they themselves marveled and said they never in their lives would have believed it."[22] Hebrew grammar may set the limits for a possible reading of the Old Testament, but only knowledge of the New Testament, and Christian faith, could truly illuminate its meaning. As Luther concludes his Letter on Translation:

> Alas, translating is not some kind of magical talent, like the crazy "Holy ones" think. It calls for a righteous, pious, true, hard-working, God-fearing, Christian, learned, experienced and trained heart. For that reason, I believe that no false-Christian or reed in the wind can translate faithfully, as we saw in the translation of the Prophets done in Worms. You can truly see a lot of of work, and it seems to follow my German almost entirely, but there were Jews there that didn't show a lot of respect for Christ—even though they had enough skill and hard work.[23]

Luther's growing aversion to Jewish teaching set him apart from humanists, Christian Hebraists, and Reformers with whom he otherwise identified. Thus, while Basel and other Protestant centers of Christian Hebraica continued to rely on medieval Jewish exegetical resources in their study of the Hebrew Bible, and indeed to defend this reliance, Luther worked hard to assemble in Wittenberg a center of Christian Hebraica absolutely untainted by Jewish influence (although in earlier years Luther had secured a series of Hebrew teachers who were converts from Judaism and had himself sought Jewish instruction in Hebrew on his 1510 visit to Rome). Luther's chief expert on all problems of Hebrew translation, Johannes Forster, distinguished himself by defining an approach to Hebrew scholarship that seconded Luther's convictions that Hebrew studies could be separated from Jewish tradition. In what amounted to a declaration of independence, Forster published a Hebrew dictionary which clearly stated this goal in the title: *New Hebrew Dictionary, Not Arranged Out of the Comments of the Rabbis Nor Out of the Foolish Imitations of Our Native Doctors But Out of Our Own Treasures of Sacred Scripture and Developed by an Accurate Collation of Biblical Passages, Annotated with Passages and Phrases from the Old and New Testaments.*[24] Forster, following Luther, set a course away from both the Jews and their "foolish imitators," the "judaizing" Christian Hebraists in other Protestant centers.

Jerome Friedman has pointed out out that "the plain fact was that . . . Forster's program was more a goal that a true possibility."[25] Nevertheless, Luther's view of his translation as devoid of Jewish influence would have been impossible to sustain only a few years earlier, even as a fantasy or goal. Luther was the first important translator from the Hebrew whose initial encounter with the language was mediated not by a Jewish or formerly Jewish teacher, but rather through a dictionary. In this regard, it is worth contrasting Luther with his great precursor in the return to the *Hebraica veritas*, Jerome. Jerome and Luther, whose translation projects frame the Middle Ages, both began to study Hebrew as monks in their cells. Jerome first learned Hebrew in the late 370s under the tutelage of a Jewish convert to Christianity and later studied with such Jewish teachers as Baraninas, whom he called his "master," to the horror of his contemporaries. Luther, in contrast, began studying Hebrew in 1508 by working his way through Johannes Reuchlin's recently published Hebrew–Latin dictionary and grammar *The Rudiments of Hebrew* (Pforzheim, 1506), which was partially adapted from and modeled on David Kimhi's late-twelfth-century Hebrew lexicon *Sefer hashorashim* (The book of roots).[26] Reuchlin's was not the first text designed to help Christians acquire Hebrew—these were Manutius of Adrianus's short introduction to Hebrew (Venice, 1500) and Conrad Pellican's grammar (Strasbourg, 1504). But Reuchlin's publication contained both a grammar and a dictionary and was ultimately much more influential.[27] Unlike Jerome, and indeed unlike Reuchlin himself, who studied Hebrew with the court physician Jacob Loans and the biblical scholar Obadiah Sforno, Luther was indebted to no Jewish "master" for his knowledge of Hebrew.

The two modes of access to Hebrew knowledge, through the expertise of the convert from Judaism or through the new scholarly apparatus being developed by Christian Hebraists and humanists, came into conflict in what some scholars consider the opening salvo of the Reformation (although the humanist Reuchlin, who was condemned by the same 1520 papal missive as

Luther, remained a Catholic until his death).[28] This conflict, which pitted Reuchlin against the convert Johannes Pfefferkorn, erupted after Reuchlin objected to Maximilian I's order that all Jewish books be confiscated, an order instigated by Pfefferkorn and the Dominicans of Cologne. In his 1511 *Recommendation Whether to Confiscate, Destroy, and Burn All Jewish Books,* Reuchlin made it clear that Pfefferkorn's Jewish birth alone could not guarantee that the convert had accurately described Jewish books. Reuchlin parades his knowledge of Hebrew in combating Pfefferkorn's accusations, for instance, that Jews curse Christians daily in their prayers: In the prayer at issue, the grammarian Reuchlin expounds, *meshumadim* cannot refer to Christians, since "the word '*meshumadim*' is a verb or a present participle in the active case that means 'those who destroy.'"[29] In Reuchlin's reading, the prayer merely expresses the unobjectionable hope that those unspecified individuals who would destroy the Jewish people might themselves be destroyed. As for the Talmud, Reuchlin acknowledges that he himself cannot fully judge its heretical or blasphemous character, since he has only read excerpts cited elsewhere. But neither, for that matter, can Pfefferkorn:

> I know of no Christian in all of Germany who has himself actually studied the Talmud. Never, moreover, in my lifetime has there ever been a baptized Jew in the German lands who could either understand or read it (except for the Chief Rabbi of Ulm, who immediately after being baptized, reportedly converted back to Judaism in Turkey).[30]

Reuchlin's critique of Pfefferkorn's Jewish knowledge goes to the heart of Pfefferkorn's claim in his various pamphlets to be exposing the "hidden transcript" of the Jews, what Jews say among themselves about Christians and Christianity. In his 1509 *Enemy of the Jews,* for instance, Pfefferkorn had provided a bilingual dictionary of Jewish curses aimed at Christ, the Virgin Mary, or Christianity in general. In Sander Gilman's words, Pfefferkorn "brings to his investigation of this vocabulary the authority of one knowledgeable in Hebrew, showing this by providing the Hebrew term, its transliteration, and then its meaning and implication."[31] Even in this regard, Reuchlin claims a superior knowledge to the former Jew, writing that Pfefferkorn often cites words "which are more than likely not rightly understood and, therefore, not properly translated into German." For instance, Reuchlin quotes Pfefferkorn as saying that when the Jews

> greet a Christian by saying: "*Seit willkum!*" [Welcome] they are really saying: "*Sed willkum!*" [welcome, devil] This a grammatical impossibility in proper Hebrew, since *shed,* which is devil in Hebrew, has a dot on the right side of the

letter *S* (shin); thus it is pronounced "sh": *shed*. Any fool can tell that if they were
to say "*Sched wilkommen*" it would sound nothing like "*Seit wilkommen*" since
"*shed*" sounds nothing like "*seit*."[32]

In exposing the illogic of Pfefferkorn's renderings of the Hebrew–German
doubletalk of the Jews, Reuchlin coolly demonstrates that Christians should
not unquestioningly accept converts from Judaism as reliable experts on or
translators of Jewish texts. On the contrary, a little knowledge of Hebrew grammar can easily trump such "genetic" knowledge as Pfefferkorn's. Reuchlin
makes no attempt, we should note, to deny that Jews *do* follow a "hidden transcript." His debunking of Pfefferkorn's transcription of this discourse rests
not on superior information about what Jews say among themselves, in fact,
not on any knowledge Reuchlin claims as his personal province. Reuchlin relies rather on the authority of language itself, as it were—that is, on the principles of grammar and pronunciation discernible to all who would make a
study of them. If the Talmud seems to be cloaked in mystery, that is not
because the Jews have deliberately concealed its anti-Christian message but
rather for purely linguistic reasons that pose an obstacle to all but the most
learned Jews and even to as accomplished a Christian Hebraist as Reuchlin.
The Talmud, Reuchlin writes, is little read or understood because "its language is not pure Hebrew . . . but rather we find in its phrasing diverse
strains from other Oriental languages, that is, among others, from the Babylonian, Persian, Arabic and Greek." Moreover, "it also contains countless ab-
breviations, so that a great effort and lengthy study is required of the reader,
which is why not many Jews can understand the Talmud, not to speak of
Christians."[33] The implication is clear: knowledge of Jewish sources is a matter of nurture rather than nature, of protracted textual and linguistic study
rather than birthright; the Talmud is inaccessible not because it is written in
a secret code, but because it is a melange of languages, Jewish and non-Jewish
alike. In a striking move, Reuchlin explains the difficulty of the Talmud
by reference to the linguistic theories of Augustine. Implicitly—and auda-
ciously—including the Talmud in the general category of Holy Scripture,
Reuchlin cites Augustine: "The precise meaning of the Holy Scripture can
only be understood according to the unique qualities of each language in
which it is written." Since "the Talmud contains the characteristics of so
many languages," Reuchlin continues, it is no wonder that hardly a Jew, not
to mention a Christian, can decipher it. Cryptic religious sources may be
found among the Jews, but it is Christian linguistic philosophy—not Jewish
insider knowledge—that best elucidates them.

Reuchlin's knowledge of Hebrew, as it turns out, was imperfect: *"meshu-madim"* is in the passive rather than active voice and various communities of Hebrew speakers from biblical times to the present have pronounced the "shin" as "sin"—it was just this inability to pronounce the Hebrew word "shibboleth" that led to the detection of the Ephraimites at the river crossing in Judges 12 (it is from this "mispronunciation" that the meaning of shibboleth as password derives).

Nevertheless, the Reuchlin–Pfefferkorn affair affords us a privileged glimpse into what R. Po-chia Hsia has called "the disenchantment of magic," a process Hsia views as integral to the theological revolution of the Reformation. In the Protestant campaign of "true religion" against "ceremonies, magic and superstition," theologians charged the Church with propagating such irrational beliefs as the veneration of saints, Marian devotion, and the eucharistic doctrine of transubstantiation as literal truth. Among the superstitions derided by Protestant theologians, Hsia notes, is "the use of the Hebrew language as a system of magical signs," a practice widespread among both Jews and Christians. "Even Protestant pastors were implicated in this penchant for the occult," Hsia writes:

> Some twenty years after the promulgation of an evangelical church ordinance for Ernestine Saxony, the home province of the Reformation was still permeated with Jewish magic. In 1543, Luther recalled with anger the 1527/28 Visitation of the Saxon Church, which turned up many magical books in the possession of village pastors and churchwardens; these forbidden prints contained the tetragrammaton—the Hebrew word for the ineffable name of God, names of angels and demons, and many prayers and incantations in Hebrew.[34]

The understanding of Hebrew as a magical language, in Hsia's view, is predicated on its opacity. Drawing upon Marcel Mauss's analysis of magic as relying on a system of "signs understood by only a small circle of practitioners," Hsia writes: "Once a magical language is dissected and studied, it loses its force of enchantment."[35] At the turn of the sixteenth century, only a handful of born Christians could lay claim to any significant knowledge of Hebrew. By the middle of the century, Friedman writes, "nearly every student could find Hebrew instruction at the majority of universities in western Europe and Germany." By 1550, in sharp contrast to what had been true only decades before, Friedman continues,

> there were many elementary and advanced Hebrew grammars, a large number of dictionaries and volumes of essays describing and detailing unusual Hebrew structures, fine points of voweling, as well as the Hebrew language's historical

development. There were critical editions of all the books of the OT and a large number of volumes in both Hebrew and Latin presenting major medieval Jewish exegetical writings. Moreover, the complete Talmud had been published under Christian auspices for those wishing to read that work in the original Aramaic with the aid of special dictionaries, grammars, and word-lists prepared for a Christian audience.[36]

The process of disenchantment Hsia describes was both cause and effect of the rapid development of Christian Hebraica in Europe. The assumption that Hebrew was a language that could be rationally analyzed and grammatically deciphered underlay Reuchlin's groundbreaking lexicographical work and those that followed. Five decades later, the ready availability of Jewish texts in the original or translation helped further dissipate whatever aura of secrecy hovered around Hebrew. Hebrew may have retained its unique status as the language of the Hebrew Bible and its God, but it was now open to all comers. In Hsia's words:

> What began as an attempt to recover the heritage of the Old Testament for Christianity resulted in a new Christian knowledge of Jewish rites and writings; no longer feared as a system of mysterious, magical signs, as it was sometimes crudely applied in popular magic, Hebrew came to treasured as a divine language in the service of the Reformation.[37]

George Steiner's distinction between language as private code and as public communication sheds light on Hsia's discussion of the transformation of Hebrew at the beginning of the sixteenth century from the language of Jews and the cognoscenti to a language well mapped by Christian grammarians and theologians. Christian Hebraists alone cannot be credited with this development; the disclosures of converts themselves, which may initially have reinforced the perception of Hebrew as the language of Jewish concealment, eventually also served to demystify Hebrew texts and the Jewish religion by the very dialectical logic of disclosure. Thus, Hsia argues that converts from Judaism played an important role in the early Reformation in the disenchantment of Hebrew; among the most important of these converts was Anthonius Margaritha, whose 1530 compendium *The Entire Jewish Faith* served as an introduction to Judaism for the early Lutheran church. Where converts like Pfefferkorn had focused on those passages or behaviors likely to be most repugnant to Christians, Margaritha (the son of Rabbi Jacob Margolis of Regensburg, whom Reuchlin had consulted on the Kabbalah) sought to present Judaism in panoramic view and in copious detail—from the Talmud and Kabbalah to Jewish liturgy, history, and ritual observance, from the social structure of Jewish communities to Jewish folk medicine and, inter alia, what Jews thought of Christians. Margaritha's monumental if thoroughly biased work represented, Hsia writes, "a sort of encyclopedia of Judaism."[38] Once works like *The Entire Jewish Faith* had become widely available, the authority of any individual convert as informant on Jewish secrets began to erode.

The exponential growth of Christian Hebraica in the very late fifteenth and early sixteenth century, and the apparatus of grammars, lexicons, and encyclopedias that accompanied this phenomenon, succeeded in forging a direct connection between the Christian translator and the Hebrew language and liberating him from what had sometimes been a humiliating dependence on Jews or converts. The convert who had historically served as a translation aid had embodied the relationship between languages—most commonly Hebrew and Latin—in his own life story; this story, moreover, suggested not the equivalence of these languages but rather the tension between them. The lexicon, by contrast, graphically rendered linguistic equivalence visible in its parallel columns; in the face of such evidence, the question of translatability was implicitly laid to rest. Lexicons neutralized the cultural, historical, and ethnic specificity of languages and stripped them of their function as "passwords," to borrow Steiner's term. From the dictionary, an unbroken line leads to the chimera of machine translation, translation without even the purely instrumental use of a human, historical translator. That this rationalizing process not only neutralizes the historical and cultural dimension of language but also arises as a form of substitution for particular historical subjects is apparent in the discourse of sixteenth-century Christian Hebraica. Christian Hebraica in this period is as much about the *absence* of Jews as it is about the acquisition and appropriation of their language. In the preface to his Hebrew-Latin lexicon, Reuchlin speaks openly of his worry that the Jews, who had so recently been expelled from Spain and Portugal, would soon be driven from all of Europe, leaving Christendom without even these reluctant resources for deciphering Hebrew texts:

> For working alone with much dedicated study I have completed a Hebrew dictionary, with exempla, and all else which you see here with your eyes and mind. I have of course borne in mind the wretched sufferings of the Jews in our time, who have been driven not only from the borders of Spain but also from our own Germany. They are compelled to seek homes elsewhere and move to the Muslims. The effect of this will be that finally the Hebrew language could cease and vanish, to the great detriment of the sacred writings. I have personally laid down the first foundations in this book, in order to pass on to Christians knowledge of the Hebrew language, in accordance with the divinely inspired constitution of Pope Clement V which concerns educators.[39]

The situation of the Jews is unfortunate, but armed with Reuchlin's dictionary, no Christian need be sorry to see the Jews go. The parallel columns of the lexicon, in severing the historical association of Hebrew with the Jews, thus inaugurates the modern period of translation on the ruins of Jewish–Christian cultural encounter.

LAWRENCE VENUTI writes of the "translator's invisibility" as the dominant characteristic of modern translation in the West. In Venuti's analysis, however, this invisibility is a function of the *operation* of translation, in particular of the ubiquitous choice of fluency as a modern translation strategy. Especially in his work *The Scandals of Translation,* Venuti is concerned with reversing this invisibility, for instance as it shapes copyright laws, royalty payments, translation commissions, and the status of the translator.[40] Nevertheless, Venuti seems curiously uninterested in the figure of the translator herself, giving virtually no attention to the particular historical, cultural, or educational circumstances that come together to produce an individual who can, at a given historical moment, mediate between languages. That a translation is required implies that not everyone who might wish to can understand the two languages in question; that translation nevertheless occurs is proof that at least one individual has transcended this more general ignorance. Venuti proceeds according to what could be called the Berlitz model of language acquisition, with its assumption that languages can be acquired by anyone for the price of a course or guidebook. By contrast, for the medievals acquiring a language might cost one's soul. Linguists speak of the phenomenon of "interference" in bilinguals but typically limit this interference to questions of syntax or pronunciation. Interference between languages, or between language-worlds, is potentially life-altering, earth-shaking. The early sixteenth-century figure of "La Malinche" (ca. 1500–1527, also known as Doña Marina and "La Lengua," literally "the tongue," for her knowledge of Nahuatl, Totonac, Mayan, and Spanish) might exemplify this: La Malinche not only served as translator between Hernán Cortés and Montezuma at their fateful initial meeting, but also bore a son to Cortés before he abandoned her, thus becoming the imagined progenitor of the Mexican people and symbol of *mestizo* culture. She is an ambivalent symbol—according to the chronicle of Bernal Díaz, she betrayed the indigenous Cholulans to the Spaniards and paved the way for the conquest of Mexico.[41] In La Malinche's case, faithfulness as a measure of accurate linguistic transfer and of loyalty to a community (although La Malinche was not herself Cholulan) collide, with far-reaching historical consequences. As with other translators who enabled and shaped the colonial encounter, La Malinche could take no neutral linguistic position between the language-worlds she was negotiating.

In this regard as in so many others, the Jews in medieval Europe were in the position of internal colonial subjects, and mediating between Jewish and Christian worlds similarly involved the crossing of a charged border. Not all converts from Judaism, of course, were translators, just as not all translators were converts. But within the small numbers of those born-Jews and Christians who bridged the two worlds, the convert had a privileged, archetypal role. Within the medieval European Jewish–Christian context, the difficulties and tensions of translation are most clearly illuminated as they parallel and overlap with the phenomenon of conversion. As with conversion, no Archimedean point existed outside of Judaism or Christianity from which a translation could be produced or judged. Venuti's project of reversing the invisibility of the translator, in Jewish–Christian translation, requires first that the figure of the translator-convert be brought back into translation history in all the peculiarities and ambivalence of its double role. It is this figure, I would further argue, that has haunted the history of translation and propelled its movement to modernity.

It is tempting to read the development of modern translation practice, with its accompanying apparatus of dictionaries and encyclopedias, as a move toward greater rationality, toward "science." Frances Yates has shown throughout her work on the development of scientific thought in the seventeenth century, however, that the scientific impulse cannot be separated at its inception from a range of influences now considered irrational or even occult: hermeticism, alchemy, and Christian Kabbalah.[42] What manifests itself from one perspective as the modern rationalization of linguistic theory, as what Hsia calls the "disenchantment" of Hebrew, must be viewed alongside the irrational conflation of Hebrew with the Jew that propelled and motivated this "rationalist" revolution. Moreover, as Susannah Heschel has demonstrated in the case of nineteenth-century Protestant historians, the scientific methods of Reformation translators were put to distinctly theological uses.[43] In relying on a lexicon as the bridge between languages, in moving from source-orientation to reader-orientation, translators have not left behind the theologically charged territory of conversion. Conversion, in Protestant translation and its modern offshoots, becomes the *aim* of translation rather than its background. Speaking not of the invisibility but rather of the "introversion" of the translator, Douglas Robinson makes the point that the assumptions behind a range of questions about the "effectiveness" of a translation—and not merely Bible translation—rely on an implicit Christian model of translation as conversion:

If the Western ideal for translation has been introversion, the introverted translator making him- or herself into a window for the SL [source language] meaning to pass through unhindered, the practical aim concealed behind and mystified by the idea has almost invariably been conversion. . . . The translator's task is to stay out of the way so that God can do his work on the TL [target language] reader. Stand between God and the TL reader, certainly, but invisibly: as an instrument, introvert, a window. The purpose behind this is to help God (conceived as the Ultimate SL Writer) convert the TL reader, but that purpose is so monolithic, so universally accepted, so hegemonically built into the entire ecclesiastical institution, that the translator need not even be aware of it, let alone be able to articulate it.[44]

As this passage implies, a direct line may be drawn between Luther's reader-orientation and the contemporary translation theorist Eugene Nida's notion of "dynamic equivalence," the correspondence between the *effect* of a text on the original reader and the reader of a translation (in contrast with "formal equivalence," in which formal rather than rhetorical or persuasive elements of the texts are reproduced in translation).[45] In both cases, theological aims are grounded in a scientific apparatus that promises a culturally neutral linguistic transparency. Beginning from the linguistic equivalence demonstrated by Reuchlin's lexicon, Luther produces a Bible in which God speaks, without impediment, not only *to* the German folk but even, as it were, as a German. Nida's project is similarly woven of scientific and evangelical strands: Nida served as translation consultant for the World Bible Society in the 1960s and 1970s and wrote a number of books celebrating missionary translation, with such titles as *God's Word in Man's Language* (1952) and *Message and Mission* (1960).[46] But Nida also laid claim to constructing a true "science of translation" in such works as *Toward a Science of Translation* (1964) and (with Charles R. Taber) *The Theory and Practice of Translation* (1969), works still taken as basic textbooks in a number of important academic centers of translation studies. Despite appearances, Nida has had not two careers but one: his later reliance on (many would say, misreading of) Noam Chomsky's theory of universal generative grammar is of a piece with the evangelical assumption that the message of the Bible is meaningful and translatable for every potential reader on the planet.[47]

For both Luther and Nida, then, the Christian dissemination of the Word derives from the transparency of the word, the dissolution of the magical— that is, insider—functions of language. Luther made explicit his understanding of Hebrew as a language of communication, that is, a language that was in principle translatable without loss, in his 1543 *On the Ineffable Name* (*Von Schem Hamephoras*). Readers led by the exotic, bilingual title of the book to expect a treatise on the power of the Hebrew letters or the divine name would be forgiven: Reuchlin in fact had published a Latin work with a very similar title—*On the Wonder-working Word (De verbo mirifico)*—elucidating the divine characteristics of Hebrew letters. In the 1494 work, Reuchlin had harnessed the power of Hebrew for Christian theology; "the wonder-working word" of the title is not the Tetragrammaton, YHWH, but rather what Reuchlin called the Pentagrammaton, or YHSWH, the five Hebrew letters Reuchlin took as the Hebrew spelling, and mystical meaning, of the name "Jesus."[48] Reuchlin's project in this and other of his works on Christian Kabbalah, from the perspective of the history of translation, is a hybrid phenomenon: on the one hand, Reuchlin adheres to a source-oriented approach to translation, paying the strictest attention to the formal dimensions of Hebrew, indeed, the very Hebrew letters; his Latin works are everywhere interspersed—unavoidably so—with Hebrew words and letters in the original and transliteration. Hebrew letters, Reuchlin learned from the Kabbalists, have a mystical significance expressed in their numerical value as much as in the words they comprise; translation, in such a symbolic system, is difficult if not impossible. On the other hand, Reuchlin can be considered a precursor to Luther not only in his grammatical and lexicographical works but also in his reader-orientation; the powers of the Hebrew letters are directed to the theological concerns of a Christian readership, pointing everywhere to Christian religious truths.

Luther, by contrast, moves away from the mystical Hebraism of Pico, Reuchlin, and the generation of Christian Kabbalists immediately preceding his own, giving acerbic expression to what I have been calling a culturally neutralized or "rational" theory of language. Where Reuchlin had *appropriated* Kabbalistic methodology for Christian purposes, Luther exposed it as Jewish irrationality and abandoned such Jewish semiotics altogether. In the first section of the book, Luther translates and discusses Salvagus Porchtus's 1315 *Victory against the Impious Hebrews,* which itself included a Latin translation in abridged form of the Hebrew manuscript *Toldot Yeshu.* The Jews, Luther reports, claim that Jesus performed his miracles through the power of the "ineffable name":

> Now Jesus the Nazarene came and learned the letters and wrote them on a parchment. Then he ripped up the flesh along his leg and placed the notes therein. And because he named the Name, nothing hurt him and the skin came together as it had been before . . . as he came home, however, he ripped open his leg with a knife and took the notes out upon which the letters of the Shem Hamphoras were written and learned them again. . . . Soon they brought a lame man who had never stood on his feet and he spoke the Shem Hamphoras over him; at that same hour he arose and stood on his feet. Then they all bowed before him and said: He is without any doubt Messiah.[49]

What infuriates Luther about this narrative is not only its claim that Jesus is a magician and trickster, and that Christianity is founded on the ludicrous sleight-of-hand of a young Jewish boy. Luther goes to extraordinary lengths to argue also against what might seem to be a secondary issue in this accusation of the Jews: that these "circumcised holy men" continue to believe in the power of Hebrew letters:

> They attribute such divine works and miracles to the Shem Hamphoras, that is the empty, dead, miserable letters, written in a book with ink, or hovering on the tongue or in the heart so that even the godless are carried along. Let the Shem Hamphoras be what it may; they are, and cannot be anything but, single, dead, powerless letters, although the Jews act as though it were the same as God's Holy Scriptures of which they prattle a lot although they don't know what they are talking about. What can letters accomplish as letters from their own power if nothing else is added?[50]

What is at stake in Jewish claims for the power of individual letters is not only the nature of Jesus's ability to perform miracles, it becomes clear, but also the principle of translating God's Holy Scriptures into another tongue. Jews blaspheme Jesus when they attribute his wonder-working to the theft of the Tetragrammaton from the Temple; but even more infuriating for Luther-the-translator is the Jewish attribution of power to the Hebrew letters. If Luther returns so insistently to the old accusation that the Jews are *Buchstabendiener*, it is because his own project is threatened by this enslavement. Where, for Augustine, Jews serve the useful function of preserving the Holy Scriptures, for Luther this attention to the letter of the text, their mistaken notion of how Hebrew *means*, forms an obstacle to his own access to the Hebrew sources. If the meaning of the Bible lies in the letters that comprise it, then translation is manifestly impossible. Luther must demonstrate, then, not only that the Jewish blasphemy of Jesus is mistaken, but that the meaning of the *Schem Hamphoras* is in principle expressible in other tongues:

> This name, Jehovah, according to grammar, is derived from the word Haja or Hava, which means in Latin: *fuit in pareterito, esse;* in German: *Wesen* or *Sein*, "to be": and the "J" could be *nota nominis verbalis,* as in Josaphat, Jesaias, Jeremias, and many other names, and amounts to the same as the Latin *Ens* or the Greek *ON*. We Germans say: *er ist's* ["he is it"]; and thus it becomes the *Trigrammaton* in Latin, *Digrammaton* in Greek, *Hexagrammaton* in German.[51]

In analyzing the Tetragrammaton grammatically, and in rendering a chain of translations of this divine name into the simplest Latin, Greek, and German words, Luther argues that Hebrew is a language among others, a medium of communication for a universal signified. Not only is God's name not "ineffable"; it is not even, strictly speaking, a *proper* name, one that, according to most translators, should be transliterated rather than translated. In deriving meaning from the Hebrew *word* for God rather than the letters that comprise this word, Luther argues for the superiority of Christian translation as an embrace of the meaning of the text over the Jewish indebtedness to the "dead" Hebrew letter. With its insistence on the translatability of the name of God, *On the Ineffable Name* also presents a strong case that the God of the Old Testament is not the tribal God of a particular people but rather a universal deity, whose meaning can be rendered in Greek, Latin, and German, as well as in philosophical, theological, and ordinary discourse.

The crude viciousness of *On the Ineffable Name* has ensured its place in the history of Christian anti-Jewish writings and, more specifically, of Luther's hostility to the Jews in his last years.[52] Whereas earlier in his career Luther had written with considerable sympathy about the plight of Jews in Europe, particularly in his 1523 pamphlet *That Jesus Was a Born Jew*, by the 1540s Luther had relinquished all hopes for the conversion of the Jews to a newly reformed Christianity and denied that the Jews could be converted. Luther makes clear in the first lines of *On the Ineffable Name* that his intention is not "to write against the Jews in the hope of converting them" but rather to "warn our Christians against them." *On the Ineffable Name*, along with its companion volume *Against the Jews and Their Lies*, thus represents Luther's position on the immutability of Jewishness: "A Jewish heart is as hard as stone and iron and cannot be moved by any means," for converting a Jew, Luther writes, is "about as possible as converting the Devil . . . into an angel, hell into heaven, death into life, and sin into holiness."[53]

The two major points of Luther's work, taken together, constitute a striking dialectic: (a) The Jews can never be converted; (b) Hebrew can be readily translated. Jews believe, perversely and blasphemously, in the power of Hebrew letters, a belief, in other words, that Hebrew is untranslatable; Luther's response to this superstition is precisely to translate, in a virtuoso multilingual display, what Jews insist is the "ineffable name." If there is logic to be found in Luther's argument, it is that the Jews cannot be converted because, in espousing the (devilish, blasphemous, absurd) principle of untranslatability, they have come to embody it. Hebrew may be translated into German, just as the biblical characters may be recreated as Germans. But the Jews of Luther's own day cannot be similarly translated. Linguistic conversion, then, becomes uniquely applicable to Hebrew at the very moment, by the very stroke, that religious conversion is declared impossible for the Jews. With this stroke, the long medieval association of Hebrew and the Jews is sundered, and the special knowledge of the convert rendered obsolete. If Venuti is right in viewing the translator's invisibility as the hallmark of modern translation, then this history might begin with Luther's fashioning of the Hebrew language into a transparent pane between God and the German people. What remains obscured by this very rationality and transparency—what stands just outside Luther's window frame, as it were—is the figure of the untranslatable Jew.

THE TRANSLATED JEW

The association of Hebrew and the Jews—however this association was valued—goes back to the earliest periods of Christianity. The power of this association may be best gauged not by the fact that Jews were assumed to know Hebrew (of course, as Reuchlin argued, many or most did not), but rather by the fact that knowing Hebrew was considered a telling symptom of Jewish background; "Hebrew and Jews were so closely identified," writes Friedman, "that observers had to assume that Nicholas of Lyra must have been Jewish to explain the rare phenomenon of an alleged Christian's knowing Hebrew. Indeed, as late as the sixteenth century many people continued to believe that knowledge of Hebrew was proof of Jewishness and on the basis of such an association [the Hebraist Martin] Bucer, for one, continually defended his family's honor from so horrid an accusation."[54]

Because Hebrew knowledge was so rare among Christians (as was knowledge of Latin or the gospels among Jews), those who wished to learn Hebrew were largely dependent on Jews, or converts, as teachers. This dependency could be humiliating; Reuchlin complained about the difficulty of finding a Jewish teacher in Germany, and Luther, too, had to negotiate with a series of converts for the Hebrew professorship at Wittenberg before he could find a born Christian for the position. In certain periods and places (Renaissance Italy, most notably), Jews openly and willingly taught Christians, whereas in other places, a would-be Christian Hebraist might have great difficulty finding a teacher. The "Jews of our country," Reuchlin had complained in the preface to his Hebrew lexicon, "wish to instruct no Christian in their language because of ill-will and ignorance." Indeed, although some authorities, including Maimonides, ruled that it was permissible to teach Christians Hebrew or Torah, other medieval rabbis forbade all Hebrew instruction to non-Jews.[55]

In the popular Christian imagination, attitudes toward the Jews as secretive or diabolical were often projected onto Hebrew. Sander Gilman tells us that "whenever Jews appear in medieval Christian religious drama, they are shown conjuring up the spirit of darkness with mock Hebrew oaths."[56] But the conflation of Hebrew and the Jews could work in the other direction, so that Jews were appreciated for their knowledge of Hebrew. Hebrew, after all, was the language of the Old Testament, the language in which God had created the world and in which the prophets had foretold the Kingdom of Heaven. Beryl Smalley famously wrote that many a Christian scholar assumed that a medieval rabbi was "a kind of telephone to the Old Testament. . . . The Jew, however despised and persecuted, could put him in touch with the patriarchs, the prophets and the psalmist."[57] Hebrew had a special role in Christian theology, as a language of Christian origins. Ora Limor has demonstrated that not only did Christians often view Jews as the heirs to legitimate traditions about the Old Testament—as might be expected—but Christian folklore also attests to a belief that Jews had special knowledge of texts, sites, and objects important to Christians. Although Jews "themselves did not accept the sanctity of the Christian tradition, they were nevertheless regarded as the ones who could identify [Christian sites and objects] and confirm their authenticity."[58] Thus, a fifth-century Christian legend reports that it was a Jew who (reluctantly) revealed the site of the True Cross to Helena, mother of the Emperor Constantine; similarly, a Jewish woman revealed to Christian pilgrims the location of the Virgin Mary's robe. Limor points out that such legends as these arose during the period when Jews were legally barred from living in Jerusalem; the physical absence of Jews from the city apparently did not negate their special, "genetic" knowledge of its secrets. The legends both "establish the authenticity of the traditions concerning the holy sites through the legitimation provided by the 'knowing Jew,' and, on the other hand, perpetually recreate the authority of the Jew and his *Judaica veritas*."[59] Limor concludes:

> The Jew is the constitutor of the Christian identity. Identity in general, as is commonly asserted today, depends on the "other" and is constituted by him, and in particular . . . by the one who is close, the neighbor, who is problematic precisely because he is so close. The "other" stands in front of us and shows us our own image, as in a mirror. Without him, we cannot see ourselves. Our identity depends on him and is formulated by him.[60]

The attribution of special knowledge to the Jews aroused both admiration and animus. This psychic ambivalence found its theological correlation in the belief that Jews had unique access to Christian truth, but they concealed this knowledge, or deliberately distorted it, or were blind to it. Augustine viewed Jews as the (blind, ignorant, or perverse) carriers of the Hebrew books that bore witness to Christian truths: "What is [the Jewish] nation today but the desks [*scriniaria*] of the Christians, bearing the law and the prophets as testimony to the tenets of the church, so that we honor through the sacrament what it announces through the letter?"[61] The Jews serve Christians as guardians (*custodes*) of their books, librarians (*librarii*), and servants who carry the books of their master's children to school but must wait outside during class (*capsarii*).[62]

The Augustinian notion of Jews as "living letters of the Law" shifted into a more unambiguously negative conception of the Jews, as Jeremy Cohen and others have argued, by the growing Christian knowledge of Jewish post-biblical literature in the eleventh and twelfth centuries; what was most fascinating and objectionable to Christians, of course, were those passages they saw as blasphemous against Christianity or—sometimes at the same time—as suppressed Jewish evidence for Christian truths.[63] Either as uniquely willing teachers of Jewish traditions, since Jews were often reluctant to study with Christians, or as "informers" about Jewish anti-Christian secrets, converts were the privileged carriers of this knowledge to a Christian world, whether this knowledge was helpful for Christian biblical exegesis or evidence of the Jews' anti-Christian sentiments. As Reuchlin had testified, the number of anti-Christian Jewish texts is small (especially when compared to the vast corpus of Christian *Adversus Judaeos* literature): nevertheless, converts played a crucial role in divulging these sources, the "hidden transcript" of the Jews, to Christian readers. Pope Clement IV, in a 1267 bull, recommended the convert Pablo Christiani as especially capable of supervising the inspection and possible eradication of Jewish books "both because he stems from the Jews, ably trained among them in Hebrew, and knows their language, the old law, and their errors, and because having been reborn at the baptismal font he embodies the zeal of the Catholic faith."[64] Given the language barrier that kept Christians from understanding Jewish sources, the "betrayal" of this hidden transcript normally required not only the Hebrew knowledge of the convert, but also his skill as a translator. So integral is translation to medieval Jewish–Christian disputation that J. D. Eisenstein's introduction to the subject refers to the Christian disputants as "the priests and their convert-translators" (*hakomarim umeturgemaneihem hamumarim*).[65] One version of the passage from the Amidah prayer translated so often by converts similarly implies an equation between converts and informers: "velamalshinim velameshumadim al tehi tikvah" (May the informers and apostates have no hope).[66]

Not all translations by converts from Judaism to Christianity were betrayals of Jewish secrets, of course—converts served in a variety of capacities as mediators or bridges between Jewish and Christian communities. Converts, for instance, translated Christian material into Hebrew, often as part of a mission to the Jews. Immanuel Tremellius, one of the first Jewish converts to the Reformed Church, translated Calvin's catechism into Hebrew; Victor von Carben "the priest, formerly a Jew," transliterated the Ave Maria into Hebrew characters; and the New Testament was translated and retranslated into Hebrew, and later Yiddish, by a succession of converts. Elisheva Carlebach has argued, however, that conversion was particularly associated with the betrayal of Jewish secrets, as proof of the convert's shift of allegiances. By the end of the medieval period, converts "and their converters had come to believe that their transformation was not complete unless it traduced Jewish secrecy, revealing how Jewish otherness was constituted."[67] The Jewish fear of betrayal by indigenous renegades ran so deep, Carlebach continues, that, according to one seventeenth-century German-Jewish compendium of customs, "It was a universal Jewish practice not to bury evil sinners near the righteous 'because the righteous are privy to the [divine] decrees, and if the sinners are buried nearby there would be no revelations to the righteous, because the sinners would eavesdrop.'"[68] In the figure of this Jewish apostate-translator, untrustworthy even in the grave, the Italian witticism, "*traduttore, traditore,*" to translate is to betray, found one historical embodiment.

Converts played a particularly critical role in the three major Jewish–Christian disputations of the Middle Ages. The Paris Disputation of 1240 was instigated by the apostate Nicholas Donin; the convert Pablo Christiani (formerly Saul of Montpellier) disputed Nachmanides at the Barcelona Disputation of 1263; and the Tortosa Disputations of 1413–14, the longest and most demoralizing of the disputations, were convened with the help of Paul of Borgos (formerly Solomon Halevi), and the chief Christian disputant was Geronimo de Santa Fe (formerly Joshua Halorki). The disputations, despite the term, did not take the form of arguments that pitted the religions against each other—the Jewish disputants were strictly forbidden from attempting to refute Christian principles. The disputations rather put the Talmud "on trial." In the Paris Disputation, the Talmud was indicted for heresy, obscenity, error, and imbecility and condemned to burning; in the Barcelona Disputations, a new tack was taken, with Pablo Christiani quoting the Talmud in an effort to "prove [to the Jews] from their own Talmud that the Messiah had come, and is Jesus."[69] In either case, the Talmud was at the center of discussion, and its translation for a Christian audience was a key dimension of each of the disputations. The Paris Disputation, for instance, both began and ended with the translation of the Talmud by a convert: in 1236, Donin began the process that led to the Paris Disputation by submitting thirty-five charges against the Talmud to Pope Gregory IX, selecting and translating those talmudic passages that blasphemously referred to Jesus, Mary, or Christianity. The Latin record of the the Disputation, along with the "confessions" of the Jewish disputants, was published in 1242 as an appendix to *Selections from the Talmud*, a collection of anti-Christian passages from the Talmud translated and assembled by the convert Thibaut de Sezanne.[70] The disputations themselves were structured as recitations of translated passages from the Talmud and other post-biblical Jewish sources; the Jewish disputants were asked to acknowledge that these passages could indeed be found in their books and then to defend these sources.[71] Thus, Donin proved the perfidiousness of the Jews and incited his Christian audience to fury by quoting a number of apparently anti-Christian passages from the Talmud. According to the Hebrew account of the Disputation, Donin reported that the Jews say of Jesus "that he was condemned to boiling excrement, and he read before them the passage at the end of the Tractate Nezikim. . . . And he said this in the vernacular before the Queen in order to make us look bad [literally, stink]."[72] (Donin actually spoke to the Queen Mother Blanche, who was presiding over the Disputation.)

From the Jewish perspective, the disputation had the character of a *forced* translation, in which Jewish secrets were "smoked out," paraded before a hostile audience. As Gilman writes about Pfefferkorn's anti-Jewish pamphlets, "Here was a Jew privy to the secret books of the Jews, written in their magical language, who had been converted to the truth and was now willing to reveal the Jews' secret mysteries to the world."[73] The rhymed opening of the Hebrew account of the Paris Disputation imagines Donin's intentions thus: "I shall ransack all the treasures [of the Talmud] and my tongue will bleat its tongue, and genius, and power."[74] The chronicler later describes Donin as "reciting in [the Christians'] ears" the passage that describes the heavenly decree that sentenced Jesus of Nazareth to stoning, and "raising his voice" when he spoke of the talmudic injunction that permits Jews to kill non-Jews.[75] It is palpable throughout the Hebrew account of the Paris Disputation that the Jews experienced Donin's translation of the Talmud for Christian ears as a profound violation, the pillage of Jewish treasure and its exposure to unfriendly eyes—nearly a sexual violation. A rabbinic participant in a later disputation used similar language in speaking of the apostate Christiani as "one who exposes the secrets of the Torah" (*megalleh razei Torah*).[76]

In this regard, medieval Christian translation from Jewish languages embodies George Steiner's thesis that translation necessarily involves a degree of aggression—although without the compensation that in Steiner's fourfold stages of translation ultimately redresses the unavoidable violence of translation. Steiner writes, "Decipherment is dissective, leaving the shell smashed and the vital layers stripped. . . . The translator invades, extracts, brings home. The simile is that of the open-cast mine left an empty scar in the landscape."[77] The movement of translation from Jewish to non-Jewish languages stripped Jewish discourse of its protective covering, forcing Jewish texts out into an unfriendly Christian world. In this, the fate of Jewish sources resembled that of their defenders; the Disputations, especially at Barcelona and Tortosa, were aimed at bringing Jews into the Christian world through baptism. At Tortosa, the parade of Jewish sources was accompanied by a parade of converts; Samuel Krauss describes it: "A spectacular scene was presented every day [of the disputation], when groups of Jews who wished to be baptized were led in, and the act was performed in the assembly hall."[78] The chief spokesperson for the Jews during the first stages of the disputation, Don Vidal, as well as another Jewish notable who had participated in the disputation, Todros Benveniste, themselves had converted by the time the disputation was halted. At Tortosa, translation and baptism were parallel campaigns, performed in the same public space, demonstrating that the Jewish world had been blown wide open.

The first line of defense for the Jewish disputants was the denial of the basic charge that the Jews inhabited a private discursive world. Although it is clear from the Hebrew account that its author bitterly despised Donin as a betrayer of Jewish secrets, Jehiel insisted to the court even before Donin could make the first of his accusations that the Talmud was an open book which Christians had long been welcome to peruse. In the opening exchange, "The rabbi turned to the Queen and said, 'Please, do not make me respond to [Donin's] words, since the Talmud is an ancient text and no one has spoken against it before. St. Jerome, after all, knew all of the Torah and the Talmud, just as other priests have, and if there is any problem to be found in it, we would have heard of it by now.'"[79] This line of defense was shot down and Jehiel was compelled to respond to Donin's indictments of the Talmud; nevertheless, he found a way to make the same point later in the disputation in answering Donin's accusation that the Talmud was hostile to Gentiles (goyim). Jehiel asserted, in what would become the standard Jewish rejoinder to that charge, that Christians were not included in the category of Gentiles, proof of which could be found in the fact that although Jews were forbidden from teaching "Gentiles" Torah, they were permitted to and in fact regularly did teach Christians Hebrew and Torah, proof of which is the number of Christian clergy who could read Hebrew books.

To the argument that the Talmud did not mean Christians when it spoke of Gentiles, Jehiel added a similar claim, but one that was much harder to sustain. Defending the Talmud against charges that it blasphemed Jesus Christ, Jehiel asserted that the Jesus mentioned in the Talmud was not the one known to Christians. According to the Hebrew account, Jehiel responded to what was undoubtedly the most explosive moment of the Paris Disputation, Donin's citation of *Neziqin*, by arguing that the Talmud

> spoke not of the God of the Christians but rather of some other Jesus who had mocked them and who did not believe in their words, like you, but only believed in the written Torah [as opposed to the Oral Torah or the Talmud]. And you should know that the text does not say "Jesus of Nazareth" but rather refers to another individual by that name who lived at a different time, because if it were the same man, he did not just reject the oral law but also corrupted the Jewish people and declared himself a God and rejected the Bible itself.[80]

It may well be doubted that Jehiel ever uttered these audacious words. Even while denying that the Talmud spoke harshly against Jesus Christ, Jehiel manages to suggest that Jesus Christ actually deserved a much harsher punishment than the one prescribed for the Jesus who merely abrogated rabbinic authority (he also implies that Donin himself should expect to burn in hell as well). Such boldness was presumably for the enjoyment of the Jewish readers of the Hebrew account. While the Latin account differs from these formulations, it confirms that Jehiel indeed asserted that the Talmud had meant a different Jesus when it rebuked a man by that name. Jehiel stuck to this argument even in regard to a passage in *Sanhedrin* that referred explicitly to a Jesus of Nazareth. The Christian disputants could hardly contain their incredulity: "Could there have been two Jesuses of Nazareth," the friars asked, "who both corrupted the people and were both hanged on the eve of Passover?" According to the Hebrew account, Rabbi Jehiel answered:

> "Not every Louis who is born is the same, and some of them are not the King of France. Has it never happened that two people in the same city had the same name and died the same kind of death? There are many such cases in the land."
>
> And the Queen said to the friars, "Why do you want to raise a stink? Here he has said to your honors that they did not open their mouths against your God and never said that he was condemned to boiling excrement and you want to force your own humiliation from his mouth? And isn't it shameful for you too to be talking about excrement?"
>
> And the Queen said to the rabbi, "On your faith, tell me the truth, is there really another Jesus?"

And the rabbi answered, "As I live and will return to my home, it was never said of him that he would boil in excrement and they never spoke of him in such words."[81]

Jehiel attempts to shield his community here through a sophisticated (or sophistic) linguistic defense rivaling President Bill Clinton's famous line, "It all depends on what the meaning of 'is' is." Between his Jewish sources and their exposure in the Christian sphere, Jehiel places a maze of intractable problems in reference and translation. In the interchange between the rabbi and the queen (mother of the Louis who *was* the King of France!), Jehiel questions the status of the proper name as what linguists call a "rigid designator," that is, a word that points to one and only one referent "in all possible worlds."[82] As if Jehiel's approach were contagious, the Queen Mother's rebuke of the friars for repeating the blasphemous and offensive passage in *Neziqin* rides on another linguistic problem, the distinction between *quoting* and articulating a forbidden utterance; the queen herself, of course, falls into the very trap she is warning the friars against. The queen thus suggests that the friars' insistence on exposing Jewish infamy contributes to the defamation of Jesus, even if it is aimed at smearing the Jews. Jehiel's concluding speech act has a similarly destabilizing effect, with its potential *double entendre:* The rabbi vows on his life that the Jews never spoke of Jesus in such words, but his vow could also be taken as an assertion that his safe return to his home depends on his saying the right thing.

Jehiel's riskiest move (even if it is made only within the Hebrew account) is to take the name "Louis" as his example to demonstrate the unreliability of the name "Jesus" as designator of the Christian God. In pointing out that the name "Louis" is shared by kings and commoners, Jehiel undermines the authority carried by the name of the King and, by implication, also suggests that Jesus is much like those other men who share his name. "Louis" and "Jesus" are emptied of their singular authority, in Jehiel's argument, becoming conventional names that refer promiscuously to a motley crew of characters roaming the streets of Roman Jerusalem and medieval Paris.

Jehiel's defense against Donin can thus serve as an exemplary episode in translation history. On the one hand, Jehiel argues, the Talmud is not a secret Jewish text and has long been accessible to all who wish to read it. On the other hand, the Talmud is of no particular relevance to Christians; even if they recognize some terms in the Talmud, Jehiel asserts that those names refer to a different cast of characters than those familiar to them. There is no equivalence between words found in the Talmud and those apparent cognates in

Christian discourse; in translation terminology, these apparent cognates are "false friends." Jehiel uses a familiar problem in translation, the difficulty of proving that signs in different languages point to the same referent, to drive a wedge between Jewish texts and their Christian translation. In asserting the difference between the Christian Jesus and the Jesus mentioned in Jewish literature, Jehiel is thus also implicitly challenging the reliability of Nicholas Donin as informer on the Jews and faithful translator of Hebrew texts. Finally, he is suggesting that Judaism and Christianity may stand in no real kinship relation—either positive or negative. If there is no contiguity between Christianity and Judaism, if Judaism is not a warped mirror of Christian belief, the convert loses his role as mediator between the religions.

CONVERSION and translation, related etymologically and, as we have seen, historically, emerge in medieval Europe as closely allied if not parallel operations. Practically, medieval conversion from Judaism to Christianity (and vice versa) implied the move to a new language, and conversion testimonies such as Hermann-Judah's twelfth-century *Short Account of His Own Conversion* (*Opusculum de conversione sua*) simultaneously served as evidence of a spiritual rebirth and a linguistic transformation—the Latin exam passed. Writing of conversion in early modern Germany, Carlebach asserts that "success in either Latin or the vernacular came to be seen as a component of a successful conversion." As evidence that such conversions were not only to Christianity but also to the German language and folk, she cites narratives in which converts speak interchangeably of "uns Teutchen" and "wir Christen."[83] In this regard, the Apostle Paul's "conversion" sets the pattern of signaling and marking religious transformation by a name-change that is also a move from Hebrew to Greek, an interlingual shift.[84] (By contrast, the transformation of Jacob to Israel in Genesis is an *intra*lingual shift.) The name-change that is traditional in medieval conversions from Judaism to Christianity is only a translation in a qualified sense, however. Although "Saul" and "Paul" refer to the same person, the name-change is meant to signify not a singular identity beneath the two names but rather a radical transformation, indeed a "rebirth" as a new person. In the move from Moses Sephardi to Petrus Alfonsi, or from Saul to Pablo Christiani, semantic equivalence is specifically ruled out.

Jewish–Christian conversion, as an interlingual speech act, thus has its closest links not with the mainstream conception of translation but rather with the particular theory that translation is transformation. In conversion, what is "contained within" an individual is radically transformed through the assumption of a new name in a new language; the new signifier (the baptismal name Pablo Christiani, for example) points to a new signified (the "reborn" Christian self). As Lewis Rambo has suggested, the Christian sense of conversion is shaped by this language of death and rebirth, which configures the scene of conversion as a violent and dramatic process.[85] The name-change, within this notion of conversion, signifies a radical transformation of the self; as a theory of translation, the name-change in conversion relies on the assumption that a new signifier points to a new signified, just as a new name points to a new self.

It may not be surprising, given the Christian investment in the stability of the signified, that the theory underlying the convert's name-change, that the new name signifies a new self, met with skepticism and was continually compelled to battle the notion—ubiquitous in medieval Europe among Jews and Christians both—that a Jewish core remained intact within the new Christian. In the popular Christian imagination, the convert, in Gilman's words, was "merely a disingenuous Jew."[86] Sometimes the very anti-Jewish zeal of the convert to Christianity was evidence that conversion was essentially a Jewish affair, an internecine struggle rather than a personal spiritual awakening. The Hebrew account of the Tortosa Disputation records that when the Jews complained about Geronimo's hostile opening remarks, the Pope replied, "You are right, but do not be so surprised at his bad behavior, for he is one of your own," and later insisted that Geronimo's attempt to shift a discussion in which he was being bested was further evidence of his Jewish nature.[87] In an essay on conversion and "immutability," Jonathan Elukin writes:

> Documents from medieval governments and the institutions of the Church identified Jewish converts in ways that preserved the memory of their conversion. That is, they appear in the surviving documents identified as *conversus* or *quondam judeus*. For example, Roger the Convert and John the Convert became favorites of Henry III of England, yet they still carried their past identities with them. Perhaps in some cases the appellation was meant to honor the commitment of the convert. I think it is more likely that concealed behind this seemingly neutral terminology, however, was distrust that could grow easily into open antagonism.[88]

Jews, on their side, signaled their sense of the fictionality of conversion, the mere "performance" of Christian identity in converts, with the principle of "yisra'el, af 'al pi shehata, yisra'el hu," a sinning (in this case, baptized) Jew remains a Jew.[89] Such suggestions that a Jewish self continued to function "beneath" the new Christian one was not just a feature of Inquisition ideology or rabbinic law: the performance of converts themselves often assumed and reinforced just such a notion. Thus, the eleventh-century polemicist

Petrus Alfonsi transcribed an imaginary Jewish–Christian disputation that pitted a character named Petrus Alfonsi against one Moses Sephardi (his former name), reconstituting conversion as a synchronic rather than diachronic process, in which Jewish and Christian selves coexisted in endless argument.[90] Indeed, the work of "professional" converts—those who served as translators, censors, and informers on the Jewish community—required that the convert's Jewish background continue to remain firmly in evidence. In the public activities of these converts, conversion was less an accomplished transformation than a continually rehearsed and repeated performance. The signature of the sixteenth-century censor Dominico Irosolimitano, for example, appeared in Hebrew letters (as Yerushalmi) on texts he expurgated; among the reasons for this choice must have been the need to signal his qualifications as censor of Hebrew books.[91] The very task of expurgation produced this effect writ large. *Sefer Hazikuk* (The book of expurgation), begun in 1594 by an anonymous Capuchin neophyte and censor but compiled largely by Irosolimitano, is composed of a list of all passages in Hebrew works to be censored—a kind of guidebook for the novice or hurried censor. Under the heading *Moreh Nevukhim* (Maimonides' *Guide for the Perplexed*), for example, *Sefer Hazikuk* cites Maimonides' warning that ascribing attributes to God risks echoing the Christian error: "But whoever believes that He is one and that He yet has many attributes says 'He is one' with his lips and believes 'He is many' in his mind. *This is like the doctrine of the Christians, 'He is one, but He is three, and the three are one.'*"[92] Here as elsewhere, the *Book of Expurgation* singled out objectionable passages to aid in the censorship of Jewish books. What was produced by the neophytes from whose notes the book was compiled, however, was an uninterrupted stream of anti-Christian criticism, from dry philosophical polemic to popular invective. As Attorney General Edwin Meese's Commission on Pornography's *Final Report* (July 1986) was an anthology far more obscene than what it was intended to combat, the neophytes produced and reproduced in concentrated form what they were attempting to eradicate, as a curious by-product of their expurgatory work. The title of Samuel Brenz's 1614 anti-Jewish pamphlet *Jüdischer abgestreiffter Schlanger-Balg* (Jewish cast-off snakeskin) conveys the ironic process whereby the transformation from Jew to Christian, by the logic of this transformation, released a visible Jewish marker, a "remainder" unassimilated by conversion. In the most visible textual performances of Jewish–Christian conversion—from naming the convert *quondam judaeus* to the production of texts documenting Jewish secrets—conversion was simultaneously named and undone, remembered and undermined, esteemed and cast into doubt.

Scholars have pointed to various cultural factors in elucidating the growing medieval skepticism over the efficacy of conversion. Among the key factors in this shift, Elukin writes, is "the discovery of the interior self among Christians [of the twelfth century], with their increasingly ambivalent ideas about the interior self of Jewish converts."[93] This skepticism has its linguistic corollary: in traditional theories of translation, the signified to which each set of signifiers refers remains intact through the process of translation, much as some interior core remains unchanged in the process of conversion. As a religion dependent on the truth value of translation, Christianity has a prime investment in the transcendence of the signified. The model of conversion that takes seriously the claim that a convert is reborn at baptism corresponds not to the traditional (Christian) theory of translation, but rather to the assumption that, because the signifier shapes the signified, a translation creates a new text in the target language. Translation is a kind of conversion, conversion a kind of translation—and these are not *parallel* but rather mutually subverting operations. Traditional theories of translation are undermined by the recognition that a new language gives birth to a new text; conversion is threatened by the notion that a person is merely renamed rather than remade at the baptismal font.

The ambiguity of conversion is most often addressed as a problem of the relationship between Jewish and Christian selves in the convert. One ubiquitous approach to this question views the Christian self as a false veneer over the unchangeable, deceitful Jew; Carlebach catalogues medieval references to the baptismal font as a *Judenbad*, merely a bathtub of which it could be said that "one who sprang out of it remained the same person as the one who jumped in," or to a convert as "un giudeo mal battezzato," a badly baptized Jew.[94] But the ambiguity inheres also in the relation between the convert and the "true" Christian; in this regard, the "badly baptized Jew" calls into question the efficacy of Christian ritual as well as the convertibility of the Jews. The relation between the born Christian and the new Christian is one of *mimesis*, the process that Augustine insists propels all Christian conversion as a never-completed work of *imitatio dei* or *Christi*.[95] In the case of the convert from Judaism, the "small difference," or, to use a translation term, "remainder," that persists beyond the conversion—as irreversible circumcision, as ineradicable accent, as the persistent memory and textual production of Jewishness—functions to undermine the solidity of "true" Christian identity and ultimately to expose all religious identities (the inherited as well as the acquired) as performative. Homi Bhabha, describing the relations between colonizers and the natives who imitate them, pinpoints the contradiction that serves to undermine colonial authority as it reproduces it. By the logic of the "epic intention of the civilizing mission," the native must imitate the colonizer; but the difference that nevertheless remains between them transforms this imitation into caricature. In this play of difference and resemblance (which it shares with translation), colonialism "often produces a text rich in the traditions of *trompe-l'oeil*, irony, mimicry and repetition."[96] While an analysis of the relations of Jewish and Christian selves in the convert can help clarify the persistent mistrust of the convert in medieval Christendom, Bhabha's reading of the colonial relation also recognizes the threat posed by the convert precisely to Christian identity. Colonial mimicry, Bhabha writes, as both "resemblance and menace,"

> is the desire for a reformed, recognizable Other, *as a subject of a difference that is almost the same, but not quite*. Which is to say, that the discourse of mimicry is constructed around an ambivalence; in order to be effective, mimicry must continually produce its slippage, its excess, its difference. . . . The effect of mimicry on the authority of colonial discourse is profound and disturbing.[97]

The literature of Jewish–Christian conversion is replete with the effects of mimicry, in which pious mimesis slips into (real or perceived) parody. In Hermann-Judah's mid-twelfth-century *Short Account*, described in the scholarly literature as the first spiritual autobiography after Augustine's, the protagonist records his halting movements toward baptism as a series of quasi-theatrical performances, in which he "tried on" various roles before finally choosing one. While Hermann records his skills as a Jewish controversialist against Christians, he also relates that, before his conversion, he astonished his fellow Jews by "preaching Christ" in the synagogue at Worms. As Hermann tells us,

> While [the Jews] were arguing whether mind and tongue agreed in all the things that I had set forth against them for defense of the Christian faith, I took fright . . . and said the following: "Since I frequently dispute with Christians, I have learned, for the greatest part, their subtle arguments against the Jews. I wanted to transfigure myself into their persona, so that, instructed by this dress rehearsal of my assertions, you would seem the better informed to them when push came to shove."[98]

Arnaldo Momigliano points out that although Hermann may have had no choice but to retreat, the account still manages to testify that Hermann "had failed as a champion of Christianity, while before he had succeeded only too well as a Jewish apologist against his Christian opponents."[99] The mask is not so easily separated from the "real" face.

The imitative dimensions of Hermann's adopting the persona of a Christian—perhaps the very Christian with whom he had earlier disputed in his role as a Jew—are not stabilized even by the ritual that should have established the authenticity and finality of his conversion. In a chapter entitled "How he was baptized, and what tricks of the Devil he endured in that baptism," Hermann relates that his public baptism before an audience of Christian dignitaries all but turned into a comedy of errors because he had not been adequately prepared for one crucial aspect of the proceedings, "that baptism entailed threefold immersion in the name of the holy Trinity." Having immersed once, and deafened by the water dripping from his head, Hermann tells us that "I at first did not willingly yield to their wish" to immerse a second time. By the third time, "almost frozen rigid by its extreme cold," Hermann submitted to the shouts of the clergy and immersed again, but confesses that he "suspected that they were making a laughingstock" of him.[100] In Hermann's fear that his converters were mocking him by forcing him to immerse repeatedly, when one immersion, to his novice mind, should have sufficed, the underlying performativity of religious ritual rises to the surface, and with it the always-present possibility of empty, wrong, or farcical ritual repetition. Gender, Judith Butler has argued, is "an identity tenuously constituted in time, instituted in an exterior space through the stylized repetition of acts."[101] Religious identity is similarly constituted through the stylized repetition of ritual—in Hermann's case, repetition is the key element for which his converters had failed to prepare him. As Butler argues about gender, and as Hermann experienced as the supreme moment of his transformation from Jew to Christian, the iterative quality of religious identity constitutes identity as an exterior and theatrical performance. In the church or synagogue as theater of religious identity, pious submission to the mimetic rules of religious adherence cannot be easily distinguished from the feigning, or "dress rehearsal," of such adherence.

If colonialism "often produces a text rich in the traditions of *trompe-l'oeil*, irony, mimicry and repetition," the history of conversion, too, has given us a variety of double-voiced texts: *Igeret al tehi ka-avotekha* (Letter: Do not be like your fathers) may be one of the most striking of such texts, occupying a middle position between pious Christian theology and covert anti-Christian polemic. The 1396 letter from Profiat Duran, the Jewish grammarian and philosopher who had been forcibly baptized in 1391, is addressed to his friend, also forcibly baptized but who had since become persuaded of the truth of Christianity. The letter is an apparent espousal of Christian dogma by a fervent convert and an attack against what "your fathers believed," for instance, that God is One. "Between the lines," however, Duran seems to be attempting to turn his friend back to Judaism. The technique has been described by Leo Strauss, who uses other examples, in his 1952 work *Persecution and the Art of Writing:* "The influence of persecution on literature is precisely that it compels all writers who hold heterodox views to develop a peculiar technique in writing, the technique which we have in mind when speaking of writing between the lines."[102] Strauss writes that, in such literature, the writer espouses the orthodox position loyally but automatically while stating "the case of the adversaries . . . clearly [and] compellingly," attracting an intelligent reader to the forbidden position while avoiding the wrath of the authorities.[103] The letter, referred to among Christians in garbled transliteration of the Hebrew as *Alteca Boteca,* is written, as Pinchas Lapide puts it, "with such subtle irony and theological skill that it was at first generally regarded as a defense of baptism and the superiority of Christianity";[104] it was cited, translated and commented on by Christians until 1420, when it was exposed as a satire (on the evidence that Duran had, in the meantime, moved to Palestine, reverted to Judaism, and published an overtly anti-Christian polemic) and publicly burned.

Duran's letter indeed seems to take the approach described by Strauss, "quoting" the Jewish position apparently under attack with a persuasive clarity not usually awarded to Jewish beliefs in Christian polemic. Moreover, Duran may also have been hinting in the opening of the letter that his words should be read as a code, since they derived from his reading of "a hidden scroll . . . with deep secrets etched upon its pages . . . and there was little I could understand from its mysteries."[105] What follows is a litany of "false" Jewish beliefs, each introduced with the phrase "do not be like your ancestors," and followed by the Christian belief that is to be preferred; for example, that God is a Trinity, or that He was incarnated in Jesus Christ and born of a virgin, and so on. The first of these is "Do not be like your ancestors who believed in the One God, never associating him with any element of plurality or partnership."[106]

If Duran's letter is indeed a parody, a "blank" imitation of a Christian theological treatise, it also thematizes the problem of religious affiliation as itself one of imitation or mimesis. What Duran's interlocutor must choose between is not "true" versus "false" belief but rather the model set forth by his ancestors versus that of his converters. The very structure of quotation in the letter suggests the character of religious belief as imitative; that a lapsed convert to Christianity can produce such an orthodox manifesto demonstrates the twin possibility of conversion as pious *imitatio* and as devious imitation. In Lapide's analysis, the writer is performing a deliberate sleight of hand, reversing on paper the beliefs he truly espouses in his own mind. But there is no reason to insist on Duran's intentional double-dealing in his letter, despite the later reversion to Judaism. The narrative of sincere conversion cannot be separated from its parody precisely because both work according to the logic of imitation (as does even the piety of a born Christian); it is this logic that constitutes both the coherence and potential instability of conversion and its textual performances.

The Vatican Hebrew New Testament translation (Vat. Ebr. no. 100 in the Vatican Library), an anonymous Hebrew translation whose provenance is unknown, represents the problem of mimicry not through an apparent parody of a sincere conversion narrative but rather through a seemingly faithful translation. Lapide hypothesizes that the translation was produced by a Jew under duress, since only such constraint could explain "the great contrast between the comprehensive range of rabbinical knowledge and familiarity with the Hebrew language shown on the one hand, and the numerous errors on the other hand which sabotage the work, undoubtedly with the intent to misrepresent the meaning of the text."[107] These errors, Lapide explains, are "due to an excessively literal rendering" and show that the text was either controlled or censored by a Christian with some knowledge of Hebrew, but whose knowledge was insufficient to catch such coded messages as, for instance, the first phrase of the introduction: *betsa'ar athil*, "I begin in sorrow (or: under duress)." The evangelists, in another of Lapide's examples, are introduced with a precise Hebrew transliteration of the "innocent" Italian or Spanish abbreviation for Saint, *s"y*, which "was undoubtedly approved by the ecclesiastical censors, while by Jewish readers it was recognized as the familiar sign for *sone yisro'el* [enemy of Israel]." In a final signal that the "faithful" New Testament translation is nevertheless not the *Christian* rendering it might appear, the manuscript ends with words *barukh sheptarani*, "Blessed be he who sets me free," an expression traditionally used after a difficult or unpleasant duty has been fulfilled.[108]

In this apparently Jewish document, we have the translated text as a sham "convert," repeating the phrases of the New Testament in "an excessively literal rendering" that is the translational equivalent of parodic mockery. Translation, as "a difference that is almost the same but not quite," occupies the ambivalent position of the convert in Christianity, threatening always to destabilize Christian authority precisely through the required mimetic performance—in this case a hypercorrect translation.[109]

THE explosion in Christian Hebraica of the first decades of the sixteenth century was inaugurated, by most accounts, by the pioneering Christian

Kabbalist Pico della Mirandola. It was Pico who introduced Reuchlin to the study of Hebrew in Rome, and Reuchlin who brought Christian Hebraica to Germany, thus opening the way for Luther's achievement as a translator and the dawn of Protestant Hebraism. If Pico's work in Christian Kabbalah is the beginning of the end of the era of Christian reliance on converts, it is also true that his work could never have proceeded without the help of his translator, perhaps the most remarkable of the translator-converts, Flavius Mithridates. Mithridates was a preternaturally gifted and prolific translator: Chaim Wirszubski considers Mithridates' own estimate of the forty folio pages a day he prepared for Pico in the summer of 1486 a not implausible one, given that he translated perhaps five thousand folio pages of the most abstruse Hebrew and Aramaic texts into Latin over the course of a few years.[110] Mithridates' work as a translator was matched by a proliferation of identities, as if this convert embodied the principles of both textual transformation and self-transformation run amok: in Shlomo Simonsohn's words, the translator Pico commissioned was "Guglielmo Raimondo Moncada, alias Flavius Mithridates, alias Siculus, alias Romanus, alias Chaldeus, a Sicilian convert to Christianity."[111] To those aliases Simonsohn might had added, alias Samuel ben Nissim ibn Faraj, the birth-name Umberto Cassuto has reconstructed from various hints strewn through Mithridates' commentaries, and alias YHWH, to whom Mithridates compared himself through the operations of kabbalistic numerology.[112] By all accounts, Mithridates was an erudite scholar of Jewish mysticism and gifted translator who set the stage for Pico's groundbreaking appropriation of kabbalistic methods in the service of Christian truth-claims. But Mithridates was far from an "invisible translator," using his Latin interpolations and commentaries as avenues to make his desires and demands known to Pico. Thus, Mithridates employed Hebrew words as a code within the Latin translation to remind Pico of his promises to pay for the translation by bringing him a beautiful boy—*na'ar yafeh*—and laced his commentaries with pseudo-mystical reveries on the mysteries of the "*tahat*," which in nonliterary Hebrew means the bottom or anus.[113] Mithridates used Hebrew numerology not only to demonstrate Christian dogmas, but also, on occasion, to settle personal scores or to repeat particularly witty Jewish interpretations; as Wirszubski writes about one such interpolation, "Almost twenty years after his conversion, Mithridates repeats an anti-Christian interpretation of the 'strange gods of the land' [*elohei nekhar*] as a prefiguration of Jesus and Mary."[114] What Mithridates was rendering visible in these interpolations was precisely the human desires, economic considerations, and power relations whose shaping of the practice of translation is only recently coming to the surface of translation studies. In his numerological translation of the divine names into their human "equivalents," Mithridates lays bare the social asymmetries obscured in such "purely linguistic" arguments about translation as Luther's; to wield knowledge of Hebrew, Mithridates seems to suggest, is to take the supreme (if not divine) position over the mere reader, who is compelled to accept the translator's word. In Mithridates' interpolations about the young boy Pico has promised to procure, the *price* of translation is inscribed into the translated text, stripping the illusion that translation is produced in a realm uncontaminated by erotics or economics. In quoting the anti-Christian interpretation, Mithridates signals the potential instability separating Jewish source from Christian translation, Jewish from Christian self. Translation in Mithridates reached not only its greatest output, but also its greatest shiftiness, in which the changing of names and translation of texts were juxtaposed in their most jarring proximity.

The sixteenth century brought a new paradigm to translation, inserting in the place of this all too visible translator the retiring Christian Hebraist, who inspired confidence in a way that no convert could. I do not mean to imply that anti-Jewish or anti-convert sentiments are solely responsible for the growing dominance of born Christians in Hebrew studies; Christian Hebraists assumed their role on the modern stage precisely because their approach and methods were modern. Carlebach writes,

> Converted Jews claimed knowledge of Judaism and its texts as a birthright. Compelled to traduce that very birthright in order to claim their place within the Christian world, they wrote books motivated by the need to expose, or invent, the dark side of Judaism. Christian Hebraists, by contrast, had been trained in the rigors of Greek and Latin grammar and Christian theology. By their painstaking but thorough acquisition of Hebrew, they intended not so much to discredit Judaism as to use its resources to enrich their study of German texts. While none acted out of a philo-Judaic motivation, the overt polemicism and sloppy methodology that characterized so many works of the converts contrasted with the scholarly accuracy and aura of professionalism in the works of the Hebraists.[115]

It can hardly be denied that the convert-translator was impelled by a variety of unsavory and covert motivations, and that with these came the clear potential for distortion. But even as respected a Christian Hebraist as Reuchlin had his ulterior, if benign, motives—chief among them to save Jewish books from the flames. This desire may well lie behind Reuchlin's "generous" mistranslation of the word *meshumadim;* the Hebrew word in fact means exactly what the convert Pfefferkorn says it means, not because this meaning can be grammatically derived (the derivation is far from transparent), but because so it was understood by Jews from the rabbinic period to our own day, not only in Hebrew but also in Judeo-German, Pfefferkorn's native tongue. Meaning, as Aristotle and Augustine, among others, have argued, is not determined by correct grammar but rather constructed through the usage of a language community. Alongside my own certainty about what *meshumad* refers to—confirmed by but not derived from a dictionary—is the emotional charge of the word, uttered, in my experience, with a hushed horror that is surely also relevant to the semantic history of the term. That Pfefferkorn the *meshumad* was implicated in—was a prime target of—precisely the Jewish attitudes he translated for the German public cannot rule him out as their reliable interpreter: Where, in Christian Europe, could one stand outside the dilemma of the convert? If Jewish–Christian polemic disqualifies the translational testimony of the convert, it also taints the Christian Hebraist.

The convert as the embodiment of a range of obstacles to "pure" translation did not disappear when Luther took the side of Reuchlin over Pfefferkorn, as is evident even in Luther's own work. In Luther's eyes, the fraudulence of Jews and particularly converts continued to be an active threat to the Christian-German folk, everywhere encroaching on their wholesome goodness. In 1528, Luther helped republish and wrote the introduction to *Liber Vagatorum* (The book of vagabonds and beggars), an anonymous booklet that had first appeared in 1512 detailing the habits and vocabulary of the vagabond underclass. In his introduction, Luther explains the importance of exposing the "secret language" of the beggars and thieves and admits that even he has been tricked on occasion by these scoundrels. Nevertheless, Luther, as a student of Hebrew, is particularly qualified to take on this project, since the jargon of the thieves catalogued in the book "has come from the Jews, for many Hebrew words occur in the vocabulary, as anyone who understands that language may perceive."[116] Sander Gilman notes that Luther, "from his newly won position as one knowledgeable in the hidden language of the Jews, is the first to point out in print that Hebrew functions as a major element of the secret language of the criminal."[117] The words that show Jewish influence in Luther's collection of tricksters' cant are actually a mixture of German and Hebrew—that is, a variety of Yiddish; in this regard, Luther's pamphlet is also the first of the various Yiddish glossaries and handbooks that were designed to "provide the institutions of society with the means to understand the Jews in spite of their hidden language."[118] For Luther and his contemporaries, such an exposé also consolidated the gains of the Reformation in claiming "pure" Hebrew, the language of Isaiah, for Christianity, while designating the German–Hebrew mixture that was the vernacular of his Jewish contemporaries as the true, corrupt, language of the Jews—and of German's vagabonds and beggars.

The bastardized German spoken by vagabonds may have been "the natural expression of the Jewish spirit," but as it turned out, this language was spoken not only by Jews; indeed, Jews or converts are mentioned only once or twice in the *Book of Vagabonds*, among the various beggars, swindlers, rogues, vagrants, knaves, and double-dealers that are said to use the trickster language. The twenty-third chapter of the *Liber Vagatorum* describes the *veranerins*, or "baptized Jewesses"; as it turns out, these "baptized Jewesses" are in fact Christian women "who *say* they are baptized Jewesses and have turned Christians, and can tell people whether their fathers or mothers are in hell or not, and beg gowns and dresses and other things, and have also false letters and seals."[119] The *Book of Vagabonds* presents a German countryside infested with friars, lepers, converts, and con artists, including Christians masquerading as converts to Christianity; the fraudulence of conversion finally threatens even the purity and wholesomeness of Christian identity.

The *Book of Vagabonds* responds to this Babelian confusion in two ways: in the rational ordering of beggar-types that is the body of the pamphlet; and in the grammatical exposition of the language of these tricksters, with the etymological roots of each mysterious word traced to its "pure" origin, that is its appendix. Thus, the first entry is "*Adone,* God. *Hebrew,* ADHONAIY, the Lord, i.e. God," while the second is "ACHELN, to eat. *Hebrew,* AKAL."[120] In this glossary, the exemplary genre of Protestant Hebraism is brought to bear on the theater of frauds that for Luther is the German countryside. Against this vision of the tricksters that plague the German folk we might set Luther's own Bible, in which the angel speaks a loving, pure German to Mary and Daniel. In Luther's biblical scenes, the characters that traverse the margins of the German landscape have been banished from view, replaced by angels and prophets who speak an unadulterated German prose. That Mary is a Miriam in German-Christian garb (as Mithridates, for one, had pointedly reminded Pico in the interpolation mentioned above), or that the angel's tongue produced the same harsh, secret syllables that grate in the speech of Luther's tricksters, is lost in the very transparency of Luther's translation. It is from this transparency, and all that it hides, that modern translation begins.

CHAPTER FOUR

———— ✳ ————

A Translator Culture

For the voice of the Bible is not to be enclosed in any space—not in the inner sanctum of the church, not in the linguistic sanctum of a people, not in the circle of the heavenly images moving above a nation's sky. Rather this voice seeks again and again to resound from outside—from outside this church, this people, this heaven.

FRANZ ROSENZWEIG, "Scripture and Luther"

IN EARLY April 1933, the National Socialist Student Association extended their anti-Jewish actions from the economic to the cultural sphere, posting twelve theses aimed at "purifying" German public life on billboards all over Germany; the seventh of these read: *"When the Jew writes in German, he lies. He should be compelled, from now on, to indicate on books he wishes to publish in German: 'Übersetzung aus dem Hebräischen' [translated from the Hebrew]."*[1] The implication that Jews were incapable of authentic German expression was itself far from original, recycling the older antisemitic stereotype that Jews were uncreative, unoriginal parasites on the "organic" German body politic. Translation here signified both this derivative cultural disposition and, as Semites ("from the Hebrew"), a constitutional foreignness to all things German. The perception that German was somehow closed to Jewish expression was palpable before and without the Nazi billboards, even—perhaps especially—to such masters of the language as Kafka. As Kafka ruefully wrote in a letter to Max Brod, the Jewish use of German was a "bumptious, tacit, or self-pitying appropriation of someone else's property, even when there is no evidence of a single solecism."[2]

Kafka's response to the challenge of writing in German was to produce a limpid prose as devoid of Jewish "flavor" as of references to Jewish culture. Other Jewish writers of the period transformed allegedly Jewish "traits" into a badge of honor, a sign of what Jews, as insider-outsiders, could contribute to German culture. Martin Buber, for instance, saw German Jews as serving a crucial role as mediators between "the Orient" and "the Occident," as he put it, at a moment of crisis for both great civilizations. "For the Jew has remained an Oriental," he proudly proclaimed in the 1916 essay "The Spirit of the Orient and Judaism." For the "world-historical mission" of a new spiritual encounter between East and West, "Europe has at its disposal a mediating people that has acquired all the wisdom and all the skills of the Occident without losing its original Oriental character."[3] These crucial "translators from the Hebrew," as we might term them, are of course the Jews. I do not mean to equate Buber's vision of the Jews as "translators from the Hebrew" with that of the Nazi students: Buber believed that Jews had "acquired all the wisdom and skills of the Occident," while it was precisely the thrust of the seventh thesis to deny them this cultural acquisition; moreover, for Buber translation carries no stigma—on the contrary. But I would point out that the perception that German Jews were consummate cultural translators, whether this was highest praise or nastiest insult, wild exaggeration or powerful insight, itself transcended the German–Jewish divide.

There were, of course, *actual* German-Jewish "translators from the Hebrew": Buber as well as his collaborator Franz Rosenzweig, and Moses Mendelssohn, Leopold Zunz, and Samson Raphael Hirsch among others. It has been argued that German-Jewish culture from the Enlightenment until its destruction in fact found exemplary expression both in Bible translation and in translation theory. An astonishing number of important Jewish translations of the Bible into German appeared during this period: aside from the translations of Mendelssohn (1780–83) and of Buber and Rosenzweig (1925–29), we can count the influential nineteenth-century versions of Zunz, Lewis Philippson, and Hirsch. Although there were a number of translations before Mendelssohn's and at least one after the first volumes of the Buber-Rosenzweig Bible began to appear (the 1934 "Berlin Bible" of Harry Torczyner, commissioned by the Berlin Jewish community), the Mendelssohn and Buber-Rosenzweig Bibles have been characterized as the "bookends" of the modern German-Jewish experience, the first ushering in the very dawn of German-Jewish modernity and the second not reaching completion until 1962, when its potential Jewish readership had largely been murdered or dispersed.[4] In addition to this plethora of Bible translations, German Jews also made crucial contributions to translation theory, most prominently in the work of Walter Benjamin and, of course, Buber and Rosenzweig.

From Mendelssohn on, the integration of Jews into the German public sphere has been closely associated with German-Jewish Bible translation, and German-Jewish integration can in turn be read as a kind of translation project. Translation from Hebrew could signal Jewish foreignness (as it did for the Nazi student organization), but it also had a range of other significations for translators and their audiences. Translation is thus both a lens for analyzing the character of German-Jewish identity and a privileged mode of its expression. In a monograph entitled *German-Jewish Bible Translations: Linguistic Theology as a Political Phenomenon*, W. Gunther Plaut writes that Mendelssohn's Bible represents "the first attempt to create a symbiosis between the [German and Jewish] cultures."[5] For Mendelssohn and those who followed, the challenge was "to render the essence of one culture into the medium of another," according to Plaut. "In Germany, each Jewish translator's solution reflected the way in which he perceived the relationship between *Deutschtum* and *Judentum*."[6] Thus, Mendelssohn's having created a work that was both "traditionally Jewish" and "cast in remarkably free and fluent German" served as a model for how to be both a good Jew and a proper German,[7] while Zunz's attempt to retain Hebrew word order as much as possible "reflected, however subconsciously, the feeling of most German Jews that they were not fully German."[8] Drawing on a similar model of translation-as-cultural-encounter, Gershom Scholem poignantly described the Buber-Rosenzweig translation as "a kind of *Gastgeschenk* which German Jewry gave to the German people, a symbolic act of gratitude upon departure. And what *Gastgeschenk* of the Jews to Germany could be as historically meaningful as a Bible translation?"[9] Even when the German–Jewish conversation has ceased, or been brought to a violent end, the Buber-Rosenzweig translation remains as a gracious reminder of and stand-in for a living Jewish presence in Germany and the German language.

The discourse that views Hebrew–German textual translation as Jewish–German cultural conversation is bolstered by the role played by the first of the great Bible translators, Mendelssohn, as emblem of the very possibility of authentic Jewish–German intercourse. Lessing's Nathan the Wise, understood as a theatrical embodiment of Mendelssohn, became the symbol of the enlightened Jew whom tolerant Christians could engage as an equal; Moritz Oppenheim's painting of Lessing and Mendelssohn playing chess (1856), according to David Sorkin, "became the iconic symbol of that relationship."[10] The strongest proponents of conceptualizing translation-as-cultural-encounter indeed emerged from this German-Jewish milieu. Rosenzweig's *Sprachdenken,* his philosophical turn from monologic to dialogic thinking, expressed itself as translation theory even before he embarked on his first translation projects (of the Blessing after Meals in 1920 and the poetry of Jehuda Halevi in 1924). Rosenzweig wrote in a 1917 letter to his cousin Rudolf Ehrenberg:

> Translating is after all the actual goal of the mind [*Geistes*]; only when something is translated has it become really *audible,* no longer something to be disposed of. Not until the Septuagint did revelation become entirely at home in the world, and as long as Homer did not yet speak in Latin he was not yet a fact. In a corresponding way, also translating from person to person.[11]

In Rosenzweig's view, translation is not a purely textual operation but rather a form—perhaps the paradigmatic form—of human speech, partaking of the openness to another voice, the unpredictable give-and-take, the intimacy and richness of living conversation; without translation, texts have no meaning, just as the isolated thought of a philosopher means nothing outside of its reception. Rosenzweig later declared that "all languages are virtually one. . . . The possibility and the function of translating, its can-be, may-be, and should-be, are based on this essential oneness of all languages, and on the command springing from that oneness that there shall be communication among all men."[12] Rosenzweig's perspective on translation has its close corollary in Buber's "philosophy of dialogue," which has had an impact on translation studies as on a host of other fields—Douglas Robinson, for instance, argues for an embodied and experiential "dialogics of translation," a notion drawn from his engagement with Buber's thought.[13] (Of course, Buber's translation approach has also been hugely influential on such Bible translators as Everett Fox and Robert Alter.) Both Buber and Rosenzweig spoke quite directly about translation as a conversation not only between individual interlocutors, but also between peoples and nations, or between one "national spirit" and another. In his essay on Luther, Rosenzweig expands the German Romantic view of language as bound up in the lifeblood of a people to characterize translation as a living encounter between two such peoples. The great translations that sometimes arise when two languages meet represent a *"hieros gamos,"* a sacred marriage, in which, as Rosenzweig lyrically put it, "the receiving people comes forth of its own desire and own utterance to meet the wingbeat of the foreign work."[14] Buber thought in similar terms. Late in his life, Buber referred to his and Rosenzweig's translation project as "the first genuine encounter of the Jewish-Hebrew Bible and the spirit of the German language."[15] Such a view of translation deviates strikingly from the more normative conception of translation as moving in a single direction, either from source to target text or from target to source, as in the Roman "plundering" of Greek literature; Schleiermacher's model offers translators the choice of bringing the reader to the text or the text to the reader—but not both! The Buber-Rosenzweig model is not entirely new: I argued in the second chapter of this book that the *Letter of Aristeas* implicitly figures Hebrew-Greek translation as Jewish–Greek negotiation, symposium, and even "romance." In Buber and Rosenzweig, and elsewhere in the discourse on Jewish–German translation, this way of imagining translation becomes explicit: the work of rendering the Bible into German is a spiritual embrace—attempted or consummated—between the Jewish and German peoples.

It hardly needs pointing out that this model of Hebrew–German translation as Jewish–German integration assumes a connection between Hebrew and the Jewish people, whether the Jews are represented by the modern monolingual German Jew or the prophet Isaiah. Such a connection is made in *The Star of Redemption*, in which Rosenzweig claims that "the Jewish people never quite grows one with the languages it speaks" because its truest attachment is always to the Holy Tongue.[16] Speaking elsewhere of the Jewish encounter with the Bible, Rosenzweig remarks that "the German, also the German in the Jew, can and will read the Bible in German—in Luther's, in Herder's or Mendelssohn's versions; the Jew can understand it only in Hebrew."[17] Rosenzweig's comments here help us see the broad outlines of this model of German-Jewish Bible translation as encounter: (biblical) Hebrew is a metonym for the (modern German) Jew, while the German language is linked to the (Christian) German people; once these equations have been established, it follows logically enough that translation from Hebrew to German embodies and expresses both the fact and the quality of the relationship between these two peoples.

One more element of this model remains to be laid out. The stage on which this encounter is enacted is the Hebrew Bible, which indeed played a pivotal role in German-Jewish culture beyond the question of its translation. Describing the importance of the Bible to the Jewish Enlightenment, Edward Breuer writes that "As a text shared by Jews and Christians, the Hebrew Bible could serve to highlight a common religious and cultural heritage, a notion that . . . reinforced the grounds for economic and social integration."[18] In a culture that provided few enough arenas for Jews and Germans to meet on equal grounds, the Bible offered just such an invaluable if symbolic site.

The model of German–Jewish translation-as-cultural-integration is so ubiquitous and transparent that the close attention I have been paying to its components hardly seems warranted. I will be arguing, however, that this model obscures at least as much as it illuminates. I should acknowledge at the outset of my argument that the logic of the model has been subjected to critical scrutiny of a different variety than I am proposing in this chapter. I am not referring here only to the Nazi denigration of Jewish "translators" as unwelcome intruders onto the German scene; German Jews themselves felt the inadequacy of translation as a vehicle for cultural communion. Scholem among others bitterly argued that German–Jewish symbiosis was no more than a flattering fantasy; the vaunted "Jewish–German dialogue" turned out to be a myth in which "the allegedly indestructible community of the German essence with the Jewish essence consisted, so long as these two essences really lived with each other, only of a chorus of Jewish voices and was, on the level of historical reality, never anything else than a fiction."[19] And on the same occasion in which Scholem called the Buber-Rosenzweig Bible a parting gift of the Jewish people to their German "hosts," Scholem spoke directly to the question of whether German-Jewish Bible translation should be seen as an expression of German–Jewish symbiosis. Revising his assessment of the translation as a gift from the Jews to the Germans, Scholem described the Buber-Rosenzweig Bible rather as "the tombstone of a relationship that was extinguished in unspeakable horror."[20] Plaut's monograph follows a similar trajectory: he begins by considering German-Jewish Bible translation as the embodiment of the developing encounter of Germans and Jews and ends his analysis with the failure of this encounter; German-Jewish translations, in every generation, inevitably ran aground on German-Jewish tensions "until there were literally no more Jews left to try. It turned out that the perfect German-Jewish translation remained elusive, as elusive as the integration of *Deutschtum* and *Judentum*—so tantalizingly alike in some respects and irreconcilably different in others."[21] If the hope for German-Jewish cultural integration depended on a cruel misreading of the Jewish place in Germany, then the notion of German-Jewish Bible translations as an expression of this cultural affinity must itself be an illusion.

My own argument with the model of Jewish-German translation-as-dialogue is not a historical one, although I am hardly disagreeing with Scholem's and Plaut's assessment of German–Jewish symbiosis. While Scholem and Plaut turn their attention to the eventual success or failure of the symbiosis toward which German-Jewish translation strived, my focus is rather on the myth itself, or rather on what is occluded by the paradigm Hebrew-German translation = Jewish-German symbiosis, leaving aside for the moment the question of whether this symbiosis or integration was either desirable or ever actually achieved. One inconsistency in the model can already be glimpsed in Rosenzweig's remarks on the relationship of Jews to the Hebrew Bible quoted above: the category of German, in the German who may read the Bible in German, includes both the German Christian and "the German in the Jew." Put otherwise, the German Jew is both "Hebrew" (as a Jew) *and* "German." In this deconstruction of Jewish identity, the category of a pure or organic German language or people prior to or outside of any "contamination" by Jews or Jewishness also collapses. When one takes into account the duality *within* the German Jew as within the German language itself, German-Jewish Bible translation emerges not as a sign of cultural symbiosis but rather as the self-presentation of a divided individual or group.[22] From this perspective, Buber's continuation of the Bible translation project after the Holocaust requires no justification, once "German-Jewish dialogue" has been recast as a form of talking to oneself. These two understandings, one social and the other psychic, one symbiotic and the other rather schizophrenic, could hardly be in greater tension.

There is another reason to complicate the model of translation-as-cultural-integration outlined above, as I have begun to suggest. If "German" cannot easily stand for Christian Germans alone, even Rosenzweig is compelled to acknowledge that Hebrew is no simple or obvious metonym for the (modern, German-speaking) Jew. The "internal" problem of widespread Jewish illiteracy in Hebrew (which, after all, made translation necessary) can be placed alongside the "external" contestation of this ostensibly self-evident link between Jews and the Hebrew language. The connection between Hebrew and the Jews clearly draws on the German linguistic philosophy of Johann Gottfried Herder, who, in the same city and during roughly the same period when Mendelssohn was working on his Pentateuch translation, described language as a natural, organic entity that arises among a people rooted in their own land, shaped by the distinctive characteristics of its climate and terrain; his *Treatise on the Origin of Language* was awarded the prize of the Royal Academy of Berlin in 1771, eight years after Mendelssohn had won it. This linguistic philosophy both suggested and ultimately undercut the claims of modern German Jews to an organic bond with Hebrew. In a range of publications, Herder praised the beauty and power of Hebrew poetry and the Hebrew language spoken in ancient Israel, a poetry suffused with the *Geist Gottes* (spirit of God), but denied that Jews residing in Europe had retained any living connection to this poetry. In a 1781 essay, "On the Effects of Poetry on the Customs and Morals of the Nations in Ancient and Modern Times," Herder diagnoses the spiritual-linguistic effect of Jewish territorial dislocation:

A ball among the nations, [the Jewish people] has everywhere adopted the customs, the way of thinking, and partly the language of the soil over which the ball
has rolled; they can neither rejuvenate their national poetry nor perhaps feel
whole and true [*ganz und treu*] in intention or effect.[23]

Herder recasts the ancient trope of Jewish literalist blindness to the meaning
of their own texts within a historical and organicist model, writing that, in
the diaspora, "The spirit retreated from [the Jews] and only the corpse of that
misunderstood, misinterpreted letter remained."[24] In this intellectual environment, it was rather a claim to be established than a fact to be presupposed
that Jews could bring the force and truth of Hebrew Scripture to the German
cultural arena.

The model of translation as dialogue takes for granted as well that the
Bible constituted a shared Jewish–Christian heritage; it is just this assumption that drives Scholem's comment that the Jews could have bequeathed the
Germans no finer gift. Certainly it was the status of Hebrew Scriptures for
both Jewish and Christian communities, a status "not necessarily commensu-
rate with religion or tradition," that encouraged modern Jews to claim "the
most intimate connection with Hebrew" as their potential contribution to
German, as Richard Cohen puts it.[25] But the view of the Bible as a platform
for German-Jewish integration was perhaps more a *Jewish* than a general
view. In the Christian camp, opinions on the subject were decidedly mixed.
The Lutheran rejection of Jewish interpretation as irremediably tainted by
rabbinic exegesis continued to shape Protestant attitudes in Mendelssohn's
and even in Buber's time. In the eighteenth century, "higher" or source criticism of the Bible drove a new wedge between the Old Testament and its traditional Jewish exegesis—now even reliance on the Masoretic text and belief
in the unity of the text, staples of Jewish translations from Mendelssohn to
Buber-Rosenzweig, could seem the mark of rabbinic delusion. The Christian
theologian, biblical scholar, and translator Johann David Michaelis took aim
at Mendelssohn's work on both these scores: that it was tainted by rabbinic
interpretation, and that it relied on outmoded notions of the divine authorship of the accents and vowels of the Hebrew Bible. Although Michaelis
praised the Old Testament, its glory registered only against the Jews of his
own time, who were incapable of appreciating what they had in it. Frank E.
Manuel calculates that "the more Michaelis glorifies the Mosaic code, the
less acceptable to him appeared the integration of contemporary Jews into
German society."[26]

Nor was the Bible a royal road to German-Jewish coexistence for Buber and

Rosenzweig. Looking back at the project from Palestine in 1938, Buber recognized that the Bible translation had partly arisen as a perhaps unconscious polemic directed at the German intellectual movement Buber called the "new Marcionites," those Protestant theologians (Buber mentions Paul de Lagarde) who "aimed at the 'Germanization of Christianity' with a 'German God' and a 'German Christ'—goals that had as their first postulate a radical severance from the 'Old Testament.'"[27] Moreover, Buber reflected, their Bible translation posed a challenge even to those German Christians who welcomed the Jews as "The People of the Book" but tended to have a rather different book in mind than their Jewish friends did. Buber recalled the "openhearted camaraderie" between Germans and Jews at the Berlin *Stammtisch* (informal club) to which he belonged in the years before the Great War:

> But some of the Jewish members seemed sometimes to themselves like excerpts of a Hebrew book read in Luther's translation; it seemed to them that what counted in the camaraderie was not the Urtext of their being but the translation, the translation that was more beautiful than true. Luther had translated the Hebrew Bible into the German of his New Testament, into a language stamped with Christian theology, and no translator, not even a Jewish translator, had been able subsequently to get free of it. Were not we ourselves, however intimate we were with our German friends, accessible to them only in a Christian translation?[28]

Even when Christians accepted the Bible as a stage for Jewish–Christian encounter, at least some Jews felt themselves to be thrust into false roles in a German biblical drama heavily scripted by Luther. The ideal of true translation leading to authentic German-Jewish integration gives way, in Buber's reading, to the image of an inauthentic encounter based on a mistranslation of Jewish identity. Buber's solution to this cultural dilemma was a translation of the Bible stripped of its Lutheran overlay, even if such a project might "aid these New Marcionites in their work."[29] The Buber-Rosenzweig Bible aimed to be not merely another *Jewish* Bible, which might aid the project of dividing German Christianity from the Jews and their "Old Testament," but rather a "real" Bible that would ring out from beyond the Jewish–Christian divide so that, as Buber, speaking with wry biblical tones after his departure from Nazi Germany, proclaims, "one day, the eyes of the people would open, and they would be astonished at what they could now see, and be amazed at themselves." From Buber's perspective, no German Bible had yet accomplished this goal.

There is yet a further complication to the model of Hebrew–German translation as Jewish–German integration. Jews in Germany had long been associated with a language other than Hebrew: Yiddish, Judeo-German, or its residual traces in *mauscheln*, the Jewish "mispronunciations" of "proper" German that posed a formidable obstacle to German–Jewish symbiosis precisely on linguistic grounds. The perception that Jews spoke an impure, specifically Jewish dialect of German persisted into the modernist period, as Sander Gilman has demonstrated. It is hard to resist the suspicion, in fact, that Rosenzweig's claim that "the Jewish people never quite grows one with the languages it speaks" makes oblique reference to and poetically revalues the phenomenon of *mauscheln*. Even when and where Jews spoke no other language than German and when their German speech or writing demonstrated mastery of the language, Jewish expression in German was felt to be somehow unnatural, an attitude made hatefully explicit in the seventh of the Nazi students' twelve theses. The contradictory impulses of German nationalist attitudes toward language thus denied the Jews linguistic expression from both directions: first in the skepticism that Jews had retained an authentic connection to the glorious language of the Bible, and second in the insistence that their German was also inauthentic, a "translation from Hebrew"!

It may be no coincidence that the most potent and influential German philosophical formulations of an organic connection between *Sprache* and *Volk* date roughly to the period and even place in which the Jewish transition to German speech was gathering momentum. Mendelssohn himself was a native Yiddish speaker who spoke and wrote in that language throughout his life, and twelve years after his arrival in Berlin and turn to German he was still struggling "to express himself smoothly in German," according to his friend Friedrich Nicolai. As Nicolai writes, "He labored with incredible tenacity to grasp, little by little, the character of this language, which was by no means his mother tongue."[30] Mendelssohn's Pentateuch translation was the crowning effort of his achievement, evidence that he did eventually acquire a firm grasp on "pure" German. That the whiff of Yiddish dogged all Jewish cultural production is evident from the critiques to which he nevertheless was subject. An anonymous reviewer of the first volume of Mendelssohn's Pentateuch praised the translation but declared that "we did not find it at all to be of such pure German (*nicht so rein deutsch*) as we might assume of such an author."[31] Even when Mendelssohn escaped censure, some reviewers still managed to betray their prejudices. Werner Weinberg describes Michaelis's grudging praise for Mendelssohn's translation of Psalms as "a masterpiece of seemingly particular praise within a collective condemnation."[32] According to Michaelis, Mendelssohn's translation has "said the new quite coherently, more coherently than I can remember having seen with the author's other coreligionists . . . in a pleasing language, in which one hardly notices some features that are not German in the true sense."[33]

The dramatic and dialectic role Yiddish played in the Mendelssohn Bible at the beginning of the Jewish transition from Yiddish to German had not completely faded even for Buber and Rosenzweig. Buber of course knew Yiddish, and his first forays into translation were the free, romantic rewritings of Rabbi Nachman's Yiddish (and Hebrew) Hasidic tales.[34] The turn to the Bible, then, was also a turn away from Yiddish, as it had been for Mendelssohn. At an early point in their work, Rosenzweig warned Buber that his translation was "remarkably German; Luther in comparison is almost Yiddish. But maybe now it's *too* German?"[35] While the Buber-Rosenzweig Bible is normally described as a meeting of Hebrew and German, there was another pairing at work in the translation, between "pure" German—which for Rosenzweig was "too German"—and the Yiddish into which even Luther was liable to fall. Buber and Rosenzweig intended their Bible to be Hebraic, source-oriented, foreign to the German ear. But in moving toward the Hebrew in German, they also ineluctably moved away from the Yiddish in German, and not only by their own account. Buber and Rosenzweig were criticized in a famous essay by Siegfried Kracauer for writing an pseudo-archaic, "Wagnerian" German:

> Under the pressure of their work—which they took upon themselves of their own free will—they have run aground of a form of language which is certainly not of today. But these tones do not resonate forth from the biblical era either, even though that is the locus to which the authors want to transfer the scene. . . . They take the Luther text "and the LORD smelled the lovely scent" and elevate it to the lofty German formulation "Thus HE scented the scent of assentment" [*Da roch ER den Ruch der Befriedigung*]. The stench of these alliterations stems not from the Bible but from runes of a Wagnerian sort.[36]

As Kracauer's critique makes clear, the Buber-Rosenzweig translation project could be formulated not only as an encounter between Hebrew and German, but also as the selection of a particular German register and style from the various historical layers, dialects, jargons, genres that comprise any language. German-Jewish Bible translation, for Mendelssohn as for Buber-Rosenzweig, involved more than a mobilization of the organic connection between a people and "its" language. German-Jewish translation inevitably involved the positioning of the translated Bible within the ideologically charged *German* linguistic and cultural palette. Finding this position meant negotiating a German literary arena permeated with both a phobia of Jewish "appropriations" and "corruptions" of German, indeed of the very linguistic mixing that is another name for translation, and the prejudice that Jews were capable only of translation and not of original creative production. Kracauer's critique of the Buber-Rosenzweig Bible warns as well of the danger of abandoning the Jewish register altogether, of producing a translation that was only and *too* German. To Kafka's notorious four German-Jewish "impossibilities," "the impossibility of not writing, the impossibility of writing German, the impossibility of writing differently . . . [and] the impossibility of writing," we might add a fifth, the impossibility of translation.[37]

The equation Hebrew = the Jews assumed in the discourse on German-Jewish Bible translation is thus a constructed stance rather than a self-evident truism. The equation, rather than faithfully representing the *existing conditions* for translation and integration, is itself part of the ideological work of both German-Jewish translations and the discourse that surrounds them. The connection between Hebrew and the Jews, along with its counterpart in a homogenous German sphere and the Bible as shared Jewish–Christian heritage, are not the *sources* of German-Jewish Bible translation as an integration project, the conditions for its production; but rather its desired *effects*. German-Jewish Bible translation advances the claim that Jews have a special kinship with Hebrew and the Bible and constructs a pure German space as its structural counterpart, and it does so in the face of both the counternarratives that would deny this claim and a German nationalist rhetoric that would grotesquely mimic it (Jews are "Hebrews") precisely to deny Jews a place in German culture (*all* Jewish expression is translation from Hebrew). German-Jewish translation is thus polemic as well as dialogue, the record of a national encounter and the narrative of a divided self.

AGAINST HYBRIDITY

In the course of the translation work that culminated in *Sefer netivot hashalom* (The book of the paths of peace), as his translated Bible was called, Mendelssohn gave a variety of explanations for his decision to undertake such an ambitious project.[38] Primary among these motivations, he wrote in the introduction to Genesis, was the education of his young sons:

> When God in his grace gave me male boy-children [*yeladim banim zekharim*] and the time arrived to teach them Torah and to instruct them in the words of the living God, as it is written, I took it upon myself to translate the Pentateuch into ornate and proper German such as that spoken in our time, and I did this for the benefit of the children.[39]

Mendelssohn continued by describing how he came to recognize the utility of his translation for German Jews in general. The existing translations were all deficient, for different reasons. Christians had produced some beautiful translations, but "Jews were endangered by reading Christian translations," Mendelssohn wrote, warning that "the Christian translators lack the traditions of our sages and do not follow the Masorah, and do not even accept the vowels and accents (*ṭa'amim*) as we know them."[40] In criticizing Christian translations, Mendelssohn set himself within the camp of the traditionalists, thus assuring his Jewish readers of the propriety of his translation. But he also argued for the necessity of a *new* Jewish version, since prior Jewish translators had lacked proficiency in both Hebrew grammar and proper German usage. Mendelssohn's collaborator Solomon Dubno spelled out the need for a new translation in their prospectus for the project, explaining that "the ways of our holy tongue have been forgotten in our midst, the elegance of its phraseology eludes us, and the loveliness of our poetry is hidden from our eyes."[41] German Jews were shamefully deficient, as well, in their knowledge of the German language, as even the rabbinic approbation Mendelssohn secured from the chief rabbi of Berlin, Hirschel Lewin, acknowledged:

> Nowadays there are many Gentile nations that, by God's grace, believe in the Torah of Moses and in the holy prophets, and understand the Scriptures. God inspired them to undertake the translation of the Bible into their several languages, "making it savory food" to their heart's delight. Yet we, the people of the children of Israel, and particularly those of us who dwell in these lands and are called Ashkenazim (Germans) . . . speak with a stammering tongue. For we are "surety for a stranger" and there is none among us who knows his way about the foreign tongue to make himself understandable in it. We merely "went about and gathered" words from the books of the Gentiles, and there resulted a very "grievous mixture."[42]

Personally recommending the translation of "Rabbi Moses of Dessau," Lewin writes that "there is not one in a thousand among them like him, who is a master of the word, and who speaks and writes their language with grace and clarity."[43] In his own introduction, Mendelssohn notes that the Bible had been translated into German (actually Judeo-German, or Western Yiddish) twice before—the two versions both came out in Amsterdam in 1670—by Yekutiel Blitz and Josel Witzenhaus; of these, Mendelssohn mentions that he has seen Witzenhaus's translation, and although it was done with the best of intentions and endorsed by the rabbinical authorities of the time, it is an unfit text, for the translator

> did not know the character of the holy tongue, and did not understand the depths of its style, and what he did glean from the text he translated into a stammering

and very corrupt language. The reader who speaks a pure language would be disgusted by it.[44]

Thus Mendelssohn's project filled a very specific need, for a translation loyal to the traditional Jewish text that was built on a solid foundation of Hebrew knowledge and rendered the Bible into correct German. In the manner traditional to German Jews of the period, Mendelssohn's German translation was written in Hebrew characters and included a Hebrew introduction. Alexander Altmann points out that Lewin's approbation directs the reader's attention to Mendelssohn's expertise in Hebrew and German, rather than to his status as philosopher and aesthete.[45] Despite this caution, Mendelssohn narrowly averted the public opposition of the chief rabbi of Altona, Raphael Kohen, by signing on the King of Denmark—Altona was then under Danish jurisdiction—as a subscriber. But writing to his fellow philosopher and friend August Hennings on June 29, 1779, Mendelssohn suggested that he had yet another rationale for the translation: to lead Jews "toward culture." Reporting to his friend that he had taken a hiatus from philosophical writing due to ill health, Mendelssohn described his turning to translation as less strenuous and more useful than philosophy:

> [I translated the Bible] to render a useful service to my children, and perhaps [also] to a considerable part of my nation, by giving into their hands a better translation and explanation of the holy scriptures than they had before. This is the first step toward culture, from which, alas, my nation is kept at such a distance that one might almost despair of the possibility of an improvement.[46]

What exactly Mendelssohn meant by his translation leading the Jewish nation to culture has been the subject of vigorous debate. Did Mendelssohn intend his translation to serve as a German-language manual, as has sometimes been contended?[47] Was Mendelssohn's translation disguised as a pious tome the better to lead unsuspecting traditional Jews down the path not of "peace" but rather of assimilation? Abigail Gillman enumerates Mendelssohn's goals in translating the Pentateuch:

> To facilitate the study of Torah; to move German Jews back to Hebrew, their own "pure," aesthetic language; to displace the Yiddish Bibles on which they had relied for over a century and to hasten the incipient renunciation of Yiddish; to advance their knowledge of German; and to introduce German Jews to culture. Only the first of these was a religious goal; the latter, cultural goals, Mendelssohn would have to justify by reframing them within the discourse of sacred history.[48]

As Gillman amply demonstrates, Mendelssohn mobilized a variety of techniques to present his translation as faithful to Jewish tradition. In personal correspondence in German, however, Mendelssohn instead was able to speak quite openly about his desire to see the translation help Jews acquire the cultural accoutrements for entering the German public sphere. Although Gillman does not mention this, Mendelssohn may have been circumspect about the more traditional goals with Henning, who wore his own religious identity more lightly than did his Jewish friend. Only a reading of his writing in *both* languages can provide a full picture of Mendelssohn's motivations in the project.

The basic model for German-Jewish Bible translation endorsed in all these writings was a solid knowledge of Hebrew grammar, combined with proper German style free of the admixture of Yiddish or Judeo-German. Both Hebrew and German were seen in Mendelssohn's translation through the clear lens of grammar: Mendelssohn's introduction ends with a detailed overview of the principles of biblical grammar, while the commentary, known as the *Bi'ur*, privileged above all the exegesis of the classic medieval grammarians known as the *pashṭanim*, those who followed the "plain sense" of the text; when these were unable to clarify the meaning, Mendelssohn relied on his own grammatical analysis to elucidate the biblical text.

This attention to Hebrew grammar was matched by a faithfulness to correct German usage. Weinberg notes that Mendelssohn's translational bias was toward the "receiver" rather than "donor" language:

> Mendelssohn did not violate the inherent laws of contemporary good German; when sacrificing had to be done, Mendelssohn sacrifices literalness. One may say that Luther's translation was in many instances more faithful to the original Hebrew, but for Mendelssohn, the aesthete, the man of letters and celebrated German stylist, there could be no compromise with the demands of the German language.[49]

"Contemporary good German" had more than one signification in the rhetoric of the Haskalah, the Jewish Enlightenment. It signified propriety in a grammatical sense that implicitly expanded to cover the range of social strictures governing bourgeois German society. If Jews could speak German well, they could also be expected to follow the myriad rules of civility that shaped the public sphere. The irony of the Jewish translator's unwillingness to "compromise with the demands of the German language," as opposed to Luther's willingness at times "to make room for the Hebrew word," is no irony at all. For Mendelssohn, his own integration and that of his coreligionists were at stake in the question of proper German style.

Good German had yet another signification: German, properly spoken, was the language of Jewish-German social transparency and thus morality.

By contrast, Yiddish was the hidden language of the Jews, by which they drew a veil around their religious and commercial behavior; the various Patents of Emancipation were united in forbidding "secret" Jewish communication as part of the condition for Jewish emancipation. Yiddish was thus wrong in a grammatical, political, and ethical sense; it constituted the barrier to Jews being trusted in the public sphere. Mendelssohn made that clear in his letter to Assistant Councilor Ernst Ferdinand Klein on the Jewish oath required by the Prussian courts of law. Vehemently rejecting the suggestion of Joseph Jonah Fränkel, rabbi of Breslau, that the use of "the Jewish-German idiom" be permitted in the oath, Mendelssohn famously wrote:

> I am afraid that this jargon has contributed not a little to the immorality of the common man; and I expect some very good results from the use of the pure German way of speech that has been coming into vogue among my brethren for some time. How annoying to me it would be for the law of the land to speak in favor, as it were, of the misuse of both languages! Herr Fraenkel might rather make an effort to translate the entire admonition into pure Hebrew so that it may be recited, according to the circumstances of the case, in pure German or in pure Hebrew or even in both languages. But let there on no account *be* a mixture of tongues! (*rein Deutsch oder rein Hebräisch . . . nur keine Vermischung der Sprachen!*)[50]

Mendelssohn's letter can provide us with a privileged view of the philosophical conceptualization of Jewish languages from the medieval period, when the Jewish oath was first formulated, to its transformation—but not repudiation—in Enlightenment Germany. The oath required of Jewish witnesses in Prussian courts to ensure that Jews spoke truthfully, in Joshua Trachtenberg's description, "was essentially a magically coercive formula, binding upon the maker and *upon God and His agents,* in the European view, and the *more judaico* was therefore designed by Christians to incorporate what they conceived to be magically binding Jewish components." Swearing by the name of God, or by "the seventy names of God" as in the Narbonne oath formula, the Jew also "was obliged to call down upon his head, in the event that he should be perjuring himself, an assortment of imprecations and curses. . . . The intent of such formulas was not only to frighten the Jew but actually to subject him automatically to the prescribed heaven-sent penalties if he swore falsely."[51] The Jewish oath thus depended for its efficacy on the shared Jewish–Christian perception of Hebrew (including the Hebrew embedded in Judeo-German formulations of the oath) as a magical language with performative powers beyond its communicative capacities. For Mendelssohn, language continues to perform a truth-guaranteeing function but in a drastically reformulated sense: National languages signify truth and morality not by their medieval magical attributes (since German is included as a possible language for the Jewish oath), nor only in their transparency (since Hebrew is also an acceptable language for the oath). Languages signify and compel virtue by their rule-bound structures and their status as discrete national languages within the human diversity of tongues. As a "jargon," Yiddish could not serve the function of emblematizing the place of the Jews among the family of tongues and nations. "Pure" German and Hebrew, by contrast, could—by a kind of Enlightenment magic—signal Jewish truth and morality on the witness stand as in the translation project.

The German of Mendelssohn's translation was not only correct German, it was also elegant and of an elevated register, signifying *Bildung* and refinement. In the translation and the commentary, readers could be made to see the affinities between the Hebrew and German as bearers of high culture. It was Mendelssohn's philosophical rendering of the Tetragrammaton as *der Ewige* or *der ewige Wesen* (the Eternal or the eternal Being) that made this most obvious. The Jewish God carried a name that was translatable into Enlightenment discourse, even if the German translation, as Mendelssohn ruefully acknowledged in the commentary, captured only a part of what was implied in the Hebrew. Mendelssohn's God also eschewed the hierarchy implicit in Luther's *der Herr*, which followed the Vulgate and Septuagint rendering of the Jewish circumlocution *Adonai*. The Hebrew God was no Old Testament tyrant—he was fully consonant with the principles of rational religious thought. In his commentary on *eheye asher eheye* in Exodus 3:14, Mendelssohn quotes a talmudic interpretation of the verse, "I will be with them in this misfortune as I will be with them in their bondage to every other kingdom" (*Berakhot* 9b), but only to draw from it a universal-philosophical rather than national-political conclusion: "I am with human beings [*beney adam*], to be gracious to and have mercy on whom I will have mercy."[52] Altmann points out that even the title of the translation, "The Book of the Paths of Peace," speaks both to a traditional image of the Torah—the phrase is taken from Psalm 3:17, a verse often applied to the Torah—and to a new philosophical-political reading of the wisdom of the Torah consonant with other of Mendelssohn's writings: "There can be no question," Altmann writes, that for Mendelssohn "this choice of title was inspired by the same sentiments that caused him to conclude the *Jerusalem* with the appeal 'Love truth! Love peace!'"[53] The title of Mendelssohn's translation was an appeal for acceptance from the rabbis and other potential opponents, sending the message that "the precepts of the Torah are designed to promote tolerance rather than militancy."[54]

There is yet another signification of the use of proper German and Hebrew rather than Yiddish, one less readily apparent. It can be gleaned, however, from Naftali Herz Wessely's foreword to the translation, "In Praise of a
Friend," which lays out his case for the importance of Mendelssohn's project.
Wessely laments that Jewish pedagogy slights the importance of learning
biblical Hebrew grammar, so that students of Torah

> mix up the past with the present and future, confuse the singular and the plural,
> masculine and feminine, and when they are told that grammar is the outer gate
> that leads to the inner holiness, and whoever abstains from it cannot approach
> the holy, they consider it a joke, and they send their children to school when they
> are four or five to teachers who teach them the Bible, and pay no attention to
> whether these teachers are stammerers . . . and after a year or so they announce
> to the fathers that their sons have succeeded in learning Mishnah and Talmud
> and there is no longer any need for them to study the Bible, and they begin to
> study one of the topics of the Torah, the laws of Marriage, Marital Contracts or
> Divorce [*Kiddushin, Ketuvot,* and *Gittin*], before the boy has learned the differ-
> ence between a male and a female [*mah beyn zakhar leneqevah*].[55]

Wessely's argument with the traditional curriculum was soon to become a familiar Haskalah refrain: children spend too much time on Talmud and too
little, or none at all, on the basics of biblical grammar. But he makes his case
with sharp wit, implying that the problem with studying the laws of marriage
and divorce before one knows Hebrew grammar—that is, the difference between masculine and feminine—is a sexual problem as well. In linking the
young boy's sexual/grammatical ignorance with the study of marriage law,
Wessely brings together two separate critiques of Jewish tradition, both of
which were to be fundamental planks in the Haskalah platform: the first, that
traditional Jewish education privileges the Talmud over the Bible and Hebrew
grammar; and the second, that Jewish adolescents are prematurely married
off, to the detriment of their sexual health.[56] Wessely's clever passage juxtaposes these two practices and implies that they are facets of the same inappropriate norms. Only grammar could help sort out what was both gender
confusion (not knowing the difference between masculine and feminine) and
premature sexuality (studying marriage law before puberty), creating a solid,
gradual, and rational foundation for a boy's sexual and linguistic maturation.

Mendelssohn's translation program was thus prescribed, only half jokingly, as a corrective to these practices—the prospectus for the translation is
called '*Alim letrufah* (Leaves for a cure). The remedy for traditional Judaism's
linguistic and sexual ailments is appropriate grammatical knowledge that

would also translate into appropriately gendered behavior. Mendelssohn, in his introduction, had mentioned only the Yiddish translations by Blitz and Witzenhaus rather than those Yiddish translations explicitly directed to women published earlier in the seventeenth century, the best known of which was the *Tsenerene*, a midrashic reworking of the Bible by Rabbi Jacob Ashkenazi. But at least a few of the later publishers of Mendelssohn's translation, when it had begun to penetrate deeper into the traditional Jewish world, saw it as a replacement specifically for the popular Yiddish translations addressed to women. The title page of the 1822 Basel edition of Mendelssohn's Pentateuch actually begins with the phrase "tse'eneh u-r'enah benot tsion," an invitation to the female reader to "come and see, O daughters of Zion" (Song of Songs), the phrase from which the *Tsenerene* took its title. The Sulzbach edition of 1810 had been perhaps even more direct, including a recommendation from the editor of Mendelssohn's translation as more refined and appropriate than the Yiddish "women's Bible": "One might argue that we already have a *Tsenerene*. This is true, and it is useful, too . . . but it is not suited for all, especially not half-grown girls, since its language is too corrupted and some passages are too lurid for the sensitivity of our morals."[57] It is startling to notice that, for the Enlighteners, traditional Judaism was *too* sexually coarse, and the model with which it was to be replaced was a restrained, bourgeois sexuality, in which young boys and girls were shielded from the "prurience" of the Talmud and traditional Jewish translations for women. Mendelssohn, we might recall, emphasized that he began translating the Pentateuch for his "male boy-children," perhaps to signal that despite appearances he had no intention of contributing to the traditional genre of translations for women or participating in an exegetical activity perceived as feminine. His translation staked out new territory for Jewish Bible translation, a German version of the Bible explicitly directed at (his own!) boys, and thus suitable for the newly growing Jewish middle class. Mendelssohn's project, then, contributed to the reformulation of traditional Jewish gender roles in the Enlightenment partly by investing translation itself with new intellectual prestige. There is some irony in the fact that Mendelssohn's traditional audience in the beginning of the nineteenth century returned him to the category of translations for women, even if as a clear improvement over his precursors in that field.

Analyzing the implicit model of Jewish identity presented in Mendelssohn's Bible, Gillman has noted that the translation closely mimics the traditional arrangement of text, translation, and commentary in the *Miqra'ot Gedolot*, the standard traditional edition of the Bible—later editions of the translation also included Rashi's commentary above Mendelssohn's *Bi'ur.* Through this and other strategies, Gillman writes, "Mendelssohn sought to mitigate the innovative nature of his work."[58] Mendelssohn's translation was supposed to appear thoroughly Jewish in order to disguise modern German values in traditional Jewish garb. Plaut sees it differently, however, arguing that the translation demonstrates that Mendelssohn wanted German Jews to be at home in German, but "while he desired their acculturation he did not wish their assimilation."[59] The "Jewish garb" of the translation was not a disguise but a proud affirmation of one facet of German-Jewish identity. In Plaut's model, the encounter between *Deutschtum* and *Judentum* is embodied in Mendelssohn's translation as a form of *Jewish* identity, in which Hebrew and German meet as linguistic equals across facing columns; in the Hebrew script in which the German is clothed, Mendelssohn also signaled that social equality could be achieved without Jews relinquishing their Jewish identity. Jews could thus be accepted if they aligned themselves with the rational principles of Enlightened life, using a well-spoken German and immersing themselves in a philosophically coherent Hebrew. Only under such conditions could a German-Jewish encounter take place, not in the mingling of languages that was Yiddish.

The difference between Gillman's approach and Plaut's, between a view of Mendelssohn's project that foregrounds its strategic duplicity and one that emphasizes Mendelssohn's striving for transparency and equality, mark a recurrent tension in Mendelssohn's biography and in the reception-history of his work. Mendelssohn championed the values of openness and tolerance but was himself compelled to live a life of circumspection. A related tension marks the reception of Mendelssohn's thought, dividing those who view Mendelssohn primarily from his own perspective and those who judge him in the larger perspective of German-Jewish history. From this second point of view, there is some significance to the fact that Mendelssohn's translation—particularly in its use of Hebrew characters for German but also in its rationalist-philosophical *Tendenz*—was largely obsolete within his own German-Jewish milieu within a decade or two of its publication, just as it is somehow relevant to Mendelssohn's philosophical project that four of his six children converted to Christianity after his death (one sense, at least, in which Mendelssohn was "the father of Jewish assimilation"). The translation embodied an approach to German-Jewish integration that had no lasting appeal: the generations of German Jews who followed him largely rejected Mendelssohn's approach to Judaism (as did his own children, for whom the translation was initially composed), either because his philosophical rationalism did not speak to their spiritual needs, or because they failed to see the value of religion altogether.

There is another perspective we can take on Mendelssohn's translation that avoids relying either on Mendelssohn's intentions or on the retrospective moralism that trots out Mendelssohn's four converted children as proof of the inefficacy of his project. The ambiguities of Mendelssohn's translation are lodged in the logic of the German-Jewish Enlightenment project itself, it seems to me. Alongside the rhetoric of cultural equality and religious tolerance, German Enlightenment discourse less openly takes part in the project of internal European colonialism, the civilizing mission to the Jews of which Mendelssohn can be called a "native agent." The eradication of Yiddish, the imposition of "proper" German expression, and the reconstruction of Jewish masculinity along Christian-European lines are all part of Mendelssohn's program (whether or not one terms this program assimilationist), and they stand in unavoidable conflict with the Enlightenment ideal of tolerance for cultural difference. These tensions worked themselves out at least partly through a strategy of displacement: some Jews might enter a German public sphere as equals, but only if Jewishness were localized in and abjected onto a "more Jewish" group. Yiddish speakers and *Ostjuden* (these categories, of course, overlapped) are exemplary in this regard. The syllogism can be reduced to its basic components: Jews deserved toleration (the Enlightenment ideal); at the same time, Jews had to show themselves worthy of toleration through the eradication of differences (the colonial subtext). It is crucial to add that the strategy of displacement by which this contradictory message expressed itself within Jewish discourse only partly succeeded in focusing antisemitic sentiments outside the circle of "good"—that is, acculturating—Jews.

Homi Bhabha, in his influential discussion of colonial discourse, has famously argued that colonialist taxonomies regularly produce not a clear separation between Self and Other but rather hybridity, "an interstitial space between fixed identifications."[60] It is precisely the *compliant* colonial subject, moreover, that generates this destabilizing effect, by expressing the split in the colonial presence "between its appearance as original and authoritative and its articulation as repetition and difference."[61] Bhabha's colonials are "almost the same but not quite," or—as Bhabha rewrites the phrase—"*almost the same but not white*";[62] the difference that begins in the mimicry required of colonials is nevertheless perceived by the colonizer as mockery or menace. This menacing hybridity is an effect not only of interstitial identities but also of language itself: The parade case of colonial doubling that Bhaba returns to again and again in his writing is the linguistic doubling that is translation, particularly the missionary translation that brought the Bible to Europe's colonies. Colonial translation inevitably opens itself to an "uncertain and threatening process of cultural transformation," for instance in the problem of conveying the importance of being "born again" to a people who all too readily accept the truth of reincarnation (the example is from A. Duff's 1839 *India and India Missions*). In such circumstances, Bhabha writes,

> The grounds of evangelical certitude are opposed not by the simple assertion of an antagonistic cultural tradition. The process of translation is the opening up of another contentious political and cultural site at the heart of colonial representation. Here the word of divine authority is deeply flawed by the assertion of the indigenous sign, and in the very practice of domination the language of the master becomes hybrid—neither the one thing nor the other. . . . The Word could no longer be trusted to carry the truth when written or spoken in the colonial world by the European missionary. Native catechists therefore had to be found, who brought with them their own cultural and political ambivalences and contradictions, often under great pressure from their families and communities.[63]

Bhabha need hardly point out that these "native catechists" inevitably produce new varieties of linguistic hybridity; in the very doubling of the sign lies its susceptibility not only to deliberate mistranslation but also to repetition as farce, to the slipperiness of language itself.

What is so striking about Mendelssohn's translation project is that it proceeds from a *resistance* to hybridity, or what Mendelssohn might call "the grievous mixture"; moreover, this project proceeded precisely through that interstitial space of translation. The German Jew, from the Enlightenment through National Socialism, was seen, of course, as a hybrid creature, "almost but not quite" German, in which some persistent reminder of the Jew's "Asiatic" or "Semitic" origins (often but not always linguistic) perpetually stymied full integration. Yiddish, in this cultural formation, both inhabits and represents the interstitial space of the European Jew, in which the Semitic language mingles grotesquely and intolerably with "pure" German to form a corrupt and corrupting "jargon." Jewish complicity in the European civilizing "mission to the Jews" thus understandably took the form of a series of displacements and abjections (projections out and "down") of this corrupt and contaminating mixture onto the Yiddish-speaking Jew, the Jewish underclass, the *Ostjude*. But the menace posed by German-Jewish difference was manifested not only in its blatant form—the distinctive garb and speech of traditional Jews—but also in its deferential form—the acculturated and German-speaking Jew who nevertheless represented a perhaps even more uncanny form of hybrid. That Mendelssohn's translation, in which German and Hebrew were symbolically differentiated and represented only in strictly policed grammatical form, nevertheless succumbed to the logic of hybridity is a linguistic manifestation of this same principle.

What the controversies over Mendelssohn's Bible demonstrate is that the linguistic phenomena of hybridity—the disruptive and unpredictable effects of colonial discourse—haunt German-Jewish translation both as motivation and effect, exciting the impulse to a translation that would separate and define the constituent parts of German-Jewish identity, as well as in the inevitable failures of this "purifying" project. In Mendelssohn's work, Yiddish, the most visible symbol of German-Jewish hybridity, has been swept not off the stage but rather under the rug—its effects continue to haunt. For all Mendelssohn's desire to substitute a transparent, rational discourse for the opacity and "immorality" of Yiddish, Mendelssohn's translational project, with its German wrapped in Hebraic garb and Mendelssohn's Hebrew-German double-talk, retains the whiff of the colonial subject's speech. Mendelssohn's translation, despite its "purity," remains almost but not quite German.

This hybridity extended to the sexual aspects of the translation. Mendelssohn's project was part of a more general Enlightenment program of reorganizing Jewish masculinity according to a series of linked European ideals: reason, grammar, and sexual restraint. It has been widely recognized that the Jewish man sought through a variety of techniques to "reinstate himself as manly in the terms of the masculinist European culture that had rejected and abused him."[64] Writing at the beginning of this process, however, Mendelssohn drew on a set of European gender norms different from those that animated *fin-de-siècle* German culture. Unlike those German Jews who turned to Zionism or psychoanalysis, Mendelssohn still lived within a Jewish culture in which "native" Jewish models of masculinity remained alive. Ezekiel Landau, chief rabbi of Prague, declined to give Mendelssohn's translation his approbation on the grounds that

> the narrator deeply immersed himself in the language using as he did an extremely difficult German that presupposes expertise in its grammar . . . it induces the young to spend their time reading Gentile books in order to become sufficiently familiar with refined German to be able to understand this translation. Our Torah is thereby reduced to the role of a maidservant to the German tongue.[65]

From the traditional standpoint, secular knowledge confers no great manliness on a young Jewish boy; only the deepest and most exclusive immersion

in the classical Jewish sources can serve that function. Hebrew was the signifier of the masculine, both as the language of male Jewish education and
in its dominant position in the hierarchy of languages. All other languages
properly serve it, in the feminine role of handmaiden/translation. To force
Hebrew into the role of helping readers master a secular tongue was an unnatural overturning of the religious as well as sexual order. In the process,
one might conclude, not only was the masculinity of Hebrew imperiled, but
also that of its traditionally male readers. Enlightenment was no road to
manliness for Jewish boys, but rather the very opposite!

A remarkably similar charge against Mendelssohn's translation was to
surface in the Zionist writings of Peretz Smoleskin, who also accused Mendelssohn of reducing Hebrew to the status of a maidservant for German—
although for Smoleskin, the insult was to Hebrew as the national language
of the Jewish people rather than as the Holy Tongue:

> [Mendelssohn took the Sacred Scriptures] which are the joy of the spirit and
> the glory of the house of Israel . . . and turned them into "confectioners and
> cooks" [1 Samuel 8:13] for the German language. Mendelssohn used the Holy
> Scriptures as a passage to the German language. This is Ben-Menachem [Men-
> delssohn], who set aside the Talmud and desecrated the honor of the Torah,
> making her a despised handmaiden [shifḥah nevazah] to teach by means of it the
> German language.[66]

In Landau's and Smoleskin's rhetoric, Mendelssohn's recruitment of Hebrew
to the service of German is both a class demotion and a sexual degradation
of the Jewish male (the "confectioners and cooks" of Smoleskin's biblical citation refer to the service of captured Israelite *women*). If Mendelssohn had
hoped to construct a proper Jewish masculinity in the face of the corrupt notions of gender in traditional Jewish society, he had ended merely by emas-
culating Jews again in his deference to German norms. The controversy over
Mendelssohn's translation is thus a classic manifestation of the double bind
of colonial discourse: Jewish men who do not capitulate to the European
model are deemed effeminate, even (in the antisemitic fantasy about circumcision) castrated, but to acculturate is to play the subservient role to the dominant group, to acknowledge its continuing power of judgment. Sander
Gilman describes the colonialist imperative in these terms: "Become like
us—abandon your difference—and you may be one with us"; but "The more
you are like me, the more I know the true value of my power, which you wish
to share, and the more I am aware that you are but a shoddy counterfeit."[67]
Drawing upon Bhabha's insight that the colonizer is undone by this impera-

tive as well, we can continue: "And the more I see myself mirrored in you, a Jew, the stranger and more unnatural do I seem to myself." The juxtaposition of Hebrew and German, German and Jew in acculturation and translation threatens the integrity of both national language and national identity.

Mendelssohn had attempted to produce a Bible translation in which his correct German would serve as soothing evidence that the Jews were suitable and respectful participants in the intellectual society of Enlightenment Berlin. Buber and Rosenzweig, a century and a half later, intended the very opposite effect; as Leora Batnitzky has it, their translation "aimed to produce shocked attention in its readers" in its strangeness and difference.[68] Batnitzky's point is that Buber and Rosenzweig hoped to unsettle all that was overly familiar about the Bible in its readers, but the shock to the familiar idioms of German certainly functioned equally as a social-political gesture: the Buber-Rosenzweig Bible was no Jewish apologetic, arguing that Jews and Germans were not, after all, so very different from one another (for example in the vein of Hermann Cohen's claim that Judaism was just a particularly refined form of Kantianism). It was part of their rebellion against what they saw as the timid assimilationism of their fathers and teachers that Buber and Rosenzweig outrightly rejected the suggestion that Jews were like Germans, if not more so. Buber and Rosenzweig rather "set out to dramatize the apparent chasm between contemporary German culture and those ancient Hebrew 'origins' that Jews claimed as their own," Peter Gordon writes.[69] If the German language could be enriched and expanded by making room for Hebrew at its most foreign, German culture could surely benefit from the inclusion of Jews precisely at their most different and alien. The strongest argument for the acceptance of Jews in German culture was not the *similarity* of Jews to Germans but rather their *difference*. There is an obvious irony in the transformation of this motif: it was precisely when the distinctions between Germans and Jews had largely faded that these differences accumulated their greatest symbolic capital, if only among Jews.

If the Buber-Rosenzweig Bible can be read as a moment of colonial resistance in contrast with Mendelssohn's colonial deference, then it too can be shown to succumb to the logic of hybridity. Mendelssohn's mimicry of "good" German produced a kind of Yiddish; Buber and Rosenzweig's resistance to proper German registered in at least one important strand of its reception not as uncannily foreign but rather as uncannily familiar—a kind of hyper-German. Bhabha's own focus is on the first of these dialectics, that of mimicry that is perceived as mockery. But Daniel Boyarin has shown that Bhabha's hybridity functions as well in the opposite case, in the moment of colonial rebellion that is also a moment of inadvertent mimicry; Zionism, the anti-colonial discourse of European Jews, thus recapitulates the very colonialist discourse it resists.

Like the Zionist mimicry of European nationalisms, Buber and Rosenzweig's anti-colonial insistence on foreignizing and Hebraizing German might be yet another apparently resistant "moment that forgets its own mimicry."[70] That the Buber-Rosenzweig translation inevitably imitated the discourse it aimed to destabilize is clear whether we accept Kracauer's charge that Buber and Rosenzweig reproduced the "stench" of Wagner's runes; or argue, with Lawrence Rosenwald and Abigail Gillman, that their Bible mimics the dissonances and directness of modernist poetry;[71] or that, as Peter Gordon has it, Buber and Rosenzweig enacted a Hebraist version of Heidegger's "return" to the Greek. To put this somewhat differently: Hebraist modernism itself has strong non-Jewish roots; as Gordon points out in arguing for the relevance of understanding the work of Rosenzweig within the German philosophical tradition, "The very notion of Jewish difference derives from sources outside the Jewish orbit."[72] All this is perhaps simply to say that the Buber-Rosenzweig Bible is translated from Hebrew into *German*, the German of its time—and it could hardly have been otherwise. In the fervor of their expressed loyalty to the Hebrew, Buber and Rosenzweig seem almost to have forgotten this.

My goal here is not to demonstrate yet again the seemingly universal applicability of Bhabha's hybridity theory but rather to illuminate a certain double bind in German-Jewish translation. This translation emerged within a distinctive cultural and philosophical situation with a number of contradictory strands. First, German Jews entered modernity in part by moving away from Hebrew and Yiddish, the Jewish languages. The language they adopted brought with it a linguistic ideology that insisted on the powerful bonds between people, soil, and language, a linguistic philosophy that bolstered as it undermined German-Jewish translation. German Romantic translation theory imagined that German was peculiarly capable of enriching itself through an encounter with the foreign, as Schleiermacher had suggested. But Jews were both too foreign (Semites rather than Greeks) and not foreign enough ("almost but not quite" German) to find their easy place within this philosophical current. German-Jewish translation thus took shape as a kind of cultural paradox—evidence for and against an organicist conception of national language, for and against the German capacity to enrich itself through cross-cultural and interlingual encounter. Both Jews and Germans were invested in these notions of an organic connection between people and language. But what the rhetoric of toleration and integration as of purity and nation could not account for were the hybrid formations, the translational mixtures, that were the inevitable expression of modern German as of German-Jewish culture.

THE POLITICS OF BREATH

While Buber and Rosenzweig weighed in on the important questions of the day, they were not eager to associate their translation work with contemporary political concerns. Buber's writings on translation barely mention the gathering Nazi storm clouds under which the work was commencing. Nevertheless, the political challenge was put to Buber and Rosenzweig immediately upon the publication of the first volume of their Bible, in the review by Kracauer that charged that their archaicizing Wagnerianism, their national romanticism (*völkischer Romantik*) "veers away from the public sphere of our social existence and into the private."[73] For Kracauer, the very notion of a contemporary Bible translation was sheer anachronism, an abdication of the public intellectual's responsibility to address the pressing issues of the day. In their published response, Buber and Rosenzweig refused Kracauer's challenge to demonstrate the relevance of their work to Weimar political discourse. If their translation was in any degree relevant to the political climate in which it was composed, they signaled this only by the subtlest choice of words, arguing that the Bible "will speak to all times, at all times, and do so in *defiance* of all times" (jeder Zeit zum Trotz).[74] Instead of entering into a debate on contemporary matters, Buber and Rosenzweig took recourse to the Hebrew text itself, claiming that it was solely their fidelity to the text, and not an allegiance to German style of one sort or another, that had dictated their translational choices. Elsewhere Buber and Rosenzweig repeated this line of argument, countering criticism of their translation by insisting on the integrity of their translation as faithful to the Hebrew, as emerging from the Bible as it was and had always been. The closeness of their engagement with, indeed identification with, the Hebrew provided a route to sidestep the question of what sort of *German* text they had produced, as well as the larger question of how their translation fit in with their own situation as German Jews, as Weimar intellectuals, as philosophers and literary modernists. Their translation *was* the Bible, and it spoke not from within their milieu but as if from utterly outside it.

Even the Jewish aspects of their translation are curiously muted in this discourse. Buber did speak forthrightly in 1938 about the translation as a

Jewish replacement of Luther's Bible, but in earlier writing, Buber and Rosenzweig accord Luther the status of a respected precursor, whose engagement with the Hebrew Bible enacted an authentic *hieros gamos;* their own translation represented not a *Jewish* alternative to Luther's Bible but rather its *modern* counterpart. Rosenzweig spoke of the Bible as a long and continuous conversation between humanity and God, not distinguishing between Paul's and Augustine's role and his own. The Jewish character of their Bible, to the extent that it was acknowledged, was significant insofar as it would make it attractive beyond the borders of the Jewish community; indeed, the commissioning of the Bible by a Christian publisher was among the factors that initially recommended the project to Buber.

Nevertheless, as Plaut and others have argued, the Buber-Rosenzweig Bible of course does indeed embody a political stance within a particular historical circumstance. In Plaut's view, Buber might not have spoken openly about the "unfavorable metaphysical and sociological situation" of the time, but his position can be gleaned clearly enough from the work itself. "Now, nearly sixty years later," Plaut writes, "one can remove the veil from their circumlocution. They knew that they were creating *a translation that Hebraized the German language. Theirs was a work of defiance, as much as it was a work of utter loyalty to the original.*"[75] Plaut adds in a note that he does not intend to represent Rosenzweig, who died in 1929, as a resister of Nazism *avant la lettre.* It is interesting to recognize, however, that Rosenzweig articulated clearly enough what he thought Jewish defiance meant in the realm of the Bible. In the last of his published writing, a review of the third and fourth volumes of the *Encyclopedia Judaica,* Rosenzweig notes with surprise and approval the practice in the *Encyclopedia* of referring to "what is commonly called the Old Testament" simply as the Bible. "But this fact," Rosenzweig writes, "which came about quite simply without being solicited, shows how the old Jewish defiance, the eternal reservation against visible, all-too-visible world history, proclaims itself, in the middle of this most modern Jewish work, in favor of the invisible."[76] For Rosenzweig, Jewish defiance is the rejection of the "visible world" in favor of what cannot be clearly discerned in history; but it is evident from the example he gives that this defiance is *at the same time* also resistance to a Christian perspective on the Bible—rendered visible in and as history—in which, Rosenzweig continues, "our own is not the whole." The politics of defiance of the Buber-Rosenzweig Bible therefore goes beyond the project of substituting a Jewish-hebraizing Bible for Luther's Christian-domesticating Bible, as their project is often conceptualized. It was not a "Jewish" Bible they published but *the* Bible, making its claim not from the confines of the Jewish tradition but from outside and "above" the Jewish–Christian divide that is history itself. And theirs was a politics that expressed itself specifically as a resistance to inhabiting the realm of the political "in favor of the invisible."

In this section of the chapter, I will be arguing for the political significance of perhaps the most invisible dimension of the Bible—that of breath, or "spirit." I have already had occasion in this work to trace the long historical associations made in translation discourse between, on the one hand, Jews and the letter and law of the biblical texts, and between Christians and its living spirit, on the other. While patristic writers had separated the spirit and the sense of the text from its written form taken as a whole, advances in the study of the biblical text led to a series of refinements of this opposition. As Maurice Olender has shown of the nineteenth-century study of linguistics, philology and biblical anthropology often drew on old Judeophobic paradigms even as they expanded the reach of these sciences beyond their religious origins.[77] In the field of biblical criticism, the Christian Hebraist discovery that the traditional Jewish vocalization and accents of the Bible were more recent than the consonantal text itself prompted some scholars to map the old theological opposition of letter and spirit onto the new scientific one of consonants and vowels. This is not a purely Christian move; the association between the Hebrew vowels and breath, spirit, and soul appears already in the *Zohar,* the classic work of medieval Jewish mysticism. In the seventeenth century, Spinoza lent this tradition scientific heft:

> In Hebrew the vowels are not letters. That is why the Hebrews say that "vowels are the soul of letters" and that letters without vowels are "bodies without soul." In truth, the difference between letters and vowels can be explained more clearly by taking the example of the flute, which is played by the fingers. The vowels are the sound of the music; the letters are the holes touched by the fingers.[78]

Although Spinoza does not make the analogy explicit, the "sound of the music" is also the breath as it is shaped by the flute. Jewish tradition considered itself the owner and player of the whole flute, breathing the soul into the "body" of the consonants as it shaped this breath through the medium of the letters. Such a conception of breath as a crucial aspect of language is also implicit in rabbinic writings; in Onkelos's translation of Genesis 2:7, for instance, the breath of God infuses Adam not only with life but also with the capacity for language (*va-ḥavat be-'adam le-ruaḥ memalelah*). Although the Masoretes had fixed the vowels and accents only in the sixth or perhaps seventh century CE, the pronunciation they recorded was an integral (if no

doubt shifting) part of the biblical text, transmitted—appropriately enough—
through the living sounds of oral tradition.

By contrast, Christian theologians sometimes took the distinction between the (ancient, true, mute) consonant and the (invisible, distorted, rabbinic) Hebrew vowel as a screen on which to project their views of Jews and
Judaism, ancient and modern. Ernest Renan, who abandoned the seminary
at Saint-Sulpice to devote himself to Hebrew philology, saw the consonantal
character of Hebrew writing as key to the Israelite mentality. In his *General
History and Comparative System of the Semitic Languages,* Renan writes that the
languages in which monotheism was first formulated, with their invisible
vowels, were impervious "rock through which no infiltration has been able
to penetrate," and thus the foundation for what Renan saw as the peculiar religious stubbornness of the Jews.[79]

Other scholars focused less on the peculiar characteristics of Hebrew
script than on what seemed to them the evident fact that, given its lack of
vowels, the true pronunciation of the Hebrew Bible had been forgotten. The
eighteenth-century Oxford professor Robert Lowth sketched out the resul-
tant difficulties for Hebraist scholarship at the beginning of his "Lectures on
the Sacred Poetry of the Hebrews":

> It is indeed evident that the true Hebrew pronunciation is totally lost. The rules
> concerning it, which were devised by the modern Jews many ages after the lan-
> guage of their ancestors had fallen into disuse, have been long since suspected
> by the learned to be destitute of authority and truth: for if in reality the Hebrew
> language is to be conformed to the position of these men, we must be under the
> necessity of confessing, not only, what we at present experience, that the Hebrew
> poetry possesses no remains of sweetness or harmony, but that it never was pos-
> sessed of any.[80]

Comparing Hebrew to ancient Greek or Latin, the correct pronunciation of
which had also been forgotten, Lowth continues, "The state of Hebrew is far
more unfavourable, which destitute of vowel sounds, has remained altogether silent (if I may use the expression) and incapable of utterance upward
of two thousand years."[81] Nevertheless, the very muteness of the Hebrew consonants of Scripture represented both an obstacle to full appreciation of the
text and a God-given opportunity. Once the Masoretic vowels had been recognized as the late, human contribution of diaspora Jews, Christian scholars
could reinvest the Hebrew text with meaning without following "blindly
those blind guides, the Jewish doctors."[82] Olender summarizes Lowth's insight: "The vowels could now sing in Christian tones."[83]

I will argue in what follows that among the major contributions of the Buber-Rosenzweig Bible is the reshaping of the discourse on the Hebrew letter into a new configuration which, while resisting anti-Jewish motifs in this discourse, drew only selectively from traditional Jewish perspectives. The Buber-Rosenzweig Bible is sometimes described as reversing the mainstream Christian translation valuation of spirit over letter, target text over source. But Buber and Rosenzweig did not merely transvalue literalism, privileging the letter over the sense or spirit of the text; they did something different and more complex. Arguing for the original Hebrew inextricability of spirit and letter (or word, since the German term for literalism is *Wörtlichkeit*), breath and body, they further targeted this very dichotomizing as the pernicious source of modern malaise. The Hebrew word, for Buber and Rosenzweig, is the root and source of spirit, understood as both meaning and breath. The implications of this approach could hardly be more ambitious: Jewish hermeneutics, in all its peculiarities and specifically at the level of the Hebrew word, nevertheless addressed the most general and urgent anguish of the human condition.

For Rosenzweig, Buber's most important contribution to their collaborative process was his keen ear for the orality of Scripture, which Buber felt must never be subsumed to its written dimension or fettered by punctuation. This applied as well to the traditional Jewish accents and vowels: although these were crucial aspects of scriptural orality, the punctuation indicated by the Masoretic system, Rosenzweig argued, had never been intended as anything other than a guide from which commentators "may and must in all modesty be permitted to diverge."[84] What was needed above all was a reading of the text based on the natural rhythms of speech:

> The bond of the tongue must be loosed by the eye. We must free from beneath the logical punctuation that is sometimes its ally and sometimes its foe the fundamental principle of natural, oral punctuation: the act of breathing.
>
> Breath is the stuff of speech; the drawing of breath is accordingly the natural segmenting of speech. It is subject to its own law . . . which for the most part mirrors directly the movements and arousals of the soul itself in its gradations of energy and above all in its gradations of time.[85]

For all Rosenzweig's emphasis on the rhythms of breath and speech, he is careful to deny that he envisions the Bible as poetry or song. It is the inner logic of the words, falling differently into short or long units, not the enraptured meters of poetry that generations of theologians and philologists had heard in the Bible, that structures the Hebrew text. In the Bible, "The inwardly rhythmic speech of the word wins out over the discrete pulses of the song; prose wins out over poetry." Rosenzweig continues:

> For poetry is indeed the mother tongue of the human race; we need not reject here the insights of Hamann and Herder. But *only* of the race . . . one day—and afterwards no one knows what day it has been—through the original language of the human race breaks the language of humanity in the human being, the language of the word. The Bible is the hoard of this language of the human being because it is prose.[86]

The Bible is not "the song of a race," it is the prosaic breath of the human being qua human, beyond racial difference. In keeping with this notion of the Bible as prose, separated into breath-units or cola expressive precisely because they are of unequal length, the Buber-Rosenzweig Bible is laid out on the page with wide margins and lines of different length. What this Bible resembles, as Lawrence Rosenwald has pointed out, is not so much prose as the free verse form of modernist poetry, rather than the more metrical and "racial" Wagnerian song whose disagreeably overwrought tones Kracauer had caught. Moreover, it is not the alliterative techniques that Wagner used to create a wash of sound but rather the roots of the Hebrew word, and the word itself, that carried the biblical message. The word, Rosenzweig hauntingly wrote, is the "gate into the nocturnal silence that enveloped the human race at its origins." I would emphasize here Rosenzweig's view of the importance of the word for "the human race." The word in Rosenzweig is not the site of opacity and linguistic difference, the place where mutual differences are most profoundly felt, in the way it has traditionally functioned in translation theory. Rosenzweig acknowledges that "the aerial view of a language's verbal landscape seems at first glance severed and radically diverse from that of every other language." The sense that languages are different from one another, Rosenzweig continues, is not heightened but rather dissolved in a closer—radically closer—view:

> The picture alters only through a more geological approach. In the roots of words the severed areas lie together; and still deeper, at the roots of meaning, the roots of physicality, there is, apart from questions regarding some possible original relatedness of languages, the unity of all human speech which the surfaces of words only let us dimly intuit.[87]

The place where languages meet is not the abstracted and "higher" *sense* but rather the word reduced to its deepest structure, which is both the linguistic root and the root of "physicality" itself. By contrast, Aristotle and Augustine had sent sense and word, meaning and physicality, down two separate tracks. For Buber and Rosenzweig, the translator must follow these winding roots in "the veins of the text itself," rather than discovering dictionary equivalents for each separate word. In the theory of the *Leitwort*, the "leading" word, it is the internal repetition of the word or word-root that provides the privileged, if subterranean, path to the Bible's meaning.

Literalist translation is here understood not in terms of rendering the biblical text through a word-for-word technique, nor as rendering the "plain sense" of the text, but rather as keeping close to the Hebrew word in its recurrence, in the word-play of names, in the "physicality" of its base-meaning. In one particularly notable explanation of their technique, Rosenzweig calls Luther to their defense. Luther had taken care to keep close to the Hebrew at particularly crucial points of the Hebrew Bible, when Christological passages were at stake; Rosenzweig argues that he and Buber adhere to Luther's method for *every* word of the Bible, since the entire Bible is potentially meaningful to the modern readers, who are (in Buber's words, now) "open," not knowing "from what place the spirit will foam up and pass into them."[88] Lawrence Rosenwald has this exactly right: Rosenzweig never defends this aspect of their technique as the traditional *Jewish* approach to the Bible as sacred in its entirety rather than at moments of Christological import. That is, the contrast both Buber and Rosenzweig separately draw between Luther's Bible and their own is not, "Luther was translating as a Christian, we are translating as Jews, our translations differ accordingly"; the contrast drawn is rather "between now and then." As Rosenwald concludes, "the translation is presented not as Jewish but as modern, not as sectarian but as universal."[89] In describing their translation technique as the only adequate response to the modern world in which they are working, Buber and Rosenzweig also accomplish another feat: they produce an apologia for literalism that severs its long associations with the imputed rigid legalism and archaic esotericism of Jewish tradition and links it rather to the open, questioning modern moment.

This submerged argument involves more than just the question of proper translation technique. At the core of the Buber-Rosenzweig project is the insistence that *Geist* cannot be separated from life, breath from spirit; nor should *Geist* be relegated to the sphere of the intellect, as in modern uses of the term. "The 'Old Testament' teaches the sacred marriage of *Geist* and life; it accordingly rejects both all enslavement of life to *Geist* and all humbling of *Geist* before life. It has, then, even here and now the power to help people today in their deepest need."[90] Discussing the problem of translating the Hebrew word *ruaḥ*, Buber insists that "the translation must let us feel how a spiritual divine act and a natural divine act are relating to each other." This recognition of the relatedness of spirit, wind and breath is necessary

> because since the time of Luther, who had to choose between *Geist* and *Wind*, *Geist* has lost its original concreteness—a concreteness it had in company with *ruah,* with *pneuma,* with *spiritus* itself—lost its original sensory character— "a surging and a blowing simultaneously.". . . This splitting of a fundamental word is not merely a process in the history of language but also a process in the history of *Geist* and life, namely the incipient separation between *Geist* and life.[91]

Buber concludes, "I have lingered over this first example in order to show what guiding power can lie in a single biblical word if we will only pursue it earnestly and commit ourselves to it."[92]

I do not mean to imply that Buber and Rosenzweig took Jewish linguistic philosophy and passed it off as modernism or vice versa. Their approach draws on both existentialist philosophical trends and certain aspects of Jewish attitudes toward language and translation, but these appear in their work in new combinations and surprisingly transformed. In particular, the notion that Hebrew roots at their most profound depths meet those of other languages perhaps extends the idea that Hebrew perfectly conforms with reality or with divine speech itself—but it is also a radical reformulation of this idea. Similarly, Buber and Rosenzweig move beyond Heidegger's obsessive valorization of a single language—Greek in his case. Rabbinic texts sometimes use Hebrew roots to demonstrate this conformity with reality, but at the expense of other languages, in which such perfection is not evident: *Midrash Genesis Rabbah* thus bases its argument that Hebrew must have been the language of creation on the similarity between the Hebrew words for man and woman:

> "She shall be called woman (*ishah*) because she was taken out of man (*ish*)" (Gen. 2:23). R. Pinhas and R. Hilkiah say in the name of R. Simon: Just as the Torah was given in the sacred tongue, so was the world created with the sacred tongue. Have you ever heard anyone say *gune, gunya; anthrope, anthropia, gavra, gavrata*? But *ish* and *ishah* are used. Why? Because the forms correspond to each other.[93]

Unlike Greek and Aramaic, where the terms for man and woman are markedly different, the closeness of these terms in Hebrew proves that Creation must have mobilized that language—since puns are notoriously untranslatable, Genesis 2:23 could hardly have been uttered in any language but Hebrew. What is implicit in this rabbinic passage is the further assumption that Hebrew—and only Hebrew—uniquely corresponds with creation—that is, with reality. Buber and Rosenzweig would certainly have enjoyed this rabbinic attention to the repetition of word-roots in the construction of biblical meaning, and indeed they rendered it explicit by translating the verse with a transliteration of the crucial Hebrew words, since German, like Greek and Aramaic, provides no such convenient word-play (although English does!):

> Die sei gerufen
> Ischa, Weib,
> denn von Isch, vom Mann, ist die genommen.[94]

Nevertheless, the Buber-Rosenzweig approach must be sharply differentiated from the rabbinic one. For Buber and Rosenzweig, the perfection of Hebrew, its union of the physical with meaning itself, provides the path that leads toward similar qualities inherent in other human languages (even if they could discover no underground channel to German for Genesis 2:23). But their universalist approach to language must also be distinguished from the more normative universalism of translation discourse. In Buber and Rosenzweig, the path to all human languages is emblematized by and channeled through the peculiar characteristics, the specific roots and physical "rootedness," of the Hebrew tongue.

The very refusal of Buber and Rosenzweig to take an overtly political stance in their writings on the Bible, to address contemporary concerns or even suggest the Jewish character of their work, is part and parcel of this approach. Only the most profound engagement with the Hebrew text can yield its message, but once it emerges, it speaks to each individual reader and to an entire era and beyond. The Bible could only speak to their audience if it did so from within the density and peculiarity of its Hebrew sources; precisely this attention to the word represented the best hope for a generation's spiritual renewal. For Buber and Rosenzweig to have openly engaged in the debate to which history has subjected their work would have been to mistranslate, to limit the force and universality of the Bible itself.

BERLIN-ALEXANDRIA

Among the ways in which critics have attempted to make sense of Benjamin's notoriously difficult 1923 essay, "The Task of the Translator," has been to read in the light of the Jewish mystical language philosophy Benjamin learned from his friend and idiosyncratic interpreter of this tradition, Gershom Scholem. Although his own major essays on the topic were not published until the 1970s, Scholem had long been interested in the subject of language within the Jewish mystical tradition and had at some point intended to write his dissertation on this subject; he shared his excitement about this research with Benjamin over the years of their friendship.

Certainly there are striking parallels between a number of *topoi* in Benjamin's writings and Scholem's later formulations of Jewish mystical language philosophy; the assumption that Scholem "influenced" Benjamin has given way, in recent work, to the view that the two thinkers mutually shaped each other's view of language, even if Scholem's work on this topic is presented as historical analysis while Benjamin's belongs to what might be called "constructive" literary theory. Benjamin's memorable image of translation as the careful fitting together of "fragments of a vessel which are to be glued together" (Scherben eines Gefässes um sich zusammenfügen zu lassen) and which thus must "follow one another in the smallest detail, although they need not be like one another,"[95] may be utterly new within the limited repertoire of figures for translation, but it is strikingly reminiscent of the Lurianic doctrine of *tiqqun*,[96] in which the mystic "repairs" a broken cosmos by piecing together the shards—including the language shards—of God's creation.[97] Benjamin's *reine Sprache,* the pure language contained within languages and toward which all languages and translations strive, has been linked with similar notions in French symbolism or the German language philosophy of Humboldt and Hamann, but it also appears as a modernist addition to the long history of mystical and theological speculation (Jewish and Christian both) about a language in some way more perfect or higher than ordinary speech—a divine language, a Holy Tongue, the *Logos* itself. Indeed, in his 1916 essay "On Language as Such and the Language of Man," Benjamin borrowed directly from this mystical-theological discourse, speaking of a language of creation and a language that links God's with human language, most ideally in the act of naming.[98] In "The Task of the Translator," pure language has a similarly transcendent function, even if the connection with a religious linguistics of a specific variety is harder to draw. Benjamin seems to invite a religious reading: there is, and not only in the passage that translates translation into *tiqqun,* a strong whiff of the messianic to the essay. Thus, "If languages continue to grow . . . until the end of their messianic time, it is translation that catches fire on the eternal life of the works and the perpetual renewal of language"; as Benjamin also writes, translation liberates "the language imprisoned in a work."[99] Even the critic who has most forcefully resisted such a "Jewish" reading of Benjamin's essay, Paul de Man, acknowledges that "at first sight, Benjamin would appear as highly regressive. He would appear as messianic, prophetic, religiously messianic."[100]

Most generally, perhaps, Benjamin's thinking on language and translation is characterized by an interest in the nature of language outside of referential communication, an interest paramount as well in Scholem's formulation of mystical language philosophy. In "The Name of God and the Linguistic Theory of the Kabbala," Scholem writes that all mystics, in all religious traditions, share a sense

> that language is used to communicate something that goes way beyond the sphere which allows for expression and formation. . . . The mystic discovers in language a quality of dignity, a dimension inherent to itself, as one might phrase it at the present time: something pertaining to its structure which is not adjusted to a communication of what is communicable, but rather—and all symbolism is founded on this paradox—to a communication of what is non-communicable, of that which exists within it for which there is no expression; and even if it could be expressed, it would in no way have any meaning, or any communicable "sense."[101]

Whether or not Scholem indeed captured something crucial about mystical linguistics, this language philosophy applies closely to Benjamin's description of the special language that emerges through translation. "To regain pure language," Benjamin writes,

> is the tremendous and only capacity of translation. In this pure language— which no longer means or expresses anything but is—as expressionless and creative Word, that which is meant in all languages—all information, all sense, and all intention finally encounter a stratum in which they are destined to be extinguished.[102]

Even the trajectory of Benjamin's two central essays on language, the 1916 "On Language" and the 1923 "Task of the Translator," mirrors the development of Jewish mysticism from the earlier theosophic speculations of the *Book of Creation* and the *Zohar*, which focus on God's creative-linguistic power through a close reading of "the alphabet of creation," to the Lurianic turn in the sixteenth century—after the exile from Spain—from creation to redemption. "On Language" begins with the role of language in creation, mining biblical territory in its search for the origins of language and the roots of its present fallen state; "The Task of the Translator" is impelled by the exilic swerve of translation itself toward the pure language that is the messianic aim of translation. Benjamin thus retraces the cosmogenic and messianic antipodes of Jewish mystical-linguistic thought, finally discovering in translation the redemptive potential of a language sundered from its wholeness at creation.

It would be wrong, however, to simply imagine Benjamin to be an acolyte of Scholem's or otherwise subsume Benjamin's work to the Jewish tradition, as has been vociferously argued by de Man among others. Denouncing the notion that Benjamin can be read in the light of a messianic tradition, de Man writes that "the man who bears a strong responsibility in this unhappy interpretation of Benjamin is Scholem, who deliberately tried to make Benjamin say the opposite of what he said for ends of his own."[103] De Man's view seems to be that attention to the kabbalistic and messianic echoes of Benjamin's work obscures what he sees as Benjamin's nihilistic conception of fragments that never ultimately cohere, that is, of translation that necessarily and inevitably fails; invoking the Messiah amidst such irredeemable shards constitutes a peculiarly postmodern sacrilege. It is true enough, though, that even before Benjamin's (also heterodox and idiosyncratic) adoption of a Marxist-historical materialist program in the early 1930s, Benjamin's interests and concerns only partly overlapped with those of his friend; and even if Benjamin did borrow a formulation or two from Scholem's analysis of mystical language philosophy, he certainly brought them into radically new territory. Whether or not the Jewish mystical tradition underlies Benjamin's thought on translation in the way (to use the analogy Benjamin draws in "Theses on the Philosophy of History") that the wizened hunchback that is theology manipulates the puppet of history from inside the chess table, the very transformation and concealment of this tradition in Benjamin renders it nearly something else altogether.[104]

It is unnecessary to rehearse here the unseemly dispute over Benjamin's legacy, the custody battle between the Jewish studies crowd and the Marxists, the theologians and the poststructuralists, that is itself a replay of the tug-of-war during Benjamin's lifetime between Scholem and Brecht. My aim is rather to expand the discussion of Benjamin's relation to the Jewish tradition beyond its ubiquitous elements: the friendship with Scholem and the fragments of kabbalistic linguistics sparked by this friendship. Aside from these touchstones, Benjamin has not been situated within a (necessarily fragmentary and ambivalent) history of Jewish translation, no doubt because such a history has rarely been advanced. The question of whether Benjamin would have known very much of this history need hardly detain us. The configurations—constellations—of Jewish translation emerge as much from political-cultural conditions as from texts, from the "sickening of tradition" that Benjamin saw in Kafka's writing as from its coherence and wholeness.

To bring the "politics of Jewish translation" to a discussion of Benjamin's writings on language and translation implies yet a further intervention. The dichotomies at play in the reception of Benjamin's work—which were visible to Benjamin himself—distinguish between his Jewish or "theological" affiliations (emblematized by Benjamin's friendship with Scholem) and his political, Marxist affiliations (emblematized by his friendship with Brecht). These dual affinities do come together in the secularized messianism that manifests itself most clearly in the last of Benjamin's essays, the "Theses on the Philosophy of History." But the political ramifications of Benjamin's writings about translation—or indeed, of Jewish mystical linguistics—have often been overlooked. Tejaswini Niranjana's postcolonial reading of "The Task of the Translator" is an exception in this regard, arguing that Benjamin's investment in history has been obscured in the dominant poststructuralist readings of the texts, de Man's above all. As Niranjana sees it, de Man reads Benjamin so that "'history' becomes just a 'linguistic complication,'" turning "the political into the poetical."[105] Niranjana deftly juxtaposes the liberating potential of translation with the redeeming of history accomplished by the historical materialist in "Theses on the Philosophy of History" to argue that Benjamin had similarly messianic goals in mind for translation and the reading of history "against the grain." Niranjana's primary concern is with combating a variety of poststructuralism (now much less dominant) that views politics and history as naively mimetic concerns; ultimately, she turns to Benjamin for a translation theory that combines a postrepresentational view of language with a call for radical political practice—specifically, literalist translation in the postcolonial setting. While I consider Niranjana's insights into Benjamin invaluable, I would strongly argue with her assumption that the Jewish echoes in Benjamin's language philosophy must be distinguished from his political aims. Niranjana writes that "although 'The Task of the Translator' draws heavily on Judaic conceptions of language, it is at the same time pointing forward to a secular notion of redemption as the function of translation."[106] The word "although" in this sentence (along with what is implied in "pointing forward") places her alongside de Man as judging all that is "Judaic" in Benjamin as apolitical, conservative, or even (as de Man has it) "highly regressive," and so to be isolated from what is truly revolutionary in Benjamin, whether that is construed as his politics (as it is for Niranjana) or as his linguistic nihilism (as it is for de Man).

The philosophy of language at play in Benjamin is *already* "political," I would argue, and precisely in its connection with "Judaic conceptions of language." Moreover, it is political in a postcolonialist sense Niranjana would recognize as related to her own project. Scholem did not doubt the revolutionary force of the Jewish mystical tradition, even in its most abstruse formulations; indeed, it was this power that attracted him to the field. Nevertheless, in the Benjamin reception the "theological" linguistics evident in such notions as a pure language or the absolute translatability of divine writ are often distinguished from those aspects of Benjamin's text that are viewed as radical—whether this religious dimension is glossed over in embarrassment (see, for instance, the end of de Man's lecture) or treated as a separate area of investigation. That these "theological" motifs and biblical references are part and parcel of Benjamin's concern for political action in the world, that the brokenness of language and the violence of history belong to the same dynamic and call for the same translation practice, has not been seriously entertained. The argument throughout this book has been, however, that conceptions of language—however "religious" they may appear—cannot be isolated from the power structures in which they arise and to which they respond; theology itself, from this perspective, is both a translational and political site.

Among the attractions of Benjamin's translation theory to such poststructuralists as not only de Man but also Derrida is its forceful rejection of the traditional theory of signification on which translation has rested at least since Augustine. In Benjamin's account, translation is not accomplished through the isolation of a signified common to both languages, but rather through the careful articulation of radically different signifiers; the freedom of Benjamin's translator lies in an abandonment of meaning altogether and in the pure focus on the distinctive contours of each separate language. But although Benjamin's essay places him as a precursor of poststructuralist translational "difference," it also situates him within the mainstream of the Jewish countertradition I have been tracing in this book. Benjamin shares with the rabbinic tradition a focus on the distinctiveness of languages, the construction of a linguistic world in which languages are not all roughly equivalent and interchangeable media. I am suggesting that there is at least a family resemblance between the rabbinic notion of the Holy Tongue (as well as other divine languages) and those Benjamin posits, from the language of Creation and its closest human derivation in the language of naming to the "pure language" toward which all translation strives. Despite this shared conceptual structure, Benjamin's notion of a higher language, and of the absolute differences between languages, swerves from the rabbinic perspective in at least one major regard: for the rabbis the difference between languages poses a formidable obstacle to translation, of the Bible above all; for Benjamin it is the very difference between languages that is the guarantee of their mutual translatability, for Scripture above all. In the mainstream of Jewish tradition, a divine language (whether one identifies it with the Holy Tongue or reserves it as a language beyond human expression) has its corollary in a suspicion about the possibilities of true translation; between Hebrew and the other languages, or between God's and other languages, opens a chasm difficult if not impossible to bridge. Benjamin's "pure language," by contrast, arises precisely in and through translation. In the most striking expression of this contrast between Benjamin's thought and normative Jewish notions of biblical untranslatability, Benjamin declares that only sacred texts put a halt to the plunging of meaning into "the bottomless depths of language" that threatens such translations as Friedrich Hölderlin's of Sophocles, which he otherwise praises. Benjamin's essay concludes:

> It is vouchsafed to no text but the holy one, in which meaning has ceased to be the watershed for the flow of language and the flow of revelation. Where a text belongs in its literalism to the "true language," to truth or to teaching [*der wahren Sprache, der Wahrheit oder der Lehre*], unmediated by meaning, this text is unconditionally translatable.[107]

Within Jewish translation history, it is precisely this character of the Bible, the absolute indissolubility of form and content, letter and meaning, that has constructed the highest barrier to translation. For Benjamin, the irrelevance of meaning to Holy Writ, the unity of text and truth, language and revelation, renders the Bible "unconditionally translatable."

If Benjamin diverges from the rabbinic path here, he also fails to follow, *avant la lettre,* the ways of the poststructuralists. No wonder, then, that de Man misses this point, reading Benjamin as a theorist of translation difference, of poststructuralist (rather than traditional Jewish) untranslatability. De Man begins his lecture on Benjamin by explaining that he has brought many

> translations of this text, because if you have a text which says it is impossible to translate, it is very nice to see what happens when that text gets translated. And the translations confirm, brilliantly, beyond any expectations which I may have had, that is impossible to translate, as you will see in a moment.[108]

If anything does emerge with clarity from "The Task of the Translator," it is that Benjamin is a prophet of translatability; this is a role so unexpected that even such careful readers as de Man, in what is surely among the most closely scrutinized pieces of writing after the Bible itself, could miss it. Benjamin, after all, not only confounds a quasi-Jewish notion of linguistic difference with a theory of unconditional translatability; he also confuses poststructuralists by coupling the now normative belief in the incommensurability of different languages with a passionate—I daresay almost religious—embrace of translation. The radicality of Benjamin's thought here can be put somewhat differently: Benjamin displaces translation from the sign theory on which it had rested since Aristotle—the separability of signifier from signified and the shared dimension of the signified as the translational pivot—without, however, relinquishing either the possibility or the necessity of translation.

How is this move accomplished? Benjamin's technique, like Buber and Rosenzweig's and indeed Aquila's, is literalism, freed completely now of the imperative of communicating meaning. Literalism, traditionally the "enslavement" to the word, becomes something else altogether in Benjamin. Free translation "does not derive from the sense of what is to be conveyed, for the emancipation from this sense is the task of fidelity." With this newly reconceptualized fidelity, it is "the task of the translator to release in his own language that pure language which is under the spell of another, to liberate the language imprisoned in a work in his recreation of that work."[109] Translation gains its own freedom and the power to liberate the pure language through its fidelity to the details of form rather than sense, word rather than sentence:

> A real translation is transparent; it does not cover the original, does not block its light, but allows the pure language, as though reinforced by its own medium, to shine upon the original all the more fully. This may be achieved, above all, by a literal rendering of the syntax which proves the word and not the sentence to be the primary element of the translator. For if the sentence is the wall before the language of the original, literalness [*Wörtlichkeit*] is the arcade.[110]

What we have in "The Task of the Translator" is a passionate defense of the long-disparaged approach of literalist translation, now associated with freedom as opposed to servitude, transparency as opposed to opacity. I made the argument in chapter 2 that the rabbinic tradition had also read literalism, in the case of Aquila, as a species of Jewish power rather than enslavement. The rabbinic defense of Aquila took shape against the specific national and religious differences of Hebrew and Greek. Benjamin's championing of literalism names no such national-linguistic markers. Nevertheless, whether or not Benjamin knew Aquila, similar structural circumstances affect their works. Aquila's translation emerges as a response to the imperial reach of the Septuagint, mobilizing Hebrew difference against it from within the translational enterprise. Benjamin's response was rather to the "bourgeois" German-Jewish assimilationism of an earlier generation, but it was similarly a repudiation of a universalism couched as linguistic philosophy. Both translators implicitly ask the question of what translation might look like if one rejected the notion of equivalence in content. Both argued for literalism as the route dictated by this insight. Aquila produced what is nearly an interlinear Bible (and which may have served as one in effect in the Greek synagogue); Benjamin championed such an interlinear Bible translation as the perfect example of translation. Like Aquila's translational practice, I would insist, Benjamin's literalism is a post-colonial technique, a reaction to earlier, more target-oriented and "fluent" translation; it is thus part of a long Jewish translation tradition—even if Niranjana separates what is "Judaic" in Benjamin from his radical position on translation.

I have postponed an analysis of how Benjamin's advocacy of literalism imagines its liberatory potential or combines with the larger themes of his essay, in particular with the notion of a pure language. Meaning is bracketed in Benjamin's thought (as it is not, for instance, in Buber-Rosenzweig), so that what traditional theory might call "form" becomes paramount. If Benjamin avoids this term, it is because he resists throughout the notion that language might function as a mere "container" for content and to speak of form is inevitably to imply its corollary in content. For mainstream translation theory, this dimension of language outside of content or meaning is the most expendable; for Benjamin, it is the most precious, the closest to the core of language. Sense-for-sense translation discards this dimension; Benjamin's word-for-word technique "releases" it. Literalist translation thus "produces" pure language by distilling the "linguisticality," the materiality and specificity, of a text. The Bible, which has never been read as providing simple "content," thus provides the most ideal conditions for translation.

Benjamin's divergence from rabbinic sources here is less stark than might at first seem. Aquila's translation produced a Hebraized Greek, a Greek made opaque in its failure to convey meaning in a familiar form; that is, Aquila produced pure language in Benjamin's sense. (For Benjamin, of course, such a juxtaposition of any two languages would have an equivalent effect.) Aquila's redemption of the Septuagint was to stamp the Hebrew onto the Greek, intimating a day in which the dominant culture would pay its respects to Semitic forms—Noah's blessing, we might recall, was interpreted by the rabbis as both already fulfilled in Aquila and to be fully realized in the messianic era. Benjamin's messianic view harkens to another, equally Jewish linguistic vision, in which "I will make the people pure of speech, So that they all invoke the LORD by name And serve Him with one accord" (Zephaniah 3:9 [NJPS]). Nevertheless, Benjamin's translational vision grows from the same insistence on linguistic particularity as Aquila's, the same belief that the Messiah will come not through the annulment of difference but rather through the strait gate that is the individual and unique word. Where Scholem sees mystical practice as the place where meaning falls silent, Benjamin insists that this dimension of language is available to translators, insofar as they practice the freedom of literalism. He thus unites two strands of Jewish mystical philosophy that have otherwise remained distinct: that of the mystical *tiqqun* that is literalist translation with that of pure language, the language beyond meaning.

Benjamin stands in similar relation to the Jewish tradition as Kafka does, in Benjamin's own view of the writer. In a famous passage on Kafka's relation to the Jewish tradition, Benjamin wrote that Kafka, along with many others, responded to the loss of "the consistency of truth" not, as other writers did, by "clinging to truth or whatever they happened to regard as truth and, with a more or less heavy heart, forgoing its transmissibility." Benjamin writes:

> Kafka's real genius was that he tried something entirely new: he sacrificed truth for the sake of clinging to its transmissibility, its haggadic element. Kafka's writings are by their very nature parables. But it is their misery and their beauty that they had to become more than parables. They do not modestly lie at the feet of the doctrine, as the Haggadah lies at the feet of the Halakah. Though apparently reduced to submission, they unexpectedly raise a mighty paw against it.[111]

Benjamin, too, it might be said, recognized the loss of "the consistency of truth" in abandoning, between the 1916 and the 1923 essays on language, the notion of one *originary* language that united the divine and human tongues. But like Kafka, Benjamin rescued from the "sickening of tradition" not consistent truth, or doctrine, or law, but rather transmissibility, the beauty and power of the modes by which "the rumor of true things (a sort of theological whispered intelligence dealing with matters discredited and obsolete)" continues to reverberate. For Kafka, narrative—Haggadah—is the arena for his messengers of discredited truths; for Benjamin, translation is the pulse that expresses the transmissibility of truth beyond all questions of origin and outside all content and meaning. Benjamin gave up the notion of a Holy Tongue in exchange for its mode of signification, finding in the specific difference of the Jewish tongue a truth about the kinship of all languages. Robert Alter titled the chapter of *Necessary Angels* in which he discusses Benjamin's essay "On Not Knowing Hebrew," insisting on the generative influence of Jewish stances on language beyond the particular uses of Hebrew. As Alter writes, "Benjamin's theory of language is Hebrew as conceived by the Kabbalah transposed into a universalized metaphysical abstraction."[112] Benjamin's depiction of translation as the fitting together of one jagged broken language-shard with another in its most intricate detail describes as well Benjamin's own construction of a theory of translational difference from the sharp corners of a Jewish stance on translation—following the shape of this Jewish attitude without regard to its history, doctrine, or law. As with Kafka's "translations," Benjamin's transmission of this Jewish stance outside of Jewish "truth" turned out to speak for an entire generation.

The arc that connects the translation of Mendelssohn with that of Buber-Rosenzweig and Benjamin can be described as a movement from the Jewish embrace of proper German idiom to an increasingly foreignizing stance toward German. For all their differences, Buber-Rosenzweig and Benjamin both espouse a translational politics of encounter-through-difference opposed to the domesticating and (in the minds of the Weimar generation) assimilating stance of Mendelssohn and at least some of his German-Jewish followers. Rudolf Pannwitz's formulation, quoted by Benjamin, provides a framework for understanding the value of this increasingly foreignizing German-Jewish cultural and translational stance:

> Our translations, even the best ones, proceed from a wrong premise. They want to germanize Hindi, Greek, English instead of hindicizing, grecizing, and anglicizing German [*sie wollen das indische, griechische, englische verdeutschen, anstatt das deutsche zu verindischen, vergriechischen, verenglishen*]. Our translators have a far greater reverence for the usage of their own language than for the spirit of the foreign works. . . . The basic error of the translator is that he preserves the state in which his own language happens to be instead of allowing his language to be powerfully affected by the foreign tongue.[113]

For translators from the Hebrew (or Yiddish), both the risks and the benefits of allowing a Jewish language to "powerfully affect" German spoke directly not only to the position of Jews in German culture but also to their own complex identities. From Mendelssohn to Buber-Rosenzweig, German Jews increasingly considered the risk to be worth taking, at least in part because the attitude toward the foreign expressed in Pannwitz promised a growing receptiveness to Jewish difference. I have already mentioned the irony in this development: Jewish difference was valued to the extent that Jewish difference (whether measured by Hebrew literacy or Yiddish speech) decreased. Plaut, Gillman, and others have made roughly this point; it is part of the argument of this last section that Benjamin too should be considered as part of this trajectory, even if his writings on translation did not take German-Jewish translation as their example and even if he himself disdained much in the Buber-Rosenzweig Bible. Benjamin, it might be said, exemplified the principle of Jewish translation difference without recourse to the linguistic particulars of this difference, or indeed to Jewishness at all. The principle of translational difference, developed within the context of German–Jewish relations, in Benjamin served to illuminate the operations of translation in general, in more radical form than Buber-Rosenzweig envisaged. For Benjamin, not cultural "encounter" but the release of a pure language beyond national communities or religious truths became the redemptive goal. In this sense, Benjamin's translation theory repeated and reversed Paul's theological universalizing of Jewish concepts. Paul separated letter from spirit, privileging the spirit and, in the process, providing a foundation for Christian translation theory (and more). Benjamin separated letter—or word—from sense, privileging the former and, in the process, providing a foundation for a poststructuralist translation theory that resisted the lure of disembodied meaning, the transcendence of a universally shared signified, and the association of any one language with truth. In the Weimar Jewish context, such a rejection of both universalism and (either German or Jewish) nationalist essentialism could hardly fail to be a radical political stance. In 1933, the Nazi student organization branded German Jews as immutable outsiders, quintessential translators from an utterly foreign language. Ten years earlier, Benjamin had written that

> unlike a work of literature, translation does not find itself in the center of the language forest but on the outside facing the wooded ridge; it calls into it without entering, aiming at that single spot where the echo is able to give, in its own language, the reverberation of the work in the alien one. . . . The intention of the poet is spontaneous, primary, graphic; that of the translator is derivative, ultimate, ideational [*abgeleitete, letzte, ideenhafte*].[114]

To be an outsider to the (German) forest, to be derivative, these were the insults by which German Jews were branded. But it is precisely in these characteristics, the outsider stance, the derivative relation to the language of the original, that for Benjamin, the greatest prize lies:

> If there is such a thing as a language of truth, the tensionless and even silent repository of the ultimate truth which all thought strives for, then this language of truth is—the true language. And this very language, whose divination and description is the only perfection a philosopher can hope for, is concealed in concentrated fashion in translations.[115]

CHAPTER FIVE

——— ✳ ———

The Holocaust in Every Tongue

The suffering of anti-Semitic persecution can only be told in the language of the victim. It is conveyed through signs that are not interchangeable.
EMMANUEL LEVINAS, *In the Time of the Nations*

THE UBIQUITY OF the Holocaust in contemporary culture is explained—when it is not merely assumed—by recourse to the singular horror of the events it names. Yet the visibility and power of the Holocaust narrative, decades after the end of World War II, was neither predictable nor inevitable. Indeed, as Peter Novick and Alan Mintz have recently reminded us, once the shock of the first newsreels had passed and the postwar reconstruction of Europe was underway, the murder of Europe's Jews appeared to be rapidly fading from memory.[1] Anne Frank's diary was initially rejected by a series of publishers, first in the Netherlands and later in Germany, England, and the United States. Annie Romein-Verschoor, who in 1947 approached the Querido publishing house with the manuscript on behalf of Otto Frank, was told that "the certainty prevailed [at Querido] at the time that interest in anything to do with the war was stone cold dead."[2] Primo Levi found a publisher for *Se questo è un homo* (translated as *Survival in Auschwitz* in 1960 and *If This Is a Man* in 1979) only with difficulty in 1947, but the memoir barely sold—it was not until its republication in 1958 that it found a wide audience. Levi later explained this curious lag by suggesting that in the late 1940s "the public did not want to return in memory to the painful years of the war that had just ended."[3] Elie Wiesel, writing in Yiddish in the mid 1950s, bitterly lamented that, in the postwar cultural climate, he had lost his faith that "a book could shake the consciousness of humanity."[4] The initial impact of reports from the death camps (which, in any case, rarely singled out Jews as victims of the Nazis) seemed to the survivors—called "refugees" or "displaced persons" in postwar culture—to have quickly evaporated.

As it turned out, Wiesel was marking not the end of the period in which "anything to do with the war" might draw the public's attention, but rather the inauguration of another era, in which the story of the murder of the Jews found an ever-increasing international reception that must have far exceeded these writers' expectations. This Holocaust discourse arose not in the immediate aftermath of the war—as might be expected in the normal course of things—but primarily and increasingly in the decades that followed, as a function of a number of significant public events: the 1952 Doubleday publication of *The Diary of A Young Girl* and, even more so, the 1955 play and 1959 film based on Anne Frank's diary (it was these events that led, by American detour, to a renewed interest in the diary in Europe); the appearance of Elie Wiesel's *Night* in French (1958) and English (1960); the Eichmann trial in 1961; and perhaps most influentially, the 1978 television miniseries *The Holocaust*. The term "Holocaust" itself seems to have first come into general usage, according to Gerd Korman, sometime between 1957 and 1959.[5]

The belated reception of Holocaust discourse can be explained not only, as Levi does, by the effects of the lingering trauma of the war but also by the process of semantic consolidation that the narrative of the destruction of European Jews had to undergo before it could be assimilated by a wider public. The coining of the term "Holocaust" to mean the Nazi genocide of Europe's Jews can metonymically stand in for the construction of this discursive shorthand. In his study of the presentation of the Holocaust on American television, Jeffrey Shandler describes "the inchoate status of the Holocaust as a historical concept" during the first postwar years:

> What would later be distinguished as a separate "war against the Jews" was not yet codified as a discrete unit of human experience with its own authoritative sources, narrative boundaries, vocabulary, historiography, and scholarly apparatus. Jews were not singled out as the quintessential victims of Nazi persecution, nor were Jewish responses regarded as central to the postwar understanding of this chapter of history. Moreover, the Holocaust had not yet been distinguished as an event of ultimate or paradigmatic stature, against which other moral issues might be measured.[6]

My intention in this chapter is to focus on a specific aspect of this (often invisible) constructedness of Holocaust discourse—the role of translation in the production and reception of Holocaust narratives. Many of the most influential of the texts that reached a wide audience were initially written in minor languages. Dozens of diaries and memoirs were composed in Yiddish or Hebrew, Czech, Polish, and Hungarian. The polyglot nature of Jewish discourse and the displacements of postwar life affected the vagaries of Holocaust literature: Paul Celan's "Todesfuge," for instance, was composed in the writer's native German, but first appeared in Romanian translation. Anne Frank's Dutch writings were translated into German by Otto Frank for his German-speaking mother to read before he attempted to find a publisher in the Netherlands for them. And a longer Yiddish version of Elie Wiesel's *Night* was published in Buenos Aires as *Un di velt hot geshvign* in 1956, two years before Wiesel's appearance on the French literary scene.

It would hardly be an exaggeration to say that the international reception of the story of Nazism's Jewish victims—and certainly what Lawrence Langer has called "the Americanization of the Holocaust"[7]—depended almost entirely on translation; those testimonies that did not find a voice in translation largely fell into oblivion. That the very language of its composition could preclude a testimonial from finding readers was already understood during the war. A Polish letter dated June 26, 1944, found near Vilna, begs whoever should find the letter to "deliver it into Jewish hands . . . so that for the 112 of us, at least one [of our betrayers] should be killed in revenge." The letter is in Polish, the writer explains, "because were someone to find a letter in Yiddish, he would burn it, but in Polish some good and decent person will read it and deliver it to the Jewish resistance."[8] Similarly, as David Roskies tells us, the "Oyneg Shabes" Archive, the collection documenting life in the Warsaw ghetto assembled under the leadership of the historian Emanuel Ringelblum, began to publish in Polish rather than Yiddish as the final liquidation of the ghetto approached:

> The last underground publication to appear within the [Warsaw] ghetto walls was *Wiadomosci*, a Polish-language news bulletin issued by the Archive for January 9-15, 1943. In April 1942, still addressing itself to the ghetto population, the Archive had published *Mitteylungen*, in Yiddish. Now that the End was in sight, the truth about the Nazi genocide had to reach the Aryan side, or further away still—the Polish government in exile.[9]

It was clear to the writers of these documents, at least, that their Yiddish mother tongue was in the same danger of eradication as the millions of its European speakers. Under the threat of such a linguistic and cultural genocide, Yiddish–Polish self-translation provided the only hope that the lives and deaths of these Yiddish speakers might be remembered or avenged. Translation in such instances meant the perhaps chimerical hope of survival— chimerical, since what survives is not the victim but his or her words, and not the victim's native speech but only its echo.

The "Holocaust," as an episode in the history of translation, thus affords us a peculiarly literal insight into Walter Benjamin's striking description of the "vital connection" between a text and its translation:

> A translation issues from the original—not so much from its life as from its after-life [*aus seinem Überleben*]. For a translation comes later than the original, and since the important works of world literature never find their chosen translators at the time of their origin, their translation marks their stage of continued life [*Fortlebens*].[10]

Although Benjamin insists that "the idea of life and afterlife in works of art should be regarded with an entirely unmetaphorical objectivity," he did not seem to have envisioned a situation in which translation would constitute the only, or nearly the only, opportunity for survival for a text, by which a text is reconstituted elsewhere—in a less endangered language—at the very moment the original is obliterated.

The connections between survival and translation did not end with Liberation. In his memoir *The Truce* (first translated as *The Reawakening*), Primo Levi describes postwar Europe as a nearly carnivalesque theater of shifting populations, through which his motley band of Italian refugees travels home, traversing linguistic as well as geopolitical borders. Levi describes the narrator's conversation with a priest in Latin; an unsuccessful attempt by one refugee to communicate with his girlfriend with an Italian–Polish dictionary (the relevant words are, as in all "decent" dictionaries, absent); business deals conducted in grotesque mime; and the efforts of his group at persuading a pair of Yiddish-speaking girls of their Jewishness by reciting the *Shema* (in a Hebrew the girls find comically un-Jewish). There is one scene among these others, however, that strikes me as emblematic of the quest for translation on the part of survivors in the aftermath of the war. Descending from the train in the town of Trzebinia, Primo finds himself surrounded by a crowd curious about his "zebra clothes," with whom he is, however, unable to communicate. Into this Babelian confusion, a cultured and multilingual lawyer serendipitously appears:

> He was Polish, he spoke French and German well, he was an extremely courteous and benevolent person; in short, he possessed all the requisites enabling me

finally, after the long year of slavery and silence, to recognize in him the messenger, the spokesman of the civilized world, the first that I had met.

I had a torrent of urgent things to tell the civilized world: my things, but also everyone's, things of blood, things which (it seemed to me) ought to shake every conscience to its foundations.[11]

Levi dramatizes here not only the urge to communicate one's story but also the potential for miscommunication that haunts all translation scenes. As the lawyer translates "his torrent of urgent things" for the crowd, Primo realizes that he is censoring his account, that the lawyer has substituted "Italian political prisoner" for "Italian Jew" in explaining his internment in Auschwitz. When he asks the lawyer why he hasn't told the crowd that he, Primo, is a Jew, the lawyer answers, "C'est mieux pour vous. La guerre n'est pas finie." (It's for your own good. The war isn't over.) The (apparent) end of the war and even the presence of interested listeners cannot guarantee that this Jewish story can or will be faithfully translated. Levi's retelling of this story in his own words, as it were, is yet another link in an ongoing chain of translation, always liable to disruption: Levi's setting down this story in Italian (with interpolated French dialogue), the translation and retranslation into English—and this trajectory does not end on the written page. As Millicent Marcus points out, Francesco Rosi's 1997 film version of the memoir, *The Truce*, "translates" this very failure of Levi's Jewish testimony to be heard into a visual, and thus universal, language. In ending this scene by pulling the camera back from the crowd in a long overhead shot, Rosi signals

his acceptance of the imperative to witness. In foregrounding the technology of the medium at the moment when the lawyer ceases his activity as translator, Rosi announces his own role as a translator of Levi's memoir, as mediator between the written word and the language of audio-visual spectacle.[12]

This scene, in all its variations, can serve as a parable for translation as a crucial component of Holocaust testimony, the vehicle whereby an act of witness is carried—or miscarried. In becoming an international discourse, historical events that largely transpired in one set of languages were brought into entirely different cultural and linguistic systems, and only through such movement were these narratives eventually heard as "the Holocaust." Translation as interlingual transfer is only one aspect of this cultural operation, which includes such literary processes as anthologizing, editing, and adapting for the stage or screen. André Lefevere argues that "contrary to traditional opinion, translation is not primarily 'about' language. Rather, language as the expression (and repository) of a culture is one element in the cultural transfer known as translation."[13] Lefevere thus prefers the term "rewriting" to translation, using the term to dislodge common notions of translation as linguistic equivalence and call our attention to the cultural constraints that shape the rewriting of a text in a new context:

> Whether they produce translations, literary histories or their more compact spin-offs, reference works, anthologies, criticism, or editions, rewriters adapt, manipulate the originals they work with to some extent, usually to make them fit in with the dominant, or one of the dominant ideological and poetological currents of their times. . . . This may be most obvious in totalitarian societies, but different "interpretive communities" that exist in more open societies will influence the production of rewritings in similar ways.[14]

In drawing on Lefevere's work, I am arguing first of all that the canon of Holocaust literature should be read as the *rewriting* of this historical event for new audiences. The translation of this canon—which became a canon, moreover, primarily in and through translation—is not merely the sum of each individual textual transfer from one language to another. Rather, broad general patterns can be discerned within the work of individual translators, editors, and other rewriters (and there is a sense in which even the "original" writer is a rewriter). The Polish lawyer at Trzebinia is thus an instantiation of a larger network of attitudes that determined, in the immediate aftermath of the Holocaust, what of Jewish experience could or would be translated; in this negotiation, we should note, not only the translator but also the translator's addressees play an important role. It is in the translations and mistranslations from minor into major languages, from Jewish to not entirely Jewish milieus, from the circle of survivors to the Polish train station or Broadway stage, that the story of the Holocaust attained its distinctive shape.

As the Polish lawyer can remind us again, translators have often acted as cultural censors, and translation can provide us a unique lens into the censorial moments that have shaped Holocaust narrative. The specificity of Nazism's Jewish victims, suppressed in the lawyer's mistranslation, is also softened in the Broadway version of *The Diary of Anne Frank*. Frances Goodrich and Albert Hackett, the husband-wife team that wrote the script, omitted Anne's entry about the suffering of the Jews, instead giving Anne these lines: "We're not the only people that've had to suffer. Right down through the ages there have been people that have had to suffer . . . sometimes one race . . . sometimes another."[15] The Hacketts' freedom with the *Diary* has been much discussed, but other translational choices are less known. Roskies has recently shown, for instance, that records of intra-Jewish discord or collaboration with the Nazis were long "placed under a ban"; thus, Yitzhak Katzenelson's *Vittel Diary*, "which names the names of his political opponents . . . was not published in full until 1988."[16] Not all the choices that shaped Holocaust narrative for an American and indeed an international audience are so clearly ideologically freighted: Anne Frank's *Diary* was edited for sexual as well as Jewish content, and Mintz points out that Holocaust anthologists have preferred concentration camp to ghetto memoirs as less foreign, ironically, for readers illiterate in Jewish culture. Taken together, this process of rewriting reveals as much about the audience for Holocaust narrative as it conceals of the events it claims to communicate.

The role of translation in Holocaust discourse, however, has rarely been recognized, in part because critics of Holocaust literature themselves frequently read this literature solely in translation. Moreover, this lack of access has failed to pose an obstacle to Holocaust scholarship. Of the dozens of dissertations, articles, and books on Elie Wiesel's *Night*, for instance, only a very few even mention (much less analyze) the Yiddish text on which it is based. The same holds true even for Anne Frank's *Diary*: at the 1959 trial against Lothar Stielau, who had claimed it was a forgery (he later shifted his charge to denying the accuracy of the German translation), the proceedings repeatedly bogged down on the problem of finding an expert witness to testify on the relationship between the Dutch and German versions.[17]

Ignorance of Jewish or minor languages does not entirely explain the neglect of translation in Holocaust discourse. Reinforcing this denial is the assumption in the critical literature on the Holocaust, accepted as an article of faith rather than as a matter of evidence, that Holocaust testimonies and memoirs are uniquely unmediated. The ghettos and death camps are directly presented in the memoirs and presentations, with the testimony of the survivor functioning, in Wiesel's words, as "the instrument of the events he recorded."[18] The critical literature on this testimony reaffirms the view that, as James Young describes the consensus, the writer "is a neutral medium through which the events would write themselves."[19] Mintz terms this position, long dominant in Holocaust scholarship, as the "exceptionalist model" as opposed to the "constructivist model," which "stresses the cultural lens through which the Holocaust is perceived." For exceptionalists, the canon of Holocaust literature remains a discreet one, referring to nothing but itself, situated in no cultural context but the concentrationary one: "Hewn out of the same void, these works of art, *no matter their different origins or languages of composition,* make up a canon of Holocaust literature with a shared poetics."[20] Neither the Romantic view that a literary work is the expression of individual genius, nor the constructivist view, which insists on the significance of the language and context of a work of narrative art, has any place in such criticism. Under the stress of such unique horrors, writers "channel" rather than shape what they have witnessed.

Young's argument with this view is directed primarily against what he calls "the critics of metaphor," those who deny the literary-critical insight about "the fundamentally metaphorical character of language, thinking, conceiving and writing" to insist that it is possible to "narrate [Holocaust] history without figurative language."[21] But his point applies as well to those who deny the relevance of translation as an instrument in shaping Holocaust discourse. Mintz himself views this denial as an aspect of the exceptionalist position, which exposes itself most clearly "when it comes to the question of translation."[22] Thus, in Lawrence Langer's *Art from the Ashes* (1995), which serves as Mintz's prime example of an exceptionalist anthological project (the first chapter is called "The Way It Was"), the issue of translation is pushed to the margins. "Try as one might," Mintz writes,

> it is only by resourceful detective work that the reader [of *Art from the Ashes*] can discover the language in which a given text was originally written. . . . The names of the translators—but not the languages translated from—are listed only in the small print of the copyright acknowledgements in the front matter of the volume and not in the body of the book. Again, this is not negligence but a kind of principled indifference. If the Holocaust constitutes a separate realm—or planet or universe, whatever the metaphor may be—then it has its own language, a language that is displaced and unnatural but at the same time unmistakable.[23]

Such a neglect of a text's linguistic history is characteristic as well of Elie Wiesel's concentration-camp memoir; "try as one might," it is impossible to discern the existence of a Yiddish original from even the closest study of the 1960 version of *Night*.[24] In the 1960 *Night*, the canon of Holocaust literature has (in part) what translation theorists call a "covert translation," that is, "a translation that enjoys the status of an original source text in the target culture."[25] I say in part, since while English-language readers of this translation could easily see from the copyright page that they were reading a translation by Stella Rodway of Wiesel's French *La Nuit* (which makes *Night* in this respect an *overt* translation), the text provided no clue of the existence of a Yiddish version that preceded the French. Here, too, one might speak of a "principled indifference" to the fact of translation. What one encounters in *Night*, after all, is Auschwitz "itself."

In the context of this general insistence on the immediacy of Holocaust testimony, the otherwise banal insight that writing—much less rewriting, editing, and translating—inevitably constitutes a powerful mode of shaping events becomes a form of bad taste if not sacrilege. And perhaps this is no surprise. The widespread assumption that diaries and memoirs constitute direct access to the horrors of the ghettos and camps has had to contend not only with those who, like Young (and myself), insist on the "literary-critical insight" that no such unmediated access is possible, but also with the much nastier claims that such testimony cannot be believed, claims put forward in such neo-Nazi brochures as *The Diary of Anne Frank—Truth or Forgery?* and *Anne Frank's Diary—The Big Fraud.*[26] (Indeed, it was Meyer Levin's attack on the reworking of Anne's diary for Broadway that inadvertently lent fuel to the revisionist charges of the diary's fraudulence.) In this charged and painful atmosphere, nearly any critical examination of the ways in which Holocaust discourse is rewritten in new contexts risks a kind of betrayal, a playing into revisionist hands. Thus does translation become an unwelcome, even scandalous, guest in Holocaust studies, the garish mistress at a dignitary's solemn funeral.

It is nevertheless my intention not only to insist on the significance of translation in Holocaust discourse, but also to trace the contours, as it were, of its invisibility. Holocaust discourse, as I have begun to argue, is profoundly reliant both on translation and on the obfuscation of its translational character. Although in this as in other respects Holocaust discourse presents what appears to be a *unicum,* there may in fact be a historical precedent for this uneasy combination in the curious career of the Hebrew Bible. The connection between the Bible and the literature of the Holocaust has been drawn before, though not, to my knowledge, in terms of their translation histories. Young discusses the literary warrants for the reading of Holocaust literature as sacred testimony, quoting Primo Levi's reference to the writings of survivors as "stories of a new Bible."[27] Wiesel's Yiddish memoir (although not his French) commences on a decidedly biblical note: "In onheyb iz geven di emune" (In the beginning there was faith).[28] Young comments that, in invoking the ancient texts, "the literary testimony of the Holocaust thus seem to accrue an ontologically privileged status . . . as privileged a status as the holy texts on which they are modeled."[29]

Holocaust writings thus stand alongside the Bible itself in the privileged category of sacred literature. But the connections with the Bible are not exhausted by recourse to the category of the sacred. The Hebrew Bible, initially available only in Hebrew and directed to the small group of Hebrew-readers, first found in the Septuagint and continues to find an international readership in translation. Once the initial translation of the Bible had been completed, no other Jewish book or narrative fully captured the attention of the non-Jewish world—until the Holocaust. Testimonies of the catastrophe in Hebrew and Yiddish, intended for a Jewish audience, eventually gave way to a vast literature outside of Jewish languages that found its way to an international audience. The Bible and Holocaust discourse are thus the two major "crossover hits" (if such language is not offensive in this context) in the history of Jewish literature.

Although, or because, the vast majority of readers of the Bible and of Holocaust literature encounter these works in translation, their status as translated text—the fact, for instance, that Jesus did not speak the King's English (or even, probably, the New Testament's Greek)—has been repeatedly denied or minimized. The Hellenistic-Jewish and Christian records of this denial indeed comprise the foundational texts of Western translation theory. In a series of variations on one pious myth, both Hellenistic-Jewish and Christian writers described the Septuagint as having emerged from the same inspired conditions that occasioned the Sinaitic transmission, making the Greek Bible as fully canonical, sacred, and true as its Hebrew source. Christian traditions record the belief that in Bible translation, as W. Schwarz writes, "The process of rendering is executed not with the help of human interpretation but through God's direct intercession. The translator is nothing but an instrument of God."[30] The problem of accepting God's word in translation was as acute for Greek-speaking Jews as for the Fathers, but the patristic sources reveal an additional anxiety: Christians were dependent on a *Jewish* translation for access to the divine word. That the world had the Bible through translation was both inescapable and unacceptable, in different ways for Jews and Christians. Translation, in this theologico-political context, was the providential messenger who must nevertheless be shot.

The view of the Greek Bible as a perfect translation suffered a series of rude shocks over the patristic period, each time the differences between Hebrew and Greek texts were made apparent. In the first centuries of the Common Era, charges and counter-charges of malicious tampering circulated widely. On the Christian side, the Jews were suspected of disguising Christian prefigurations or otherwise deliberately falsifying texts out of anti-Christian animus; Justin Martyr, for instance, declared that the scope of Jewish tampering with Scripture exceeded in its enormity the "calf which they made."[31] As I discussed in chapter 1, the Talmud, in retelling the story of Ptolemy's commissioning of the Septuagint from the Jewish community, essentially agrees with the Fathers, that the Septuagint is an imperfect translation altered by the Jews, rather than with Philo, who argued for its perfect equivalence. What is different about Christian charges that the Jews tampered with the biblical texts and the Jewish acknowledgments that these alterations were in fact made is that the Fathers thought the Jews mistranslated out of anti-Christian malice, while the rabbis explained any differences between the Hebrew and Greek Bibles as a product of Jewish discretion, the inevitable self-censorship of a minority community.

Under these conditions, it is no surprise that new translations began to compete for canonical status. For the Jews, the Greek Bible that Philo had praised as a perfect sister of the Hebrew lost its status when it became the Christian Bible, and the second century CE saw the three recensions of Aquila, Symmachus, and Theodotion. These Jewish and Jewish-Christian re-translations of the Hebrew Bible sought to bring the Greek closer to its Hebrew sources—the most radical of these, Aquila's, attempted to reproduce in Greek even the Hebrew word order.

The historical vagaries of what has been called the first major translation project of the West, the rendering of the Hebrew Bible into Greek, are shaped by theological concerns (the sacredness of the text) and political concerns (the movement of a text from a minority to a majority culture). The translation of the Holocaust, too, I would argue, poses both theological and political issues. Taking biblical history as his prime example, Willis Barnstone has argued that "translation denies itself," since the derivativeness implied by translation is an embarrassment for religion; thus, Barnstone writes, *"translation is frequently a historical process for creating originals."*[32] Douglas Robinson has similarly argued that the difficulty translation posed for the category of sacred texts has given rise to a structure of taboo around translation even in secular contexts, demanding that translating be carried out and discussed only under a cloak of mystification.[33] The "embarrassment" of translation, it seems to me, holds as true for Holocaust discourse as it does for the Bible, and the structure of taboo Robinson describes can account for at least some of the neglect of translation in Holocaust scholarship.

But the parallels between the Bible and the Holocaust as translation phenomena—particularly in the political dimension of these translations—are more specific than such a general account might suggest. The first centuries of the Common Era are worlds away from the second half of the twentieth century, and the Gentile reception of a narrative of Jewish catastrophe in which it itself is deeply implicated must differ from its embrace of the Hebrew Bible. Nevertheless, the transport of the Bible from Hebrew to Greek, from the Jewish camp to all corners of the world, may provide us (in drastic simplification) with a heuristic model for understanding the movement of the Holocaust from a Jewish catastrophe to a paradigmatic narrative that spoke "in every tongue." The first phase is that of the free translation of a relatively unknown primary text. If this translation is so successful as to introduce a new sacred text into the world, what follows is a second stage, the canonization of the translation as a perfect text. The third stage is the contestation of this perfection; it is inevitable that a sacred text would be subject to the kind of scrutiny that might demonstrate to those who have access to both the original and the translation that the "perfect" translation is (inevitably) shockingly flawed. It is probably also inevitable that different interpretive communities should trace any discrepancies to different sources. The rarity of bilingual readers hampered the process of contestation during the first few centuries, but it could not stem it entirely; once Origen's *Hexapla* appeared in the third century, with its six or seven biblical versions in parallel columns, scholarly comparison was greatly eased. The fourth stage is also predictable: the retranslation "toward" the original—though such retranslations hardly settle the issue. If they are canonized, the entire cycle may begin again.

The process by which the Holocaust has come to matter to nearly the entire world has been both an enormously successful one and an enormously ambivalent one. The "successes" are, I think, clear enough. The ambivalences are so much still with us that they are perhaps less easily seen—and it is here that the history of the Bible in translation may help us. Holocaust discourse in American Jewish culture follows the path, roughly speaking, of the Bible in Greek. Translators and editors handled Holocaust diaries and memoirs with the impunity with which first-time authors are often treated. In translating Anne's work into German for the benefit of family and friends, Otto Frank copied "only the essentials" of his daughter's diary, omitting whatever he felt would "prove of no interest"; the *Diary*'s first Dutch publishers later omitted other sections they considered "unsuitable or indecorous."[34] The title Primo Levi chose for his concentration camp memoir was changed to *Survival in Auschwitz,* presumably to make the text's content more transparent to a casual browser. It was only after such works had achieved their sacred and canonical status that their early history risked becoming embarrassing; in the "myths of origin" that develop around these now-sacred texts, all such evidence of textual manipulation was itself edited from the narrative.

This first era, in which the jagged seams of translation are disguised, is characterized by an implicit belief in the power and perfection (or, to put it differently, the irrelevance) of translation—or adaptation: thus, as Lawrence Graver has noted, many people took for granted that the famous closing line of the play and film, Anne's affirmation "In spite of everything, I still believe people are really good at heart," is also the last line of the *Diary*.[35] In Novick's words, "the majority of reviewers stressed how *faithfully* the play (and later the movie) followed Anne's diary."[36] As in the cultural context within which the Septuagint emerged, this trust in translation was accompanied by a belief in the fundamental translatability of human experience—more particularly, of Jewish experience. Eisenhower's America has something in common, then, with the Alexandria where Philo dreamed of a Torah from whose beauty "the greater part, or indeed the universal race of mankind, might be benefited."[37] As Novick has argued, the late 1940s and the 1950s saw a "universalist framing" of the Holocaust, "with an emphasis on the diversity of the victims of Nazism rather than on what was singular about Jewish victimhood."[38] Jews, too, Novick stresses, sometimes viewed Nazism in such "universal" terms; one American Jewish leader, for instance, described the Nazis as having targeted "Judeo-Christian civilization."[39] While the Holocaust later became emblematic of Jewish suffering, in the first decade after the war the destruction of European Jewry was only one part of a larger narrative American Jews saw themselves as sharing with the world.

Echoes of the Jewish-Hellenistic shift from unmitigated reverence for the Septuagint to the heated charge that the translators had grossly "betrayed" their source can be heard, however faintly, in the changing fortunes of Anne Frank on the stage. The contestation of the American Anne Frank begins with Meyer Levin, who fought to stage the version he himself had written, which he insisted was truer both to Anne's Jewishness and the fate of the Jews to which she too had succumbed (although his initial objection to the version by Goodrich and Hackett was merely that the dramatists were non-Jews).[40] This era of contestation is far from over: Cynthia Ozick's recent liturgical lament over the "evisceration" of the *Diary* "by blurb and stage, by shrewdness and naiveté, by cowardice and spirituality" ends with her imagining a "more salvational outcome: Anne Frank's diary burned, vanished, lost."[41] Ozick's rhetoric here is matched only by that of the rabbis, who wrote that when the Bible was translated into Greek, the world sank into darkness for three days.[42] It is not surprising, in this context, that Holocaust literature has entered the stage of retranslation: newer editions of Levi's work render his titles more closely than the early editions did. But it is the changing fortunes of Anne Frank's diary that perhaps best illustrate the dialectical stages of the Holocaust in translation.

The first editors and publishers of Anne Frank's diary (including Otto Frank) freely reworked the various writings Anne Frank had left, editing, trimming, and censoring for a range of ideological and stylistic reasons.[43] Only after the 1959 trial, in which the "authenticity" of the diary was subjected to judicial attention, were attempts made to establish a definitive text. One result is the 1988 *Critical Edition* of the *Diary*, which reproduces in precise detail the variety of texts from which Otto Frank culled a manuscript: Anne Frank's original journals and her own "polishing" in 1944 of these journals. Anne herself, in the last months before the capture of the Franks, was reworking and polishing her earlier work with an eye to its eventual publication. The edition presents Otto Frank's collation (and censorship) of these two (incomplete) sets of documents and provides information about the translations and adaptations of this material into various languages and media. The *Critical Edition*, it may be superfluous to point out, is the *Hexapla* of our own day, although with only three columns to Origen's six or seven. What emerges from this careful documentation is that Anne Frank's "diary," rendered in the singular in the title of every edition of her work and graphically shown (bound in red plaid fabric) on the stage and screen, was only the first of the journals, notebooks, and unbound sheets on which Anne Frank wrote and revised, with both overlapping sections and chronological gaps for which Anne's writing has apparently been lost. Even so, American readers were presented in 1995 with an English-language edition edited by Otto Frank and Mirjam Pressler that called itself *The Definitive Edition*, without, however, indicating with entire clarity what might constitute such definitiveness within such a complex textual history.[44] The edition received a kind of imprimatur when the 1997 stage production of *The Diary of Anne Frank* announced its intention to restore Anne Frank's words through fidelity to the now critically reconstructed text. By the 1990s, the cavalier treatment of the diary that had shaped its early history was no longer thinkable. Nevertheless, the fact that any readable or watchable version of "The Diary" was *unavoidably* a product of editorial choice (was Anne's first or rewritten draft more "authentic"?) had also become nearly impossible to acknowledge. The era of retranslation, then, had inaugurated its own new canon.

In at least one way, Holocaust literature stands in contrast with its biblical antecedents: for the Greek Bible, history records only the legends about the composition alongside the attacks on or defenses of the translation; the processes by which the translation actually took place are lost to memory. For *The Diary of Anne Frank*, we have enough evidence about the process of translation and adaptation to begin to explore the merits of the charges and countercharges. As in the patristic era, "the Jews" who disseminated the text were charged with falsifying their texts out of animus against the Gentiles; Stielau and those who followed him argued that the Diary was actually co-written by Otto Frank and Meyer Levin(!), as a way to generate sympathy for Jews and hatred of Germans.[45] The parallel is even more precise: just as the rabbis agreed, in some limited sense, with the Christian charge that Jews had altered the biblical text in translation, a host of Jewish opinion beginning with Levin has insisted that Jews *had* falsified Anne Frank's (very real) testimony. These alterations, though, stemmed not from anti-Gentile malice; quite the contrary, they were the expressions of the "universalizing" self-censorship of a timid Jewish community, eager to pacify and pander to a non-Jewish audience.[46] While we have no real evidence for the rabbinic story that the Bible was altered to avoid offending Greek readers, it is clear that such motivations helped shape at least the German translation of the Diary. As Anneliese Schütz, the German translator, candidly remarked to *Der Spiegel*, she had made certain changes in the text because she believed that "a book intended after all for sale in Germany . . . cannot abuse the Germans."[47] We should not be shocked at Schütz's impulse here; even the rabbis understood the workings of patronage and power on the most sacred text they knew.

If Holocaust discourse has replayed some of the scenes that followed upon the composition of the Septuagint, it is for two reasons: because the taboo-laden atmosphere of the sacred text has encompassed Holocaust testimony as completely as it did the Bible, and because Holocaust discourse has taken the path laid out by the Bible from Jewish to non-Jewish language-worlds (and halfway back again). As occurred with the Bible, the initial theological assumptions of translational perfection that were implicit in the early reception of Holocaust discourse have been decisively shaken. And as with the Jewish response to the initial success of the translated Bible, early "universalizing" Holocaust translations and adaptations have given way to more "Jewish" versions. The processes of translation and sacralization, each complex in its own right, are made more so by their uneasy juxtaposition: on the one hand, we have the theological phenomenon of a sacred text and the myth of its immediacy; on the other, the mediation of experience is not only inevitable, it is also inevitably shaped by conditions that might be called political in the most quotidian sense. In translation, the theological serves as both the final product of political negotiations and the mask for its unseemly operations.

It may be no coincidence then that the term Holocaust itself is derived from the Septuagint, where it and its variants occurs more than two hundred times as a translation for the Hebrew term *'olah* (a burnt whole offering or sacrifice); the term is translated as *holocaust* in the King James Bible, which would render it familiar to literate English speakers. Various accounts have been given of the first uses of the term and its general adoption. Although earlier instantiations of the term to refer to the genocide of the Jewish people have been found (some as early as the first years of the war), Zev Garber credits the popularization of the term to Elie Wiesel in the late 1950s.[48] In reconstructing the motivation for the term, Garber suggests that Wiesel intended to "preserve the specialness of the tragedy as a Jewish tragedy," particularly through bringing to bear on the genocide the biblical intertext of the *'Aqedah*, the Binding of Isaac.[49] In a speech delivered in 1980, Wiesel made these connections explicit:

> The Akedah is the most mysterious, one of the most heartbreaking, and, at the same time, one of the most beautiful chapters in our history. All of Jewish history can actually be apprehended in that chapter. I call Isaac the first survivor of the Holocaust because he survived the first tragedy. Isaac was going to be a burnt offering, a *korban olah*, which is really the Holocaust. The word "holocaust" has a religious connotation. Isaac was meant to be given to God as a sacrifice.[50]

In David Roskies' view, public acceptance of the term implied no general understanding of the theological connotations Wiesel and others may have had in mind. At most, the term "establish[ed] a vague connection to the Bible for both Jews and Gentiles," and this vagueness worked in favor of the absorption of the term, "for it was precisely the nonreferential quality of 'Holocaust' that made it so appealing."[51]

The term has met with increasingly open dissatisfaction in recent years. For Berel Lang, "Theological or at least mediating overtones [of the term] . . . are confined to the viewpoint of the victims, and they fail to suggest the specific role of genocide as it figured in the deeds of the Third Reich."[52] In drawing out the implications of the analogy of the murdered Jews as a ritual sacrifice, Garber points out that "Holocaust" is more than just inadequate to its referential task: if the Jewish victims are the ritual sacrifice, "in effect one cast the Nazis into a quasi-'priestly' role."[53] Although Garber acknowledges that Wiesel chose the term precisely to indicate that the Holocaust was "a Jewish tragedy," it seems clear to him that the time has come to find a new, less exalted or "beautiful" language for the genocide. "To turn the Jewish genocide into a sacrifice," Garber writes, "makes it a 'biblical' event rather than an event of our own time—a myth rather than a reality."[54]

What I would add to this discussion is that "Holocaust" carries with it the aura not so much of the Bible, as Roskies, Garber and others have pointed out, but more specifically of the *translated* Bible. Roskies implies as much when he writes that the term suggests the Bible *"for both Jews and Gentiles."*

What is significant about the term is not only that, as Garber writes, it renders the genocide a "biblical" event, but that it renders it an event of the "Judeo-Christian" Bible, the Bible that bridged the worlds of Hebrew and Greek, Jew and Christian, whether as the Septuagint or the King James. For it is clearly not the biblical referent itself that differentiates "holocaust" from *sho'ah* or *hurban* (pronounced in Yiddish *khurbm*); these last two terms, after all, also carry biblical or theological weight.[55] What reverberates in the term "holocaust" is rather the specific tone of Jewish Hellenism.

G. W. Bowersock and Jan Assmann have recently argued that Hellenism served not as a distinctive cultural formation in Late Antiquity but rather as the matrix in which a range of indigenous traditions could find Greek expression. As Bowersock puts it, "Greek was the language and culture of transmission and communication . . . a flexible medium of both cultural and religious expression."[56] Assmann further argues that such indigenous cultural and religious expressions were transformed in moving into Greek:

> As they were translated into the common semiotic system of Hellenism, the borders between the different *traditions* tended to become much more permeable than they had been within the original language barriers. A process of interpenetration took place which not only for Jews and Christians but also for the "pagans" themselves made the differences between them much less evident than what they had in common. Hellenism, in other words, not only provided a common language but helped discover a common world and a "cosmopolitan" consciousness.[57]

Assmann may be painting too rosy a picture of Hellenism; as he himself points out, there were "frequent clashes and tensions between indigenous traditions and the world of the gymnasium." Paula Fredriksen introduces her section on Hellenistic Judaism by remarking that "Judaism both resisted and embraced the seductive reasonableness of syncretistic Hellenism."[58] In both its harmonious and unhappy modes, the semiotic model of Hellenism outlined by Bowersock and Assmann can be fruitfully applied to the beginnings of Holocaust discourse in the 1950s. Anne Frank's words, invented by the Hacketts for the Broadway version of her diary ("We're not the only people that've had to suffer. There have always been people that've had to . . . sometimes one race . . . sometimes another"), are a modern, secular form of *theokrasia,* the archetypically Hellenistic discovery of equivalences between religions and gods.[59] In the case of Wiesel, translation was accompanied and in part accomplished by that Hellenistic invention, the *theological,* the marriage between Greek philosophy and Hebrew religion in which the differences between Jews and Christians became "much less evident than what they had in common." What comes into discourse with the Hebreo-Greek "holocaust," then, is this history of (the fantasy of) a shared language.

Assmann ruefully acknowledges that the moment has passed for his vision of reciprocity and mutual translation, exemplified for him in Hellenism. "The cultural imperative, today," he writes, "points in the opposite direction: to regionalism, the preservation (or invention) of dying languages and traditions, and the emphasis on otherness."[60] Assmann is speaking in general here, but his diagnosis can serve to illuminate the current mood in Holocaust studies as well. There are very good reasons, it seems to me, to have swung away from the syncretism of the 1950s, and Jewish scholars need not share Assmann's regret at the move toward "an emphasis on otherness." Hellenism, in Alexandria and New York, has often been an ambivalent enterprise for Jews. And if this ambivalence, which led to new retranslations of the Bible in the second century, produces new ways of thinking about the Holocaust in our own, so much the better.

It is nevertheless worth remembering that the Septuagint was as "authentic" a Jewish cultural product as the retranslations that followed. So, too, is the term "Holocaust," to which this Greek Bible gave rise. Moreover, it was the "universalist" Holocaust discourse of the 1950s that brought the Jewish genocide not only to world consciousness, but also to the consciousness of the world's Jews. Like the Jews of Alexandria, the Jews of America received the Torah primarily in translation. In our disdain for the unseemly operations of translation, its complicity with the forces of assimilation and the marketplace, we are forgetting its power to communicate experience and forge identities—indeed rejecting the very cultural ground on which we stand.

ELIE WIESEL AND THE SCANDAL OF JEWISH RAGE

It may not have been Elie Wiesel's *Night* that first sounded the note of silence or elicited it from its readers. *Night*, though, is its purest, most powerful expression, as a work and in the literature that has arisen around it. The theme of silence, in its theological, existential, and linguistic dimensions, dominates the commentary on *Night* (this commentary cannot be called criticism in the usual sense): the mystery of God's silence in the face of evil; the muteness of the dead; and the incommensurability of language and the events of the Holocaust—the naming of these enormities, in other words, as unnameable, unsayable. To these one might add a fourth silence, the proper awed stance of the reader and spectator in the face of Holocaust testimony. The only thing more predictable than this injunction to silence is the regularity with which it is broken. And even this has been said before.

Let me be clear: the interpretation of the Holocaust as a religious-theological event is not a tendentious imposition on *Night* but rather a careful reading of the work. In the description of the first night Eliezer spends in the concentration camp, silence signals the turn from the immediate terrors to a larger cosmic drama, from stunned realism to theology. In the felt absence of divine justice or compassion, silence becomes the agency of an immense, murderous power that permanently transforms the narrator:

> Never shall I forget that nocturnal silence which deprived me, for all eternity, of the desire to live. Never shall I forget those moments which murdered my God and soul and turned my dreams to dust. Never shall I forget these things, even if I am condemned to live as long as God Himself. Never.[61]

This famous and powerful passage describes a loss of faith, but faith can be lost in many ways. In Wiesel's description, the murder of God does not collapse eternity or strip it of religious mystery. Where the eternal God once reigned, henceforth shall live the eternal memory of the witness. In the aftermath of God's abdication, the site and occasion of this abdication— "the Holocaust"—takes on theological significance, and the witness becomes both priest and prophet of this new religion. "Auschwitz," Wiesel has said, "is as important as Sinai."[62] The near-religious silence that pervades *Night* also appears in Wiesel's accounts of its composition. Wiesel begins the essay "An Interview Unlike Any Other" by explaining not so much why he became a writer, but rather why he did not write his Holocaust memoir sooner:

> I knew the role of the survivor was to testify. Only I did not know how. I lacked experience, I lacked a framework. I mistrusted the tools, the procedures. Should one say it all or hold it all back? Should one shout or whisper? Place the emphasis on those who were gone or on their heirs?
>
> How does one describe the indescribable? How does one use restraint in recreating the fall of mankind and the eclipse of the gods? And then, how can one be sure that the words, once uttered, will not betray, distort the message they bear?
>
> So heavy was my anguish that I made a vow: not to speak, not to touch upon the essential for at least ten years. Long enough to see clearly. Long enough to learn to listen to the voices crying inside my own. Long enough to regain possession of my memory. Long enough to unite the language of man with the silence of the dead.[63]

La Nuit was written, then, only after Wiesel's decade-long, self-imposed moratorium on speech had elapsed. But it was also written, as the essay goes on to explain, at the insistence of the French Catholic writer and Nobel Laureate François Mauriac, who was its first reader and shepherded its publication. When, at the end of their first fateful meeting, Mauriac asked why Wiesel had not written about "those events," the young journalist replied that he had taken a vow not to speak. But Mauriac would not relent. Escorting Wiesel to the elevator, he spoke again: "I think you are wrong. You are wrong not to speak. . . . Listen to the old man that I am: one must speak out—one must also speak out." Wiesel continues, "One year later I sent him the manuscript of *Night*, written under the seal of memory and silence."[64]

This image of the former concentration-camp inmate, speaking haltingly and reluctantly from within "the silence of the dead," unites Wiesel's account of how *Night* came to be written with the final passages of that text. For *Night*, we should remember, depicts not only a witness to the Holocaust but also a survivor—one might say *the* survivor. In the final lines of *Night*, when the recently liberated Eliezer gazes at his own face in a mirror, the reader is presented with the survivor as both subject and object, through his inner experience and through the outward image of what he has become. And while the emaciated boy who is the corpse in the mirror may have changed, the man he becomes has never forgotten this deathly reflection (in the French, the sense that this gaze of the corpse remains within the survivor is even stronger). Precisely because the image of the corpse in the mirror is so unfamiliar, so unassimilable to the living consciousness of the survivor, that image must live on; the survivor will always, in some sense, be a corpse:

> One day I was able to get up, after gathering all my strength. I wanted to see myself in the mirror hanging from the opposite wall. I had not seen myself since the ghetto.
>
> From the depths of the mirror, a corpse gazed back at me.
>
> The look in his eyes, as they stared into mine, has never left me. (Son regard dans mes yeux ne me quitte plus.)[65]

Read together, the text of *Night* and Wiesel's account of its composition form a single portrait of the artist as a young survivor, haunted by a cosmic, deathly silence he can break only at the urging of another. This portrait has come to stand for the ineradicable effects of the Holocaust on the psyche of those who experienced its horrors. Because *Night* has nearly always been received as an unmediated autobiographical account, the complexity of Wiesel's interpretive craft, his *writing,* in other words, has been very nearly invisible.

It is a measure of the profundity of the influence of *Night* on the discourse of Holocaust literature that its distinctive tone and approach have come to seem simply inevitable, the only response imaginable.

Yet an alternative to this image of the survivor, this set of responses to Jewish catastrophe, exists in Wiesel's own writing. The reluctant young journalist whom Mauriac had to implore to speak ten years after his liberation had already written a Holocaust memoir called *Un di velt hot geshvign* (And the world kept silent). According to Wiesel's 1994 memoir, *All Rivers Run to the Sea*, the Yiddish memoir was composed and submitted for publication in 1954, several months before his fateful interview with Mauriac; Mark Turkow, the Buenos Aires–based Yiddish editor and publisher, accepted *Un di velt* for inclusion in his series *Dos poylishe yidntum* (Polish Jewry) not long afterward. *Un di velt* was written, Wiesel recounts, on board a ship to Brazil, where he had been assigned to cover Christian missionary activity among poor Jews: "I spent most of the voyage in my cabin working. I was writing my account of the concentration camp years—in Yiddish. I wrote feverishly, breathlessly, without rereading. I wrote to testify, to stop the dead from dying, to justify my own survival."[66]

Night emerged on the scene of European writing in 1958 as a work that stood alone. By contrast, when *Un di velt* had been published in 1956, it was volume 117 of Mark Turkow's series, which included more than a few Holocaust memoirs. The first pages of the Yiddish book provide a list of previous volumes (a remarkable number of them marked "Sold out"), and the book concludes with an advertisement/review for volumes 95–96 of the series, Jonas Turkow's *Extinguished Stars*.[67] In praising this memoir, the reviewer implicitly provides us with a glimpse of the conventions of the growing genre of Yiddish Holocaust memoir. Among the virtues of Turkow's work, the reviewer writes, is its comprehensiveness, the thoroughness of its documentation not only of the genocide but also of its victims:

> At the end of the second volume is an index that includes eight hundred names of actors, writers, poets, and various other artists, not all of whom are well known, demonstrating that the writer collected a mass of details and names he mentions and remembers. Not only has he erected a monument on the graves of these wandering stars, but he has also included much useful historical material that can serve as a primary resource for historians of Yiddish theater from the beginning of the Second World War until its tragic destruction.[68]

For the Yiddish reader, Eliezer (as he is called here) Wiesel's memoir was one among many, valuable for its contributing an account of what was certainly an unusual circumstance among East European Jews: their ignorance, as late as the spring of 1944, of the scale and nature of the Germans' genocidal intentions. The experiences of the Jews of Transylvania may have been illuminating, but certainly none among the readers of Turkow's series on Polish Jewry would have taken them as representative. As the review makes clear, the value of survivor testimony was in its specificity and comprehensiveness; Turkow's series was not alone in its preference. Yiddish Holocaust memoirs often modeled themselves on the local chronicle (*pinkes*) or memorial book (*yizker-bukh*) in which catalogs of names, addresses, and occupations served as form and motivation. It is within this literary context, against this set of generic conventions, that Wiesel published the first of his Holocaust memoirs.

Although the 1960 English translation closely follows the original French version of *Night*, the relationship between the published Yiddish and French texts is more complex. *Un di velt* has been variously referred to as the original Yiddish version of *Night* and described as more than four times as long; actually, it is 245 pages to the French 158 pages.[69] What distinguishes the Yiddish from the French is not so much length as attention to detail, an adherence to that principle of comprehensiveness so valued by the editors and reviewers of the Polish Jewry series. Thus, whereas the first page of *Night* succinctly and picturesquely describes Sighet as "that little town in Transylvania where I spent my childhood," *Un di velt* introduces Sighet as "the most important city [*shtot*] and the one with the largest Jewish population in the province of Marmarosh."[70] The Yiddish goes on to provide a historical account of the region: "Until the First World War, Sighet belonged to Austro-Hungary. Then it became part of Romania. In 1940, Hungary acquired it again."[71] And while the French memoir is dedicated "in memory of my parents and of my little sister, Tsipora," the Yiddish names both victims and perpetrators: "This book is dedicated to the eternal memory of my mother Sarah, my father Shlomo, and my little sister Tsipora—who were killed by the German murderers."[72]

The Yiddish text may have been only lightly edited in the transition to French, but the effect of this editing was to position the memoir within a different literary genre. Even the title *Un di velt hot geshvign* signifies a kind of silence very distant from the mystical silence at the heart of *Night*. The Yiddish title indicts the world that did nothing to stop the Holocaust and allows its perpetrators to carry on normal lives; *La Nuit* names no human or even divine agent in the events it describes.[73] From the historical and political specificities of Yiddish documentary testimony, Wiesel and his French publishing house fashioned something closer to mythopoetic narrative.

Even more radically transformed in the move to French than "the most important city in Marmorosh" was the image of the survivor. In both the Yiddish and the French, the narrator criticizes the other survivors for thinking of nothing but food, and "not of revenge." The following passage is taken from the Yiddish, but the French is similar:

> The first gesture of freedom: the starved men made an effort to get something to eat.
>
> They only thought about food. Not about revenge. Not about their parents. Only about bread. And even when they had satisfied their hunger—they still did not think about revenge.[74]

But the Yiddish continues: "Early the next day Jewish boys ran off to Weimar to steal clothing and potatoes. And to rape German girls [*un tsu fargvaldikn daytshe shikses*]. The historical commandment of revenge was not fulfilled."[75] In French this passage reads: "Le lendemain, quelques jeunes gens coururent à Weimar ramasser des pommes de terre et des habits—et coucher avec des filles. Mais de vengeance, pas trace."[76] Or, in Stella Rodway's English rendition: "On the following morning, some of the young men went to Weimar to get some potatoes and clothes—and to sleep with girls. But of revenge, not a sign."[77]

To describe the differences between these versions as a stylistic reworking is to miss the extent of what is suppressed in the French. *Un di velt* depicts a post-Holocaust landscape in which Jewish boys "run off" to steal provisions and rape German girls; *Night* extracts from this scene of lawless retribution a far more innocent picture of the aftermath of the war, with young men going off to the nearest city to look for clothes and sex. In the Yiddish, the survivors are explicitly described as Jews and their victims (or intended victims) as German; in the French, they are just young men and women. The narrator of both versions decries the Jewish failure to take revenge against the Germans, but this failure means something different when it is emblematized, as it is in Yiddish, with the rape of German women. The implication, in the Yiddish, is that rape is a frivolous dereliction of the obligation to fulfill the "historical commandment of revenge"; presumably fulfillment of this obligation would involve a concerted and public act of retribution with a clearly defined and more appropriate target. *Un di velt* does not spell out what form this retribution might take, only that it is sanctioned—even commanded—by Jewish history and tradition.

If the two versions characterize the larger group of survivors differently, they also present different views of the recently liberated Eliezer. *Un di velt* presents us with the writer gazing at his deathly reflection, but it does not end there as *Night* does, nor does the Yiddish suggest that the image will stay with Elie for the rest of his life; the last few paragraphs of *Un di velt* follow the young survivor out of the camp and into the larger world of postwar Europe:

> Three days after liberation I became very ill; food-poisoning. They took me to the hospital and the doctors said that I was gone.
>
> For two weeks I lay in the hospital between life and death. My situation grew worse from day to day.
>
> One fine day I got up—with the last of my energy—and went over to the mirror that was hanging on the wall.
>
> I wanted to see myself. I had not seen myself since the ghetto.
>
> From the mirror a skeleton gazed out.
>
> Skin and bones.
>
> I saw the image of myself after my death. It was at that instant that the will to live was awakened.
>
> Without knowing why, I raised a balled-up fist and smashed the mirror, breaking the image that lived within it.
>
> And then—I fainted.
>
> From that moment on my health began to improve.
>
> I stayed in bed for a few more days, in the course of which I wrote the outline of the book you are holding in your hand, dear reader.
>
> But—
>
> Now, ten years after Buchenwald, I see that the world is forgetting. Germany is a sovereign state, the German army has been reborn. The bestial sadist of Buchenwald, Ilsa Koch, is happily raising her children. War criminals stroll in the streets of Hamburg and Munich. The past has been erased. Forgotten.
>
> Germans and antisemites persuade the world that the story of the six million Jewish martyrs is a fantasy, and the naive world will probably believe them, if not today, then tomorrow or the next day.
>
> So I thought it would be a good idea to publish a book based on the notes I wrote in Buchenwald.
>
> I am not so naive to believe that this book will change history or shake people's beliefs. Books no longer have the power they once had. Those who were silent yesterday will also be silent tomorrow. I often ask myself, now, ten years after Buchenwald:
>
> Was it worth breaking that mirror? Was it worth it?[78]

By stopping when it does, *Night* provides an entirely different account of the experience of the survivor. *Night* and the stories about its composition project the recently liberated Eliezer's death-haunted face into the postwar years when Wiesel would become a familiar figure. By contrast, the Yiddish sur-

vivor shatters that image as soon as he sees it, destroying the deathly existence
the Nazis willed on him. The Yiddish survivor is filled with rage and the desire to live, to take revenge, to write. Indeed, according to the Yiddish memoir,
Eliezer began to write (or at least to outline his memoir) not ten years after the
events of the Holocaust but immediately upon liberation, as the first expression of his mental and physical recovery. In the Yiddish we meet a survivor
who, ten years after liberation, is furious with the world's disinterest in his history, frustrated with the failure of the Jews to fulfill "the historical commandment of revenge," depressed by the apparent pointlessness of writing a book.

There are two survivors, then, a Yiddish and a French—or perhaps we
should say one survivor who speaks to a Jewish audience and one whose first
reader is a French Catholic. The survivor who met with Mauriac labors under the self-imposed seal and burden of silence, the silence of his association
with the dead. The Yiddish survivor is alive with a vengeance and eager to
break the wall of indifference he feels surrounds him. The question of how
he can hope to break through the world's apathy by writing, to his "dear
reader," in Yiddish is one Wiesel never raises in *Un di velt* nor explicitly answers anywhere else. But the answer is implicit in the gap between volume
117 of the Polish Jewry series and the familiar slim paperback of *Night*. Wiesel
found the audience he told his Yiddish readers he wanted. But only, as it
turns out, by suppressing the very existence of this desire, by foregrounding
the reticent and mournful Jew who will speak only at the urging of the older
Catholic writer. Wiesel began by preaching to the Jewish converted, but soon
enough, one might say, the preacher himself underwent a kind of conversion. By the time Wiesel was negotiating with his French publishers, the survivor who pointed an accusatory finger at Ilsa Koch, then raising her children
in the new postwar Germany, had been supplanted by the survivor haunted
by metaphysics and silence. As David Roskies has written, the Yiddish and
French versions of *Night* have a different message:

> Themes of madness and existential despair are not as highlighted in the Yiddish
> narrative, which ends with the engagé writer's appeal to fight the Germans and
> anti-Semites who would consign the Holocaust to oblivion. Since no one in the
> literary establishment of the 1950s was ready to be preached to by a Holocaust
> survivor, existentialist doubt became the better part of valor.[79]

It is the second version of how *Night* came to be written that has attained
mythical status, most directly because it appears in Mauriac's foreword to the
work (included in each new edition and translation). And the myriad works
of commentary on Wiesel have seized upon the theme of silence, producing

endless volumes on the existential and theological silences of his work, on the question of what has been called "the limits of representation." What remains outside this proliferating discourse on the unsayable is not (only) what cannot be spoken but what cannot be spoken *in French.* And this is not the "silence of the dead" but rather the scandal of the living, the scandal of Jewish rage and unwillingness to embody suffering and victimization. The image that dominates the end of *Night*—the look, as Mauriac describes it, "as of a Lazarus risen from the dead, yet still a prisoner within the grim confines where he had strayed, stumbling among shameful corpses"—is precisely the image that Wiesel shatters at the end of his Yiddish work.[80] And resurrects to end the French one.

IF WE HAVE two memoirs, the Yiddish and the French, we also have two stories about how the French version came to be. Both Mauriac and Wiesel have written accounts of the fateful 1954 interview that resulted in the publication of the French memoir. The two versions, from different perspectives, describe a meeting that began uncomfortably and ended with a strong and by all appearances absolutely sincere friendship, but only after the young East European journalist and the older French Catholic writer had overcome the reticences native to the situation and painfully confronted both what united and what separated them. Of the two versions, it is Mauriac's that serves as the foreword, and something of a frame text, to *Night.* The foreword begins with a description of his unease at the prospect of being interviewed by a foreign journalist: "I dread their visits," Mauriac confesses to us, "being torn between a desire to reveal everything in my mind and a fear of putting weapons in the hands of an interviewer when I know nothing about his own attitude toward France. I am always careful during encounters of this kind."[81] Mauriac, apparently speaking as a spokesperson for France, a sort of minister of its defense, does not explain why he should be worried about a foreign journalist's opinion of his country; in the next passage, however, he goes on to talk about the Occupation years, although the transition from his mistrust of journalists (particularly those writing for Israeli papers?) and his decision to confide in this one is left unexplained:

> I confided to my young visitor that nothing I had seen during those somber years had left so deep a mark upon me as those trainloads of Jewish children standing at Austerlitz station. Yet I did not even see them myself! My wife described them to me, her voice still filled with horror. At that time we knew nothing of Nazi methods of extermination. And who could have imagined them! Yet the way these lambs had been torn from their mothers in itself exceeded anything we had so far thought possible. I believe that on that day I touched for the first time

upon the mystery of iniquity whose revelation was to mark the end of one era and the beginning of another. The dream which Western man conceived in the eighteenth century, whose dawn he thought he saw in 1789, and which, until August 2, 1914, had grown stronger with the progress of enlightenment and the discoveries of science—this dream vanished finally for me before those train-loads of little children. And yet I was still thousands of miles away from thinking that they were to be fuel for the gas chamber and the crematory.

This, then, was what I had to tell the young journalist. And when I said, with a sigh, "How often I've thought about those children," he replied, "I was one of them."[82]

Having identified himself as a survivor, the young journalist tells Mauriac of his experiences and, more particularly, of his loss of faith in God. There is no evidence from the interview that Wiesel, who raged against non-Jewish indifference in the Yiddish memoir he had so recently completed, implied by word or gesture that the French writer need examine his own actions as a witness to the Jewish deportations (though, as Mauriac makes clear, hardly a witness at all, except second-hand, and one who was "thousands of miles away" from even the thought that these Jewish children were to be mur-dered) or those of France, whose national honor Mauriac is inclined to de-fend. The introduction does speak of passivity, of the failure to act, in the next passage, in which Mauriac recommends the book he is introducing because it speaks of "the fate of the Jews of the little Transylvanian town called Sighet, their blindness in the face of a destiny from which they would still have had time to flee; the inconceivable passivity with which they gave themselves up to it, deaf to the warnings and pleas of a witness who had himself escaped from the massacre, and who brought them news of what he had seen with his own eyes; their refusal to believe him, taking him for a madman."[83] With that, the vexed question of political responses to Nazi terror is left squarely in the Jewish court.

What interests Mauriac even more profoundly than the blindness of the Transylvanian Jews, their "inconceivable passivity," is the innocence of the story's protagonist and narrator, whom Mauriac refers to throughout as a "child":

> The child who tells us this story here was one of God's elect. From the time when his conscience first awoke, he had lived only for God and had been reared on the Talmud, aspiring to initiation into the cabbala, dedicated to the Eternal. Have we ever thought about the consequences of a horror that, though less apparent, less striking than the other outrages, is yet the worst of all to those of us who have faith: the death of God in the soul of a child who suddenly discovers ab-solute evil.[84]

With this passage, Mauriac lays out an implicit hierarchy of Holocaust horrors; for people of faith what was "worst of all" about the murder of six million Jews was "the death of God in the soul of a child."[85] The foreword ends with Mauriac's reaction to the story Wiesel tells about how he lost his faith:

> And I, who believe that God is love, what answer could I give my young questioner? Did I speak of that other Jew, his brother, who may have resembled him—the Crucified, whose Cross has conquered the world? Did I affirm that the stumbling block to his faith was the cornerstone of mine, and that the conformity between the Cross and the suffering of men was in my eyes the key to that impenetrable mystery whereon the faith of his childhood had perished? Zion, however, has risen up again from the crematories and the charnel houses. The Jewish nation has been resurrected from among its thousands of dead. It is through them that it lives again. We do not know the worth of a single drop of blood, one single tear. If the Eternal is the Eternal, the last word for each of us belongs to Him. This is what I should have told this Jewish child. But I could only embrace him, weeping.[86]

Mauriac describes Wiesel as his "young questioner," but by Mauriac's own account, Wiesel questions neither God nor the person to whom he relates his story. On the contrary, Mauriac quotes Wiesel's description of Rosh Hashanah in the camp: "That day, I had ceased to plead. I was no longer capable of lamentation. On the contrary, I felt very strong. I was the accuser, and God the accused." It is Mauriac who responds to this story as if he had been asked for counsel. With Wiesel's implicit invitation to theological meditation in hand, Mauriac explains how the Jewish boy's loss of faith is an impetus to his own, that the contradiction Wiesel feels between the suffering of the Jews and God's love for them is only an illusory one. But presumably because he respects Wiesel's right to interpret his own experience, the Catholic writer weeps and keeps silent. The story of the Holocaust, after all, is a Jewish one to tell.

Or is it? Mauriac, in a paradoxical assertion, claims for himself the virtue of silence, presenting a Christian perspective while framing it as tactfully and respectfully withheld—despite an implicit Jewish invitation to express it. The foreword begins by acknowledging the position of European non-Jews as witnesses to the deportation of Jewish children, but only to divert the implicit indictment of such witnesses in two distinct ways. Mauriac describes the scene his wife witnessed at Austerlitz station as the end and antithesis of everything France and enlightened Europe stand for. But he also speaks of that day as the beginning of a new era, with a new kind of knowledge: even as Mauriac insists that he was far from imagining the fate of the Jewish "lambs" at Austerlitz, that day was a "revelation" of "the mystery of iniquity."

By contrast, Mauriac couches the Transylvanian Jews' response to evidence of Nazi intentions in the language of deafness, blindness, refusal to believe (the same language, not coincidentally, of the Jewish rejection of Christ's divinity). His own disbelief points to his innocence—he cannot even imagine the possibility of such evil—while his dawning comprehension gains its significance only as a philosophical and theological event. Whether as French humanist or Catholic initiate, Mauriac distances himself from the charge of having been a cowardly bystander of the Nazi genocide. And by drawing attention to the narrative of the protagonist's loss of faith, Mauriac frames the Jewish catastrophe within existentialist religion and then reasserts his own authority as a religious thinker. The effect of all these moves is to place the Jews in the position of those who do not know and to assert Mauriac's own privileged access to the knowledge they lack.

As both participants acknowledge, the meeting between Mauriac and Wiesel was strained; but it would probably have been far more strained if the French-Jewish writer had not opened a theological channel for Jewish–Christian communication. If the survivor's complaints were primarily directed against God, all of Europe might breathe easier. Moreover, as Mauriac makes clear, Christian faith need not be troubled by Jewish doubts, since "the stumbling block of [Wiesel's] faith was the cornerstone of mine."

I do not mean to imply that Mauriac is undisturbed by the Holocaust because he believes the Jews to be guilty of crucifying Jesus. For Mauriac, Jewish suffering is theologically meaningful in the same way as the suffering of "that other Jew." Mauriac responds to Wiesel's story by constructing a reverse typology: the fate of Elie's father, for instance, is described as "his martyrdom, his agony, and his death."[87] Nor is the resurrection missing, in the rise of Zion from the ashes of the Holocaust. Mauriac, in his Christological reframing of the Jewish Holocaust, never touches on the question of Jewish guilt for Christ's crucifixion; but what also vanishes in his reading of Jewish catastrophe is the other half of that story—the historical animosity of Christian against Jew.

WIESEL published his own account of the interview, although not until 1978, twenty-four years after it had taken place. He also confessed to an unease before the interview began, for reasons different from the ones Mauriac implies. Wiesel was far from wanting to acquire anti-French ammunition from Mauriac; he writes, in fact, that the request for a meeting with the writer was no more than a journalist's ploy—what Wiesel wanted from the well-connected writer was an introduction to the Jewish prime minister of France,

Pierre Mendès-France, whom the journalist very much hoped to interview. Wiesel describes how he reproached himself for manipulating the old man: "Impostor, I thought, I am an impostor."[88] But his guilt dissipated, Wiesel writes, when he realized that "the Jewish statesman had ceased to interest me, the Christian writer fascinated me."[89] The friendship between the older Christian and younger Jew began, then, with Wiesel relinquishing his aim of manipulating Mauriac for Jewish purposes and turning, in all sincerity, to the man himself. With this psychological shift, Wiesel also began his transformation from Hebrew journalist and (still unpublished) Yiddish memoirist to European, or French, writer.

Mauriac's interest in Jews is just as strongly subjective as, if less obviously manipulative than, Wiesel's initial interest in him. As Wiesel describes it, Mauriac spoke at length about the chosen and martyred people of Israel, but only as that suffering echoed the martyrdom and divinity of the Jew Jesus. Mauriac's "impassioned, fascinating monologue," Wiesel recalls, "was on a single theme: the son of man and the son of God, who, unable to save Israel, ended up saving mankind. Every reference led back to him."[90]

Mauriac, by his account, began by speaking of Jewish children and tactfully refrained from mentioning Jesus, whereas by Wiesel's account Mauriac began by speaking of Christ, not mentioning the suffering of Jewish children until the Hebrew journalist demanded that he do so. What Mauriac claims to have thought but not said in response to Wiesel's story becomes, in this version, what he said, apparently unprovoked by anything the interviewer asked. And Wiesel remembers Mauriac as at least hinting at the adversarial relationship between Jesus and Israel, whom he was "unable to save," a tension Mauriac only implies by his reticence in speaking to a Jew. After listening to Mauriac with growing annoyance, Wiesel writes, he responded with anger and "bad manners":

> "Sir," I said, "you speak of Christ. Christians love to speak of him. The passion of Christ, the agony of Christ, the death of Christ. In your religion, that is all you speak of. Well, I want you to know that ten years ago, not very far from here, I knew Jewish children every one of whom suffered a thousand times more, six million times more, than Christ on the cross. And we don't speak of them. Can you understand that, sir? We don't speak of them."[91]

After Wiesel's outburst, Mauriac questioned the emotional and apologetic journalist about his experiences, and Wiesel responded, "I cannot, I cannot speak of it, please, don't insist." It was then that Mauriac implored him to write; Wiesel's acquiescence, though always qualified by silence, is implied in the final sentence of the essay: "One year later I sent him the manuscript of *Night*, written under the seal of memory and silence."[92]

In this version of the interview between the two men, the burden of silence is shouldered by the Jew, not the Christian. Where Mauriac writes that he suppressed his religious reaction to the survivor's story, Wiesel describes his unwillingness to tell his story to the older man. And both men tell their stories from within a paradoxical affirmation of silence; the two essays end with nearly parallel descriptions of stifled or self-censored expression. But where Mauriac's foreword is "silent" on the Christian reading of Jewish martyrdom, Wiesel's essay presents the genocide itself as unspoken by both Christian and Jew, only belatedly reminding the pontificating Christian of the Jewish children of whom "we"—the referent is ambiguous—"don't speak." That Mauriac or the French may have been implicated in the genocide or in the silence that accompanied and followed the genocide of the Jews remains outside this narrative, just as it is pushed below the surface of Mauriac's—except for the mild accusation implied in the phrase "not very far from here." (Mauriac's own measure of the gap between French civilians and the murder of Jewish children vacillates between the proximity of Austerlitz station and the distance of "a thousand miles.") And even this accusation is softened by the journalist including himself among those who have been silent on the fate of the Jews: "*We* don't speak of them." In the passive-aggressive logic of the Jewish–Christian post-Holocaust encounter, every utterance must be introduced and framed by a declaration of silence, and only by proclaiming a reluctance to speak can the speaker—Jewish or Christian—hope to heard. The Jewish survivor's desire for an audience he also mistrusts cannot, it seems, be uttered in earshot of that audience. Of all the silences inherent to "Holocaust representation," this one has least often been breached.

THE French reworking of *Un di velt hot geshvign* and Mauriac's framing of this text together suggest that *La Nuit*—read so consistently as authentically Jewish, autobiographical, direct—can be read as a compromise between Jewish expression and the capacities and desires of non-Jewish readers, Mauriac first among them. I do not mean to suggest that this compromise, these negotiations, were either calculated or hypocritical; any conversation is a balancing act between two speakers, any text a reflection of its audience as much as its writers. That Wiesel wrote his Yiddish memoir first and to a Jewish audience makes it no more "authentic" than his better-known French work; the Yiddish genre in which Wiesel participated imposed its own set of cultural conventions. If I choose to focus on these operations, this cultural translation of Jewish into Catholic idioms, in the encounter between Wiesel and Mauriac, it is because what happened between the two men has turned out to have the farthest-ranging of repercussions.

The question I would put to the 1954 interview, then, is this one: What happened between these two men to explain the tranformation of *Un di velt hot geshvign* into *La Nuit*, the survivor's political rage into his existentialist doubt? The encounter, it seems to me, could be described as a series of delicate negotiations, in which the survivor's first concession was to relinquish all talk (if not thought) of Jewish revenge—and why not?[93] As an author whose audience crossed ethnic borders, it made sense for Wiesel to suppress an impossible fantasy whose clearest effect would be to alienate Christians. It is only in later writings that Wiesel makes the further move of seeing this failure to take revenge as a sign of Jewish moral triumph—a nearly Christian turning of the other cheek—rather than the unfortunate result of cowardice or realism. In an open letter "To a Young Palestinian Arab," Wiesel compares the Jewish response to their victimization with that of the Palestinians:

> We [survivors] consistently evoked our trials only to remind man of his need to be human—not of his right to punish. On behalf of the dead, we sought consolation, not retribution.
>
> In truth, the lack of violence among these survivors warrants examination. Why deny it? There were numerous victims who, before dying, ordered him or her who would survive to avenge their death. [. . .] And yet . . . with rare exceptions, the survivors forced themselves to sublimate their mandate for revenge.
>
> Whereas you . . .[94]

There is something disingenuous, it seems to me, about Wiesel's description of the Jews as having "sublimate[d] their mandate for revenge." This sublimation, after all, was their ticket into the literature of non-Jewish Europe.

Wiesel's second concession was to narrow the target of his anger to avoid accusing Mauriac or his countrymen of the crimes of complicity or silence. Even more significantly, the survivor redirected his complaints against the Jewish God—while the Christian God remained unscathed. With these moves, Wiesel established channels of communication between Jewish survivor and Christian theologian while rendering the Holocaust harmless for Catholic pieties and French loyalties. The survivor is no longer the enraged seeker of revenge but rather a religiously potent emblem of martyrdom, and Jewish martyrdom in particular.

What Mauriac gave Wiesel in return for this transformation was the weight of his moral authority and the power of his literary status. Mauriac introduced Wiesel to his own publisher and wrote his first and most glowing reviews; in short, Mauriac found and secured Wiesel the larger audience he wanted. And in conversation with Mauriac and the publisher Mauriac introduced him to, Wiesel developed a language to talk about the Jewish genocide that could hold the attention of Jews and Christians, a considerable achievement indeed.

When this book was already in press, a new translation of *Night* appeared to some notice, and Wiesel's memoir followed *The Diary of Anne Frank* into the era of retranslation. The 2006 edition is, inevitably, another "rewriting," in Lefevere's sense of the term, a reworking of the text rather than the restoration of an "original" in its pristine state. And how could it be otherwise? What exactly is the original of *Night*? The experience "itself"? The lengthy Yiddish manuscript from which the published Yiddish version was culled? *Un di velt hot geshvign*? The French manuscript, before the publisher's editing? *La Nuit*? Given this confusing textual history, it is no wonder that the *New York Times* initially reported that the new translation was from the Yiddish, a misstatement it corrected three days later.[95]

In the preface to the new edition of *Night*, Wiesel pulls the curtain open—if only partway—on the textual evolution of the book, acknowledging the existence of a Yiddish precursor to *La Nuit* and discussing the text in its various forms and languages. Wiesel translates selections from the Yiddish, including the passage at the end of *Un di velt hot geshvign* that indicts the world's indifference to the memory of the Holocaust (Wiesel does not quote the references to the smashing of the mirror that frame this passage). The new translation is not entirely an invitation to critical analyses of the evolution of *Night*, suggesting that these transformations of the Yiddish into French were largely a matter of length; nor can these changes be identified as the work of a single hand, whether Wiesel's or his publisher's:

> Though I made numerous cuts, the original Yiddish still was long. Jérôme Lindon, the legendary head of the small but prestigious Éditions de Minuit, edited and further cut the French version. I accepted his decision because I worried that some things might be superfluous.[96]

This portrait of the uncertain, unknown writer submitting to the dictates of his French publisher stands in some contrast with the image of Wiesel sending Mauriac "the manuscript of *Night*, written under the seal of memory and silence."[97] Revelations of the untidy and commercial processes of literary production, editing, and publishing are the very hallmark of the era of retranslation.

In the case of a text as canonical—one might say, as sacred—as *Night*, re-translation has its evident risks. As Wiesel asks, "Why this new translation, since the earlier one has been around for forty-five years? If it is not faithful or good enough, why did I wait so long to replace it with one better and closer to the original?"[98] The danger of retranslation, these questions suggest, is that the new, "better" translation will draw attention either to the "failings" of the earlier translation or to awkward differences between versions. The very attempt to resolve discrepancies inevitably gives rise to new ones, as the title of Edward Wyatt's *New York Times* article implied: "The Translation of Wiesel's 'Night' Is New, but Old Questions Are Raised."[99] As Wiesel writes in the preface, he had taken the opportunity of the new translation by his wife "to correct and revise a number of important details."[100] These details, teased out in Wyatt's article, include a revision *of* the French as well as revisions *toward* the French. Among the minor corrections, as the *Times* reported, was a reference to the age of the book's narrator when he arrived in 1944 at Birkenau, the entry point for Auschwitz. The French version, and its first English translation, had recorded that age as "not quite fifteen," Wyatt writes, "but the scene takes place in 1944. Mr. Wiesel, born on Sept. 30, 1928, would have already been 15, going on 16. In the new edition, when asked his age, he replies, '15.'"[101]

As with other retranslations, Wiesel's new version, and its corrections, were almost certainly occasioned by contestations of the earlier text; the *Times* article quotes Daniel R. Schwarz's question in *Imagining the Holocaust*, "Is not this age discrepancy one reason why we ought to think of *Night* as a novel as well as a memoir?"[102] What neither Schwarz nor the *Times* mentions is the context for Wiesel's misstatement: it is in the urgent exchange with a more-experienced inmate who warns both father and son to lie about their ages to Dr. Mengele when they pass before him during the infamous "Selection":

> "Here, kid, how old are you?"
> It was one of the prisoners who asked me this. I could not see his face, but his voice was tense and weary.
> "I'm not quite fifteen yet."
> "No. Eighteen."
> "But I'm not," I said. "Fifteen."
> "Fool. Listen to what *I* say."[103]

It is clear enough, in the narrative, why Eliezer would be urged to lie about his age to Mengele. But what are the forces—infinitely less extreme—that might have led Wiesel to describe or remember himself to his *readers* as not quite fifteen at his internment? That people lie about their age is something our culture fully knows and often accepts (and not only when it is Mengele who is asking). The reasons people tell untruths about their age, moreover, are as revealing about their cultural surroundings—its drinking laws, its erotic ideals, its respect for elders or horror of aging—as they are about those misrepresenting themselves. Why, then, might a still-young survivor, as Wiesel was in 1956, describe or remember himself as younger, even by a year, than he actually was when he first entered a concentration camp?

It is not, I think, hard to understand this impulse. In a lecture delivered at Northwestern University in the 1970s, Wiesel described himself as "a very young boy, extremely religious, extremely naïve and innocent" when he "arrived into a kingdom that was a kingdom of curse and malediction." After an inmate warned the boy and his father that they were destined to die in its flames, "that little boy turned to his father and said, 'It is impossible. I don't believe it.'"[104] The story Wiesel tells derives enormous power from the heart-wrenching contrast between his own innocence and the experience of Nazi evil. Wiesel was not alone in viewing the concentration camp experience in these stark terms. For Mauriac, too, it is the image of Wiesel as "the child" (as he refers to him five times in the space of the brief Foreword) that arouses his fiercest compassion and invites the most exalted of his theological meditations; the adult Jews of Sighet, with their "inconceivable passivity," elicit a far more ambivalent response.[105] And it is certainly no coincidence that the first great Holocaust testimony to find an international audience was the diary of a young girl. What the rhetoric of innocent childhood conceals is an ugly corollary: that the adult victims of Nazi crimes are not innocent but naive, not pure but blind, not victimized but passive. In this discursive environment, who could blame Wiesel if he hedged his bets by describing or imagining himself as just a little younger when he was interned in the concentration camp? If I am right about the privileging of youthful victims in Holocaust discourse, then these misstatements implicate Wiesel's readers as much as they do the author himself.

In another paradox of retranslation, the gesture of restoration, the fantasy of disclosing a truer text, simultaneously exposes the anxious moment in which the need for a new translation makes itself felt. The 2006 translation of *Night*, intended as "better and closer to the original," is thus also a phenomenon of our own time.[106] The passage Wiesel quotes in the preface to the new translation, from the last page of the Yiddish novel, is not merely of historical interest for him, as evidenced by his changes to the Yiddish in English translation. While the Yiddish version (quoted above) laments that "Germans and antisemites persuade the world that the story of the six million Jewish martyrs is a fantasy," Wiesel's new English translation of the Yiddish renders this as "Today, there are anti-Semites in Germany, France, and even the United States who tell the world that the 'story' of six million assassinated Jews is nothing but a hoax."[107] The translation difference registers the gap between 1956, when the category of "Germans and antisemites" was a perfectly coherent one, and our own world, in which antisemites and Holocaust deniers are spread across a wider terrain but are no longer associated with the German people as a whole. Wiesel's "today" (only implied in the Yiddish) thus has more than a single reference, shifting between the 1950s he is representing and the contemporary moment. The decision to translate this particular passage—which is also the decision to rework this sentence for a new context—expresses both Wiesel's dismay that Holocaust denial continues into the present and his attunement to its shifting demographics ("even the United States"). Because this sentence comes to Wiesel's 2006 readers from 1956, as it were, it works as prophetic indictment, though this is a prophetic indictment that is, at least in one small part, constructed after the fact.

For all my fascination with these transformations, I would argue against Schwarz's suggestion that *Night* should be read as a novel as well as a memoir. Such a distinction leaves intact the possibility that a memoir can be found that is *not* also "a novel." It suggests, moreover, that truth lies only with the memoir, and the novel, or what is novelistic within the memoir, is the site of untruth. But it seems to me that the transformations of *Night* I have been tracing permit no clear categorization into truth and untruth; Wiesel's unstable text is at least as illuminating as a perfectly "correct" text or retranslation would be. Nor do I believe that attention to the mediations and reworking of the text inevitably collapses the important difference between minor slips and wholesale fabrication. It is rather the chimera of the sacred text that courts the radical disenchantment of readers, once the first cracks appear. And it is not only Holocaust literature but also victims and survivors that we hold to an unreal standard, as if the immensity of Nazi evil must signify the absolute goodness of its victims. Within the Manichean coloration of Holocaust discourse, a writer like Wiesel cannot be flawed—can barely be human. It is just this humanness that is glimpsed in the changing fortunes of Wiesel's memoir, its translation and retranslation; and the story that emerges turns out to be about more than Wiesel, encompassing his early readers and editors and his translator-wife and Oprah Winfrey. If the past keeps changing, it is because it is alive within and around us.

In an earlier published version of this study of the Yiddish and French versions of Wiesel's memoir, I ended my analysis by asking a final question, one that echoed and reversed the question that ends *Un di velt hot geshvign:*

Was it worth it? Was it worth translating the Holocaust out of the language of the largest portion of its victims and into *the language of those who were, at best, absent, and at worst, complicitous in the genocide?* Was it worth "unshattering" the mirror the Yiddish Elie breaks, reviving the image of the Jew as the Nazis wished him to be, as the Christian is prepared to accept him, the emblem of suffering silence rather than living rage? In the complex negotiations that resulted in the manuscript of *Night*, did the astonishing gains make good the tremendous losses? It is over this unspoken question that the culture of Holocaust discourse has arisen and taken shape.[108]

My question implied a more deliberate stance on Wiesel's part than I would now argue. What we see in the transformation of the French version of *Night* is also the transformation of its author. Ron Rosenbaum, in a response to the published article, put it clearly enough, writing that I "seem to imply a kind of bad faith on Wiesel's part as an explanation for the excision of his thoughts about anti-German revenge; that he was attempting to make his persona more palatable to the Christian West, to curry favor." Rosenbaum goes on to suggest another explanation for the Yiddish–French changes, arguing that Wiesel's "thinking might genuinely have *changed* between the Yiddish version and the French revision."[109] While I did write, and continue to believe, that Wiesel's friendship with Mauriac was accompanied by a genuine self-transformation on the part of the Jewish writer, there is something to Rosenbaum's critique that my reading of Wiesel amounts to an unfair accusation. If my thinking on this subject has changed since 1996, it is not only because of a number of intelligent responses to the published article; in the larger context that is this book, I now read Wiesel's self-translation as part of the tradition of safeguarding Jewish privacy. From this point of view, the implicit charge that Wiesel was "unfaithful" to the original Yiddish text can be nearly reversed, to highlight his faithfulness to the Jewish community. This recontextualization within a tradition of Jewish translation practice does not, I think, annul the argument that Wiesel's cultural negotiations traded away elements of his Yiddish work, but it lends historical weight to both the necessity (real or perceived) and value of these transactions.

It also seems clear to me now that Wiesel's Yiddish–French revisions should be read not in the rather stricter light of ordinary translation but as part of the more flexible and fascinating practice of self-translation, of creating "second originals."[110] From this perspective, Wiesel's move from Yiddish to French provides a map of the intellectual, but also political and religious, development of a young writer. Any apparent contradiction between these two points—Wiesel as keeper of Jewish secrets, and Wiesel as budding existentialist—is a function, I think, of the ambivalent operations of self-translation. The case of Wiesel's self-transformation is all the more fascinating because it is not unique. For many survivors, the years after the war of rebuilding their health and their communities represented a comparable if not identical cultural-linguistic journey.

For other critics, what Rosenbaum saw as the accusatory tone of my interpretation of Wiesel was not only unfair; it was disrespectful, even blasphemous, and ultimately, as Eli Pfefferkorn and David Hirsch put it, it was "more corrosive than Holocaust revisionism."[111] It would be easy enough to attack the philosophical incoherence of such Holocaust fundamentalism, by which I mean the insistence on the unmediated character of Holocaust testimony. But I would rather draw attention to a suppressed ethical dimension of the work I am doing here. To take Holocaust literature out of the realm of representation, of human culture, is to deny its writers a specific social, cultural, and psychological context. If the Nazi genocide succeeded in wiping out nearly every trace of East European Jewish culture, memorializing the Holocaust must also work to keep the richness of this culture alive, including the culture of that first wave of survivors of Nazi terror. From this perspective, a cultural analysis of survivor testimony does not "corrode" Holocaust memory but rather—it is my hope—enlivens it.

IN PRAISE OF MISTRANSLATION

In his *Heidegger and "the jews,"* Jean-François Lyotard suggests that "the jews" represent the unrepresentable, what must be forgotten in Heidegger's (indeed in Western) thought; Lyotard makes clear that he means by "the jews" not "real Jews" but rather the phantamagoric object of Europe's terror, dismissal, and persecution. Although this meditation on what "the jews" signify, or fail to signify, for European thought mostly brackets the reality of "real Jews," Lyotard turns in one passage to the phenomenon of the Jewish failure to recognize Nazi designs on their lives:

> The little child of Sighet writes: "The Germans were already in the town, the Fascists were already in power, the verdict had already been pronounced, and the Jews of Sighet continued to smile." One might say this indicates an inexplicable absence of political awareness, culpable innocence, passivity, and the like. The extermination falls upon them, and they are unable to represent it to themselves. Incredulous, they have to learn from others that it is they who are to be exterminated, it is they who have been represented as the enemy in the Nazi madness. . . . They have no means to represent to themselves the abjection and the extermination of which they are the victims.[112]

In this passage, Europe's failure to see "the jews" as they are is met by the failure of the Jews to see how they are seen, to recognize themselves as the objects of Europe's madness and "abjection." Lyotard captures not only this mutual misapprehension (which has sharply differentiated effects) but also, in the passage that follows, the horror it evokes in the observer. This horror is not unrelated to the murderous impulse itself, a desire to hit the Jewish target that is propelled by the very impossibility of finding the mark. This failure perpetuates the uncanny survival, beyond representation and beyond genocide, of "the jews." And so the cycle of persecution and innocence continues.

As disturbing as Lyotard's analysis is, there can be no doubt that it accurately reflects one of the characteristic features of post-Holocaust discourse: the peculiarly intense outrage directed at Europe's Jews, for not knowing sooner what the Nazis had in store for them, for not leaving Germany in 1933 or Poland in 1939, for not resisting Nazism more successfully. The ready responses to these challenges—were the Jews supposed to know Nazi intentions before the Final Solution was formulated? Which countries opened their doors to the Jewish refugees? Did the Warsaw Ghetto Uprising not hold back the German forces longer than the Polish army had?—are ineffectual for perhaps the reasons Lyotard intimates, that these questions arise not from any genuine interest in Jewish experience or concern for Jewish survival but rather from the same irrational and inchoate horror of "the jews" that is the psychic source of anti-Jewish persecution. That such accusations of "culpable innocence" seem to be directed primarily (or only?) at Jewish victims, and that they remain impervious to the usual forms of argumentation, suggests that they operate outside the political realities they pretend to engage.

I would propose, though, that Lyotard has missed something in his analysis of Jewish "culpable innocence," though he accurately captures how it is perceived by European eyes. From the Jewish perspective, the gap between how the Jews are seen and how they see themselves is a source of more than just passive bewilderment or neglect. The theater of misapprehension is something Jewish culture knows well; this misapprehension is mined for its comic potential and exploited for Jewish advantage as often as it is mourned or decried (as Wiesel does in Lyotard's citation of *Night*). It may be true that these cultural tools were ineffectual in the face of Nazism. Nevertheless, that Jewish culture recognizes that it misrecognizes, and sometimes mobilizes this misrecognition, complicates the rhetoric of Jewish ignorance that has long soured Holocaust memory.

In the first few decades of Holocaust discourse, the narrative of Jewish resistance shouldered the burden of defending Jewish honor (especially in

Israel, where Jewish heroism was at a new premium). It has taken half a century for a different counterrhetoric to emerge, this time not denying, minimizing, or explaining Jewish passivity or ignorance but rather recasting such Jewish responses as another kind of heroism. I am referring here especially to the 1998 Roberto Benigni film *Life Is Beautiful,* which makes a case (the viewer will have to decide how strong a case) for the viability, in the teeth of the Nazi genocide, of misapprehension as a mode of Jewish survival.[113]

Life Is Beautiful was widely criticized, especially initially; critics were not shy about asserting that they loathed it. It is not hard to understand why. The film sins against at least one cardinal rule of Holocaust representation: not to mitigate the horrors of the Nazi crimes against the Jews. The very title *Life Is Beautiful,* given that half the film is set in a concentration camp, grates on the ear; the genre, romantic comedy, seems hardly suitable to the subject portrayed; to make matters worse, *Life Is Beautiful* presents a series of implausible scenarios, the central one being the survival of a young child, more or less unscathed, in the Auschwitz concentration camp. The critics are united in decrying the impossibility of such a scenario. David Denby, who reviewed the film twice for the *New Yorker,* once when it was released and again a few months later to protest its popularity, writes, "Surely Benigni knows that any child entering Auschwitz would be immediately put to death. . . . Benigni wants the authority of the Holocaust without the actuality."[114] In his harshest assessment, Denby adds that the fact that audiences could leave the film feeling happy was evidence that *Life Is Beautiful* "is a benign form of Holocaust denial."

There is a growing number of critics who defend the film, however. Hilene Flanzbaum, taking note of the widespread critique of Benigni's unfaithfulness to Holocaust realities, argues that "the absolute demand for verisimilitude placed on artistic representations of the Holocaust in our culture may once have been necessary, but today they have little use."[115] Speaking of Holocaust representation in general, Millicent Marcus concurs:

> If the purpose of Holocaust witness is dynamic transmission . . . then the narrative must remain open to constant elaboration, adaptation, and rearticulation in ways that will recommend it to new generations of readers. To insist on a documentary approach to the representation of the Holocaust is to consign it to the archives, to embalm it and distance it in a way that will deprive this history of its urgent moral claim to our attention.[116]

Writing in the same mode, Sidra DeKoven Ezrahi establishes the genre of Begnini's film as fable, beginning with the "patently artificial, romantically

Edenic space" constructed in the opening scenes of the film. The comic quality of the film, Ezrahi writes,

> provides a continual alternative to history's implacable verdict. The comic is constructed as an act of revolt based on faith in a higher truth, in History-as-it-was-and-will-be. It is a protest against a set of generically rendered facts about the fate of Jews during World War II. . . . Any consideration of the comic must therefore engage with what is essentially its counterhistorical pretense, its daring attempt at erasure in the foreground of what remains its historical backdrop.[117]

Although Roberto Benigni is not Jewish, Ezrahi reads his film in the context of a "cultural Jewish attitude, that of the story as a meliorative version of history." Central to this story is a familiar roster of Jewish characters, "*shlemiels* in varying degrees of incredulity and heroic self-invention."[118]

The achievement of *Life Is Beautiful*, all would concur, is not in the realm of Holocaust documentation; in fact, it is precisely the documentary approach to history that is rejected in and by the film. The counterargument to the rhetoric of Jewish passivity and ignorance put forward by *Life Is Beautiful* asserts that it is not *knowledge* of the hateful enemy that safeguards the Jew but rather a principled blindness to a repulsive reality. In *Life Is Beautiful*, the protagonist Guido keeps his son Giosuè alive in Auschwitz by persuading him, through a series of antics, that the concentration camp is the setting for an elaborate game in which he must play hide-and-seek all day and refrain from whining for food or for his mother. If he wins, he will be awarded the grand prize of "a real tank," the toy he has long coveted.

As Ezrahi has suggested, Guido's actions are part of a counterhistorical Jewish tradition that includes the *deliberate* failure to recognize oneself as the object of antisemitism. The scene, late in the film, in which Guido carries his sleeping son past what appears to be an open mass grave emblematizes this strategy. Marcus writes:

> The image of the man holding his sleeping child against this phantasmagoric background presents, in germinal form, the entire narrative of the film's second half. Guido's job is to keep Giosuè "asleep" to the horrors that await them in the pit. The mortal stake of Guido's game emerges here . . . to keep the child from falling into the despair that would mean surrender to Nazi attempts at dehumanization.[119]

Although in this scene it is the innocence of a child that is being preserved, his father Guido, as played by Benigni, treats Nazism as a farce from the earliest scenes of the film, ridiculing fascist rhetoric and blithely discovering in an array of threats against him an opportunity for mimicry and buffoonery.

Life Is Beautiful takes every opportunity to present Guido as dedicated to the preservation of his own happy ignorance of Nazi threats, even before such ignorance becomes a concerted strategy to fool his son into making it to the end of the war.

In a pivotal and brilliant scene that follows soon upon the arrival of father and son in the camp, it becomes clear that the echoes of the Jewish comic tradition Ezrahi discerns in Benigni's Italian film are also echoes of the more specific Jewish tradition of comic mistranslation. In the first scene that takes place in the barracks, the SS corporal calls for a prisoner to translate his barked German into Italian. Although he knows no German, Guido takes the opportunity to volunteer for the job, and then to mistranslate the cruel orders into benign announcements of the rules of the game for the benefit of his son, who is standing among the prisoners. "Attention! I'm only going to say this once!" barks the German. Guido, standing at his side, barks: "Okay, the game begins! If you're here you're here, if you're not, you're not!" The corporal continues: "You are here for one reason. To work!" Guido "translates": "The first one to score a thousand points wins. A real tank!" And, a few lines later, when the corporal shouts, "You are privileged to work for our great Germany, building our great empire!" Guido echoes, "We play the part of the mean guys who yell! Whoever's scared loses points!"[120] In a rapid, tour-de-force sequence, Guido mimics not only the rhythm and tone of the German guard, but also his counting off three rules on his fingers, transformed in Guido's Italian into something far less menacing.

> CORPORAL [in German]: There are three very important rules. One: Never attempt escape. Two: Obey all orders without asking questions. Three: Any attempt at organized riots will be punished by hanging.
> (*loudly*)
> Is that clear?
> GUIDO: You can lose all your points for any one of three things. One: If you cry. Two: If you ask to see your mother. Three: If you're hungry and ask for a snack!
> (*loudly*)
> Forget it![121]

This mistranslation is, on the most basic level, a ploy to secure Giosuè's cooperation in his father's attempts to save his life by translating the Nazi war machine into—literally—child's play. The most effective way Guido ensures that Giosuè will not register the disruption of his world is in cutting the Nazis down to size. As Marcus writes, "By becoming simply 'those bad guys who yell' [the Nazis are turned into] hyberbolic versions of the strict teachers, irritable parents, and grumpy neighbors who temporarily darken the horizons of all normal childhood experience."[122] It is not only the Nazi who is transformed in this translation, from the incarnation of demonic evil into an oafish bully; the Jewish prisoner (to the viewer if not to his son) is transformed as well, from a dehumanized victim into a clever manipulator (through the eminently Jewish tool of language) of his very circumscribed situation. In the translation scene, which juxtaposes the sad-clown face of Benigni with the bullet head of the guard, the ratio of difference between Nazi and Jew is both registered and recalculated.

The tradition of creative mistranslation traced in this book has primarily involved rendering Jewish into non-Jewish languages rather than mistranslating murderous non-Jewish discourse into comic Jewish language. But the mistranslation at the heart of *Life Is Beautiful* is a cousin to the one in the Talmud: Ptolemy's cells are not so far off from Guido's barracks, and the preservation of a Jewish language-world, in the face of an overwhelming attempt to break it down, is the goal of both narratives. (Both are also fictional rewrites—mistranslations—of history rather than accurate representations of it.) And both stories cast the Jewish mistranslator as the hero, who manipulates the differences between languages and cultures in favor of Jewish lives and truths.

In the film's most audacious move, Guido's machinations turn out to be not only brave but also successful. Although he himself is eventually shot, his son survives and at the end of the film even gets his prize, when the American liberation forces roll into the camp and a soldier lifts him high onto his tank. In the final scene, Giosuè is reunited with his mother, who has survived the women's camp and is in a convoy of prisoners streaming past the tank. As she embraces her son, he exclaims, "We won!"

In insisting that being "asleep" to the antisemitic representation of "the jew" is a viable strategy for Jewish survival, Benigni makes his strongest defense not only of Guido's "culpable innocence" but also of the film's own artistic stance. The praise of mistranslation advanced in *Life Is Beautiful* thus acts as an apology for the film's own mistranslations, its transformation of unrelieved horror into a kind of comic redemption. The two mistranslations, Guido's strategic use of mistranslation to save his son and the film's transformation of the Holocaust into a romantic comedy, thus work in tandem: only in this fantastic world can a mistranslation lead to a child surviving Auschwitz; and only the survival of an innocent child can justify such filmic misrepresentation.

What is at stake in Benigni's work? Is it the integrity of the Jewish imaginary or the survival of Jewish children? In presenting Giosuè with his "real tank" at the end of the film, *Life Is Beautiful* seems to imply that the two cannot be separated. As the camera pulls back from the embracing mother and son, the narrator's voice (it is now clear that he is Giosuè) intones, "This is my story." As Benigni seems to be saying, what counts in film is the subjective experience of an individual, or, to put it differently, the viability of the Jewish imagination. If Guido's comic recasting of Nazi evil into a child's game can save his son, then Benigni's production of a comic film set in Auschwitz may have similar redemptive powers.

How are we to take Benigni's defense? Does this misrecognition, this refusal of realism, *really* work as Jewish political strategy? The conundrum posited by the film calls, it seems to me, for a Kafkaesque solution:

> Many complain that the words of the wise are always merely parables and of no use in daily life, which is the only life we have. . . .
>
> Concerning this a man once said: Why such reluctance? If you only followed the parables you yourselves would become parables and with that rid of all your daily cares.
>
> Another said: I bet that is also a parable.
>
> The first said: You have won.
>
> The second said: But unfortunately only in parable.
>
> The first said: No, in reality: in parable you have lost.[123]

If it is among the tasks of Holocaust discourse to salvage the memory of Europe's Jews, then we must also remember a Jewish tradition of comic, salvific ignorance. Whether Benigni should be read as a filmer of parables or as offering counsel in the "real world," the brute facts of history cannot silence Jewish fantasy. In this era as in the Talmud's imagined Ptolemaic Alexandria, mistranslation reminds us that there are worlds that remain untouched, undreamed, under the regime of "correct" translation.

CHAPTER SIX

✳

Translation and Assimilation

Singer in America

Yiddish into English follows in the footsteps of American Jewry, and Bashevis was all too eager to move in that direction. Had he not been willing, and perhaps eager, to cross the street, he would undoubtedly have been left behind. But he wanted more than to cross over—he wanted to be able to move in two directions at once. For the most part he succeeded, but even he could not walk the tightrope without occasionally falling.

    IRVING SAPOSNIK, "A Canticle for Isaac: A *Kaddish* for Bashevis"

Singer... did not become a writer for all seasons in the twinkling of an (evil) eye. What's amazing is that he did it at all. For a time when life is so fragmented that only in a scholarly journal can one even speak anymore of a coherent Jewish culture, it is comforting, if not downright miraculous, to have someone living in our midst who managed to pull all the pieces together.

    DAVID ROSKIES, Introduction to *Prooftexts* issue on I. B. Singer

THE POIGNANT truth that underlies Cynthia Ozick's hilarious novella "Envy; or, Yiddish in America" is that translation is the only means of survival for secular Yiddish literature. As the title implies, to be translated is an enviable condition indeed, catapulting the Yiddish writer from the claustrophobic sphere of Yiddish letters into the larger realm beyond. "Envy" is propelled by the desperate search for a translator by Edelshtein, an aging Yiddishist embittered at a world that exalts one of his peers (arbitrarily and unfairly, to Edelshtein's mind) into the higher regions of literary fame while consigning all other Yiddish writers to oblivion. In a soliloquy worthy of a

Yiddish King Lear, Edelshtein rages at the one writer who has escaped the dark fate of Yiddish literature:

> Ostrover was released from the dungeon of the dailies, from the *Bitterer Yam* and even seedier nullities, he was free, the outside world knew his name. And why Ostrover? Why not somebody else? Was Ostrover more gifted than Komorsky? Did he think up better stories than Horowitz? Why does the world outside pick on an Ostrover instead of an Edelshtein or even a Baumzweig? . . . Why only Ostrover? Ostrover should be the only one? Everyone else sentenced to darkness, Ostrover alone saved? Ostrover the survivor? As if hidden in the Dutch attic like that child. His diary, so to speak, the only documentation of what was. Like Ringelblum of Warsaw. Ostrover was to be the only evidence that there was once a Yiddish tongue, a Yiddish literature? And all the others lost? Lost! Drowned. Snuffed out. Under the earth. As if never.[1]

Ozick's story reverses the usual American perspective on Jewish literature: Edelshtein refers to Anne Frank, whose name is familiar across the globe, as "that child," while he lists his circle of unknown Yiddish writers by name after unfamiliar name. From his own overwhelmingly *literary* perspective, it makes sense that Edelshtein thinks of Anne Frank as the lone survivor of a general catastrophe—although Frank did not in fact survive the war. From this same perspective, the Yiddish writers who did not find an audience in translation are like victims of the Holocaust, although there is nothing to suggest that they succumbed to antisemitic violence rather than the ecumenical indifference of the publishing world. What counts in this skewed tally is *whose work will be read;* in this worldview, it is translation alone that spells the difference between living on and being "snuffed out."

Ozick marshals a range of narrative devices to drive home the connection between translation and physical survival. For Edelshtein, translation signifies not only the possibility of finding a readership but also human contact and a reprieve from the death sentence that came swiftly to most of the world's Yiddish speakers and which hangs over his own head. Ozick's unflinching prose juxtaposes this literary and corporeal mortality, signaling the desperation of the Yiddish writer's situation in his obsession with the decay of the body as in his feverish desire for the attentions of the young (it is no coincidence that Edelshtein worries that "he might be, unknown to himself all his life long, a secret pederast").[2] Edelshtein, leaving his friends' apartment in quest of his translator, looks back as the old sleeping couple: "How reduced they seemed, each breath a little demand for more, more, more, a shudder of jowls."[3] Literature and life are both a fierce struggle for survival.

Edelshtein is not alone in viewing Yiddish literature against the backdrop of death. In a major essay on Yiddish and translation, Anita Norich has suggested that the cultural survival of Yiddish in postwar America can hardly be separated from the Holocaust, from the recognition, as Edelshtein puts it, that Yiddish was "lost, murdered. . . . Of what other language can it be said that it died a sudden and definite death, in a given decade, on a given piece of soil?"[4] In Norich's view, the "old culture wars" about the role of Yiddish in Jewish life "have given way to a debate about survival itself. And, inevitably in modern Jewish culture, that debate evokes the Holocaust."[5]

The politics of translation in this cultural atmosphere is complicated by the fact that translation rescues only a select few, deciding with peremptory arbitrariness "who shall live and who shall die." It is Ozick's particular genius to tell the story of "Yiddish in America" from the perspective of one not chosen. The novel, too transparent in its allusions to the larger Yiddish scene to merit the title of roman à clef, gives us a glimpse of the Yiddish literature cast in the shadow of its great and singular success story. Ostrover is clearly a stand-in for Isaac Bashevis Singer; it is part of the story of Yiddish in America that no other contender comes close. As for whom Ozick had in mind in the figure of Edelshtein, there are enough contenders to fill those shoes: David Roskies mentions the Yiddish poet Jacob Glatstein, whose name (sometimes rendered as Yankev Glatshteyn) rhymes nicely with Edelshtein's.[6] Although Glatstein (unlike Edelshtein) did in fact publish some poetry and memoirs in English translation, his disdain for Bashevis was no secret. Speaking with some understatement, Glatstein wrote in 1965 that "the Yiddish reader is much less enthusiastic about Isaac Bashevis Singer's unpleasant stories than his non-Jewish reader."[7] But there are other candidates, including the novelist Chaim Grade—who also appeared in English, to somewhat greater notice, and whose status as Singer's chief rival and "unjustly neglected" Yiddish writer is carried on by his widow, Inna, who openly declares her loathing for Singer. During the centennial celebrations for Isaac Bashevis Singer in 2004, the *New York Times* published an article on the hatred (not limited to Inna Grade) Singer inspired in the world of Yiddish:

> "I profoundly despise him," said Mrs. Grade, the 75-year-old widow of the Yiddish writer Chaim Grade. "I am very sorry that America is celebrating the blasphemous buffoon."
>
> At even the slightest mention of Singer's name—which she will not allow herself to pronounce—Mrs. Grade (pronounced GRA-duh) becomes virtually unhinged. "I despise him especially because he is dragging the Jewish literature, Judaism, American literature, American culture back to the land of Moab," she

said, referring to the biblical region where Lot and his daughters began an incestuous affair. "I profoundly despise all those who eat the bread into which the blasphemous buffoon has urinated." Grade was of course referring to the famous scene in Singer's best-known story, "Gimpel the Fool," in which Gimpel urinates into the town's bread.[8]

Echoes of the fictional Edelshtein's lament over the exclusive attention to an unworthy writer can be heard as well in the writings of the very real Yiddish literary critic Irving Saposnik, although he never cites Ozick's story (except perhaps indirectly in the first sentence):

> From the beginning, Singer's success has been both the wonder and the envy of the Yiddish world. Many asked: Why him? Why not Khayim Grade, who wrote better, or Singer's brother, who far eclipsed him and would surely have been more successful had he not died young? But Singer was more than just a writer; he was an entrepreneur, a skillful marketer of both his image and his imagination. Much like his most famous character Gimpel, he was shrewder than he pretended to be, far more the wily peasant than the impish old man who loved to feed the pigeons in the park. Singer often read his American audience better than they read him, and he proceeded to give them what they wanted, all the time concealing both his literary and literal Yiddish originals. With both Yiddish originals effectively concealed, the selling of Singer began. Sharp edges were smoothed, ethnic quirks turned into old world charm, *shtetl* superstitions passed for venerable wisdom, and Bashevis crossed over from the mundane obscurity of a Yiddish writer to being the darling of the literary world.[9]

From Saposnik's perspective, and he is not alone, Singer's success in English translation is a product of neither native talent, nor dumb luck, nor even the congruence between a particular style and the tastes of an available readership. Singer's triumphs derive from his skill at marketing himself, his pulling the wool over the eyes of a clueless English-speaking world. Translation in this view is trickery, and Singer is the snake-oil salesman. This paranoid scenario, in which America represents both the great prize for a Yiddish writer and the betrayal of all ideals, echoes Edelshtein in yet another of his harangues. Describing the contemporary American-Jewish literary scene with his characteristic mixture of envy and contempt, Edelshtein sneers at the "writers of Jewish extraction," the "*Amerikaner-geboren:* Spawned in America, pogroms a rumor, *mamaloshen* a stranger, history a vacuum." Although Edelshtein is certain he does not envy them, "he read them like a sickness."[10]

Yiddish into English follows this American-Jewish historical trajectory from the immigrant generation to the superficial, vulgar, and ignorant writers that come in their wake, in both Edelshtein's and Saposnik's schemas. Not only is the literary scene transformed by this generational shift, but those few Yiddish writers who succeed in finding a home in the world of this second generation do so only by bowing to its dictates. Translation follows a single route, that of assimilation; in Singer's (and Ostrover's) case, this translation-as-assimilation is aggravated because it takes the form—as Saposnik sees it—of a deliberate and devious act of self-transformation to please a new public. David Roskies similarly suggests that Singer's entry into the American scene was a calculated act of cultural infiltration: Singer "began to practice the art of seduction, and when his Yiddish readers proved too skeptical or too preoccupied to be trapped in the writer's web, the demon-writer found a new pool of unsuspecting victims in the native born readers of America and still later—in their children."[11] This view of Singer as a slippery operator is no doubt compounded by the difficulty in locating the Yiddish versions of some of his English works (many of which appeared only in the Yiddish press), by his self-mythologizing as impish sage, and by the bewildering variety of different names (Bashevis, Singer, Warshavsky, and the recently identified D. Segal) under which he published in various genres, languages, and contexts; Saposnik refers to these phenomena as a whole as evidence of "the concealed Yiddish originals" of Isaac Bashevis Singer.

It is worth drawing a distinction here between the *truly* concealed Yiddish original of Elie Wiesel's *Night,* the existence of which was not generally known before Wiesel wrote of it in the preface to the new translation (2006), and the Yiddish originals of Isaac Bashevis Singer, which while not easily accessible to those who could read them, are universally known to exist, indeed in some sense underwrite the charm, the "Yiddishness" (I do not say *yidishkeyt*), of Singer's work. What Singer's English readers want is Yiddish-in-translation, a Yiddish that "real Yiddishists" might claim is tainted by exoticism, vulgarity, and kitsch. And it is this Yiddishness that Singer—unlike Wiesel—so readily (to his critics, mendaciously) supplies.

It would have been out of character for Singer himself to express reservations about his life in translation, but the Yiddish literary world had no such difficulty. Ozick's Edelshtein, to take a fictional example, saw the potential losses of translation as clearly as he envisaged its benefits. If translation tenders a reprieve to the mortal writer and dying language, it is an ambiguous and partial—if not completely illusory—reprieve. Yiddish lives on in English translation only in crippled or deracinated form, as something utterly unfamiliar to itself. Norich writes that the issue of translation from Yiddish is complicated by the question of "how a Jewish language steeped in Jewish ritual and culture can hope to be understood in non-Jewish languages."[12] The question is not a new one. In one of his first published writings, a review of a number of Yiddish-German translations that had recently appeared, Gershom Scholem put it with characteristic force, and with a typically exalted view of the Hebrew *"Sprachgeist"*:

> The problem of translating Yiddish literary works in a way that would be in principle unimpeachable is among the most difficult in the art of translation. This difficulty derives from the specific duality of the Yiddish language, which in its innermost form is already a translation. Speaking strictly linguistically, the translator then faces, *in principle,* the task—which appears paradoxical only on superficial observation—of reproducing the entire spiritual structure of a literary work, indeed in a deeper sense of the language as a whole . . . in what was originally a parallel sphere; he thus has an incomparably difficult problem before him. The inner form of Yiddish, whose highest and most distinct spiritual structure derives not from itself, but from Hebrew, is a reproduction of the Hebrew linguistic spirit in German which provides its substance to a certain extent, and so anyone who wishes to translate today from Yiddish into German has to repeat this reproductive process.[13]

Given the mutual entanglement of Hebrew and German within the Yiddish language, Scholem continues, translation from Yiddish into German requires a nearly impossible feat: the restitution of the Hebrew dimension in a language that lacks it. Translation into German then inevitably threatens to strip Yiddish of "its highest and most distinct spiritual structure," leaving it "soulless and cold."[14] What is "highest" in the Yiddish is its Hebrew component, and that is precisely what must be both reconstituted and relinquished in translation.

The case of translation from Yiddish into English is not so different: it is the "Jewish" component of Yiddish that often complicates the translational process, while the non-Jewish component may be translated into English with no more than the usual difficulties. While the marriage of Hebrew and German in Yiddish emblematizes this complication for Scholem, what I have called the Jewish component is not limited to the Hebrew elements in Yiddish; there is a sense, indeed, in which the Hebrew within a Yiddish text, for instance its allusions to the Hebrew Bible, represents the *most* translatable aspect of Yiddish, given the path paved for the Bible in other languages. In another sense, the Hebrew *within Yiddish* is often only apparently part of a shared Jewish–Christian biblical heritage. In a haranguing letter to Hannah, the young woman he fruitlessly hopes to make his translator, Edelshtein writes:

Also: please remember that when a goy from Columbus, Ohio, says "Elijah the Prophet" he's not talking about *Eliohu hanovi*. Eliohu is one of us, a *folksmensh*, running around in second-hand clothes. Theirs is God knows what. The same biblical figure, with exactly the same history, once he puts on a name from King James, COMES OUT A DIFFERENT PERSON.[15]

The Western literary tradition remembers the Bible in the King James Version, rarely recognizing the distance between the exalted English diction and the various indigenous Hebrew-Jewish traditions within which biblical tropes evolved and were domesticated. For Edelshtein, the ready translation pair of Eliohu and Elijah turns out to be composed of "false friends." In the fuzzy realm of "Judeo-Christianity," the obstacles to and channels for translation cannot always readily be distinguished.

Translation, whether it results in the exalted tones of the King James Version or the exotic "types" of Ostrover's stories, parallels the cultural movement of assimilation; the survival of a Jewish language is often at the cost of a drastic reconfiguration, a mutilation of its most distinctive features. Edelshtein's envy for the translated Ostrover is thickened rather than diminished by the disgust he feels for what translation has wrought in Ostrover: positioning him as exotic sage and rendering his distasteful and barely veiled literary gossip into profound existential conundrums for the Freud-loving deracinated Jewish literati of Manhattan's Upper West Side. The choice before the Yiddish writer is, as Edelshtein puts it in the letter to Hannah, between "death through forgetting or death through translation."[16]

In a provocative passage in her essay, Norich suggests that what I have highlighted here as Edelshtein's double bind is generally characteristic of the survival of Yiddish as a whole after the Holocaust:

Yiddish, in this context, can be understood as resistance, and translation as an act of collaboration in the destruction of a culture, a betrayal of the language in which it flourished and the millions who spoke it. Yet at the same time, and in apparent contradiction to this view of translation as a kind of violation, the cultural valence of contemporary Yiddish suggests that translation, too, is an act of resistance to history. Increasingly, everything one does with or in Yiddish—speaking, reading, writing, teaching, translation, scholarship—will be understood as a defiant gesture aimed at preserving the traces of a culture that has undergone startling and dreadful transformations in this century. Faced with the indisputably declining population of Yiddish readers, we cannot ignore the likelihood that Yiddish texts may only continue to flourish in translation. This, in turn, places an extraordinary demand on translators to be meticulously accurate and utterly literal in their translations.[17]

Translation from Yiddish is thus a particularly fraught cultural activity, expressing itself both as betrayal and as redemption, as resistance and as assimilation. It is within a literary environment which Norich characterizes as demanding absolute fidelity to the Yiddish original, moreover, that Singer's translation enterprise emerges: in fact, the translations of Singer's work into English, whether done under or outside Singer's supervision, are not "meticulously accurate and utterly literal," as Norich goes on to note. Singer has defended the freedom of his English renderings by pointing to his own involvement in their translation, a move Seth Wolitz characterizes as "a brilliant sleight of hand": Insisting that he edits and supervises all the translations of his work, Singer has proposed that they be read as "a second original." The translations "are in many ways more direct, more to the point."[18] The paradigmatic figure of the Yiddish writer in English, then, confounds the very terms by which Yiddish literature has confronted the promise and peril of translation, resisting its strict hierarchy of original and translation, Yiddish and English, authenticity and betrayal.

Although Yiddish in many ways represents a unique case study, many of the issues in Yiddish translation are also recognized in the field of postcolonial translation (whether or not Yiddish is considered part of this field). As postcolonialist translation theorists have long recognized, the colonial or minority literature navigates an unequal linguistic field, in which the dominant culture of the target language exerts what is often felt to be a disproportionate advantage over that of the source literature. This dominance is expressed first of all in the choice of which writers will be translated, and thus which writers will come to "represent" an otherwise unknown literature in the First World metropolis. But the dominance of the target culture is felt as well in the shape of the translation, which will often follow target-language norms in its bid for a place in the dominant culture. Taking Salman Rushdie as his prime example, Timothy Brennan has written that the privileging of those he calls "cosmopolitan" writers as "interpreters and authentic public voices of the Third World" is a function of the compliance of these writers with a "metropolitan audience's tastes" for certain types of narrative.[19] Drawing on a vocabulary of international commerce, sanctions, preferences, and trade imbalances in his essay on "Embargoed Literature," Edward Said has described the operations of crosscultural censorship in determining which Arabic writers are considered worthy of translation and which are not. "There almost seems to be a deliberate policy," Said writes, "of maintaining a kind of monolithic reductionism where the Arabs and Islam are concerned; in this, the Orientalism that distances and dehumanizes another culture is upheld, and the xenophobic fantasy of a pure 'Western' identity elevated and strengthened."[20]

In an article entitled "Translation, Colonialism and Poetics: Rabindranath Tagore in Two Worlds," Mahasweta Sengupta draws attention to the second of the concerns raised above, the influence of target-culture norms on the translational process. Sengupta charts the English self-translation of the Bengali poet Rabindranath Tagore, who received the Nobel Prize for Literature in 1913 (the first time the prize was awarded to a non-European). Tagore's translational stance affected both his choice of poems to translate—he rendered only the more devotional or spiritual ones—and the ornate Victorian register into which he rendered them. As Sengupta writes, although his Bengali style was "in the colloquial diction of the actual spoken word," in English Tagore emulated the older and more conservative generation of British poets:

> What is apparent is that Tagore deliberately chooses to write like these poets when he translates his own poems into English; he makes adjustments to suit the ideology of the dominating culture or system, and therefore his translations fit the target-language poetics quite easily. He fits perfectly into the stereotypical role that was familiar to the colonizer, a voice that not only spoke of the peace and tranquility of a distant world, but that also offered an escape from the materialism of the contemporary Western world.[21]

There is a critique implicit in Sengupta's analysis of Tagore "between two worlds," a suggestion that Tagore betrayed his Bengali style and sold his soul to a middlebrow English reading public. It is thus with some satisfaction that Sengupta reports that, since literary styles changed almost immediately upon Tagore's great success, the Tagore fashion in England turned out to be as short-lived as it was intense.

What is implicit in Sengupta's essay on Tagore exploded to the surface of the Yiddish literary world, reinforced perhaps by the evidence that the Singer phenomenon is no passing fad. The stakes of English translation were also much higher for Yiddish writers: while Tagore could find a Bengali audience whether or not he succeeded in attracting attention in London, Yiddish writers could only expect an increasingly shrinking readership. Moreover, Tagore split his time between India and England, keeping his audiences separate; Singer (or, to put it otherwise, Ostrover), by contrast, rose to prominence on the American literary stage (the auditorium of the Ninety-Second Street Y, that is) in full view of his Yiddish-writing rivals. The contrast with Tagore should yield another insight as well: while Tagore gained a stage by speaking to the Western hunger for simplicity and the spirit, Ostrover (or

Singer) directs his work to the appetite among the New York intelligentsia for folkloristic erotica. What the metropolis wants from its translated authors— a mirror of its own preoccupations or Orientalist difference (or, as in Singer, both at the same time)—is not always predictable.

In giving voice to the Yiddish writers in the shadow of the translated, successful writer, "Envy" presents us with the drama of postcolonial translation from an unusual perspective, not that of the translated (if mutilated) writer or of the appreciative (if hoodwinked) audience, but that of the writer who has been left completely out of this traffic, who lacks even the *opportunity* to "sell out." From the perspective of the target audience, the translated writer represents the entire culture and literature of his source language. From the perspective of the writers untouched by success, the translated writer embodies the unsavory character of interlinguistic commerce, as both wily manipulator of an unsuspecting readership and obsequious servant to alien norms.

Ozick gives us little of Ostrover's motivations unfiltered by the envy and disdain of his Yiddish peers. In the case of Singer himself, though, we are fortunate to possess the writer's own meditations on the problems of language and style. There is crucial evidence, in fact, that the piquant combination of traditionalism and modernism that struck such a chord with American readers was developed—rather late in Singer's career, but well before he was first translated—not with an eye to a potentially larger audience but rather because of the *internal* literary conditions of Yiddish in America, as he encountered them after his 1935 immigration. The approach he laid out in 1943 could hardly have been taken with translation in mind, since it set up a host of fresh problems for prospective translators. The 1943 essay Singer published after a long period in which he was unable to respond creatively to the American context could be read as a manifesto for the Yiddish writer in America and for Singer's particular resolution of the problems posed by American Yiddish. The Yiddish that had developed on American shores, Singer declared, was unusable for Yiddish fiction because of its impoverishment and falsity:

> A great number of Yiddish words and phrases are so tightly bound to the old country that, when used here, they appear not only to be imported from another land, but borrowed from a completely alien conceptual system, half obliterated by time. In general, it can be said that however poor the Yiddish lexicon was on the other side of the Atlantic, here its impoverishment has become even greater. . . . Words, like people, sometimes endure a severe disorientation when they emigrate, and often they remain forever helpless and not quite themselves. This is precisely what happened to Yiddish in America.[22]

Given the impoverishment of Yiddish in America, the Yiddish writer has only one choice, to seek his subject in those "places and periods Jews spoke Yiddish." If he chooses to write in Yiddish,

> the Yiddish writer is bound to the past. His boundaries are, spatially, the borders of Poland, Russia and Rumania, and, temporally, the date of his departure for America. Here he must, in a literary sense, dine on leftovers; only food prepared in the old world can nourish him in the new. . . . Yiddish literature is a product of the ghetto with all its virtues and faults, and it can never leave the ghetto.[23]

Nevertheless, Singer continues, a Yiddish writer need not be old-fashioned in his approach, even if he dines on leftovers from the Old Country: "Psychoanalysis can be applied to a story from the past just as well as to a slice of life still warm with reality."[24]

This combination of a modern perspective and a dense, rich, and traditional Yiddish idiom, the necessity for which Singer argues in this essay, captures more than just the specific flavor of Singer's prose style. It also serves to explain both the welcome Singer found in the contemporary American literary scene and his own growing estrangement from a Yiddish literary world that shared his language but not his thematic and stylistic norms. Certainly Yiddish forged its own brands of modernism, and some of Singer's greatest critics were also champions of one or another Yiddish modernism; but Singer's kind of modernism, with its traditional referents and grotesque eroticism, was considered both literarily unsophisticated and thematically vulgar: in Glatshteyn's view, Singer "dehumanizes" his characters "by forcing them to commit the most ugly deeds. He brutalizes them and makes them so obnoxious that the Jewish reader is repelled."[25] By contrast, both the traditional world Singer described (or invented)—now a site of memory and loss—and the particular modernist perspective Singer brought to it provided a bridge to a readership at once less familiar with the traditional world than Singer's fellow Yiddish writers and more familiar with the psychoanalytic worldview in which it was framed. Thus, Singer could be treasured as both modernist and traditionalist—although not by "his own."

Despite this bridge, Singer's Yiddish is unusually difficult to translate. Singer often draws heavily on a premodern idiomatic repertoire (often but not always linked to Yiddish's Hebrew component), including the semantic field that Weinreich calls *lehavdl loshn*, the "differentiating language" that distinguishes between what is Jewish and what is not. This semantic field is untranslatable in part because English lacks the capacity to mark these distinctions—the interjection *"lehavdl,"* a verbal marker used to distinguish between a Jewish and non-Jewish phenomenon mentioned in uncomfortably or misleadingly close proximity, should serve as sufficient example; it has taken me eighteen words to "translate" what is conveyed in a single Yiddish word. Because *lehavdl loshn* often draws on the Hebrew component of Yiddish, as less understandable to a non-Jewish eavesdropper, translating this idiom comes up against the bilingualism of Yiddish itself, its amalgam of Hebrew and German, Slavic and other non-Jewish components. (Derrida has repeatedly pointed out the challenges posed by multilingual texts to translation.) Finally, *lehavdl loshn* represents an obstacle to translation because it constitutes the "hidden transcript" of East European Jews, a potentially offensive and inflammatory dimension of Jewish discourse if uttered in earshot of its non-Jewish targets. While Yiddish possesses a "neutral," high-culture lexicon from which Singer might easily have drawn (avoiding both *lehavdl loshn* and the immigrant "potato Yiddish"), the stories that appeared after his long post-immigration creative hiatus draw a considerable share of their power and wit from precisely the richly Jewish idiom of Singer's Yiddish. These stories often find their sharpest effects in the creative juxtaposition of traditional Yiddish speech and the break with Jewish tradition.

The translational difficulties I have been outlining, then, are not epiphenomenal to Singer's literary project; that is, they do not arise only in the American "afterlife" of his fictional universe. Rather, they derive from a thematic tension that resides at the heart of Singer's stories, in Yiddish as in English, between a Jewish language and a world it cannot always comfortably express or contain. To put it somewhat differently, the stories Singer wrote after 1943 are in some way *about translation*. This is especially true of the second story I will read here, "Zeidlus the Pope," in which the figure of the apostate-translator takes center stage. But "Gimpel the Fool," too, Singer's best-known story, addresses the question of truth and lies, both in the Jewish world and within the broader horizons of the literary imagination. The drama of Singer's transport to the American literary stage is foreshadowed in his wandering storytellers and transgressors of Jewish borders. From this point of view, there is no "pure" Yiddish realm from which these transgressions, translations, and assimilations proceed. It is Singer's signature to have resisted the fantasy of an originary space of authentic speech; the critic must do so as well. What I am arguing for here is a third way of reading Singer, one that accepts the integrity of both Yiddish and English versions as well as the play between them.

In "Envy," Edelshtein lays out a translational conundrum: "death through translation" or "death through forgetting." But Ozick's story itself presents a third translational option, not through criticism (as I offer) but rather through an English literature in which Yiddish is given honest expression. In "Envy," Edelshtein *is* preserved in English, finding a woman translator (Ozick), a fancy publisher (Schocken), and a voice precisely in the American-Jewish literature he treated with such disdain. Edelshtein's poem is even reproduced—finally!—in English; nor do we fail to hear his "authentic" Yiddish words transliterated in the story. Yet "Envy" is finally a work of American-Jewish fiction. Ozick embeds her cast of fictional Yiddish writers within a coarse, physical, "Freudian" setting far removed from the literary norms that framed their own subculture. To put it differently, Ozick has written a story about a Yiddish writer who is supposed to be the antithesis of Singer while mobilizing a host of techniques and even settings (the large, drafty apartments and gritty streets of the émigré Upper West Side) familiar from Singer's stories. The characters, from this point of view, are grotesque literary "types" rather than loving (sentimental, we might unkindly say) portraits from life. Ozick's story thus "recovers" these lost Yiddish figures but does not fail to also (inevitably?) mutilate them, in the familiar language and images of Singer himself. Singer may by now be inescapable; which is to say, the effects of translation may be impossible to reverse.

WHO'S THE FOOL? GIMPEL IN ENGLISH

The first of Isaac Bashevis Singer's works to appear in English translation, published in 1950 by Knopf, was his novel *The Family Moskat*. It was Saul Bellow's much-admired 1952 translation of the short story "Gimpel the Fool," though, that truly inaugurated Singer's remarkable career in English. The story, first published in Yiddish in 1945, takes place in the shtetl of Frampol and describes the travails of Gimpel, the town fool, whose extravagant gullibility renders him the butt of Frampol's jokesters. As Gimpel recounts,

> When the pranksters and leg-pullers found that I was easy to fool, every one of them tried his luck with me. "Gimpel, the czar is coming to Frampol; Gimpel, the moon fell down in Turbeen; Gimpel, little Hodel Furpiece found a treasure behind the bathhouse." And I like a golem believed everyone.[26]

Gimpel's life takes a dramatic turn when he is persuaded by the townspeople to marry Elka, "Zi iz geven a veybl, hot men mir ayngeret az zi iz a moyd" (She was no chaste maiden, but they told me she was virgin pure).[27] Five months later a son is born, who Elka swears is Gimpel's. Although Gimpel is (justifiably) suspicious, he comes to love Elka and accepts the child as his own. The story describes Gimpel's dawning awareness of his wife's multiple infidelities and, more generally, of the cruelty of his fellow towns-people. Embittered by Elka's deathbed confession, Gimpel takes impulsive revenge on Frampol by urinating in the dough he is preparing as the town baker but quickly repents of his action, burying the loaves and then taking leave of Frampol for a life of harsh exile.

The story charmed the critics, with its ear—discernible in Bellow's transla-tion—for idiomatic Yiddish speech and its rich, unsentimental portrait of the shtetl. In the American literary arena of the 1950s, Singer's narrative world was still utterly exotic; as one reviewer put it, Bellow's English version of Singer captured "the barbaric, oriental flavor that one associates with Eastern Jews." Sensitive critics realized that "Gimpel the Fool" was not only ethno-graphical portraiture, it was also modernist literature. As "simple" as Gimpel is, he is also a complex and fully realized character, both thoroughly immersed in his traditional milieu and isolated from the main currents of its commu-nity life. With the appearance of Irving Howe and Eliezer Greenberg's *Trea-sury of Yiddish Stories*, which included Bellow's translation of "Gimpel," Sidra DeKoven Ezrahi writes, "1953 becomes the year that inaugurates the Ameri-can attempt to reclaim a lost Jewish place and a severed Jewish story."[28]

Bellow's translation, all agreed, was a masterpiece, discovering a voice in English that both was new and seemed somehow to have always been there. Bellow had not only brought Singer's Yiddish into literary English; he also succeeded in fashioning a Yiddish-infused English utterly removed from the "coarse" immigrant speech with which Yiddish had previously been associ-ated. As with all translations, however, there were also measurable losses: Chone Shmeruk and Anita Norich have (separately) drawn attention to the leveling, in the English, of the Yiddish story's very first lines.[29] While the Yid-dish begins "Ich bin Gimpel tam. Ich halt mikh nisht far keyn nar," Bellow rendered the two distinct terms *tam* and *nar* with forms of the word "fool": "I am Gimpel the fool. I don't consider myself foolish." *Tam*, of Hebrew der-ivation, means something like "simple" or "innocent" (familiar as the third of "the four sons" in the Passover Haggadah).[30] The German-derived *nar*, by contrast, lacks any positive connotations and more simply refers to a fool. As Norich writes, "Erasing the crucial distinctions between *tam* and *nar*, Bellow elides the folkloric and religious resonances of *tam* as well as the numerous linguistic derivations from *nar*."[31] The English, perhaps unavoidably, fails to register fully the difference between the *tam* Gimpel acknowledges as part of his name and the *nar* he denies that he is. With the publication of the Ger-man translation of the story (from the English) in 1968, entitled "Gimpel der Narr," the difference between foolishness and simplicity so crucial to the story's Yiddish opening was completely forgotten.[32] Gimpel was, the title asserted, exactly what the townspeople considered him—a *Narr*.

There was another serious translation loss in Bellow's version, one less often discussed by the critics. Janet Hadda's biography of Singer recounts that the translation also elided what Hadda calls "the anti-Christian references" in "Gimpel the Fool." While the translation problem of *tam/nar* rested primarily on linguistic difficulties—Norich points out that "Gimpel the Simple" would have introduced an inappropriate rhyme—the issues involved in translating Singer's references to Christianity were rather a matter of cultural politics. Hadda describes how these passages were transformed. As it turns out, it may not have been Bellow, but rather Eliezer Greenberg, Singer's European-born editor and friend, who was responsible.

> The real break for Bashevis, his introduction to American readers who could appreciate him, was the 1952 appearance, in the prestigious *Partisan Review*, of "Gimpel the Fool," masterfully translated by Saul Bellow. Although not European-born, Bellow was ideally suited to render Singer into English for a cosmopolitan audience. He spoke fluent, richly idiomatic Yiddish and, like Singer, had grown up in a strictly orthodox home, complete with one grandfather who was a khosid and one grandfather who was a misnaged (an opponent of Hasidism); he understood the milieu that Singer had created. Nonetheless, he was at first reluctant to undertake the assignment. Approached by Eliezer Greenberg, Bellow initially declined. He was teaching at Princeton University and finishing his novel, *The Adventures of Augie March*. He simply didn't have the time, he told Greenberg. But Greenberg, undeterred, suggested he could come to Bellow and read the Yiddish to him; Bellow could translate right onto the typewriter.
>
> And so it was—which allowed Greenberg to exercise a bit of deception. He omitted the overt anti-Christian references contained in the Yiddish original.[33]

Janet Hadda does not list the anti-Christian omissions of the translation, but they are easily gleaned from a comparison of the two versions. Two are brief references to Elka, comparing her first, in appearance, to a *shiksa* and then, in her swearing, to a *goy*. But it is the third and longest reference that is most striking. Greenberg omitted an entire line, the final one, from a scene that begins with Gimpel's confronting his wife, who has given birth suspiciously soon after their wedding. In Bellow's version:

> "How can he be mine?" I argued. "He was born seventeen weeks after the marriage." She told me then that he was premature. I said, "Isn't he a little too premature?" She said, she had had a grandmother who carried just as short a time

and she resembled this grandmother of hers as one drop of water does another. She swore to it with such oaths that you would have believed a peasant at the fair if he had used them. To tell the plain truth, I didn't believe her; but when I talked it over next day with the schoolmaster, he told me that the very same thing had happened to Adam and Eve. Two they went up to bed, and four they descended.

"There isn't a woman in the world who is not the granddaughter of Eve," he said.

That was how it was; they argued me dumb. But then, who really knows how such things are?[34]

While the English passage ends there, the Yiddish continues with the sentence Greenberg omitted in his dictation to Bellow: "Ot zugt men dokh, az s'yoyzel hot in gantzen keyn tatn nisht gehat."[35] Or in my own translation: "After all, they say that Yoyzl didn't have a father at all."

It is worth reflecting on why Greenberg may have perceived the line "they say that Yoyzl didn't have a father at all" as an anti-Christian reference. The insult to Christians (except perhaps in the "affectionate" diminutive "Yoyzl," or "little Jesus") seems indirect at best. This indirection can be clarified, though, by reference to the conversation earlier in the passage between Gimpel and the schoolmaster, who cites the Talmud in a way that Gimpel hears as reaffirming the possibility that his wife indeed gave birth very prematurely but which is heard by the more sophisticated reader (and who is not more sophisticated than Gimpel?) as drawing an association between Elka and Eve as sexual sinners: "There isn't a woman in the world who is not the granddaughter of Eve." Similarly, when Gimpel seems to take at face value the proposition that Yoyzl had no father, the reader understands that Gimpel's naïveté extends beyond his wife's evasions to include even the "absurdities" of Christianity. The reference is anti-Christian, then, because it assumes that the reader will see in it evidence of the extremity of Gimpel's foolishness: he is such a fool, the omitted line implies, that he believes the one thing that no other Jew has ever swallowed—that Jesus's mother Mary (like his wife, Elka) was a virgin!

Given his initial audience, Singer hardly needed to make any of this explicit. Yiddish speakers would be fully aware of the long tradition, going back to the Middle Ages if not earlier, which presented a Jewish counterhistory to the Gospel accounts of Jesus's origins. In all of its various versions, Jesus is an illegitimate child whose mother is a woman who consorted with Roman soldiers or was tricked into sex by a neighbor, but in any case conceived Jesus through the usual human channels. Greenberg's apparently minor omission, then, does more than just skip over the anti-Christian sentiments in the story; it also contributes to the erasure of the entire (often comic) tradition of Jewish attitudes toward Christianity. Greenberg's censorship of the Yiddish in his recitation to the American-born Bellow is not surprising. Yiddish as well as other Jewish languages preserve Jewish attitudes toward non-Jews, Christianity, and Jesus only in coded form, in language specifically designed to be incomprehensible to any non-Jewish listener. The *Toldot Yeshu*, the "History of Jesus," circulated underground in Jewish communities in the medieval and early modern period; it remained unpublished because it was perceived, for good reason, to be a document that could endanger the Jews if it fell into the wrong—that is, non-Jewish—hands.

As modernizing Jewish communities moved away from Jewish languages to speak the languages of their co-territorialists and share in their cultural assumptions, these linguistic artifacts of premodern Jewish discourse were largely left behind, not translated. In the English-speaking world that American Jews shared with non-Jews, gleeful Jewish tales about Mary's sexual adventures could no longer be circulated in a purely Jewish "code." But Jewish society had also, in an important sense, moved past the attitudes that underlay these anti-Christian traditions and embraced a liberal, tolerant cultural politics. No wonder, then, that Greenberg (instinctively or with calculation) skipped Singer's mention of "Yoyzl." Not only would Bellow's American audience probably fail to get the joke, but for those English readers—Jewish or not—who did get it, the line might well be construed as tasteless or offensive. Greenberg's omission of the line about "Yoyzl" is part and parcel, then, of Jewish Americanization. The trajectory of this cultural self-transformation is laid out clearly enough in the vagaries of "Gimpl tam": from Singer as Yiddish writer, to Greenberg as an emissary from the world of Eastern Europe in his friendship with Irving Howe, major figure in the New York literary scene, and finally to Bellow in Princeton and ultimately the Nobel Committee in Stockholm. It is simply to be expected that a Jewish joke that depends for its punch line on Mary's sexual peccadilloes was quietly dropped along the way.

It is also possible that Greenberg (or Bellow) found these moments not so much offensive to Christian sensibilities as simply untranslatable. The Yiddish makes full use of the universe of discourse Gimpel inhabits, the *lehavdl loshn* of traditional Ashkenaz. In the English, the (relatively) neutral range of the words "goy" and "shiksa" is vacated—they can *only* be heard as insults. And "Yoyzl," with its combination of an almost affectionate familiarity and barely disguised contempt—the contempt for Christian notions of Jesus's divinity implied in the very Yiddishizing of Jesus through the familiar diminutive (as in Primo Levi's Piedmontese humanizing designation of Jesus as Odo, that *man*)—is also dependent on the concerted workings of Yiddish grammar and Ashkenazic culture. In these cases, there *is* no "faithful" translation or transliteration. Nevertheless, the effect of these omissions, for an American audience, is to transform "Gimpel" into a story that is solely about Jews. That these exotic Jews might themselves have a critical perspective on non-Jews is lost at precisely the moment the story becomes available to non-Jewish readers.

The loss is not minimal. Singer's reference to Jesus, although it is only a single line, is crucial to understanding the story. "Gimpel the Fool" refers to the New Testament throughout, and not only in the one line that makes these Christian allusions explicit. This is not to deny the presence of other important intertexts. Sheldon Grebstein has made a strong case for the allusive presence of the Garden of Eden story in "Gimpel," demonstrating the centrality of bread and childbirth, linked in God's punishment of Adam and Eve, to a reading of the story.[36] But although Grebstein's work appears in a collection dedicated to recovering the Yiddish portion of Singer's oeuvre, he fails to note that Elka is intertextually linked in the Yiddish with *both* Eve and Mary (and the very link between the two suggests that this is a Mary who repeats rather than undoes Eve's sin). Gimpel is not only Adam, who accepts a fallen wife and makes a life with her, but also a modern-day Joseph, a cuckold who takes his unfaithful bride into his home and accepts her bastard son as his own. And it is not only Joseph who is recalled in Gimpel's marital situation. In a recurring theme of Jewish folklore, Christians in general are viewed as sexually gullible, naively taken in by Mary's "virginity"; Gimpel, in this sense, is like a Christian, willing to believe in something as patently outrageous as a virgin birth. Because English readers failed to see "Gimpel the Fool" as a Jewish retelling of the Gospels, they neatly reversed the story's ironic thrust, presenting Gimpel's foolishness as archetypically *Jewish*—that is, as either "Oriental" and barbaric or as an allegory for Jewish piety. Thus, Paul Kresh writes that Gimpel "is the quintessential Jew taunted and dispossessed but preferring to wait for his reward in the next world rather than seek revenge on his tormentors in this one."[37] In Singer's Yiddish version, though, Gimpel is somehow *un*-Jewish, insofar as Jews are, almost by definition, too clever to be taken in by philandering women and too sensible to turn the other cheek.

If this excised line is only indirectly anti-Christian, it is also not completely anti-Christian. The implied analogy between Joseph and Gimpel, Mary and Elka, is an ambivalent one, reflecting in both directions. The analogy renders Gimpel and Elka somewhat "Christian" (as when Elka is described as looking like a *shiksa*), but it also reminds us that Joseph and Mary were, after all, Jewish. Although Elka's infidelities are ultimately made perfectly clear, Singer also encourages us to see her from Gimpel's perspective, to respect the lengths to which he will go to believe his wife and salvage his family life (including citing Jesus's birth as prooftext!). Gimpel's naïveté, that is, comes with its own near-religious justification. The passage I cited above continues: "I began to forget my sorrow. I loved the child madly, and he loved me." Gimpel's foolishness, here and elsewhere, is at least partially redeemed by his capacity for love, a capacity inextricable from what could be called his willing suspension of disbelief. As Grebstein writes, "When Gimpel looks into the face of a sleeping baby, born of his wife but from another man's seed, and yet spontaneously loves it as though it were his own, in that instant he not only becomes the child's true father, he also ascends into the realm of divinity."[38] Gimpel is a saint, perhaps "one of the thirty-six humble and righteous whose existence redeems us until the Messiah comes." Grebstein continues, "In any case, I suggest that the story is a parable about the Jews."[39] My own sense is that Gimpel's actions are of interest precisely because they deviate from those seen as normatively Jewish; the parable is about those *other* Jews, whose credulity—especially about women—sets them apart from the Jewish community. If I am right, then the redeemed Gimpel, as foolish as a Christian, implicitly redeems the foolish, love-struck Christians, too.

What is so striking, and so modern, about Singer's take on the Gospel account is that while he renders Jesus's origins with as much skepticism as earlier Jewish narratives, he finds a new hero in the story that neither Jewish nor Christian sources have ordinarily discerned: Joseph, the father of Jesus. It is he who is the hero of the Gospels, not despite his status as cuckold but precisely because of it. Christianity, by replacing the "legal" patrilineage traceable through Joseph with a supernatural link with God, obscured not only its Jewish roots but also the human heroism of its not-quite-founding father. The history of the Jewish "reclamation" of Jesus in the modern period is well known. What has been hidden in this translation is that Singer participated in this history and even went a step further—to reclaim Joseph not as the foster-father of God, but precisely in the full human indignity of his role as the husband of a fallen woman.

"Gimpel the Fool" thus casts its story of skepticism and naïveté, virginity and promiscuity, against the drama of Jewish–Christian difference, where the questions of religious and sexual belief, of believing in God and believing in your wife are intimately linked. Gimpel's famous defense of his condition—"Today it's your wife you don't believe; tomorrow it's God Himself you don't take stock in"—has a persuasiveness in Christianity that Gimpel refigures as native Jewish insight. Singer's conflation of Christianity with quasi-Jewish piety is radical indeed. His story itself is evidence for the degree to

which skepticism—rather than naive belief—is marked in the Yiddish as a
Jewish trait. When, at the beginning of the story, Gimpel is informed that his
mother and father have arisen from the grave, he responds that although he
knew the report was "nisht geshtoygen nisht gefloygen," he thought he might
as well go and see for himself. "Nisht geshtoygen nisht gefloygen," of course,
means "baloney!" (Bellow renders it "I knew very well that nothing of the
sort had happened.")[40] More literally, though, the idiom means "neither rose
nor flew"—appropriately enough for denying a resurrection. In reactivating
the literal meaning of this stock phrase, Gimpel also reminds us of its possible derivations in the Jewish disbelief that *Christ* ever arose from the grave,
much less "flew." The ubiquity of the phrase in common Yiddish speech signals the extent to which Jewish identity in a Christian world, *in a variety of
contexts,* is constructed by skepticism about the divinity of Jesus. To be a Jew,
that is, means not to believe in Jesus's resurrection. Gimpel is part of this culture that links skepticism with Jewish rejections of Christian claims, but he
is also different, an orphan and eternal optimist who, although he knows better, thinks he has nothing to lose by hoping for the best—parents who rise
from the grave, a wife who is faithful to him, and children he can honestly
call his own.

It is tempting, especially when we use a Christian lens, to view Gimpel as
a "holy fool." I think this reading is misguided: Gimpel, from beginning to
end, somehow knows he is being fooled, and his character is made considerably less saintly by a barely suppressed rage that finally does erupt. When
Gimpel, at the end of the story, goes into "exile," his leavetaking of the children perfectly captures the tension between his simple goodness and stub-
born pride. On the one hand, he distributes his possessions among them as
token of his continued paternal support; on the other hand, he abandons
them and never looks back—it *does* matter, in the final analysis, that the children are not his own.

If "Gimpel the Fool" resolves the tension between skepticism and belief,
it does so only at the very end of the story, in the realm of the imagination.

> I wandered over the land. . . . I heard a great deal, many lies and falsehoods, but
> the longer I lived the more I understood that there were really no lies. Whatever
> doesn't really happen is dreamed at night. . . . Going from place to place, eating
> at strange tables, it often happens that I spin yarns—improbable things that
> could never have happened [*nisht geshtoygn, nisht gefloygen*]—about devils, magi-
> cians, windmills and the like.[41]

From this perspective, Gimpel's vision of Elka as a *tsadeykes* (saintly
woman) finds its level of truth in the alchemy of the dreaming mind rather

than the Frampol court of opinion. As a yarn-spinner, Gimpel also delivers a manifesto for the modernist Yiddish writer on the European stage who finds his place beyond Jewish–Christian oppositions, in an arena in which shtetl demons rub shoulders with Cervantes's windmills. Indeed, Singer reportedly told one of his biographers, in a Flaubertian mode, "I am Gimpel."[42] If Singer is Gimpel, the artist-storyteller belongs as profoundly to Christianity as to Judaism. And it is the *Yiddish* version of the story that makes this explicit, rather than the English; in English, Gimpel is returned to his Jewish milieu. But if "Gimpel tam" has anything to say about the relationship between Christianity and Judaism, religion and literature, it is that kinship stakes a double claim: through the mechanics of biology and through the irrational persuasions of fantasy and love.

Singer's story, so apparently evocative of an insular East European Jewish world, was eventually to be the first of his stories to cross over into the larger world of American-Jewish letters. But it had already done so in spirit, as it were, within a purely Jewish linguistic realm. It was in what would eventually be international translation, ironically, that Gimpel's world would narrow, and that he would be made to stand as a parable of Jewishness. The concluding words of Singer's Nobel Lecture should have warned otherwise: "In a figurative way Yiddish is the wise and humble language of us all, the idiom of a frightened and hopeful humanity."[43]

CONVERSION AND TRANSLATION
IN "ZEIDLUS THE POPE"

David Roskies has suggested that "Gimpel the Fool" and "Zeidlus the Pope," two stories Singer published near the beginning of the resumption of his writing career after the long hiatus that followed his immigration to America, should be read as companion pieces, representing two facets of a single narrative problematic. Zeidel "is a person who is destroyed because he is all mind and rationalism," while Gimpel is a fool who "achieves transcendence through the school of hard knocks."[44] In Roskies' reading, the two stories represent a modernist revision, and a splitting into two separate narratives, of one of the classic Hasidic stories of Nachman of Bratslav, the story of the wise man and the fool. Gimpel is the wise fool who triumphs because he has given up all vanity for the sake of love, while Zeidel is the foolish sage brought down by vanity.

Although Roskies does not spell this out, both men are also solitaries, the butt of children's teasing. "Gimpel the Fool" opens with a tour-de-force litany of names Gimpel is given at school—"imbecile, donkey, flax-head, dope, glump, ninny, and fool,"[45] while Zeidel seldom ventures out of his house after his baptism "because when he did Jewish schoolboys ran after him in the streets shouting, 'Convert! Apostate!'" (in the Yiddish, *meshumed*).[46] Both men eventually leave their shtetls—Frampol and Janov, respectively—in search of broader horizons. For all the critical attempts at viewing Singer's fiction as representing traditional Jewry, even as parables for the Jewish condition, it is clear that at least these stories depict alienation as much as tradition, the ragged edges of East European life as much as its center.

Roskies contends that it was the destruction of Europe's Jews that contributed to the resurgence of Singer's creativity in 1943, the "annus mirabilis" of his career. (The premature death of his older and more successful brother, Israel Joshua Singer, the following year, cemented the gains.) Speaking with what I hope is some exaggeration, Roskies writes that "Singer was not only unshaken by the Holocaust; he felt vindicated by it. Now liberated from the petty politics and illursory dreams of the entire Yiddish writers' club, he was ready to strike out on his own."[47] Indeed, "Zeidlus the Pope" (1943) and "Gimpel the Fool" (1945) dramatize the loosening of the stifling hold of Jewish community: "Gimpel the Fool" represents this trajectory both thematically, through its Christian intertextual allusions, and geographically, in Gimpel's self-imposed exile from Frampol. In "Zeidlus the Pope," the transgression of Jewish boundaries is the explicit theme of the story: Zeidel is a learned Jew who converts to Christianity. The closing paragraphs of "Gimpel the Fool" describing Gimpel as a wandering storyteller suggest at least one way of understanding Singer's identification with his character. "Zeidlus the Pope" also describes the journey of a Jew beyond the narrow confines of the traditional Jewish world; and indeed Joseph Sherman's reading of "Zeidlus the Pope" (*Zaydlus der ershter*, or Zeidlus the first, in Yiddish) constructs a connection between Singer and Zeidlus the would-be Pope, as well:

> Thirty-five years after this story was first published—in America—Bashevis, in the persona of I. B. Singer, became the first, and only, Yiddish writer to be honored with the Nobel Prize. The arrogance of his would-be Jewish pope—to become Zaydlus *der ershter*, "the first"—can be read as a self-reflecting irony on the Faustian bargain his creation had every intention of making himself. Bashevis may not have been *der ershter*, "the first," Yiddish writer to covet the glories that attend acceptance into the canon of Western literature; as I. B. Singer he was certainly *der eyntsiker*, "the one and only," to enjoy them.[48]

The already disturbing insinuation that Zeidel's conversion to Christianity represents a prefiguration of Singer's success in English, as a betrayal of

Singer's integrity and of the Jewish community for the sake of worldly glory, is made more disturbing still if one recognizes that this story was written in, as Roskies puts it, "the year of Our Lord Nineteen Hundred and Forty-Three, when evil of metaphysical proportions was unleashed on the Jews by nations that professed to be Christian."[49] Sherman's reading of "Zeidlus the Pope" introduces the issue, discussed earlier in this book, of translation as conversion, as going over to the enemy and the enemy's language. I would argue, though, that Sherman's provocative analysis depends on a misreading of Singer's story.

"Zeidlus the Pope" describes the apostasy of a bookish and learned Jew in the small town of Janov, orchestrated by the *yeytser hore*, the Evil Inclination (translated here as "the Evil One" or "the Tempter"), who discovers Zeidel's single weakness, vanity. The story is narrated by the Evil One, who approaches Zeidel one night to extol his brilliance and Jewish learning; when Zeidel wonders why he is singing his praises, the Evil One answers:

> "I'm telling you because it's not right that a great man such as you, a master of Torah, an encyclopedia of knowledge, should be buried in a God-forsaken village such as this where no one pays the slightest attention to you, where the townspeople are coarse and the rabbi an ignoramus, with a wife who has no understanding of your true worth. You are a pearl lost in the sand, Reb Zeidel."[50]

As the Evil One explains, Zeidel's great gifts can only be truly appreciated among the Gentiles, not among his fellow Jews. The Christians "don't care what else a man is: if he is great, they idolize him." The Evil One even prophesizes that if Zeidel uses his Jewish knowledge to

> "throw together some hodgepodge about Jesus and his mother the Virgin, they will make you a bishop, and later a cardinal—and God willing, if everything goes well, they'll make you a Pope one day. Then the Gentiles will carry you on a gilded chair like an idol and burn incense around you; and they'll kneel before your image in Rome, Madrid and Crakow."
> "What will my name be?" asked Zeidel.
> "Zeidlus the First."[51]

Zeidel does indeed convert to Christianity, changing his name not to Zeidlus but rather to Benedictus Janovsky, and sets out to become famous by writing a polemic against the Talmud, in the footsteps of "Petrus Alfonzo, Pablo Christiani of Montpelier, Paul de Santa Maria, Johann Baptista, Johann Pfefferkorn, to mention only a few. . . . Now that he converted and Jewish children abused him in the streets, he suddenly discovered that he had never loved the Talmud." But Zeidel never completes his great tractate against the Jews, and fails to find the acclaim he had expected:

> Many times he was promised a seminary appointment but somehow he never got one. A post as librarian in Crakow which was to be his went to a relative of the governor instead. Zeidel began to realize that even among the Gentiles things were far from perfect.[52]

After long years in the library, Zeidlus ends his life as a blind beggar at the steps of the Cathedral in Krakow, murmuring passages from the Talmud and the psalms. "The Gentile theology he had forgotten as quickly as he had learned it; what remained was what he had acquired in his youth." In the final scene of the story, Zeidel dies and is brought down to hell, where two mocking imps burst out laughing at his approach: "'Here comes Zeidlus the First,' one said to the other, 'the yeshiva boy who wanted to become Pope.'"[53]

Told in this way, "Zeidlus the Pope" appears to be a cautionary tale, warning against the barren lures of the Christian world: not only will the Christian world ultimately disappoint ambitious yeshiva boys, but the reward for such ambition is the mockery of hell's imps. Sherman, in fact, so interprets the story, linking "Zeidlus the Pope" with a Yiddish folkloric and literary tradition of Jewish pope stories.[54] This fantasy, or fear, of a Jewish pope, Sherman writes, "lies deep in the biblical story of Joseph, with its overtones of Jewish self-eradication through assimilation."[55] Roskies goes even further, darkly comparing Zeidel's with such "other Jewish heresies" as Communism, which "saw a host of Jewish commissars trying desperately and disastrously to be *frimer farn poyps*, more Catholic than the pope. Singer had one response to these yeshiva students turned masters of dialectical materialism: he sent them all to hell."[56]

For both Roskies and Sherman, Singer's damning of Zeidlus is more powerfully felt in the Yiddish, in which the very language of the story serves to condemn Christianity and, by implication, the Jew who converts to that religion. Speaking of the translation of the *yeytser hore* into English, Roskies writes:

> In his English persona, the devil who inveighed so relentlessly against the church not only has his mouth washed out, but he also becomes something of an expert in Christianity. English is, after all, a language steeped in Christian culture, and so a neutral "string of beads" (*shnur patsherkes*) easily suggests a rosary; he lived at the priest's (*baym galekh*) becomes "he lived in the priest's rectory"; and the toughly worded Zeidel "no longer wished to bow down before the little Jesus" [*zikh bukn tsum yoyzl*] is prettified into "nor was he inclined to kneel before an altar." Made to sound downright ecumenical, this

devil is less of an embarrassment to American Jews in the late-fifties (when "Zeidlus the Pope" was first translated) and may in fact represent the mellowing of Singer in the face of America's more tolerant brand of Christianity. But it wrecks the story. Once there's no one left to draw the line between truth and falsehood, the devil also becomes a moral relativist and Zeidel's rise and fall become an exercise in absurdity. This makes the story more modernist, and much less Yiddish.[57]

Sherman similarly writes that, in the English translation, "Bashevis's determination to avoid at all costs giving offense to his Gentile and Christian readers led him significantly to weaken, if not wholly adulterate, one of the more pressing of his artistic concerns."[58] For Sherman, this concern is the indictment of "learning divorced from moral responsibility," that is, of Jewish learning put to Christian—or merely worldly—uses. It is this indictment, for Sherman, that is conveyed through the Yiddish, and particularly through *lehavdl loshn*.[59]

"Zaydlus der ershter" mobilizes a full range of Yiddish anti-Christian phrases, effectively marshalling the resources of the language to express disdain and disapproval of Christianity. Sherman points out that what is translated as "the Church" in the sentence "After years of effort, he was so fatigued that he could no longer distinguish between right and wrong, sense and nonsense, between what would please and what displease the Church," is *di reshoim*, the wicked ones. What is called in English Zeidel's "treatise" is in Yiddish his *treyf-posl*, an abomination—the term for a forbidden book. Other examples might be added to Sherman's: The church in his home town or the cathedral in Krakow—both important places in Zeidel's post-baptismal life—are unfailingly referred to as the *tifleh* or *beys hatume*, dysphemistic code terms that refer to churches as places of impurity. Zeidel, at his baptism, becomes not a Christian (as the Christian scenario would have it), but rather a *goy* (as the most unworldly Jew might see it). Once this *lehavdl loshn* is abandoned for the sake of the Gentile reader, Sherman argues, the force of the critique embedded in the *lehavdl loshn* is lost. "Obliterate these distinctions," Sherman writes, "and Jewish demons are obliterated as well."[60]

Taken together, Roskies and Sherman provide an elegant reading of "Zeidlus the Pope" in its Yiddish and English versions. Both stories describe an apostasy; but in the Yiddish, Zeidel's conversion is harshly condemned, while in English a more tolerant and ecumenical attitude is taken. This very softening of the anti-Christian critique in translation makes the author (whose collaboration with his translators was acknowledged and known) himself a kind of apostate, a betrayer of Jewish values for the sake of worldly glory.[61] The implications of this reading are fascinating: Singer, in effect, described his treason in advance but did not enact it. On the contrary, in Yiddish he proves himself a loyal Jew. Only in the treason of the unfaithful translation did the author take on the characteristics of the apostate he had described. That is, only in translation do the author and his story become one.

There are a number of problems, however, with this reading. The first is that the critical voice condemning Christianity in such phrases as *"beys hatume"* (house of impurity) uses the *lehavdl loshn* of a pious Jew, but divorced from the usual values associated with this idiom. The narrator, after all, is the *yeytser hore*, the Evil Inclination who tempts Zeidel to convert, all the while speaking of Christianity with utter disdain: the Evil Inclination both denies that God gave Moses the Torah at Sinai and asserts that "Jesus was a bastard from Nazareth." He is not a proponent of traditional Judaism any more than he is a believer in the Virgin birth. At least as expressed to Zeidel, he is an equal-opportunity skeptic. To associate this narratorial voice with a critique only of Christianity is to diminish Singer's singular creation here.

It is no surprise that Singer, at this stage of his career, chose as narrator the *yeytser hore*. In the manifesto on Yiddish writing in America published the year "Zaydlus der ershter" appeared, Singer announced his turning to the traditional world, without, however, abandoning his interest in modernism, an interest sexual above all. The *yeytser hore*, even in rabbinic literature, is a psychic concept, the internal temptations that lure us to transgress, as well as a personified character, a kind of little devil at perpetual war with our instincts toward goodness. The character of the Evil Inclination, then, could move between two worlds, one occult and supernatural and the other worldly and psychological. What makes the *yeytser hore* in "Zeidlus the Pope" so fascinating is that he is both thoroughly Jewish and absolutely amoral, the embodiment of *Jewish* impiety. Whatever disapproval can be read into the Evil Inclination's use of *lehavdl loshn* to chart Zeidel's life as a Christian must be set against his professional investment, as it were, in human sin.

Whether the Evil Inclination is a character out of the rabbinic imaginary or an externalization of Zeidel's id, it seems clear to me that his narratorial voice must be read as continuous with Zeidel's—after all, it is *his* Evil Inclination. To say that Zeidel's journey through Christendom is narrated by the Jewish Evil Inclination is to say as well that Zeidel, even after he becomes a Christian, continues to see his new world with the old lenses. To complicate matters a bit further, the story is told in what narratologists calls "free indirect discourse," a narrative technique that purports to convey a character's mental language while maintaining third-person reference and past tense.[62] In "Zeidlus the Pope," this technique mediates between the perspective of an omniscient narrator (the Evil Inclination) and that of a protagonist with a specific, limited perspective (Zeidel). Thus, it is also *his* perspective on Jesus—not only that of the Evil Inclination—that we hear in the phrase "Er hot oykh mer nisht gevolt zikh bukn tsum yoyzl" (he no longer felt like bowing to the little Jesus).[63] The language in which he frames his reluctance to kneel at the altar (as the published translation has it) itself explains the reluctance: the statue before which Zeidel is supposed to bow is, as he clearly recognizes, nothing more than that all-too-human figure of Jewish folklore, Yoyzl. Before *him*, who would be inclined to bow? Once one recognizes the narratorial voice, in all its disdain for Christianity, as an extension of Zeidel's, it becomes clear that Zeidel is as little a good Christian as he was a good Jew.

The effect at which Singer aims is inextricably connected to the simple fact that this story is told, narrated, and "thought" in traditional Yiddish. There is no escape from this language and its habitual patterns, even in apostasy—so long as this apostasy is described and experienced in Yiddish. Zeidel's return to Jewish learning at the end of his life has nothing to do with "repentance"— it merely underlines what has been implicit in the story until this point. Zeidel lives as a Christian from within a Jewish idiom that is woven into the linguistic fibers of his being—that, we might say, *is* his being. What this produces *in the Yiddish text* is precisely the dizzying moral relativism Roskies decries in the English translation. The criticism of Zeidel's apostasy should not be ascribed to Singer; it is carried by the very language of the story—that is, by Zeidel himself. But if this language sits in judgment on Jewish apostasy, it also fails to serve as a moral compass. What we have in this story, it seems to me, is no prophetic voice castigating apostasy, but rather something much more impish, harder to pin down, and dedicated to a worldly—one might say, literary—form of pleasure.

Perhaps the major pleasure of this story for Yiddish readers—and one nearly impossible to translate—is the disjunction between Zeidel's conversion to Christianity and the language in which this conversion is narrated. This *lehavdl loshn* "follows" Zeidel into Christianity, so that Zeidel's experiences after his conversion are described not within a neutral Yiddish vocabulary but from a fully judgmental Jewish perspective. Roskies and Sherman certainly notice the critique, but they fail to remark on just how comical is this odd mismatch of plot and perspective. The Evil Inclination tells Zeidel that, *imyirtseshem*, God willing, if all goes well they will make him a Pope, prefacing his ungodly prediction with the automatic piety with which every traditional Jew superstitiously anticipates the future. Similarly, the narrator describes Zeidel's anti-Jewish work as promising to be *"lehavdl, a goyisher Yad hazakah,"* (forgive the comparison, a *goyish Strong Hand*—Maimonides' great treatise).[64] The combination of pride in Zeidel's talents and care to distinguish his *goyish* accomplishment from the Maimonidean one to which it is nevertheless compared is hardly captured by the insight, expressed in Roskies and Sherman, that Singer wields Yiddish idiom as a critical tool against Jewish apostasy. Nearly every sentence yields such a delicious jolt. When Zeidel's qualifications for producing his great anti-Jewish work are enumerated, the Yiddish tells us that "no one was as prepared to write such an abomination [*treyf-posl*] as Zeidel, the sharp-witted and knowledgeable [*der horif un boki*], the kabbalist and philosopher." The yeshiva vocabulary that differentiates types of talmudic prodigies—the *horif* excels at close textual analysis while the *boki* has broad knowledge—is directed here to praising Zeidel's qualifications for the worst kind of anti-Jewish writing. The very hyperboles themselves are formulaic, the language by which great scholars are described in the approbations typically printed as front matter in their learned volumes. In applying such highly stylized pieties to the very impious circumstances of Zeidel's conversion, Singer produced a sharp dissonance between Jewish narrative language and Christian narrative content. Perhaps the funniest use of this technique occurs in the scene immediately after Zeidel's baptism: among the options Zeidel's new *goyish* friends propose for him (the translation calls them his Gentile friends) is that "er zol khasene hobn mit a farmeglekher orelis in der gegent un vern a poritz"—that is, they "suggested that he marry a wealthy local woman and become a squire."[65] The Yiddish version, however, calls the wife Zeidel's friends envision for him not a "woman" but rather an *orelis,* that is, an uncircumcised woman! Singer introduces into the story a rare (if not absolutely unique in Yiddish letters) female derivation for the word *orel,* "uncircumcised one," one of the various terms of denigration for non-Jew available in the traditional Yiddish repertoire. The point here is not moral censure of intermarriage or the disparaging of Gentile women for failing to observe the sacred commandment of circumcision. Singer is rather characterizing Zeidel (or his evil inclination) as a Jew whose deepest impulses have hardly been touched by the baptismal waters. Conversion has not changed—perhaps *could* not change—his perspective on non-Jews; they are still alien and unappealing creatures, even if Zeidel has deliberately thrown in his lot with them.

If it is in Yiddish that the curious persistence of Zeidel's Jewishness beyond the baptismal font is most evident, it is also in Yiddish that Singer most openly invites the reader to recognize the continuity between the pre- and post-baptismal Zeidel, or to put it otherwise, between Judaism and Christianity. Among the ways in which the Evil Inclination entices Zeidel to convert is by assuring him that his life after apostasy will be much the same as his life as a Jew: "Vest vayter zitsen un lernen, trogn a lange zhupitse, a yarmulke un shmekn tabak."[66] The translation renders this as "You'll continue to study, to wear a long coat and skullcap."[67] What is missing in the English (aside from the snuff Zeidel will continue to take, inexplicably omitted) is the Jewish specificity of what Zeidel will do and wear as a Christian. What will sit on his head is not a non-denominational skullcap but rather a perfectly Jewish yarmulke (albeit "God willing" in cardinal red). What the Christian Zeidel can expect to do with his days is "zitsen un lernen," the idiomatic Yiddish term for "sitting and learning" *Talmud* (which is exactly what the Christian Zeidel does fill his days with, now with the object of writing an antitalmudic treatise!). And as an overcoat he will wear, not just any long coat but the gabardine of the Hasidic rebbe. Being a Christian of the bookish variety is not, finally, all that different from being a Jew of the same sort. This prophecy conveys something of Zeidel's trajectory in a nutshell: Zeidel converts but maintains a Jewish language and Jewish perspectives on his very Christianity. What Roskies writes about the Jewishness of the Evil Inclination holds true as well for Zeidel:

> This walking encyclopedia of Jewish self-deception ... is also a talking thesaurus of Jewish hostility toward the values of a secular world. The Yiddish he speaks, which insists on dissociating itself from everything Christian, cuts to the heart of Bashevis' argument that Yiddish will either be an expression of Jewishness or nothing at all.[68]

Given Singer's insistence on Yiddish as a vehicle for Jewishness, a Yiddish story about an apostate would have to produce the range of comic effects so evident in "Zeidlus the Pope." Because the story is in Yiddish, and because it is told in a voice that is associated with Zeidel (both because it is his Evil Inclination and because the narrative uses free indirect discourse), Singer was able to convey a double story—of Zeidel's incomplete apostasy, and of Zeidel's cold Jewish eye on the Christianity he has joined. The result, far from the unalloyed critique of Christianity in the name of authentic Jewish values that Sherman and Roskies discern, is a comedy of hybridity, an allegory for the mutual implication of language and identity. Zeidel's conversion, read in this way, is not a sin—as Sherman insists—but rather an illusion, a mistaking of one kind of yarmulke for another.

Even the final scenes do not provide an ultimate moral perspective on Zeidel's apostasy, as Roskies implies they do. At the end of his life, Zeidel is plagued by the weightiest and most consequential of questions:

> Was there a Creator or was the world nothing but atoms and their combinations? Did the soul exist or was all thought mere reverberations of the brain? Was there a final accounting with reward and punishment? Was there a Substance or was the whole of existence nothing but imagination?

Zeidel's last exchange is with the Evil Inclination, now in the form of an Angel of Death:

> "Where are you taking me?" he asked.
> "Straight to Gehenna."
> "If there is a Gehenna, there is also a God," Zeidel said, his lips trembling.
> "This proves nothing," I retorted.
> "Yes it does," he said. "If Hell exists, everything exists. If you are real, He is real. Now take me to where I belong. I am ready."[69]

As Shalom Rosenberg has pointed out, the argument between the narrator and Zeidel is expressed in the Yiddish text as a kind of talmudic dispute. To Zeidel's syllogistic derivation of the existence of God from the existence of hell, the Evil Inclination responds "s'iz ken raye nisht," that's no (talmudic) proof, and Zeidel insists, "s'iz yo a raye," it is; Zeidel makes his argument, Rosenberg writes, using "the Talmudic reasoning of an *a fortiori* argument (if there is a Gehenna, there is also a God), while Zeidel and his Evil Inclination dispute the legitimacy of Zeidel's thinking in traditional yeshiva terminology."[70]

The argument is concluded not by the Angel of Death, but rather by Zeidel, whose claim to know that God exists is never substantiated. After finishing Zeidel off with his sword, the narrator swoops down to hell with Zeidel's soul:

> In Gehenna the Angels of Destruction were raking up the coals. Two mocking imps stood at the threshold, half-fire and half-pitch, each with a three-cornered hat on his head, a whipping rod on his loins. They burst out laughing.
> "Here comes Zeidlus the First," one said to the other, "the yeshiva boy who wanted to become pope."[71]

The important thing for Zeidel in his last moments is not whether Judaism or Christianity is the true religion, or even whether he will be punished or rewarded for his conversion, but whether there is a God—that is, whether there are any grounds for adjudicating. The story, it seems to me, does not finally answer the question: we are shown imps and angels, but the Man Himself fails to make an appearance. What Zeidel encounters in hell is not a divinity above the Jewish–Christian divide that has marked his life, or ultimate answers to his existential questions. The hell to which Zeidel is consigned is the familiar *gehenem* of Yiddish folklore, complete with Yiddish-speaking imps and angels. The scene in fact perfectly reproduces the last scene of Y. L. Peretz's 1888 poem "Monish," in which the title character is similarly dispatched to hell. Thus, while Singer ends "Gimpel the Fool," his strictly Jewish story, by setting Gimpel against the broad horizons of European literature, he ends "Zeidlus the Pope," his story about apostasy, with a vision drawn from Yiddish literature. To Zeidel's question of whether anything exists beyond the imagination, Singer responds not with Truth or Substance but rather in the only way he can: with more products of the literary imagination. Whether or not God exists cannot be established, but the Yiddish underworld is palpable and intact in this story, as it must be, given the Yiddish idiom that animates it not only beyond Zeidel's conversion but even beyond his death.

THE obstacles to translating such a story should be readily apparent. The *lehavdl loshn* that lends the story its piquancy, that is so important in both establishing and undermining its plot of conversion, can hardly be rendered in another language. What might seem natural in the idiom of the Yiddish-speaking narrator, the habitual turns of phrase that come with the East European Jewish territory—even for one who has left this world for Christianity—sounds, in a literal translation, like a deliberate insult; when such an insult comes from a recent convert (as I have argued we should read the narratorial voice), this idiom becomes nearly incomprehensible. Why is Zeidel calling his own magnum opus a *treyf-posl*, an abomination? How can he think of himself, after baptism, as a *goy*? For Singer's English-reading audience, a literal translation risks missing the point of the story. Only an anti-Christian judgment ingrained in the very language of narration, and thus impervious to the baptismal waters, can capture the particular resonance of Zeidel's split consciousness, as an apostate within whom the value system of traditional *yiddishkeit* continues to echo.

But it is not simply the case that "Zeidlus" is untranslatable. In at least some passages of the story, translation is actively resisted. In the passage that describes Zeidel's decision to write an anti-talmudic treatise, the details of what might be included in such a work are omitted. In the English, we learn that Zeidel studied the work of the "many Jewish converts to Christianity

[who] had become famous by writing polemics against the Talmud." But he is disappointed by reading their work:

> He soon discovered they were all much alike. The authors were ignorant, pla-giarized from one another liberally, and all cited the same few anti-Gentile passages from the Talmud.[72]

In the Yiddish, though, the catalogue of these anti-Gentile passages is enu-merated: "Ale hobn banutst mit di eygene por memres, vi a shteyger: to'es goy mutr, kusi sheshobas hayev misa, toyv shebagoyim harog."[73] The examples listed are: "A Gentile's mistake may be excused; a Cuthite [Samaritan] that observed the Sabbath deserves the death penalty; kill the best among the Gentiles." The citations are given in cryptic shorthand, without context; the implications are that they are sufficiently familiar to need no explanation. This very familiarity is what cannot be transmitted in the English context; once one has expanded the shorthand to render the citations comprehen-sible, the notion that such phrases formed a well-worn pack of anti-Jewish cards in the pocket of antisemites is lost. But it may also be that the transla-tors, or Singer as their guide, preferred not to parade this litany of the anti-Gentile passages in rabbinic literature before an audience unfamiliar with them—an audience that perhaps could not be trusted with such an arsenal.

Whatever the reason for this translational decision, it is worth pointing out that neither Zeidel nor Singer ultimately rendered this material into a non-Jewish language (as I am doing here). Zeidel, after all, failed to complete his great (presumably Latin) work against the Talmud; only the Yiddish nar-rator records the material that might have appeared in it. Zeidel, as it turns out, is not a Pfefferkorn or Christiani; he never, in the story, exposes Jewish secrets to a hostile Christian audience. The same material Zeidel fails to translate and publish is also what fails to appear in the English version of Zeidel's story.

Joseph Sherman, in the closing paragraph of his essay on "Zeidlus the Pope," implies that Singer is another Zeidel, working with an eye to the ap-probation of a non-Jewish literary public. To repeat the most damning line of this indictment: "The arrogance of his would-be Jewish pope—to become Zaydlus *der ershter*, 'the first,'—can be read as a self-reflecting irony on the Faustian bargain his creator had every intention of making himself."[74] Both writers—Zeidel and Singer—are traitors to the Jewish community: Zeidel in opting for glory over truth and morality, and Singer in weakening the Yiddish critique of Zeidel in English translation (emblematic, Sherman hardly needs to say, of a whole career of kissing up to Gentiles). But Singer's failure to render the Yiddish *lehavdl loshn,* the absence in the English of so many details of the Yiddish disparagement of the non-Jewish world, is as much a protective gesture as an assimilationist one. In the translation of "Zeidlus the First," as of "Gimpel the Fool," the English is shaped by a closing of the Jewish ranks. If Zeidel gets off easy in English, it is not to protect *his* reputation but rather that of the traditional Jewish world as a whole. Singer, I would argue, is keeping the faith in his mistranslations, not abandoning it. If Zeidel the apostate, then, is a stand-in before the fact for the translated Singer, then he expresses more than Singer's move beyond the borders of the Yiddish-speaking world. Zeidel can also represent the ties that continue to connect the heretic Singer with a Yiddish ethos, even—especially—in its mistranslation.

———— ✳ ————

Endecktes Judenthum?

A Translator's Note

IN THE early stages of the writing of this book, my friend and colleague Daniel Boyarin jokingly suggested that I call it *Endecktes Judenthum* (Judaism Unmasked), the title of Johann Andreas Eisenmenger's notorious tract exposing the anti-Christian attitudes of the Talmud and other Jewish works.[1] The joke was characteristically sharp and it stayed with me, although the book, as you can see, is differently titled. As the scope of the book broadened, the part of my project that involved discussion—and thus exposure—of those aspects of Jewish texts and culture not intended for public consumption became less dominant; nevertheless, much of my analysis of the Jewish barriers to translation involved this "hidden transcript" of the Jews. By discussing in English this concealment of Jewish secrets, I was inevitably also reversing it. There was a superficial but uncomfortable similarity between my work and that of not exactly Eisenmenger but perhaps some of the Jewish apostates who contributed to the store of Church knowledge of Jewish texts.

Nevertheless, my intended audience—unlike that of the apostate-translators who were as fascinated as I am by the intimate discourse of Jewish communities—is not the Church or any other group who might be suspected of misusing such potent information. My primary audience is Jews and those we can count as friends (including our friends in the contemporary churches!)— that is, for whom we do not have to edit our words. From this perspective, the work of remembering what has been lost in translation is not *mesirah*, "informing" on the Jewish community, but rather the thoroughly traditional practice of *mesoret*, tradition itself.

Gershom Scholem is said to have expressed open skepticism that non-apologetic research in Jewish Studies could be published in a non-Jewish language.[2] But Scholem lived in a different world than we do, and I think I am not alone among those who publish in English to attempt to prove him wrong. The world is different not only because antisemitic uses of Jewish research are now marginal enough that we need not allow them to influence our work. It is different as well in that we can no longer retreat to a "safe" and private Jewish discourse in which to discuss sensitive internal matters; even Hebrew no longer functions in quite that way. Yiddish is no longer the language of (Ashkenazic) Jewish intimacy, in which things could be said among a community understood to consist of insiders. For many Jews it is the language of an earlier generation; it is the Jews of my generation who are now in the position of outsiders to these stories. What I often hear from second-generation Jewish immigrants is that Yiddish was the language their parents spoke "so we wouldn't understand." It is the internal Jewish loss of this understanding that my research attempts to combat.

Among the lines I pursue here is the association between apostasy and the disclosure of Jewish secrets. But this is not the only narrative in which the breakdown of the borders of Jewish discourse can be told. The emergence of Jews on the American cultural scene, as Sidra DeKoven Ezrahi has shown, was accompanied by a gradual fissuring of the walls that had separated Jewish from non-Jewish discourse. Ezrahi writes that in the early years of Jewish performance in the European vernaculars, the "anti-Christian echoes in the Purim *shpil* were, of course, kept as Jewish secrets. . . . On the New York stage and in the Hollywood of the late 1920s and 1930s, some Jewish secrets began to be leaked to general audiences in carefully measured doses."[3] By the 1960s this process was in full flower: *Portnoy's Complaint*, Ezrahi argues, was scandalous not merely for its sexual and excremental boldness; the scandal was that these were *Jewish* genitals and bowels being discussed on the American literary stage. These exposures were transgressive, but they also signaled and cleared the way for a new openness, a genuine Jewish–Gentile rapprochement possible perhaps only in the New World. Lenny Bruce's boldest monologues and Philip Roth's raunchiest novels hit the American scene not so long after the first guarded translations of Wiesel and Singer, but they are the hallmark of a new stage in American Jewish culture. This era eventually swept up even the cautious field of Jewish scholarship, and if I were to locate my own project within a cultural history, it would be in this one.

I do not mean to suggest that the stories I have told here about the translational difference that long separated Jews from the non-Jewish world are of purely historical interest, remnants of a world in which we no longer live.

The phenomena I am describing here may be less dominant in contemporary Jewish culture, but they are increasingly relevant to the larger world in which Jews live. In the aftermath of the attacks of September 11, 2001, when I was writing this book, a steady stream of anxious reports attested to the linguistic gaps that separated the West from Islam; this gap was not new, but it now urgently mattered. Translators could not be found in sufficient numbers to cope with the communiqués and the "chatter," or to communicate America's own image of itself to the Arabic-speaking masses. When translators were found, their reliability and faithfulness to the American cause they were hired to serve were regularly put into question. At Guantanamo and elsewhere in this country's "War on Terror," translation and espionage emerged as newly linked concepts. All the medieval themes of the Jewish–Christian encounter I had been diligently tracking in the library stacks seemed to be resurfacing on the evening news, although this time with Muslims as the West's "other." The insights of the postcolonial translation theorists of the 1990s, that translation can never evade the complexities of asymmetrical political encounters, now seemed startlingly prescient.

While I was writing this epilogue, the world serendipitously reminded me also of the heroic potential of translation in the story of the Ukrainian sign-language interpreter whose mistranslation helped spark what is being called "the Orange Revolution." The *Wall Street Journal* reported on Monday, November 29, 2004, that the sign language interpreter for UT-1, the Ukrainian state television network, a woman by the name of Natalia Dmytruk, deliberately failed to report the official news that Viktor Yanukovich had won the recent presidential election.

> Conspiring with her makeup artist, Ms. Dmytruk tied an orange ribbon inside her sleeve. Orange is the color of Mr. Yushchenko's campaign, and of the spreading protest movement that many Ukrainians now call the Orange Revolution. Then after interpreting the news broadcast for the deaf on Nov. 25, Ms. Dmytruk bared her wrist. "Everything you have heard so far on the news was a total lie," she says she told viewers in sign language. "Yushchenko is our true president. Goodbye, you will probably never see me here again."

Dmytruk's story can perhaps serve as a bookend to my father's; mistranslation, in both cases, tells another kind of truth. It was my father's spirit that guided this book from its start. At the very last moment, another mistranslator (born, perhaps, not so far from my father's Galicia, now Western Ukraine) ushered me to the finish line as well.

Notes

INTRODUCTION

1. My father could not recall who had said this, but Henri de Bornier (1825-1901) wrote, "Every man has two countries, his own and France!" (Tout homme a deux pays, le sien et puis la France!) (*La Fille de Roland*, act 3, scene 2, p. 65 [1909]). Jules Michelet, *Le Peuple*, chap. 6, quotes an American philosopher as saying that "for every man the first country is his native land and the second is France." A translation names Thomas Paine as the philosopher (Jules Michelet, *The People*, trans. John P. McKay [Urbana: University of Illinois Press, 1973], 191). I want to thank David Bates for these references.

2. Lawrence Venuti, *The Translator's Invisibility: A History of Translation* (New York: Routledge, 1995).

3. Eugene Nida, who served for decades as Executive Director of Translations of the American Bible Society and founded the journal *Bible Translating*, introduced the concept of dynamic equivalence—that is, the equivalence of effect on the original reader and the reader of the translation—in *Toward a Science of Translating* (Leiden: Brill, 1964).

4. Max Weinreich, *The History of the Yiddish Language*, trans. Shlomo Noble (Chicago: University of Chicago Press, 1973), 185.

5. Ibid., 195.

6. For a discussion of Yiddish speech as "performance," see Jeffrey Shandler, *Adventures in Yiddishland: Postvernacular Language and Culture* (Berkeley and Los Angeles: University of California Press, 2006), 126-54.

7. James C. Scott, *Domination and the Arts of Resistance: Hidden Transcripts* (New Haven: Yale University Press, 1990).

8. Sander Gilman, *Jewish Self Hatred: Anti-Semitism and the Hidden Language of the Jews* (Baltimore: The Johns Hopkins University Press, 1986); Elisheva Carlebach, "Attributions of Secrecy and Perceptions of Jewry," *Jewish Social Studies* 2:3 (spring/summer 1996): 115-36.

9. Scott, *Domination*, xi.

10. Tejaswini Niranjana, *Siting Translation: History, Post-Structuralism, and the Colonial Context* (Berkeley and Los Angeles: University of California Press, 1992), 47.

11. Aleida Assman, "The Curse and Blessing of Babel; or, Looking Back on Universalisms," in *The Translatatibility of Cultures: Figurations of the Space Between*, ed. Sanford Budick and Wolfgang Iser (Stanford, Calif.: Stanford University Press, 1996), 95.

12. Joseph II, "Edict of Tolerance," in Raphael Mahler, ed. and trans., *Jewish Emancipation, A Selection of Documents* (New York: American Jewish Committee, 1941), 19.

13. Thibaut de Sezanne, ed., *Extractiones de Talmut* (Paris, 1242); in English, see Hyam Maccoby, ed. and trans., *Judaism on Trial: Jewish-Christian Disputation in the Middle Ages* (Oxford: Littman Library, 1982), 163–67.

14. Jehiel of Paris, "The Disputation of Jehiel of Paris" (Hebrew), in *Collected Polemics and Disputations*, ed. J. D. Eisenstein (New York: Hebrew Publishing Company, 1922), 81–86.

15. Niranjana, *Siting Translation*, 21.

16. Ibid., 47–48.

17. Ibid., 47 n. 1. Emphasis in the original.

18. Vicente L. Rafael, *Contracting Colonialism: Translation and Christian Conversion in Tagalog Society under Early Spanish Rule* (Durham, N.C.: Duke University Press, 1993), 21.

19. See Daniel Boyarin, *A Radical Jew: Paul and the Politics of Identity* (Berkeley and Los Angeles: University of California Press, 1994).

20. Walter Benjamin, "Die Aufgabe des Übersetzers," in *Illuminationen* (Frankfurt am Main: Suhrkamp, 1969), 58.

21. Walter Benjamin, "The Task of the Translator," trans. Harry Zohn, *Illuminations: Essays and Reflections*, ed. Hannah Arendt (New York: Schocken, 1968), 71.

22. André Lefevre, *Translation, Rewriting and the Manipulation of Literary Fame* (London: Routledge, 1992).

23. Primo Levi, *The Periodic Table*, trans. Raymond Rosenthal (London: Abacus Books, 1986), 11. Although I am not familiar with Jewish Piedmontese, my guess is that Odo is a shortened version of *oto ha'ish*, that man, an Ashkenazic reference for Jesus.

24. Weinreich, *History of the Yiddish Language*, 185.

25. George Steiner, *After Babel: Aspects of Language and Translation*, 3rd ed. (Oxford: Oxford University Press, 1998), 242.

26. Philo, *On the Life of Moses* 2.7.43, 44, in *The Works of Philo*, trans. C. D. Yonge (N.p.: Hendrickson, 1993), 494.

27. In *Masechtaot ketanot* (Minor tractates) (Jerusalem: Makor, 1970).

28. Stephen Prickett, "The Changing of the Host: Translation, Transgression and Interpretation," in *Translating Religious Texts: Translation, Transgression and Interpretation*, ed. David Jasper (New York: St. Martin's, 1993), 4.

29. Solomon Grayzel, "The Bible and I: A Translator Reflects," *Sh'ma* 7, no 123 (December 10, 1976): 19.

30. Franz Rosenzweig, "Zeit ists . . . Gedanken über das jüdische Bildungsproblem des Augenblicks," in *Zur jüdischen Erziehung* (Berlin: Schocken, 1937 [1917]), 12.

31. Eugene Nida, "Bible Translation," in *The Routledge Encyclopedia of Translation Studies*, 2nd ed., ed. Mona Baker (London: Routledge, 2000), 22–23.

32. Michael Alpert, "Torah Translation," in Baker, *Routledge Encyclopedia*, 270.

33. Ibid., 269. Alpert does not acknowledge that his is a midrashic reading of the verse (taken from *b. Megilla* 3a), and that very few scholars take Nehemiah 8:8 as historical evidence of translation in that period — the phrase just means "clearly" or "distinctly." See Michael Fishbane, *Biblical Interpretation in Ancient Israel* (Oxford: Oxford University Press, 1985), 109, and Joseph Blenkinsopp, *Ezra-Nehemiah* (London: SCM Press, 1989), 288.

34. *Nachlass Hennings*, no. 22, letter 8, fol. 11 r.-v. Quoted in Alexander Altmann, *Moses Mendelssohn: A Biographical Study* (Birmingham: University of Alabama Press, 1973), 344. Frederick Greenspahn, "How Jews Translate the Bible" (unpublished paper), discusses this phenomenon.

35. Max Margolis, *B'nai Brith News* 4, no. 2 (November 1910): 11.

36. For a discussion of this colonial trope, see Niranjana, *Siting Translation*, 33 and passim.

37. Yuri Slezkine, *The Jewish Century* (Princeton: Princeton University Press, 2004).

38. The major work on this topic remains the 1893 historical and bibliographical work of Moritz Steinschneider, *Die hebräischen Übersetzungen des Mittelalters und die Juden als Dolmetscher* (repr. Graz: Akademische Druck, 1956). See especially xv–xxiv.

39. Primo Levi, *If Not Now, When?* trans. William Weaver, intro. Irving Howe (New York: Summit, 1985), 164; Italian original, *Se non ora, quando?* (Turin: Einaudi, 1982).

40. Sander Gilman, *Inscribing the Other* (Lincoln: University of Nebraska Press, 1991), 311.

41. Slezkine, *Jewish Century*, 19.

42. Edward L. Greenstein, "What Might Make a Bible Translation Jewish?" in *Translation of Scripture*, ed. David M. Goldenberg (Philadelphia: Annenberg Research Institute, 1990), 87.

43. Edward L. Greenstein, "Theories of Modern Bible Translation," *Prooftexts* 3, no. 1 (January 1983): 19.

44. Ibid.

45. Ibid.

46. Jacques Derrida, "What is a 'Relevant' Translation?" trans. Lawrence Venuti, in *The Translation Studies Reader*, 2nd ed. (New York: Routledge, 2004), 431.

47. Maimonides, *Letters of Maimonides* (Hebrew), vol. 2, letter 35, ed. and trans. (from Arabic) Isaac Shailat (Maale Adumim: Ma'aliyot Press, 1988), 532. Maimonides goes on to list two Arabic sense-for-sense translators of Aristotle and Galen of whose methods he approves and another translator whose word-for-word technique he considers misguided.

48. Abraham ibn Ezra, commentary to Exod. 20:1.

49. Jan Assmann, "Translating Gods: Religion as a Factor of Cultural (Un)Translatability," in *The Translation of Cultures: Figurations of the Space Between*, ed. Sanford Budick and Wolfgang Iser (Stanford: Stanford University Press, 1996), 28.

50. Ibid., 29.

51. Ibid., 32.

52. The Sybilline Oracles (1.137-40), in R. Merkelbach and M. Totti, *Abrasax* (Oplanden: Westdeutscher Verlag, 1992), 2.131, quoted in J. Assmann, "Translating Gods," 309 n. 33.

53. *Aristeas to Philocrates* (Letter of Aristeas) 16, ed. and trans. Moses Hadas (New York: Harper, 1951), 102-3.

54. See Steiner, *After Babel*, 257; John F. A. Sawyer, *Sacred Languages and Sacred Texts* (London: Routledge, 1999), 85.

55. A. Assmann, "Curse and Blessing," 89.

56. Ibid., 86.

57. Willis Barnstone, *The Poetics of Translation: History, Theory, Practice* (New Haven: Yale University Press, 1993), 63.

58. Ibid., 71.

59. Martin Buber, "Two Types of Faith," in *Jewish Expressions on Jesus: An Anthology*, ed. Trude Weiss-Rosmarin (New York: KTAV, 1977), 57.

60. *Sifre Deuteronomy* 33:2, ed. Eliezer Aryeh Finkelstein, 3rd ed. (New York: Jewish Theological Seminary, 1993), 395. The next, equally well known, midrashic interpretation of Deut. 33:2 begins "When the Holy One, Blessed Be He, revealed himself to give the Torah to Israel, he revealed himself not only to Israel but to all the nations" (395-96).

61. Much of the debate on the rabbinic rejection of the Septuagint hinges on the dating of the line in *Megillat Ta'anit Batra* that claims that three days of darkness fell upon the earth when the Torah was translated into Greek. Although earlier scholars like M. Friedländer assumed an early date for the *Megillah*, scholars like Jellicoe and, more recently and forcefully, Giuseppi Veltri, argue that the passage is part of a Gaonic appendix to the tannaitic body of the *Megillah*. See *Megillath Ta'anith Batra*, ed. A. Neubauer (Oxford: Anecdota Oxon, vol. 4, 1895). For a discussion of its dating see Sidney Jellicoe, *The Septuagint and Modern Study* (Oxford: Clarendon, 1968), 76, and Giuseppi Veltri, *Gegenwart der Tradition: Studien zur jüdischen Literatur und Kulturgeschichte* (Leiden: Brill, 2002), 144-50.

62. Markus Hirsch Friedländer, *Geschichte der jüdischen Apologetik* (Vienna, 1906), 16, quoted in Veltri, *Gegenwart der Tradition*, 146.

63. Marc Hirshman, *Torah for All Humankind* (Hebrew) (Jerusalem: Magnes, 1999), 112.

64. Marc Hirshman, "Rabbinic Universalism in the Second and Third Centuries," *Harvard Theological Review* 93, no. 2 (2000): 102-3.

65. Ibid., 115.

66. Solomon Schechter, "The *Mekhilta Deuteronomy,* Pericope *Re'eh*" (Hebrew), in *Tif'eret Yisra'el: Festschrift zu Israel Lewy's siebzigsten Geburtstag,* ed. M. Brann and J. Elbogen (Breslau, 1911), 189.

67. Azzan Yadin, "The Hammer on the Rock: Polysemy and the School of Rabbi Ishmael," *Jewish Studies Quarterly* 10, no. 1 (May 2003): 17.

68. Veltri has recently made a very similar point, arguing that we should not take for granted that the rabbis renounced translation once the Septuagint had become the Bible of the Christian Church; rabbinic literature rather advanced an alternative model of translation. Unlike those readings that suggest that rabbinic models of internal-midrashic translation arose in reaction to Hellenism or Christianity, Veltri claims that rabbinic and Jewish-Hellenistic approaches to translation must both be understood against the philosophical background of translation in antiquity (Veltri, *Gegenwart der Tradition,* 45-52).

69. Emanuel Levinas, "The Translation of the Scripture," in *In the Time of the Nations,* trans. Michael B. Smith (Bloomington: Indiana University Press, 1994), 39.

70. Ibid.

71. Ibid., 41.

72. Ibid., 46.

73. Emanuel Levinas, *Otherwise than Being; or, Beyond Essence,* trans. Alphonso Lingis (Pittsburgh: Duquesne University Press, 1998), v.

74. Ibid.

75. Roger Ellis, Introduction to *The Medieval Translator: The Theory and Practice of Translation in the Middle Ages,* ed. Roger Ellis (Cambridge, England: Brewer, 1989), 4.

CHAPTER ONE

1. Lori Chamberlain, "Gender and the Metaphorics of Translation," *Signs* 13 (1988): 454-72, repr. in *The Translation Studies Reader,* 2nd ed., ed. Lawrence Venuti (New York: Routledge, 2000), 315, following Barbara Johnson, "Taking Fidelity Philosophically," in *Difference in Translation,* ed. Joseph Graham (Ithaca: Cornell University Press, 1985), 142-48.

2. That the rabbis rejected the accuracy of the Septuagint has recently been contested by Giuseppi Veltri in a monograph entitled *Eine Tora für den König Talmai: Untersuchungen zum Übersetzungsverständnis in der jüdisch-hellenistischen und rabbinischen Literatur* (Tübingen: Mohr, 1994). While most scholars consider the rejection of the Septuagint to have been a result of its adoption by Christians, Emanuel Tov argues, in a review of Veltri, that the Jewish revision of the Septuagint commenced well before the translation was used by Christian readers, although the Christian embrace of the LXX exacerbated the negative Jewish view of the translation. See Tov, Review of *Eine Tora für den König Talmai, Scripta Classica Israelica* 14 (1995): 178-83, repr. in *The Greek and Hebrew Bible: Collected Essays on the Septuagint* (Leiden: Brill, 1999), 81-82.

3. Translations are my own, unless otherwise indicated.

4. Harry Orlinsky views the '*almah–parthenos* crux as one of the two sites of Jewish–Christian hermeneutic difference, the other being the also much-discussed *ruah–pneuma* (wind/spirit or Spirit). See Orlinsky, "The Role of Theology in the Christian Mistranslation of the Hebrew Bible," in *Translation of Scripture,* ed. David M. Goldenberg (Philadelphia: Annenberg Research Institute, 1990), 127-32.

5. Justin Martyr, *Dialogue with Trypho the Jew* 67:1, trans. A. Lukyn Williams (London: Society for the Promotion of Christian Knowledge, 1930), 139.

6. For a riveting account and analysis of the controversy see Peter J. Thuesen, *In Discordance with the Scriptures: American Protestant Battles over Translating the Bible* (Oxford: Oxford University Press, 1999), 93-119. At issue in the RSV controversy of the 1950s was not only, as Thuesen puts it, "the quest for an undefiled book," but also the anti-Communist fervor rocking the country. The RSV was denounced in some quarters for having been composed by Communist sympathizers. This charge took a vicious anti-Jewish turn when "fundamentalists set their sights on Harry Orlinsky, the sole Jewish member of the committee. . . . Never before in Anglo-American history had a Jew served on a major Christian Bible translation project" (109-10).

7. Raymond Brown, *The Birth of the Messiah: A Commentary on the Infancy Narratives in Matthew and Luke* (Garden City, N.Y.: Doubleday, 1977), 146 n. 37.

8. There is, of course, an immense literature on this question. For somewhat overlapping summaries of the scholarly discussion of the terms *'almah* and *parthenos*, see R. G. Bratcher, "A Study of Isaiah 7:14," *The Bible Translator* 9 (1958), 97-126, and Adam Kamesar, "The Virgin of Isaiah 7:14: The Philological Argument from the Second to the Fifth Century," *Journal of Theological Studies*, n.s., 41, no. 1 (April 1990): 51-75.

9. The Liddell and Scott Greek Lexicon gives a number of examples of the use of the word *parthenon* or its semantic relatives in which the meaning "virgin" would normally be ruled out, for instance in the word *parthenios*, which refers to "the son of an unmarried girl." The Lexicon cites *Iliad* 16.180, where the word explicitly means an illegitimate son. The word seems to have come to imply virginity in later Greek literature, and it *is* used unambiguously in that sense in a number of LXX passages other than Isaiah 7:14. See *Liddell and Scott's Greek-English Lexicon* (Oxford: Clarendon, 1996), 1339.

10. Kamesar, "Virgin of Isaiah 7:14," 58-62.

11. Jerome, *Against Jovinianus* 1.32, trans. W. H. Fremantle, Nicene and Post-Nicene Fathers ser. 2 vol. 6 (1893), repr. in *The Principal Works of St. Jerome* (Peabody, Mass.: Hendrickson, 1994), 370.

12. Kamesar demonstrates that the rabbis, too, derive a similar meaning from *'almah* in a midrash on Moses' sister, who is also referred to as an *'almah* in Exodus 2:8: "Why does the text refer to her as *almah*? . . . R. Samuel said, because she concealed her words [i.e. her identity and intention]" *Exodus Rabbah* 1.25, quoted in Kamesar, "Virgin of Isaiah 7:14," 64.

13. Ibid., 68. Emphasis added.

14. Most notably, Isaiah's prophecy that "she," the young woman, would name the child is changed, in Matthew, to the prophesy that "*they* will call him Emmanuel," perhaps to avoid contradiction with 1:25, where it is Joseph who names the child Jesus (a name that arguably is synonymous with Emmanuel—"God will save" and "God is with us"). It is also possible that Matthew used a no-longer-extant LXX variant.

15. For a brief overview of Jewish and Christian charges and countercharges of falsification, see William Adler, "The Jews as Falsifiers: Charges of Tendentious Emendation in Anti-Jewish Christian Polemic," in Goldenberg, *Translation of Scripture*, 1-27. Emanuel Tov is among the few LXX scholars who are inclined to believe the talmudic account of deliberate Jewish alterations in the Greek translation *prima facie*, arguing that the alterations mentioned in the Talmud that are not attested in extant manuscripts—nine of fourteen—represent earlier versions that were later "corrected" toward the Hebrew. See Tov, "The Rabbinic Tradition concerning the 'Alterations' Inserted into the Greek Translation of the Torah and Their Relation to the Original Text of the Septuagint," in *The Greek and Hebrew Bible*, 1-20.

16. See Justin, *Dialogue with Trypho* 71.

17. Brown, *Birth*, 149.

18. Jacques Derrida, *Dissemination*, trans. Barbara Johnson (Chicago: University of Chicago Press, 1981), 220-21. For Derrida, the "hymen," which signifies both marriage and virginity and can thus serve as a countersignifier to the phallus in its (fictional) unity, "is inscribed at the very tip of this indecision [of signifying systems]."

19. Daniel Boyarin, "Why Augustine Was Right" (paper presented at the conference "Augustine and the Disciplines," Villanova University, November 2000). Boyarin's paper constitutes ironic Jewish advice to a group of Christian scholars *not* to turn to Jews and their sources at the expense of Church tradition. There is a further irony: It is Augustine in his defense of Christian exegetical tradition who relies on the consensus of Jewish translators in the Septuagint, while Jerome overthrows both in his return to the Hebrew sources.

20. Martin Hengel, "The Septuagint as a Collection of Writings Claimed by Christians: Justin and the Church Fathers before Origen," in *Jews and Christians: The Parting of the Ways, A.D. 70 to 135*, ed. James D. G. Dunn (Grand Rapids, Mich.: Eerdmans, 1992), 50.

21. For a discussion of Ebionites and the virgin birth, see Marcel Simon, *Verus Israel*, trans. H. McKeating (Oxford: Oxford University Press, 1986), 252-54 (French original, 1964). Simon goes on to complicate the picture, arguing that Jewish Christians, Ebionites among them, were described as split on the issue of the virgin birth, or even as conforming with other Christian groups in their beliefs; Simon reconciles these differences by arguing for a gradual assimilation of Ebionite Christology to orthodox claims. In any case, the connection between a reliance on the Septuagint and a belief in Mary's virginity stands.

22. For a discussion of the possible contradiction between the genealogies and the claims that Mary was a virgin, see Geza Vermes, *Jesus the Jew: A Historian's Reading of the Gospels* (Philadelphia: Fortress, 1973), 215-22.

23. See Brown, *Birth*, 440.

24. Ibid.

25. So, too, did rabbinic writers develop a discourse that spoke of the miraculousness of birth (*any* birth!), with God as the active begetter of children. Galit Hasan-Rokem's unpublished paper (2002) on "Memories of Birth, the Birth of Memory" discusses this motif in *Leviticus Rabbah.*

26. Aphraates' views are summarized in Simon, *Verus Israel*, 160–61. Cyril of Alexandria quotes Diodore as saying that Jesus was conceived as a human and only received his divine soul after birth. Cyril of Alexandria, *Fragments against Diodore of Tarsus*, Library of Fathers of the Holy Catholic Church, vol. 47, trans. Edward B. Pusey (Oxford: James Parker and Rivington's, 1881), 330.

27. Jane Schaberg, *The Illegitimacy of Jesus: A Feminist Theological Interpretation of the Infancy Narratives* (Sheffield: Crossroads, 1995), 62.

28. Ibid., 67.

29. Vermes, *Jesus the Jew*, 213–14.

30. I do not mean to imply that Hellenistic Judaism was the only factor in the rise of Christianity, much less rabbinic Judaism. Rosemary Ruether supplies a number of other cultural components to the prehistory of Christianity, particularly Second Temple Jewish sectarianism and messianism; her analysis, of course, makes no claim to be exhaustive. See Rosemary Radford Ruether, *Faith and Fratricide: The Theological Roots of Anti-Semitism*, 2nd ed. (Eugene, Ore.: Wipf and Stock, 1995), 40–48. 1st ed., 1974.

31. Paula Fredriksen, *From Jesus to Christ: The Origins of the New Testament Images of Christ* (New Haven, 1988), 14.

32. "Die Bibel deren Gott *Yahveh* heisst, ist die Bible eines Volk, die Bibel deren Gott *kurios* heisst, ist die Weltbibel" (A. Deissmann, *Neue Jahrbücher für das klassische Altertum* 11 [1903]: 174).

33. The term "romance" is that of Henry Barclay Swete, the eminent Septuagint scholar. "Though the Story as 'Aristeas' tells it is doubtless a romance, it must not be hastily inferred that it has no historical basis" (*An Introduction to the Old Testament in Greek* [Cambridge: Cambridge University Press, 1900], 35).

34. Erich Gruen, *Heritage and Hellenism: The Reinvention of Jewish Tradition* (Berkeley and Los Angeles: University of California Press, 1998), 208–9.

35. Victor Tcherikover, "The Ideology of the Letter of Aristeas," *Harvard Theological Review* 51 (1958): 218. See also Moses Hadas's introduction to his edition of *Aristeas to Philocrates*: "Broadly speaking, Aristeas is obviously in the tradition of 'apologetic' Alexandrian Jewish writings whose general aim was to demonstrate the high antiquity and respectability of Judaism, for the purpose of strengthening the self-esteem of the Jews themselves and perhaps heightening their esteem in the eyes of their dominant environment." (Introduction to *Aristeas to Philocrates [Letter of Aristeas]* [New York: Harper, 1951], 60).

36. Tcherikover, "Ideology," 219.

37. Aristeas tells us that after its completion, any alteration was forbidden "inasmuch as the translation has been well and piously made and is in every respect accurate," *Aristeas*, 221 (verse 310). The prohibition against revising the Septuagint is often taken as evidence of the disturbing number of LXX variants circulating in the second century BCE.

38. Ibid., vv. 302–7.

39. Ibid., 102–3, vv. 15–16. Hadas comments in a note on v. 16 that only a (fictional) pagan could voice the equivalence of Jewish and Greek gods; a Jew, speaking in his own voice, would find such an idea blasphemous.

40. As D. W. Gooding puts it, the Septuagint legend would "assure Alexandrian Jewry that their Hebrew text, and the Greek translation made of it, were true representatives of the Law; they came directly from the High Priest in Jerusalem with his authority and blessing" ("Aristeas and Septuagint Origins: A Review of Recent Studies," in *Studies in the Septuagint: Origins, Recensions, Interpretations*, ed. Sydney Jellicoe (New York: KTAV, 1974), 378–79. This legitimation was particularly crucial in a community with competing textual variants: the LXX was translated using a Hebrew *Vorlage* from a tradition different from the proto-Masoretic texts of Babylonia.

41. Gruen, *Heritage and Hellenism*, 220–21.

42. Ibid., 222.

43. According to Moses Hadas, the Greek translation of the book of Exodus—of particular interest to Egypt-

ian readers—functioned partially as a Jewish counter-discourse to such popular Greco-Egyptian histories as those collected by Manetho (ca. 300 BCE), which describe the Jews as a pariah people who had been expelled from Egypt as lepers (Introduction, 71 n. 99).

44. The question of whether Philo knew of the *Letter* or was recounting a separate tradition is discussed in Hadas, Introduction, 21-26.

45. Philo, *On the Life of Moses* 2.7.37, in *The Works of Philo*, trans. C. D. Yonge (N.p.: Hendrickson, 1993), 494.

46. Hindy Najman writes that because the Greeks denigrated the written law and exalted "the law of nature," Philo "therefore undertook to show that the written law was in fact a perfect copy of the law of nature" ("The Law of Nature and the Authority of Mosaic Law," *Studia Philonica Annual: Studies in Hellenistic Judaism* 11 [1999]: 72).

47. Philo, *On the Life of Moses* 2.6.36-7-.39, in Yonge, *Works*, 494.

48. Douglas Robinson's *Who Translates? Translator Subjectivities beyond Reason* (Albany: SUNY Press, 2001) is an extended meditation on the persistent (self-) characterization of the translator as a spiritual medium or "channeler" of the source author/text.

49. Philo, *On the Life of Moses* 2.6.40, in Yonge, *Works*, 494.

50. Francesca Calabi, *The Language and the Law of God: Interpretation and Politics in Philo of Alexandria*, trans. Michael Leone (Atlanta: Tyndale House, 1998), 20.

51. Philo, *On the Cherubim* 2.17.56, in Yonge, *Works*, 86. "All the rest of the human race gives names to things which are different from the things themselves, so that the thing which we see is one thing, but the name which we give it is another; but in the history of Moses the names which he affixes to things are the most conspicuous energies of the things themselves, so that the thing itself is at once of necessity its name, and is in no respect different from the name which is imposed on it."

52. Ronald Williamson, *Jews in the Hellenistic World: Philo* (Cambridge: Cambridge University Press, 1989), 103.

53. Ibid., 104.

54. Calabi, *Language and Law of God*, 21 n. 36.

55. David Winston, "Aspects of Philo's Linguistic Theory," in *Festschrift Earle Higert: The Studia Philonica Annual* 3 (1991): 122.

56. The notion of vertical and horizontal translation is borrowed from Karlheinz Stierle, "*Translatio Studii* and Renaissance: From Vertical to Horizontal Translation," in *The Translatability of Cultures: Figurations of the Space Between*, ed. Sanford Budick and Wolfgang Iser (Stanford: Stanford University Press, 1996), 55-67. But where Stierle describes a shift from a medieval *translatio* that signaled a vertical, hierarchical relationship between a privileged or "divine" source and a debased reproduction to a horizontal Renaissance translation theory, secularized, nonhierarchical, and mutual, my own interest is in the shift from an initially horizontal translation narrative in Aristeas, in which languages meet as "equals," to the dominant, vertical mode that governs Christian translation theory from Philo certainly through the Middle Ages through a transcendent source of meaning beyond human language.

57. Ruether, *Faith and Fratricide*, 38.

58. For this opposition, see especially Romans 2:29, 1 Corinthians 10:18, 2 Corinthians 3:6, Galatians 3:7, and Philippians 3:3.

59. Aleida Assmann, "The Curse and Blessing of Babel; or, Looking Back on Universalisms," in *The Translatibility of Cultures: Figurations of the Space Between*, ed. Sanford Budick and Wolfgang Iser (Stanford: Stanford University Press, 1996), 87.

60. Irenaeus, *Against Heresies* 3.21.1, quoted in Hadas, Introduction, 24-25.

61. This notion was expressed by Eusebius and Irenaeus. For a discussion, see Adam Kamesar, *Jerome, Greek Scholarship and the Hebrew Bible: A Study of the* Quaestiones Hebraicae in Genesim (Oxford: Oxford University Press, 1993), 33.

62. Augustine, *On Christian Doctrine* 2.15, trans. D. W. Robertson (Indianapolis: Bobbs-Merrill, 1958), 49.

63. Pseudo-Justin, *Exhortation to the Greeks* 13, trans. Henry St. J. Thackeray. Loeb Classical Library. (Cambridge: Harvard University Press, 1919).

64. Philo, *The Decalogue* 17.82, in Yonge, *Works*, 525.

65. Winston, "Aspects." 124-25.

66. Ibid., 125.

67. Jacques Derrida, "Semiology and Grammatology: Interview with Julia Kristeva," in *Positions*, trans. Alan Bass (Chicago: University of Chicago Press, 1981), 20.

68. Epiphanius, *On Weights and Measures* 3-11, quoted in Hadas, Introduction, 76.

69. Eusebius, *Ecclesiastical History* 2.7.8, 17. For a discussion see J. Edgar Bruns, "Philo Christianus: The Debris of a Legend," *Harvard Theological Review* 66 (1973): 141.

70. Philo, "On the Contemplative Life or Suppliants" 3.32-33, 4.85, in Yonge, *Works*, 701, 706.

71. Robinson, *Who Translates?* 52. My own reading rests on Robinson's argument that the translator's subjectivity has been suppressed in translation, although for the purposes of the argument developed here I distinguish more sharply than Robinson does between the status of the perfect medium, as in Philo, whose "subjectivity" fully corresponds with the message transmitted, and the "empty channel" developed by the Fathers as surety against Jewish contagion.

72. In a telling slip, Douglas Robinson refers to the Jewish translators as monks in his discussion of this passage, ibid., 5. The "conversion" to Christianity by Eusebius and others not of the translators but rather of Philo is well known. See Bruns, "Philo Christianus," 141-45.

73. Mark Hart, "Gregory of Nyssa's Ironic Praise of the Celibate Life," *Heythrop Journal* 33, no. 2 (1992): 4.

74. *Anonymous Coptic Apophthegmata* 42, ed. M. Chaine (Institut Français d'Archéologie Orientale, Bibliothèque des Études Coptes, 1960), 92, cited in Peter Brown, *The Body and Society: Men, Women, and Sexual Renunciation in Early Christianity* (New York: Columbia University Press, 1988), 222.

75. Ibid., 273.

76. Douglas Robinson, *Translation and Taboo* (DeKalb: Northern Illinois University Press, 1996), 102.

77. Ibid., 52-54, and passim.

78. Raymond E. Brown, *The Virginal Conception and Bodily Resurrection of Jesus* (New York: Paulist Press, 1973), 67.

79. Tertullian, *Apologia* 9.8.

80. See, for instance, the fifteenth-century illuminated manuscript *The Rohan Master Book of Hours* (New York: Braziller, 1994), 40.

81. Jerome, *Against Jovinianus* 1.32.

82. Gustav Volkmar, *Die Religion Jesu und ihre erste Entwicklung nach dem gegenwärtigen Stande der Wissenschaft* (Leipzig, 1857), 52, quoted in Susannah Heschel, *Abraham Geiger and the Jewish Jesus* (Chicago: University of Chicago Press, 1998), 161. Heschel has revised her translation (pers. comm.) from "virgin lap" to "virgin womb."

83. Marina Warner, *Alone of All Her Sex: The Myth and the Cult of the Virgin Mary* (New York: Knopf, 1976), 35.

84. Justin, *Dialogue* 71.

85. Justin, *Apology* 1.33, in *The First and Second Apologies*, trans. Leslie William Barnard, Ancient Christian Writers: The Works of the Fathers in Translation 56 (New York: Paulist Press, 1997), 46.

86. Origen, *Against Celsus* 1.32, trans. Henry Chadwick (Cambridge: Cambridge University Press, 1953), 31.

87. The "ben Pantera" texts occur in *t. Hullin* 2.22, 23; *y. Shabbat* 14d; *y. 'Avodah Zara* 27b.

88. *M. Yevamot* 4.13.

89. For a discussion of this passage, see Tov, "Rabbinic Tradition."

90. *Midrash Hagadol* Exodus 4:20 refers more explicitly to "the eighteen details which our Rabbis changed in the Torah in Greek." As Tov writes, while the Jews were more likely to view the Greek as having been altered, Christian tradition took differences between the "Jewish" and "Greek" (from their viewpoint, Christian) versions to be alterations in the opposite direction: "a few Church Fathers claimed that the LXX reflects the true form of God's words, and that it was the Jews who had falsified them in their Bible" ("Rabbinic Tradition," 13).

91. Jonathan Boyarin, *A Storyteller's Worlds: The Education of Shlomo Noble in Europe and America*, foreword by Sander Gilman (New York, 1994), 10. Daniel Boyarin similarly speaks of the rabbis as tricksters in a chapter comparing the Christian ideal of martyrdom and the rabbinic model of escape through quick wit: "If Esau was

the legendary ancestor of Rome," Boyarin writes, "Jacob, his brother, was the exemplary rabbinic male" (*Dying for God* [Stanford: Stanford University Press, 1999], 49).

92. James C. Scott, *Domination and the Arts of Resistance: Hidden Transcripts* (New Haven: Yale University Press, 1990), 34.

93. Tov regards *all* the alterations as deriving from actual changes by the Seventy; that many of these alterations are not found in our version suggests to Tov that the LXX was corrected to bring it closer to Hebrew sources. In fact, as he remarks, "There were no two identical or nearly identical scrolls for any book of the LXX" in the pre-Christian era ("Rabbinic Tradition," 9). His argument for this, especially in relation to the translation of the word *arnevet*, is persuasive, but it only determines the antiquity of the tradition of an altered text, not the revision of the Septuagint legend (ibid., 8–15).

94. Or rather, in Tov's reconstruction, *śe'irat raglayim*, "hairy-footed," a Greek synonym for "hare."

95. Derrida, *Positions*, 20 (emphasis added).

96. A vast scholarship exists on the differences between the Infancy Narratives in Matthew and Luke, some of which labors to resolve these differences by recourse to the hypothesis that one derives from a tradition that can be traced through John to Mary while the other derives from Joseph. For a discussion, see Brown, *Birth*, 88–90.

97. This version is from the Strasbourg manuscript (defective in various details), which Samuel Krauss indicates has some intertextual links with Matthew's Infancy Narrative, e.g. Matthew 1:18 *archē geneseos*, which is glossed in the Strasbourg manuscript as *tehilat bri'ato*, in Krauss's view (*Das Leben Jesu nach jüdische Quellen* [Berlin: S. Calvary, 1902], 38 n. 1). The critical edition (and German translation) of the various versions of the *Toldot Yeshu*, which was first published by J. C. Wagenseil in his *Tela ignea Satanae; sive, Arcani et horribiles Judaeorum adversus Christum, Deum, et christianem religionem libri* (Fiery darts of Satan; or, The secret and horrifying books of the Jews against the Divine Christ and the Christian religion) (Altdorf: Schönnerstadt, 1681), remains that of Krauss.

98. Joseph Kimhi, *The Book of the Covenant* (Hebrew) (Cassuto, 1270), in J. D. Eisenstein, ed. *Otsar vikuḥim* (Collected polemics and disputations) (New York: Hebrew Publishing Company, 1922), 73.

99. *Protevangelium of James*, in *The Apocryphal New Testament*, ed. and trans. J. K. Elliot (Oxford: Clarendon, 1993), 65.

100. Rutebeuf, *Le Miracle de Théophile*, ed. Grace Frank (Paris: Champion, 1925), 20, lines 492–97.

101. Rebecca Lyman, *Christology and Cosmology: Models of Divine Activity in Origen, Eusebius, and Athanasius* (Oxford: Clarendon), 159.

102. Colm Luibheid, *The Council of Nicaea* (Galway, Ireland: Galway University Press, 1982), 75.

103. Virginia Burrus, *"Begotten Not Made": Conceiving Manhood in Late Antiquity* (Stanford: Stanford University Press, 2000), 67.

104. Ibid., 57.

105. Ibid., 67–68.

106. It was a scurrilous (in his view) critique of Jerome's "free" translation of Epiphanius's letter to John of Jerusalem that was the occasion behind Jerome's letter (395 CE) to Pammachius "On the Best Method of Translating," in *Letters and Selected Works*, trans. W. H. Fremantle, Nicene and Post-Nicene Fathers 6 (New York: Scribners, 1893), 112–19. A new translation of this letter by Kathleen Davis appears in Venuti, *Translation Studies Reader*, 2nd ed. (2004), 21–30, but I have kept to the Fremantle translation for consistency with Jerome's other letters.

107. Jerome, *Preface to Hebrew Questions on Genesis*, translated with introduction and commentary by C. T. R. Hayward (Oxford: Oxford University Press, 1995), 401.

108. Jerome, *Letter 125.12*, in Fremantle, *Letters and Selected Works*, 248.

109. Ibid.

110. Jerome is not unique in suggesting that the Septuagint cannot be considered a perfect copy of the Hebrew Bible. Origen, of course, had demonstrated as much in the *Hexapla*, and even Augustine had suggested that the Septuagint might after all be different from the Bible. But the Septuagint remained the Christian Bible: Eusebius believed that God prompted Ptolemy to commission a Bible that Christians could read, although

he also presumed that the LXX was perfectly accurate; even Origen, who knows better, makes use of the Hebrew only to establish an authoritative LXX text. The most dramatic formulation of the LXX as the Christian Bible is that of Hilary of Poitiers, who argues that the Seventy were recipients of a secret oral tradition, "guided by divine Providence, in order that the Gentiles be brought over to the true faith" (Kamesar, *Jerome: Greek Scholarship*, 33).

111. Jerome, *Preface*, 29.

112. Ibid., 31.

113. In his letter 124 to Pammachius of 400, Jerome refers to "a certain person" who found fault with him for "having had a Jew as a teacher," and who dared to "bring forward against me the letter I wrote to Didymus calling him my master." This letter, Jerome continues, "has been held over so long to discredit me," although it contains nothing but "courteous language" (*Letters and Selected Works*, 176). Jerome seems to be referring to Rufinus here, who taunted Jerome that he preferred Barabbas (as he deliberately distorted Baraninas's name) to Christ (Rufinus, *Apologia* 2.12.21).

114. Jerome, Letter to Pammachius (letter 57), 114–15.

CHAPTER TWO

1. George Steiner, *After Babel: Aspects of Language and Translation*, 3rd ed. (Oxford: Oxford University Press, 1998), 283.

2. Notable exceptions include Nabokov, who writes: "The term 'free translation' smacks of knavery and tyranny. It is when the translator sets out to render the 'spirit'—not the textual sense—that he begins to traduce his author. The clumsiest literal translation is a thousand times more useful than the prettiest paraphrase" (Vladimir Nabokov, "Problems of Translation: *Onegin* in English," *Partisan Review* 22 [1955]: 498–512, repr. in *Theories of Translation: An Anthology of Essays from Dryden to Derrida*, ed. Rainer Schulte and John Biguenet [Chicago: University of Chicago Press, 1992], 127). For illustrating a modern English rejection of the sense-for-sense approach, critics often invoke Louis and Celia Zukofsky's remarkable renderings of Catullus, which privilege the sound of the words and even syllables over their lexical meaning (Louis and Celia Zukofsky, *Catullus* [London: Cape Goliard Press, 1969]).

3. Marcus Tullius Cicero, "The Best Kind of Orator," in *Rhetorical Treatises*, vol. 2, trans. H.M. Hubbell, Loeb Classical Library (Cambridge: Harvard University Press, 1949), 364–65.

4. Horace, in his *Art of Poetry* (20 BCE), writes: "You may acquire private rights in common ground, provided you will neither linger in the one hackneyed and easy round; nor trouble to render word for word with the faithfulness of a translator," trans. E. C. Wickham, in *Western Translation Theory from Herodotus to Nietzsche*, ed. Douglas Robinson (Manchester, England: St. Jerome Press, 1997), 15.

Barnstone's translation, "Nor should you try to render the original word for word like an obedient (faithful) *interpres*," appears as an epigraph in his *The Poetics of Translation: History, Theory, Practice* (New Haven: Yale University Press, 1993), 32.

5. Eugene Nida, *The Theory and Practice of Translation* (Leiden: Brill, 1969), 204.

6. Ibid., 205.

7. Barnstone, *Poetics*, 31–32.

8. Dryden's 1680 *Preface* to his translation of Ovid's *Epistles* is included, as "On Translation," in Schulte and Biguenet, *Theories of Translation*, 18.

9. Nida, "Bible Translation," in *Routledge Encyclopedia of Translation Studies*, 2nd ed., ed. Mona Baker (London: Routledge, 2000), 26.

10. Cicero, "Best Kind of Orator," 365; Nida, "Bible Translation," 26; Octavio Paz, *Traducción: Literatura y Literalidad* (Barcelona: Tusquets Editores, 1981), quoted in Barnstone, *Poetics*, 31.

11. It is generally assumed that Aquila's translation of the Hebrew Bible into Greek, sometime around 130, derived from a growing alienation from the Septuagint on the part of Jewish communities (probably in Palestine). Sidney Jellicoe, however, connects this retranslation also with the fixing of the Hebrew canon that took place at the turn of the first century: "It was a natural corollary [of the canonization of the Bible] that the hith-

erto "official" translation, circulating so widely in the Graeco-Roman world, should be corrected to standard both for the edification of the practicing Jew and, in view of an ever-widening breach between the Old and New Israel, to provide an accurate rendering for controversy with Christians. The outcome was the version of Aquila" (*The Septuagint and Modern Study* [Oxford: Clarendon, 1968], 76).

That Aquila's version functioned within Jewish–Christian polemic is suggested from at least two of his readings: most famously, Aquila rendered the Hebrew word *'almah* as *nēanis*, or young girl, rather than the Septuagint's *parthenos*. He also translated *mashiaḥ* in Ps. 2:2 as *eleimmenos* rather than *christos*, both of which mean "anointed." For a discussion, see Karen H. Jobes and Moises Silva, *Invitation to the Septuagint* (Grand Rapids, Mich: Baker Academic, 2000), 39.

What is not a matter of conjecture is the popularity of Aquila's version: Origen and Jerome both attest to its use in contemporary Jewish circles, and a novella of the Emperor Justinian (527–65) permits its use in the synagogue, "although the author is of an alien race and his translation shows not inconsiderable differences from that of the Septuagint" (ibid., no. 19).

12. Origen, *Letter to Africanus* 2, quoted in Jellicoe, *Septuagint and Modern Study*, 76.

13. Jerome, "To Pammachius on the Best Method of Translating" (letter 57, 395 CE), in *Letters and Selected Works*, trans. W. H. Fremantle, Nicene and Post-Nicene Fathers 6 (New York: Scribners, 1893), repr. in *The Principal Works of St. Jerome* (Peabody, Mass.: Hendrickson, 1994), 118.

14. Although Jerome does not mention this, Aquila also "overzealously" rendered the word *bereshit* as *en kephalou*, or "in the heading," in an attempt to render visible the Hebrew root for beginning, which derives from the root meaning "head."

15. A. J. Maas, "The Greek Versions of the Bible," *The Catholic Encyclopedia*, ed. Charles G. Herbermann (New York: Appleton, 1912), 7:242; Henry St. John Thackeray, *A Grammar of the Old Testament in Greek According to the Septuagint* (Cambridge: Cambridge University Press, 1909), 1.9; Sebastian Brock, "The Phenomenon of Biblical Translation in Antiquity," in *Studies in the Septuagint: Origins, Recensions and Interpretations*, ed. Sidney Jellicoe (New York: KTAV, 1974), 561; Bruce Metzger, *The Bible in Translation: Ancient and English Versions* (Grand Rapids, Mich.: Baker Academic, 2001), 19.

16. Julio Trebolle Barrera, *The Jewish Bible and the Christian Bible: An Introduction to the History of the Bible* (Leiden: Brill; Grand Rapids, Mich.: Eerdmans, 1998), 8.

17. Frederick E. Greenspahn, "How Jews Translate the Bible," in *Biblical Translation in Context*, ed. Frederick W. Knobloch (Bethesda: University of Maryland Press, 2002), 51.

18. Simon Bernfeld, introduction to *Die Heilige Schrift: Torah, nevi'im uketuvim: nach dem masoretischen Text*, trans. and comm. Simon Bernfeld, 3rd ed. (Frankfurt a. M.: J. Kaufmann, 1919), xxiii–xxiv.

19. Walter Benjamin, "The Task of the Translator," trans. Harry Zohn, in *Illuminations: Essays and Reflections*, ed. Hannah Arendt (New York: Schocken, 1968), 78; "Die Aufgabe des Übersetzers," in *Illuminationen* (Frankfurt a. M.: Suhrkamp, 1969), 65.

20. E. A. Speiser, *Genesis*, Anchor Bible 1 (New York: Doubleday, 1964), lxxiii.

21. www.lxx.org\about\historyseptuagint.html, page 3.

22. Henry Barclay Swete, *An Introduction to the Old Testament in Greek* (Cambridge: Cambridge University Press, 1900),41.

23. George Campbell, ed. and trans., *The Four Gospels, Translated from the Greek. With Preliminary Dissertations, and Notes Critical and Explanatory* (London: A. Trahan and T.Cadell, 1789), 456–57.

24. Jacques Derrida, *Of Grammatology*, trans. Gayatri Chakravorty Spivak (Baltimore: The Johns Hopkins University Press, 1976; French original, 1967).

25. On Buddhist preferences for sense-for-sense translation, see Eva Hung and David Pollard, "The Chinese Tradition," in Baker, *Routledge Encyclopedia*, 368. For similar concerns in Arabic translation, see Mona Baker, "The Arabic Tradition," ibid., 320–21. I discuss Sa'adia's, Maimonides', and ibn Ezra's non-literalist approach to translation briefly in chapter 1 above.

26. Thus, for instance, the twelfth century saw an impassioned defense of word-for-word translation in the Preface to the Latin translation of St. John Chrystostom's *Homilies on the Gospel of John* (early 1170s) by the translator-theologian Burgundio of Pisa. Burgundio writes that "in fear that, if I wrote in my own idiom when

translating this holy father's commentary, I would be changing the true meaning of one or more propositions of these two very wise men [i.e., John the Evangelist and John Chrystostom], and would be incurring the risk of altering so great an original (for these are words of faith) through my own error, I resolved to take a more difficult journey and preserve in my translation not only words with the same meaning as in the original Greek but also the same style and order of words" (Burgundio of Pisa, "The Risk of Altering So Great an Original," Preface to St. John Chrystostom, *Homilies on the Gospel of John*, trans. Edward Capps III, in Robinson, *Western Translation Theory*, 41). See also Steiner's discussion of Nicholas von Wyle, a fifteenth-century translator who "demanded a total concordance, a matching of word for word: '*ain jedes wort gegen ain andern wort.*' Even errors must be transcribed and translated as they are an integral part of the original." (*After Babel*, 276-77, citing Rolf Kloepfer, *Die Theorie der literarischen Übersetzung: Romanisch-deutscher Sprachbereich* [Munich, 1967]).

27. Jerome, "To Pammachius," 113. Jerome's sincerity is doubted not only because his Bible translation is considered often "free" rather than "literal," but also because the examples he gives of defensible free renderings are themselves biblical, drawn either from the Septuagint or from the Gospel's citations of the Hebrew Bible. Thus Jerome writes that Matthew's attribution of a verse from Zechariah to Jeremiah or his misquotation of Hosea, for instance, is irrelevant to his point.

28. Aristeas and Philo are frequently represented in anthologies and discussions of Western translation, but the Talmud and Maimonides are not. Aristeas and Philo, of course, derive their importance to the field from their influence on patristic translation discourse. But the absence of rabbinic and post-rabbinic discourse on translation allows the impression that Western translation has a continuous history and speaks in a single voice, which turns out to be predominantly Christian.

29. Plato, *Cratylus*, 436a, in *The Dialogues of Plato*, trans. Benjamin Jowett (Oxford: Clarendon, 1970), 189.

30. Susan A. Handelman, *The Slayers of Moses: The Emergence of Rabbinic Interpretation in Modern Literary Theory* (Albany: SUNY Press, 1982), 5.

31. Daniel Boyarin, *A Radical Jew: Paul and the Politics of Identity* (Berkeley and Los Angeles: University of California Press, 1994), 14-15.

32. Translation, in this system, becomes the transfer of a soul from one body to another. Ulrich von Wilamowitz, in his introduction to Euripides' *Hippolytus* (1891), put it precisely in such language, writing that in translation, "the soul remains, but the body is changed: true translation is metempsychosis" (es bleibt die Seele, aber sie wechselt den Leib: die wahre Übersetzung ist Metempsychose; Steiner, *After Babel*, 281). The translation is my own. However mystical or occult such a notion might seem, translation can hardly do without it.

33. Aristotle, *On Interpretation* 16a.3-8, in *The Basic Works of Aristotle*, trans. E. M. Edghill (New York: Random House, 1963), 40.

34. Handelman writes that "putting all his Greek and Jewish learning to the task of discrediting Jewish law, he radicalized the antithesis of letter and spirit and applied it to Scripture in an unprecedented way" (*Slayers of Moses*, 86).

35. Boyarin thus insists that Paul's hermeneutic theory "by which the literal Israel, literal history, literal circumcision, and literal genealogy are superseded by their allegorical, spiritual signified is not necessarily anti-Semitic or even anti-Judaic. From the perspective of the first century, the contest between a Pauline allegorical Israel and a rabbinic hermeneutics of the concrete Israel is simply a legitimate cultural, hermeneutical, and political contestation. The denotation of 'Israel' was to a certain extent up for grabs" (*Radical Jew*, 105). It is a related error to read Paul as if in opposing the letter of the law to its spirit he were opposing Christian faith to "works-righteousness," as Luther saw it. Contemporary scholars from Krister Stendahl to Richard Hays and John Gager have stressed that Paul's interest in Corinthians and elsewhere is not to denigrate the importance of the law for Jews but rather to proclaim the superiority of its spiritual interpretation for and to the Gentiles.

36. Jonathan Z. Smith, "Fences and Neighbors: Some Contours of Early Judaism," in *Imagining Religion: From Babylon to Jonestown* (Chicago: University of Chicago Press), 1982, 11.

37. Rosemary Radford Ruether, *Faith and Fratricide: The Theological Roots of Anti-Semitism* (Eugene, Ore.: Wipf and Stock, 1974), 37.

38. Philo, *On the Migration of Abraham* 16.93, in *The Works of Philo*, trans. C. D. Yonge (Hendrickson, 1993), 262.

39. Nicholas de Lange, *Origen and the Jews* (Cambridge: Cambridge University Press, 1976), 105-6.

40. Ibid., 110.

41. Augustine, *Tractatus aversus Judaeos* 7.9, in Daniel Boyarin, *Carnal Israel: Reading Sex in Talmudic Culture* (Berkeley and Los Angeles: University of California Press, 1993), 1.

42. See Origen, "Letter to Africanus" 2, trans. Frederick Crombie, in *Tertullian, Part Fourth; Minucius Felix; Commodian; Origen, Parts First and Second*, Ante-Nicene Fathers 4 (Buffalo: Christian Literature, 1885, repr. Edinburgh: T & T Clark; Grand Rapids, Mich.: Eerdmans, 1994), 386, for an explicit acknowledgment of the usefulness of Aquila's version. And Jerome's appreciation for Aquila is implicit in the frequent citations of his translation throughout Jerome's work.

43. Cohen writes: "The doctrine of Jewish witness took shape against the backdrop of several major themes in Augustine's theology and writings: the interpretation of the Old Testament, especially Genesis; the appraisal of terrestrial history; and the assessment of human sexuality" (*Living Letters of the Law: Ideas of the Jew in Medieval Christianity* (Berkeley and Los Angeles: University of California Press, 1999), 43.

44. Ibid., 51.

45. Boyarin, *Carnal Israel*, 1.

46. In addition to *Sifre Numbers*, see also *b. Berakhot* 31b, *Yevamot* 71a, *Ketuvot* 67b, a long discussion in *Nedarim* 3a, *Gittin* 41b, *Kiddushin* 17b, among other passages. Both of these approaches, I should point out, have resulted in a variety of "literalist" analyses or translation *techniques;* one would have to concede that literalism, on closer examination, is a portmanteau term covering both a translation method that views the word or even root as the primary unit of translation, and an exegetical approach that directs its attention to the "plain sense" (however that might be defined) of the biblical text and, in translation, manifests itself as a sense-for-sense approach. Put otherwise, attention to the "letter" of the text might result in a careful word-as-unit approach or an expansive midrashic approach; the word-for-word literalism of Aquila and the (alternative) "literalism" of Onkelos's maximalist Aramaic translation which never hesitates to expand on the text in clarifying it, are very diverse manifestations of rabbinic attention to the letter. Given the range of approaches that go under the rubric of literalism, it might be more accurate (as has been suggested by Devorah Schoenfeld, pers. comm,), to consider the term as primarily polemical: either as a way of defending one's own approach as "closer" to the biblical text than that of some adversary (in the way it is sometimes used by American evangelicals), or as a term of opprobrium, to denigrate an adversary who is overly attached to the words over the content. The texts I explore in this chapter employ the term in this second sense.

47. Ephraim E. Urbach, *The Sages: Their Concepts and Beliefs*, trans. Israel Abrahams (Cambridge: Harvard University Press, 2001), 248. Hebrew original, 1975.

48. Ibid., 224.

49. Ibid., 235.

50. Ibid., 216.

51. Boyarin, *Carnal Israel*, 5-6.

52. *Tanhuma Tsav* 14 (Warsaw: Avigdor ben Joel, 1849), cited in Boyarin, *Radical Jew*, 37.

53. Ibid.

54. *Exodus Rabba* 30:12 (Vilna: Widow Romm Press, 1878).

55. As Neusner points out, converts did not pose a problem for the notion that Judaism was passed from generation to generation through kinship ties, since "they were held to be children of Abraham and Sarah, who had 'made souls,' that is, converts, in Haran," as the rabbinic literature understood it. Jacob Neusner, "The Doctrine of Israel," in *The Blackwell Companion to Judaism*, ed. Jacob Neusner and Alan J. Avery-Peck (Malden, Mass.: Blackwell, 2000), 237.

56. In a similar text from the medieval kabbalistic classic, the *Zohar*, it is Onkelos, the translator into Aramaic, who may not study Torah until he is circumcised, "because the Israelites are imprinted with a holy sign in their flesh [i.e. they are circumcised], and they are recognized as being His, the sons of his palace." *Zohar*, Leviticus 72b-73a. Access to the Hebrew letters of the Torah, and to *God's* palace (as opposed to Hadrian's, that is), is through the portal of the Judaized body, a body that is sanctified through circumcision.

57. Philo, *Life of Moses* 2.7.37, in Yonge, *Works*, 494.

58. Although earlier scholarship seems to have assumed the historical accuracy of the *Historia Augusta,* which explains the revolt by saying that "the Jews went to war because they were forbidden to mutilate their genitals," recent scholarship has cast this assumption in doubt. See, for instance, Aharon Oppenheimer, "The Ban on Circumcision as a Cause of the Revolt: A Reconsideration," in *The Bar Kokhba War Reconsidered,* ed. Peter Schäfer (Tübingen: Mohr Siebeck, 2003), 55-69, and Ra'anan Abusch, "Negotiating Difference: Genital Mutilation in Roman Slave Law and the History of the Bar Kokhba Revolt," ibid., 71-91.

59. For direct or indirect references to such a ban, see *b. Shabbat* 130a, *Ta'anit* 18a, and *Rosh Hashana* 19a; as well as *Megillat Ta'anit* 12 and *Leviticus Rabba* 32:1.

60. See, for an exposition of this argument, Boaz Cohen, "Letter and Spirit in Jewish and Roman Law," in *Essential Papers on the Talmud,* ed. Michael Chernick (New York: NYU Press, 1994), 400 and n. 9, where Cohen paraphrases Aristotle's *Rhetoric* 1.13, "General laws are those based on nature," and quotes various Church Fathers on the opinion that Scripture cannot contradict nature, either.

61. Smith, "Fences and Neighbors," 10-11.

62. Ibid., 11; Abusch, "Negotiating Difference," 84-91.

63. Shaye Cohen, *The Beginnings of Jewishness: Boundaries, Varieties, Uncertainties* (Berkeley and Los Angeles: University of California Press, 1997), 39-49.

64. See also *Scriptores Historiae Augustae, Vita Hadriani* 14.2, cited in Oppenheimer, "Ban on Circumcision," 55.

65. *Genesis Rabbah,* ed. Judah Theodor and Chanokh Albeck (repr. Jerusalem: Shalem, 1996), 1:458. Strangely, the metaphor is cross-gendered, since fig (te'enah) is feminine in Hebrew, so that the midrash literally reads, "except for her stem." For a discussion of rabbinic responses to Greco-Roman views of circumcision as unnatural, see B. Cohen, "Letter and Spirit," 412. Cohen also mentions a similar midrash, in *Gen. Rab.* 46:4, which compares circumcision to the perfection of a matron who clips a too-long fingernail.

66. In Exodus 6:12. I owe this observation to Dina Stein.

67. For these approving citations, see *y. Megilla* 10.9, *y. Qiddushin* 1.1, *y. Hagiga* 2.1, *Leviticus Rabbah* 30:8 (ed. M. Margolius [New York: JTS Press, 1993], 2:707), *Lamentations Rabbah* 1:1 (ed. Salomon Buber [repr. Hildesheim: Olms, 1967], 42); *Pesiqta Rabbati* 23 (ed. M. Friedmann [Vienna: Joseph Kaiser, 1880], 116b-17a), among many others.

68. Thus Philo writes that "enlarge Japheth" means that he will have numerous good things, including "good health, and a vigorous state of the outward senses, and beauty, and strength, and opulence, and nobleness of birth, and friends, and the power of a prince," etc. Noah "prays on behalf of the man who has those things which are around and exterior to the body, that he may dwell in the house of the wise man; so that attending to the rules of all good men he may see and regulate his own course by their example" (Philo, *Questions and Answers on Genesis* 2.76, in Yonge, *Works,* 838).

69. *Targum Pseudo-Jonathan: Text and Concordance,* ed. E. G. Clark (Hoboken, N.J.: KTAV, 1984), 10.

70. Steven Fine, "'Their Faces Shine with the Brightness of the Firmament': Study Halls and Synagogues in the Targumim to the Pentateuch," in Knobloch, *Biblical Translation in Context,* 70-72. The similar texts to which Fine refers are two marginal glosses in *Targum Neofiti.*

71. Jerome, *Hebrew Questions on Genesis,* translated with introduction and commentary by C. T. R. Hayward (Oxford: Clarendon, 1995), 38. Hayward comments that Jerome "seems aware that the 'tents' of Shem were interpreted by Jews as referring to a Study hall, a Beth Ha-Midrash, which Shem, and later Eber, had headed. His comment sounds suspiciously like a Christianized version of PJ [*Pseudo-Jonathan*] of this verse. . . . Jerome's language strengthens the suspicion. He speaks of Christians 'who are engaged in' (Latin, *versamur*) Scripture learning; the verb may equally be translated 'who are turned to,' suggesting a conversion from former paganism to Christianity" (137). See also Robert Hayward, "Shem, Melchizedek and Concern with Christianity in the Pentateuchal *Targumim,*" in *Targumic and Cognate Studies: Essays in Honour of Martin McNamara,* ed. K. J. Cathcart and M. Maher (Sheffield: Sheffield Academic Press, 1996), 72.

72. *Genesis Rabbah* 36:26-27. Although a discussion follows concerning a verse in Nehemiah that seems to permit translation, the rabbis prefer a verse from the Pentateuch as prooftext in matters of Jewish law.

73. James Kugel, "Two Introductions to Midrash," in *Midrash and Literature,* ed. Geoffrey Harman and Sanford Budick (New Haven: Yale University Press, 1986), 92.

74. *B. Megilla* 9b.

75. *Y. Megillah* 1.71c (Bar Ilan system).

76. For an insightful reading of these etymological connections and their implications, see Barnstone, *Poetics*, 15.

77. This vision should not be confused with missionary impulses that view translation as a tool for winning souls, since it is the perfection of the Greek language rather than Greek proselytes that Aquila's version wins for the side of Shem; that Aquila himself is a proselyte does not change the status of his Bible as a version for Jews. On translation as a tool of conversion, see Douglas Robinson, *The Translator's Turn* (Baltimore: The Johns Hopkins Press, 1991), 209-17.

78. The Palestinian Talmud relates that Aquila was a disciple of Akiva (*Qiddushin* 59a), whose hermeneutic methods—his insistence that every letter and particle, every peculiar grammatical construction or syntactic repetition must have significance—have long been detected in Aquila's translational techniques. Jerome also describes Aquila as a disciple of Akiva: "scribae et Pharisaei quorum suscepit scholam Akybas, quem magistrum Aquilae proselyte autumant" (*Commentary on Isaiah* 8:14). A number of midrashic commentaries more particularly describe Akiva's understanding of the words *et* in Genesis 1:1, the same verse Jerome thought Aquila had rendered so strangely. Elaborating on the verse "In the beginning God created the heaven and the earth," the commentaries relate that R. Ishmael asked R. Akiva about the significance of the *et* in Genesis 1:1. "He said to him . . . The *et* governing the word 'heaven' includes the sun, moon, and constellations; and the *et* governing the word 'earth' includes trees, grass and the Garden of Eden" (*Genesis Rabbah* 1:14, 12).

R. Akiva's midrash here is expansive, while Aquila's is limited to rendering the particle *et* with another single Greek word. Nevertheless, Aquila's use of the word *sun* in Genesis 1:1 and elsewhere for *et* can be described as a midrashic form of literalism, a translational equivalent to Akiva's principle of *ribuy* (amplification), which reads each *et* as an extension of the "plain meaning" of the text.

79. Augustine, *Against Faustus*, 12.12.341-42, in J. Cohen, *Living Letters*, 29.

80. Such a tradition is recorded in Justin, *Dialogue with Trypho* 17, as well as Eusebius, *Ecclasiastical History* 4.18.7.

81. For a discussion, see Douglas Robinson, *Translation and Empire: Postcolonial Theories Explained* (Manchester, England: St. Jerome Press, 1997), 46-62.

82. Friedrich Nietzsche, "On the Problem of Translation," from *Die fröbliche Wissenschaft* (1882), trans. Peter Mollenhauer, in Schulte and Biguenet, *Theories of Translation*, 68-69.

83. Rita Copeland, "The Fortunes of 'Non Verbum Pro Verbo'; or, Why Jerome Is Not a Ciceronian," in Ellis, *Medieval Translator*, 20.

84. Ibid., 29.

85. As Karlheinz Stierle writes, "Latin got a new function as the lingua franca of intellectual communication and particularly as the language of that spiritual imperium of Christian religion which asserted itself at the moment when the political empire began to collapse. It was in the context of the posthistory of the Roman Empire that *translatio* first acquired a prominent function" ("Translatio Studii and Renaissance: From Vertical to Horizontal Translation," in *The Translatability of Cultures: Figurations of the Space Between*, ed. Sanford Budick and Wolfgang Iser [Stanford: Stanford University Press, 1996], 55). Eric Cheyfitz, in stressing the continuity between Roman models of *translatio* and those that drove the Christian imperial mission, insists that Roman translation theory had effects long transcending the history of the Roman Empire: "The [Roman imperial] *translatio* . . . is inseparably connected with a "civilizing" mission, the bearing of Christianity and Western letters to the barbarians, literally, as we have noted, those who do not speak the language of the empire. From its beginning the imperialist mission is, in short, one of translation: the translation of the "other" into the terms of the empire" (*The Poetics of Imperialism: Translation and Colonization from* The Tempest *to* Tarzan [Philadelphia: University of Pennsylvania Press, 1997], 112).

86. Jerome, "To Pammachius," 114-15.

87. Hugo Friedrich, "On the Art of Translation," in Schulte and Biguenet, *Theories of Translation*, 12. Friedrich continues: "This is one of the most rigorous manifestations of Latin cultural and linguistic imperialism, which despises the foreign word as something alien but appropriates the foreign meaning in order to dominate it through the translator's own language" (13).

88. Jerome, *Hebrew Questions*, 29.

89. Auguste Comte, *System of Positive Polity*, 4 vols. (London: Longmans Green, 1875–77), 2:213, cited in Pierre Bourdieu, *Language and Symbolic Power*, ed. John B. Thompson, trans. Gino Raymond and Matthew Adamson (Cambridge: Harvard University Press, 1991), 43.

90. F. de Saussure, *Course in General Linguistics*, trans. Wade Baskin (1959, repr. Glasgow: Collins, 1974), 199, cited in Bourdieu, *Language and Symbolic Power*, 43.

91. Johann Gottfried Herder, *Über die neuere Deutschen Litteratur: Fragmente*, in Robinson, *Western Translation Theory*, 208.

92. Moses Hadas's editorial note on this line explains Aristeas thus: "The logic is that the Jews are a single people because they are subject to a single Law. Courtesies could therefore not be logically extended to one portion of the Jewish people and requests made of them while the king himself was responsible for holding another portion in bondage" (Introduction to *Aristeas to Philocrates [Letter of Aristeas]* [New York: Harper, 1951], 101).

93. This connection between translation and population transfer is at least as evident in the Greek as it is in English, in which 12–14 contains numerous uses of the terms for transfer and transplantation (*metagagen, metokizen*), which resonate with the initial mention of the text as being worthy of transcription (*metagraphes aksia*) in *Aristeas* 10. Aristeas thus supplies a concrete realization for the final stage of George Steiner's fourfold scheme of translation, in which he suggests that an ethical translation must attempt to give something back to the source text or culture in exchange for the unavoidable damage it has done. "The hermeneutic motion" that initiates translation "is dangerously incomplete," Steiner writes. "We 'lean towards' the confronting text (every translator has experienced this palpable bending toward and launching at his target). We encircle and invade cognitively. We come home laden, thus again off-balance, having caused disequilibrium throughout the system by taking away from 'the other' and by adding, though possibly with ambiguous consequence, to our own. The system is now off-tilt. The hermeneutic act must compensate. If it is to be authentic, it must mediate into exchange and restored parity" (*After Babel*, 316). Steiner's translational economy is ethical as well hermeneutic, but it is not yet consciously political. It would take the next wave of translation studies, postcolonial studies, to uncover the historical underpinning of such rhetoric—in its appropriative and ethical modes—in the mutual implication of translation and empire.

94. Robinson, *Translation and Empire*, 56.

95. *Midrash Tanhuma Mishpatim* 5.5 (Warsaw edition). The Buber edition is missing the line in which Aquilas compares the circumcised man to a soldier.

96. One exception to this rule is the following brief but suggestive passage: "By virtue of the languages spoken, the speakers who use them and the groups defined by possession of the corresponding competence, the whole social structure is present in each interaction (and thereby in the discourse uttered). That is what is ignored by the interactionist perspective, which treats interaction as a closed world, forgetting that what happens between two persons—between an employer and an employee or, *in a colonial situation*, between a French speaker and an Arabic speaker or, in the postcolonial situation, between two members of the formerly colonized nation, one Arabic-speaking, one French-speaking—derives its particular form from the objective relation between the corresponding languages or usages, that is, between the groups who speak those languages" (Bourdieu, *Language and Symbolic Power*, 67). My emphasis.

97. Niranjana, *Siting Translation: History, Post-Structuralism, and the Colonial Context* (Berkeley and Los Angeles: University of California Press, 1992), 172.

98. Ibid., 185.

99. Ibid., 183.

100. Bourdieu, *Language and Symbolic Power*, 122.

101. Yehuda Amichai, *Open Closed Open*, trans. Chana Bloch and Chana Kronfeld (New York: Harcourt, 2000), 148; Hebrew original, *Patuah sagur patuah* (Jerusalem: Schocken, 1998), 157.

102. Ibid., 147; Hebrew, 156.

103. Ibid., 149; Hebrew, 157.

104. Ibid., 151; Hebrew, 161.

105. Robinson, *Translator's Turn*, 3.

106. Ibid, 4.

107. Ibid, 5-6.

108. Ibid., 26.

109. *Tosefta Megillah* 4 [3].41.

110. Steiner, *After Babel*, 316.

111. "Akilas the Proselyte once came to R. Eliezer and asked: Is all the love the Holy One bestows upon a proselyte shown only in giving him bread and clothing (as it says that God befriends the proselyte/stranger, 'providing him bread and clothing' (Deut. 10:18)? I have so many peacocks and peasants even my servants pay no attention to them. R. Eliezer said: The thing that the patriarch [Jacob] begged for in prostration, saying 'and give me bread to eat and clothes to wear,' you hold this unimportant?

"Akilas then came to R. Yehoshua's home. . . , who said: Bread means Torah, s says, 'Come, eat of my bread' (Prov. 9:5). Clothing means a sage's *tallith*. When a man acquires Torah, he acquires such a tallith. More: proselytes may marry off their daughters into the priesthood, and children of their children may become high priests.

"It is said: But for R. Yehoshua's patient treatment of Aquila, he might have reverted to his evil past. To R. Yehoshua was applied the verse 'He who is slow to anger is better than the mighty.'" (*Gen. Rab.* 70:5 and, with slight variations, *Eccl. Rab.* 7:8).

112. Bourdieu addresses speech as embodied most directly in his contrasting the (feminine) pursed lips, the *bouche*, of the dominant group with the open mouth of the dominated but virile speech of the French working class (*Language and Symbolic Power*, 86-87).

113. As Bakhtin describes this social situatedness of language, "The word, directed toward its object, enters a dialogically agitated and tension-filled environment of alien words, value judgments and accents, weaves in and out of complex interrelationships, merges with some, recoils from others, intersects with yet a third group. . . . As a living, socio-ideological, somatic thing, as heteroglot opinion, language, for the individual consciousness, lies on the borderline between oneself and the other . . . the word does not exist in a neutral and impersonal language (it is not, after all, out of a dictionary that the speaker gets his words!), but rather it exists in other people's mouths, in other people's contexts, serving other people's intentions" (Mikhail Bakhtin, *The Dialogic Imagination*, trans. Caryl Emerson and Michael Holquist [Austin: University of Texas Press, 1981], 276, 293-94).

114. Irenaeus, *Against Heresies* 3.21.1, quoted in Hadas, Introduction, 24-25.

115. Epiphanius, *On Weights and Measures*, 14-15.

116. The tale describes a misunderstanding between R. Yehoshua b. Perahyah and Jesus that revolves around the fact that there is a single Aramaic word for inn and a female innkeeper, *akhsanya*. At an inn where they both are lodging,

R. Yehoshua said: "How beautiful is this inn[keeper]." Jesus said to him: "Rabbi, her eyes are bleary." R. Yehoshua said to him: "Wicked one, is it about such things that you are concerned?" He took out four hundred trumpets and excommunicated him. . . . Jesus came to him several times and said "Receive me," but R. Yehoshua paid him no attention. One day R. Yehoshua was reading the Shema when Jesus came to him. He decided to receive him and made a sign with his hand. Jesus thought that R. Yehoshua was rejecting him. He went and erected a tile and worshipped it. (*b. Sanhedrin* 107b)

117. Daniel Boyarin, *Dying for God* (Stanford: Stanford University Press, 1999), 20.

118. The note, in its entirety, reads: "To be sure, to a certain extent, the Rabbis were in general antihistoricistic in their approach, to use a somewhat anachronistic term. However, the presence of pagan Rome is everywhere felt in the texts, and often, I think, disguises through anachronism the Christian Rome that is both context and referent for the text. Christianity was, I think, too close for comfort too often" (ibid. 148 n. 89).

119. *y. Ḥagiga* 2.1.

120. *Tanhuma Bereshit* 5, ed. Chanokh Zundel (Vilna, 1833), 17.

121. Galit Hasan-Rokem has demonstrated that the midrashic literature also enjoyed imagining Hadrian acknowledging Jewish religious and moral wisdom, for instance in the story in *Lamentations Rabbah* 2:2 (Buber edition) in which Ben-Kozbah's head is brought to the Roman emperor, and when Hadrian doubts that his own

soldiers have killed the Messianic hero, Ben-Kozbah's body is brought to him and, indeed, there is a snake curled on his knees. Hadrian says: "Had his God not slain him, who could have beaten him? To fulfill the verse, 'unless their Rock had sold them, and the Lord had shut them up'" (Deut. 32: 30). As Hasan-Rokem points out, "Paradoxically, the tragic hero is Hadrian who . . . becomes aware of the divine power ruling the world. In this story, Hadrian is the one who interprets the event in the moral-religious perspective fitting the text's broader system of norms" (Galit Hasan-Rokem, *Web of Life: Folklore and Midrash in Rabbinic Literature*, trans. Batya Stein [Stanford: Stanford University Press, 2000], 168).

122. Harry M. Orlinsky, "The Role of Theology in the Christian Mistranslation of the Hebrew Bible," in *Translation of Scripture*, ed. David M. Rosenberg (Philadelphia: Annenburg Research Institute, 1990), 123. Such exegetical choices do, of course, inform later translations, and it is of primary concern for Orlinsky, the chair of the Jewish Publication Society's Bible translation committee, whether modern English translations render *ruah* in Genesis 1:2 as wind (which he considers the Jewish translation) or spirit (which he sees as the Christian rendering).

123. R. Judah bar Pazzi propounds that "In the beginning the world consisted of water upon water," proving his proposition by citing the second verse of Genesis, *"veruah elohim merahefet 'al peney hamayim"* (And the *ruah* of God moved over the face of the waters) (*y. Hagiga* 2a). The ensuing discussion lists a number of elements created on the first day, including water and wind. The Babylonian passage similarly lists ten elements created on the first day: "heaven and earth, *tohu* and *bohu*, light and darkness, wind and water, day and night" (*b. Hagiga* 12a). In such a list, it would be counterintuitive to read *ruah* as "spirit," much less "Spirit"!

124. St. Augustine, *Confessions*, trans. John K. Ryan (Garden City, N.Y.: Image Books, 1960), 339.

125. Mikhail Bakhtin, *Rabelais and His World*, trans. Helene Iswolsky (Bloomington: Indiana University Press, 1984), 19-20.

126. François Rabelais, *The Histories of Gargantua and Pantagruel*, trans. J. M. Cohen (Harmondsworth: Penguin, 1983), 541. The French reads, "Ilz meurent tous hydropicques tympanites; et meurent les hommes en petant, les femmes en vesnant. Ainsi leur sort l'ame par le cul." Rabelais, *Pantagruel* (Strasbourg: Éditions Brocéliande, 1961), 4:160.

CHAPTER THREE

1. For a detailed list of these earlier vernacular Bibles and their relation to Luther's Bible, see John L. Flood, "Martin Luther's Bible Translation in its German and European Context," in *The Bible in the Renaissance*, ed. Richard Griffiths (Burlington, Vt.: Ashgate, 2001), 45-70.

2. Ibid., 48. By "original text," Flood here seems to mean the Vulgate!

3. Martin Luther, *Sendbrief*, in *Werke: kritische Gesammtausgabe* (Weimar: H. Böhlau, 1883-), 30:636. Hereafter WA, i.e. "Weimarer Ausgabe."

4. Luther, *Briefwechsel* (WA, 4:481-85).

5. "Der vorige deutsche Psalter ist an viel orten dem Ebreischen neher, und dem deutschen ferner, dieser ist dem deutschen neher, und dem Ebreischen ferner" (WA, 10.1:509).

6. "Luther's most important contribution to translation theory lies in what might be called his 'reader-orientation'" (*Western Translation Theory from Herodotus to Nietzsche*, ed. Douglas Robinson [Manchester, England: St. Jerome Press, 1997], 84). Robinson continues: "When he formulates the standard principle that translations should be made out of good target-language words, idioms, syntactic structures and the like . . . he personalizes [the target language], humanizes it, blends it with the vitality of his own sense of self. In so doing, significantly enough, he socializes it: what he internalizes is no solipsistic fantasy-system but language as social communication, language as what people like him (members of his class) say to each other in real-life situations."

7. WA, 30:637.

8. Franz Rosenzweig, *Die Schrift und Luther* (Berlin: Lambert Schneider, 1926), 12-13. English translation from Martin Buber and Franz Rosenzweig, *Scripture and Translation*, trans. Lawrence Rosenwald with Everett Fox (Bloomington: Indiana University Press, 1994), 51.

9. WA, 30:639. Luther also ridicules the literal translation of Daniel "*Ish ḥamudot*" as "man of desires" rather than "Daniel darling."

10. Werner Schwarz, *Principles and Problems of Bible Translation: Some Reformation Controversies and their Background* (Cambridge: Cambridge University Press, 1955), 53.

11. *Sendbrief,* WA, 30:639.

12. Lawrence Venuti, *The Translator's Invisibility: A History of Translation* (London: Routledge, 1995), 1.

13. Friedrich Schleiermacher, "On the Different Methods of Translating," trans. Waltraud Bartsht, in *Theories of Translation: An Anthology of Essays from Dryden to Derrida*, ed. Rainer Schulte and John Biguenet (Chicago: University of Chicago Press, 1992), 42. "Entweder der Übersetzer läßt den Schriftsteller möglichst in Ruhe, und bewegt den Leser ihm entgegen; oder er läßt den Leser möglichst in Ruhe, und bewegt den Leser ihm entgegen" ("Methoden des Übersetzens," in *Sämmtliche Werke*, vol. 3: *Zur Philosophie* [Berlin: Reimer, 1938], 2:233).

14. Antoine Berman, "La Traduction et la lettre, ou l'auberge du lointain," in *Les Tours de Babel: Essais sur la traduction* (Mauvezin: Trans-Europ-Repress, 1985), 87–91. I am quoting the summary in Venuti, *Translator's Invisibility*, 20. Venuti goes on to qualify the notion that translation is a site of true encounter by stating that of course Berman recognizes that this "foreign" element is "never manifested in its own terms, only in those of the target language."

15. Ibid., 63.

16. Robert Stapylton, *Dido and Aeneas The Fourth Booke of Virgils Aeneid now Englished* (London, 1634), A2, in ibid., 49.

17. Berman in fact begins his study of translation and "the foreign" in German Romanticism with Luther, who in his view inaugurates the ongoing role of translation in the German culture. The importance of Luther's Bible suggests to Berman that "*the formulation and the development of a national* [German] *culture of its own can and must proceed by way of translation, that is, by an intensive and deliberate relation to the foreign*" (*The Experience of the Foreign: Culture and Translation in Romantic German*, trans. S. Heyvaert [Albany: SUNY Press, 1992], 32) (emphasis in the original).

18. *Tudor Royal Proclamations*, ed. Paul L. Hughes and James F. Larkin (New Haven: Yale University Press, 1964), 1:193, in Richard Duerden, "Authority and Reformation Bible Translation," in *The Bible as Book: The Reformation*, ed. Orlaith O'Sullivan (New Castle, Del.: Oak Knoll Press, 2000), 14.

19. Albert Schaeffer, "Bibel-Übersetzung, Zweites Stück (Aus Anlaß der lutherischen)," *Preußischer Jahrbücher* 206 (1926): 50–51, cited in Peter Eli Gordon, *Rosenzweig and Heidegger: Between Judaism and German Philosophy* (Berkeley and Los Angeles: University of California Press, 2003), 250.

20. WA, 38:9-17.

21. Harry Orlinsky makes the point that all the Reformation Bibles, from Luther's to the King James Version, were so influenced by Jewish exegesis as to be essentially Jewish in content ("The Role of Theology in the Christian Mistranslation of the Hebrew Bible," in *Translation of Scriptures*, ed. David M. Goldenberg [Philadelphia: Annenberg Research Institute, 1990], 118). He quotes the well-known ditty mocking Luther for his dependence on Nicholas of Lyra, "Si Lyra non lyrasset, Lutherus non saltasset" (If Lyra hadn't played the lyre, Luther would not have danced) and composes another to make his point: "Si Rashi non composuisset, Lyra non lyrasset" (If Rashi had not composed the music, Lyra would not have played the lyre) (118-19). Orlinsky also argues, however, that Jewish translations have also been influenced by Christian readings, for instance of *ruaḥ* as "spirit."

22. WA, 30.640.

23. Ibid. Luther's argument here is somewhat incoherent, since he accuses the translators of both borrowing from him and relying on Jews, but the point that only a true Christian may translate stands. Luther here is blaming the translators of the Worms *Prophets* (Hans Denk and Ludwig Haetzer, in 1527) both of stealing from him and of relying on Jews too heavily.

24. Jerome Friedman, *The Most Ancient Testimony: Sixteenth-Century Christian-Hebraica in the Age of Renaissance Nostalgia* (Athens: University of Ohio Press, 1983), 170.

25. Ibid.

26. Johannes Reuchlin, *Rudimenta Hebraica* (Pforzheim: Thomas Anselm, 1506).

27. For an account of the publication and impact of Reuchlin's grammar, see Friedman, *Most Ancient Testimony*, 24–27.

28. Elisheva Carlebach, however, cautions against viewing the Reuchlin controversy as "a struggle between the tolerant and enlightened forces of 'humanism' against the obscurantist clerical forces of 'scholasticism,'" reminding us that "this view is not consistent with the violent anti-Judaism of most of the 'humanist' figures and Reformation leaders." Reuchlin stood apart from many of the Reformation leaders in this regard. Moreover, "Reuchlin never advocated a break from the Catholic Church" (Critical Introduction to Johannes Reuchlin, *Recommendation Whether to Confiscate, Destroy, and Burn All Jewish Books*, trans. and ed. Peter Wortsman [New York: Paulist Press, 2000], 20–21.

29. In German, "das Wort '*meshumadim*' [ist] verbum oder participium activum praesentis temporis, und haißt 'die verdilker'" (Reuchlin, *Gutachten über das jüdische Schrifttum (Ratschlag ob man den Juden alle ire bücher nemmen, abthun und verbrennen soll)*, ed. Antonie Leinz-v. Dessauer [Stuttgart: Thorbecke, 1975], 45).

30. Reuchlin, *Recommendation*, 40; *Gutachten*, 43.

31. Sander Gilman, *Jewish Self-Hatred: Anti-Semitism and the Hidden Language of the Jews* (Baltimore: The Johns Hopkins University Press, 1986), 37.

32. Reuchlin, *Recommendation*, 47.

33. Ibid., 40.

34. R. Po-chia Hsia, *The Myth of Ritual Murder: Jews and Magic in Reformation Germany* (New Haven: Yale University Press, 1988), 135.

35. Ibid., 148.

36. Friedman, *Most Ancient Testimony*, 12.

37. Hsia, *Myth of Ritual Murder*, 148.

38. Ibid., 149.

39. Reuchlin, *Rudimenta*, iii.

40. Lawrence Venuti, *The Scandals of Translation: Towards an Ethics of Difference* (London: Routledge, 1998).

41. See Bernal Díaz del Castillo, *The Conquest of New Spain*, trans. J. M. Cohen (London: Penguin, 1963). For a discussion of La Malinche's multilingualism and her role in the conquest of Mexico, see Frances Karttunen, *Between Worlds: Interpreters, Guides and Survivors* (New Brunswick, N.J.: Rutgers University Press, 1994), 1–23. Karttunen also documents the roles of Sacajawea and Sarah Winnemucca in the European exploration of the American West.

42. See, especially, Frances A. Yates, *Giordano Bruno and the Hermetic Tradition* (London: Routledge and Kegan Paul, 1964).

43. See Susannah Heschel, "Revolt of the Colonized: Abraham Geiger's *Wissenschaft des Judentums* as a Challenge to Christian Hegemony in the Academy," *New German Critique* 77 (spring/summer 1999): 61–85. Heschel writes, "While claiming to write history, liberal Protestant theologians in the last decades of the nineteenth century merely attempted to use the latest techniques of historical investigation to promote traditional theological claims regarding Christology. Even while engaging in sophisticated debates over the dating of the gospels and expressing skepticism regarding the authenticity of the sayings and teachings attributed to Jesus, they retained what they called Jesus's unique inner religious consciousness as the basis for his originality that is different from Judaism" (65).

44. Douglas Robinson, *The Translator's Turn* (Baltimore: The Johns Hopkins University Press, 1991), 209–10.

45. Ibid., 288 n. 1.

46. Eugene A. Nida, *God's Word in Man's Language* (New York: Harper and Row, 1952); *Message and Mission: The Communication of Christian Faith* (New York: Harper and Brothers, 1960).

47. For a critique of the evangelical assumptions and what he considers the misuse of Chomsky in Nida's approach to translation, see Edwin Gentzler, *Contemporary Translation Theories*, 2nd ed. (Clevedon, England: Multilingual Matters, 2001), 52–65. Arguing that Chomsky's theories of generative grammar as expressed in his early work were too tentative and hypothetical to serve as a basis for practical methods of translation, Gentzler

writes that "while Nida's *Toward a Science of Translation* appears to be grounded in modern linguistics, the *non-dit* always present is a Protestant subtext . . . he fails to provide the groundwork for what the West in general conceives of as a 'science'" (58-59).

48. C. Lloyd Jones discusses Reuchlin's *De verbo mirifico* in his introduction to the 1983 translation of Reuchlin's 1517 *De arte cabalistica*. Although he does not specifically note that Reuchlin's Hebrew spelling of Jesus omits the *'ayin* critical for the etymological reading of "Jesus" as Savior, an omission striking in the grammarian who introduced Kimhi's analysis of the Hebrew root system to his Christian peers, Jones describes *De verbo mirifico* as "the work of a beginner." See C. Lloyd Jones, Introduction to *The Art of the Kabbalah*, trans. Martin Goodman and Sarah Goodman (Lincoln: University of Nebraska Press, 1983), 17. Moshe Idel, in an additional introduction to the 1993 reissue, notes that Jewish texts derive forms from the Tetragrammaton at least as bizarre as Reuchlin's.

49. Luther, WA, 53:582, 583. Translation taken from Gerhard Falk, *The Jew in Christian Theology: Martin Luther's anti-Jewish Vom Schem Hamphoras, previously unpublished in English, and other milestones in church doctrine concerning Judaism* (Jefferson, N.C.: McFarland, 1992), 168-69.

50. WA, 53:591-92; Falk, *Jew*, 175.

51. WA, 53:606-7; Falk, *Jew*, 188. The question of how to translate both the name and God's grammatical exposition of it at the burning bush in Exodus 3:14 continued to exercise translators, particularly in German. The passage is difficult; in any language, as Peter Eli Gordon has commented, "the phrase is at once palindrome and tautology" ("Rosenzweig and Heidegger: Translation, Ontology, and the Anxiety of Affiliation," *New German Critique* 77 [spring/summer 1999], 138). Luther rendered Exodus 3:14 thus: "Gott sprach zu Mose: Ich werde sein, der ich sein werde," and, in the following sentence, in which God tells Moses to relate his name to the Israelites, "Ich werde sein hat mich zu euch gesandt" (I will be has sent me to you). Moses Mendelssohn's translation took Luther's approach further, rendering "Ich bin das Wesen, welches ewig ist" (I am the Essence, which is Eternal). The Buber-Rosenzweig Bible, by contrast with both Luther and Mendelssohn, has "Ich werde dasein, als der ich dasein werde" (in Gordon's translation, "I will be-there, as that which I will be-there"), and, in the following verse, "ICH BIN DA schickt mich zu euch" ("I AM THERE sends me to you"). As Gordon has shown, the shift from Mendelssohn to Buber-Rosenzweig parallels the move in German thought from ontological idealism to existentialism, from God as an abstract entity to God as an ongoing being in-the-world. "As being in-the-world, [Dasein] signals human finitude as against the unknown and unworldly being of God."

52. Thus, the book is cited extensively in Mark U. Edwards Jr., "Against the Jews," in *Essential Papers on Judaism and Christianity in Conflict from Late Antiquity to the Reformation*, ed. Jeremy Cohen (New York: NYU Press, 1991), as evidence of Luther's late attitudes toward the Jews. It also forms the centerpiece of Gerhard Falk's tracing of anti-Jewish sentiment in Christian theology in *The Jew in Christian Theology* (cited above), where it is translated in its entirety, with copious notes by Falk.

53. Luther, WA, 53:579-80; Falk, *Jew*, 362.

54. Friedman, *Most Ancient Testimony*, 16.

55. H. J. Zimmels, *Ashkenazim and Sephardim: Their Relations, Differences and Problems as Reflected in the Rabbinical Responsa*, 2nd ed. (London: Oxford University Press, 1969), 276-79.

56. Gilman, *Jewish Self Hatred*, 24.

57. Beryl Smalley, *The Study of the Bible in the Middle Ages*, 3rd ed. (Oxford: Blackwell, 1983), 362-63.

58. Ora Limor, "Christian Sacred Space and the Jew," in *From Witness to Witchcraft: Jews and Judaism in Medieval Christian Thought*, ed. Jeremy Cohen (Wiesbaden: Harrassowitz, 1997), 58.

59. Ibid., 77.

60. Ibid. It is striking that the language of Jewish-Christian polemic has often alluded to mirrors. Thus, Pfefferkorn's anti-Jewish pamphlet of 1508 was called *Judenspiegel*, and Reuchlin's retort was titled *Augenspiegel*. These pamphlets' titles were apparently meant to imply an improved perspective on the subject in question, but they also managed to suggest that what was involved in the Jewish-Christian encounter was as often projection as vision, a subjective mirroring of the self as an objective description of the other.

61. Augustine, *Against Faustus*, 12.23.351, in Jeremy Cohen, *Living Letters of the Law: Ideas of the Jew in Medieval Christianity* (Berkeley and Los Angeles: University of California Press, 1999), 29.

62. Ibid., 36.

63. The argument that the Augustinian attitude toward the Jews, which admitted of some tolerance due to their special status as "living letters of the Law," shifted in the twelfth century is summarized in Jeremy Cohen, *The Friars and the Jews: The Evolution of Medieval Anti-Judaism* (Ithaca: Cornell University Press, 1982), 19–32.

64. *Bullarium Ordinis Fratrum Praedicatorum, I*, ed. Thomas Ripoll (Rome, 1724), 488, quoted in Jeremy Cohen, "The Mentality of the Medieval Jewish Apostate: Peter Alfonsi, Hermann of Cologne, and Pablo Christiani," in *Jewish Apostasy in the Modern World*, ed. Todd M. Endelman (New York: Holmes and Meier, 1987), 36.

65. Judah David Eisenstein, Introduction to *Collected Polemics and Disputations* (Hebrew) (New York: Hebrew Publishing Company, 1922), 12.

66. This prayer was translated first by Nicholas Donin and later republished in transliteration and translation first by the convert Victor von Carben and then by Pfefferkorn. See Elisheva Carlebach, *Divided Souls: Converts from Judaism to Christianity, 1500–1750* (New Haven: Yale University Press, 2001), 27. Many different versions of the prayer exist, in part because of voluntary or coerced expurgation.

67. Elisheva Carlebach, "Attributions of Secrecy and Perceptions of Jewry," *Jewish Social Studies* 2, no. 3 (spring/summer 1996): 120.

68. Carlebach cites Loewe Kircheim, *Sefer Minhagot Warmaisa*, ed. Israel Mordechai Peles (Jerusalem: Miphal torat ḥakhmei ashkenaz, 1987), 316, no. 10.

69. On the Barcelona Disputation, see Robert Chazan, *Barcelona and Beyond: The Disputation of 1263 and Its Aftermath* (Berkeley and Los Angeles: University of California Press, 1992). In a fascinating survey of the earlier literature on the disputation, Chazan argues that scholars of previous generations tended to argue that either the Jewish or Christian side had "won," and that one or another of the accounts was closer to the truth. In the contemporary academic arena, Chazan writes, "No longer could members of the two communities [of scholars] write comfortably for internal consumption" (6). Only one truth could reign, then. "In an ironic way," Chazan continues, "the old theological battle was transformed into a new historiographic battle" over which sources could better be trusted. Chazan's own approach is to view each account through the recognition that "it is in the nature of public partisan engagement to generate polar perceptions. . . . One cannot brand one perception a lie and the other the truth. It is possible to investigate the divergent views as such, attempting to ascertain the basis for both the Christian and Jewish sense of success" (14–15).

70. The "confessions" of the rabbis, as they are titled, are actually summaries of the arguments as they appear in the Hebrew version, with parenthetical notations by the friar noting that the rabbis are not telling the truth (Thibaut de Sezanne, "Extractiones de Talmut," Bibliothèque Nationale, ms. no. 16,558, f. 231). These are translated in Hyam Maccoby, ed. and trans. *Judaism on Trial: Jewish–Christian Disputation in the Middle Ages* (Oxford: Littman, 1982), 165.

71. It is tempting to conclude that the presence of the Jews was required at these disputations at least partly for the very purpose of confirming the accuracy of the convert's citation and translation of Jewish sources. Thus to say, as Maccoby does, that "the Rabbis did not admit any of the charges [in the Paris Disputation], except in the trivial sense that they agreed that the quotations put before them were verbally correct" (ibid., 164) is to miss the degree to which this confirmation is central to the function of the Jewish participants in the Disputation.

72. *The Disputation of Jehiel of Paris* (Hebrew) was first published in Latin translation by Wagenseil in 1681 and by Samuel Grünbaum in Hebrew in 1873. I have translated from *The Disputation of Jehiel of Paris*, in Eisenstein, *Collected Polemics*, 83. Maccoby has a somewhat different translation, "this is in order to make us Christians stink" (*Judaism on Trial*, 156). Some scholars view this passage as evidence that the disputation was conducted in Latin; the especially egregious nature of this passage compelled Donin to add a vernacular translation, to make sure that the Queen would understand as well.

73. Gilman, *Jewish Self-Hatred*, 34.

74. *Disputation of Jehiel*, 81–82.

75. Ibid., 84.

76. Judah M. Rosenthal, "A Religious Disputation between a Jew called Menahem and Pablo Christiani" (Hebrew), in *Studies in Jewish Themes by Contemporary American Scholars*, ed. Menahem Zohori (Tel Aviv: Book Gallery, 1974), 62, cited in Cohen, "Mentality," 40.

77. George Steiner, *After Babel: Aspects of Language and Translation*, 3rd ed. (Oxford: Oxford University Press, 1998), 314.

78. Samuel Krauss, *The Jewish-Christian Controversy: From the Earliest Times to 1789*, ed. William Horbury (Tübingen: Mohr, 1995), 175.

79. *Disputation of Jehiel*, 82.

80. Ibid., 83-84.

81. Ibid., 84-85.

82. The term "rigid designator" is used by the philosopher Saul Kripke to mean a singular term that refers to the same thing in every possible world in which it refers to anything. Kripke argues that proper names are rigid rather than "flaccid" designators, which refer to a shifting group of referents in terms of their attributes. In the sentence "Aristotle was the greatest philosopher," "Aristotle" is the rigid designator while "greatest philosopher" is a flaccid designator (*Naming and Necessity* [Cambridge: Harvard University Press, 1980]). While Kripke would insist that "Jesus" is a rigid designator, and thus refers to the same individual in all "possible worlds" (the concept is borrowed from Leibniz), Jehiel's argument might be taken not only as a warning that a proper name does not *always* function as a rigid designator—as Kripke of course would concede—but also as a suggestion that even such a proper name as Jesus may refer differently in a Jewish as in a Christian context. I want to thank Ami Kronfeld for this reference.

83. Carlebach, *Divided Souls*, 160.

84. I set the term "conversion" in quotes here as a recognition of the influential argument put forth by Krister Stendahl in 1963 that Paul "was called, not converted," since Christianity did not exist as a separate religion for Paul (*Paul among the Jews and Gentiles* (Philadelphia: Fortress, 1976), 1-23. The ensuing debate is not at issue here, since my point is only that whether or not Paul in fact "converted" (and I am inclined to agree with Stendahl that he did not), his transformation was taken as a model for the more indisputable cases of Jewish-Christian conversion of later periods.

85. Lewis Rambo, *Understanding Religious Conversion* (New Haven: Yale University Press, 1993), 70.

86. Gilman, *Jewish Self-Hatred*, 41.

87. Solomon ibn Verga, *Shevet Yehuda*, in Eisenstein, *Collected Polemics*, 105; Maccoby, *Judaism on Trial*, 171.

88. Jonathan M. Elukin, "From Jew to Christian? Conversion and Immutability in Medieval Europe," in *Varieties of Religious Conversion in the Middle Ages*, ed. James Muldoon (Gainesville: University of Florida, 1997), 174.

89. For a discussion of the development and motivations of this precept, see Jacob Katz, "Although He Has Sinned, He Remains a Jew" (Hebrew), *Tarbiz* 27 (1958): 203-17.

90. Petrus Alfonsi, *Dialogus Petri cognomento Alphonsi, ex Judaeo Christiani et Moysi Judaei* (Cologne, 1536). For more, see Moritz Steinschneider, *Die hebräischen Übersetzungen des Mittelalters und die Juden als Dolmetscher* (Graz: Akademische Druck, 1956), 933.

91. A photograph of the signature on a copy of Abravanel's *Perush ha-Torah*, vol. 3 (Venice, 1584), dated 1612, appears in William Popper's classic 1899 study, *The Censorship of Hebrew Books* (1899, repr. with introduction by Moshe Carmilly-Weinberger (New York: Ktav, 1969), plate 3.

92. Quoted ibid., 84. The emphasis is Popper's.

93. Jonathan M. Elukin, "The Discovery of the Self: Jews and Conversion in the Twelfth Century," in *Jews and Christians in Twelfth-Century Europe*, ed. Michael A. Signer and John Van Engen (Notre Dame, Ind.: Notre Dame University Press, 2001), 72. Elukin continues, "It is deeply ironic that the very human quality of his or her interior self now made it so difficult for a Jew to become a Christian in the eyes of other Christians. . . . Jews were condemned to remain apart from Christians not because Jews were perceived to be fundamentally different kinds of human beings or less than human, but precisely because they were human beings who had to cross what seemed an insurmountable distance to come to a fuller understanding of God."

94. Carlebach, *Divided Souls*, 35-36.

95. For a discussion of Augustine's doctrine of conversion as a never-completed process, see Karl Morrison, *Understanding Conversion* (Charlottesville: University Press of Virginia, 1992), 24-25.

96. Homi K. Bhabha, *The Location of Culture* (London: Routledge, 1994), 85.

97. Ibid., 86 (emphasis in the original).

98. Herman-Judah (as Morrison terms him), *Short Account of His Own Conversion*, ed. and trans. Karl Morrison, in *Conversion and Text: The Cases of Augustine of Hippo, Herman-Judah, and Constantine Tsatsos* (Charlottesville: University Press of Virginia, 1992), 105.

99. Arnaldo Momigliano, "A Medieval Jewish Biography," in *History and Imagination: Essays in Honour of H. R. Trevor-Roper*, ed. Hugh Lloyd-Jones, Valerie Pearl, and Blair Worden (London: Duckworth, 1981), 32.

100. Herman-Judah, *Short Account*, 108.

101. Judith Butler, *Gender Trouble* (London: Routledge), 140.

102. Leo Strauss, *Persecution and the Art of Writing* (New York: Free Press, 1952; repr. Chicago: University of Chicago Press, 1980), 24.

103. Ibid., 24-25.

104. Pinchas E. Lapide, *Hebrew in the Church: The Foundations of Jewish-Christian Dialogue*, trans. Errol F. Rhodes (Grand Rapids, Mich.: Eerdmans, 1984), 39.

105. Profiat Duran, "Do Not Be Like Your Fathers" (Hebrew), in Eisenstein, *Collected Polemics*, 95.

106. Ibid.

107. Lapide, *Hebrew in the Church*, 48.

108. Ibid., 49. One such occasion is at the bar mitzvah of a son, when the parents congratulate themselves on having reached the stage in their child's upbringing in which he is held accountable for his own misdeeds.

109. We might recall here that the convert is often stereotyped as "hypercorrect," more zealous than the practitioner born into a faith. Aquila's "hypercorrect" Hebrew translation was seen in such terms by the Fathers, though not by the rabbis, who approved of his zeal.

110. Chaim Wirszubski, *Pico della Mirandola's Encounter with Jewish Mysticism* (Cambridge: Harvard University Press, 1989), 5-7.

111. Shlomo Simonsohn, "Giovanni Pico della Mirandola on Jews and Judaism," in J. Cohen, *From Witness to Witchcraft*, 407.

112. Umberto Cassuto, "Wer war der Orientalist Mithridates?" *Zeitschrift für die Geschichte der Juden in Deutschland* 5 (1934): 230-36. On Mithridates' proving, through the operations of *gematriya*, that he is identical to YHWH while Pico is merely equal to Elohim, a lesser divine name, because "he couldn't or wouldn't leave women alone," see Wirszubski, *Pico's Encounter*, 116-18.

113. Wirszubski quotes the "intrusion" of this theme in Mithridates' translation, "Liber Redemptionis," Codex Vaticano Ebraico 190, fol. 415v (ibid., 115). In a salacious parenthetical remark that builds on the etymological meaning of the Hebrew vowel sign *pataḥ* as "to open," Mithridates tells Pico to "note the great mystery that the punctuation of *na'ar* [boy] is with a *pataḥ*, which means to open, because he ought to open his *taḥat* ["bottom," also punctuated with the *pataḥ*]." Devorah Schoenfeld helped me decode this line.

114. Ibid., 118.

115. Carlebach, *Divided Souls*, 200.

116. Martin Luther, *The Book of Vagabonds and Beggars, with a vocabulary of their language (Liber Vagatorum)*, ed. and trans. John Camden Hotten (London: Penguin, 1932), 3.

117. Gilman, *Jewish Self-Hatred*, 69.

118. Ibid., 74.

119. Luther, *Book of Vagabonds*, 39 (emphasis added).

120. Ibid., 49.

CHAPTER FOUR

1. Geoffrey J. Giles, *Students and National Socialism in Germany* (Princeton, N.J.: Princeton University Press, 1985), 131 (emphasis in the original); Giles writes, "The notorious twelve theses the students prepared for ritual declamation during the burnings were not exclusively directed against Jews and the 'Jewish spirit': Among the other targets were Marxism, pacifism, and the 'overstressing of the instinctual life' (that is, 'the Freudian School and its journal Imago'). It was a rebellion of the German against the 'un-German spirit.' But the main thrust of the action remained essentially anti-Jewish; in the eyes of the organisers, it was meant to extend anti-Jewish ac-

tion from the economic domain (the April 1 boycott) to the entire field of German culture." See also Victor Klemperer, *Notizbuch eines Philologen* (Leipzig: Reclam, 1965), 35.

2. Franz Kafka, *Letters to Friends, Family, and Editors,* trans. Richard Winston and Clara Winston (New York: Schocken, 1977), 288.

3. Martin Buber, "The Spirit of the Orient and Judaism," in *On Judaism,* ed. Nahum Glatzer (New York: Schocken, 1967), 75, 78.

4. Mendelssohn's translation of the Pentateuch, *Sefer netivot ha-shalom* (Book of the paths of peace), began to appear in 1780 and was completed in 1783 (Berlin: Abraham Proops). The Buber-Rosenzweig Pentateuch (Berlin: Lambert Schneider) appeared in installments between December 1925 and May 1927, followed by a complete Pentateuch, *Die fünf Bücher der Weisung,* from the same publisher in 1930. Buber revised the Pentateuch in 1954 and completed the full translation of the Bible in 1961, with the final volume appearing in 1962. For a more complete bibliography, see L. S. [presumably the publisher], "Vorbemerkung des Verlages: Zur Geschichte der Bibelverdeutschung," *Die fünf Bücher der Weisung* (Heidelberg: Lambert Schneider, 1987), 5-6.

5. W. Gunther Plaut, *German-Jewish Bible Translations: Linguistic Theology as a Political Phenomenon,* Leo Baeck Memorial Lecture 36 (New York: Leo Baeck Institute, 1992), 4-5.

6. Ibid., 19.

7. Ibid., 10.

8. Ibid., 12.

9. Gershom Scholem, "At the Completion of Buber's Bible Translation," trans. Michael A. Meyer, in *The Messianic Idea in Judaism* (New York: Schocken, 1971), 318.

10. David Sorkin, *Moses Mendelssohn and the Religious Enlightenment* (Berkeley and Los Angeles: University of California Press, 1996), 151.

11. Franz Rosenzweig, Letter of 1 October 1917 to Rudolf Ehrenburg, quoted in Barbara Galli, *Franz Rosenzweig and Jehuda Halevi: Translating, Translations, and Translators* (Montreal: McGill-Queen's University Press, 1995), 322.

12. "The Function of Translation," in *Franz Rosenzweig: His Life and Thought,* ed. and trans. Nahum N. Glatzer (New York: Schocken, 1961), 254.

13. Robinson, *The Translator's Turn* (Baltimore: The Johns Hopkins University Press, 1991), 92-100.

14. Franz Rosenzweig, "Scripture and Luther," in Martin Buber and Franz Rosenzweig, *Scripture and Translation,* trans. Lawrence Rosenwald with Everett Fox (Bloomington: Indiana University Press, 1994), 53.

15. Buber's remark to his student Ernst Simon is cited in Michael Brenner, *The Renaissance of Jewish Culture in Weimar Germany* (New Haven: Yale University Press, 1996), 108.

16. Franz Rosenzweig, *The Star of Redemption,* trans. William W. Hallo (Notre Dame, Ind.: University of Notre Dame Press, 1970), 310.

17. Franz Rosenzweig, "Zeit ists . . . Gedanken über das jüdische Bildungsproblem des Augenblicks" (1918), in *Zur jüdischen Erziehung* (Berlin: Schocken, 1937), 12.

18. Edward Breuer, *The Limits of Enlightenment: Jews, Germans, and the Eighteenth-Century Study of Scripture* (Cambridge: Harvard University Press, 1996), 20.

19. Gershom Scholem, "Against the Myth of German-Jewish Dialogue," trans. Werner J. Dannhausser, in *On Jews and Judaism in Crisis: Selected Essays* (New York: Schocken, 1989), 63.

20. Scholem, "At the Completion," 318.

21. Plaut, *German-Jewish Bible Translations,* 19.

22. For a historical model of the German Jew as split, see Paul Mendes-Flohr, *Divided Passions: Jewish Intellectuals and the Experience of Modernity* (Detroit: Wayne State University Press, 1990).

23. Johann Gottfried Herder, "Über die Würkung der Dichtkunst auf die Sitten der Völker in alten und neuen Zeiten," in *Sämmtliche Werke,* ed. Berhard Suphan (Berlin: Weidmann'sche Buchhandlung, 1877), 8:355.

24. Ibid., 362.

25. Richard I. Cohen, "Urban Visibility and Biblical Visions: Jewish Culture in Western and Central Europe in the Modern Age," in *Cultures of the Jews: A New History,* David Biale, ed. (New York: Schocken, 2002), 763.

26. Frank E. Manuel, *The Broken Staff: Judaism through Christian Eyes* (Cambridge: Harvard University Press, 1992), 262.

27. Buber, "The How and Why of Our Bible Translation," in Buber and Rosenzweig, *Scripture and Translation*, 209.

28. Ibid., 208-9.

29. Ibid., 210.

30. Moses Mendelssohn, *Gesammelte Schriften*, ed. G. B Mendelssohn (Leipzig, 1843), 5:205 n., quoted in Alexander Altmann, *Moses Mendelssohn: A Biographical Study* (Birmingham: University of Alabama Press, 1973), 39.

31. *Allgemeine deutsche Bibliothek* 44, no. 1 (1780): 227-55, quoted in Altmann, *Moses Mendelssohn*, 378.

32. Werner Weinberg, "Moses Mendelssohn's Pentateuch Translations," *Hebrew Union College Annual* 55 (1984): 216.

33. Johann David Michaelis, "Die Psalmen. Übersetzt von Moses Mendelssohn," in *Orientalische und Exegetische Bibliotek*, 22 (Frankfurt am Main, 1783), 57.

34. For a sharp critique of Buber's extremely loose treatment of the Hasidic tales (and Buber's privileging of the tales over other Hasidic genres in formulating his views of Hasidism), see Steven T. Katz, "Martin Buber's Misuse of Hasidic Sources," in *Post-Holocaust Dialogues: Critical Studies in Modern Jewish Thought* (New York: NYU Press, 1983), 52-93.

35. Buber, "From the Beginnings of Our Bible Translation," in Buber and Rosenzweig, *Scripture and Translation*, 180.

36. Siegfried Kracauer, "Die Bibel auf Deutsch: Zur Übersetzung von Martin Buber und Franz Rosenzweig," *Frankfurter Zeitung* 70, no. 308 (April 27, 1926), repr. in *Schriften*, vol. 5.1, *Aufsätze 1915-26*, ed. Inka Mülder-Bach (Frankfurt: Suhrkamp, 1990), 355-68; cited from "The Bible in German: On the Translation by Martin Buber and Franz Rosenzweig," in *The Mass Ornament: Weimar Essays*, trans. and ed. Thomas Y. Levin (Cambridge: Harvard University Press, 1995), 195.

37. Kafka, *Letters*, 288.

38. Mendelssohn was the translator, chief editor, major commentator, and driving force behind the translation, but he had the help of a number of people. Mendelssohn solicited and received comments on his translation from Solomon Dubno and others among his collaborators. Mendelssohn and Dubno each wrote an introduction to the book of Genesis; Mendelssohn eventually included a part of Dubno's introduction along with his own. Mendelssohn wrote the commentary for the first chapters of Genesis and nearly all of Exodus. Dubno wrote the commentary for the rest of Genesis and the Masoretic notes and glosses on Mendelssohn's Exodus commentary. Naftali Herz Wessely wrote the commentary on Leviticus, and Mendelssohn wrote the commentary on Numbers and Deuteronomy with the help of his friends Aaron Zechariah Friedenthal and Herz Homberg.

39. Moses Mendelssohn, Introduction (Hebrew) to *The Book of Paths of Peace* (German in Hebrew script, with Hebrew title) (Vienna: Franz von Schmidt, 1846), xxv.

40. Ibid. Solomon Dubno, in the prospectus to the translation project, similarly warned, in a rhetoric abounding in biblical proof texts, that Jewish youth "'running to and fro to seek the word of the Lord' (Amos 8:12) and desiring to understand the Scriptures and to taste the savor of its poetic style in a language with which they are familiar . . . supply themselves with the works of the Gentiles (Isa. 2:6) using the translations of non-Jewish scholars who disdain the trusted interpretations of our sages of blessed memory and who refuse to accept their unblemished tradition, while interpreting Scriptures according to their own fancy and spoiling the vineyard of the Lord of Hosts" (Dubno, "Leaves for Healing," in Mendelssohn, *Jubilee Ausgabe*, 14:27, quoted in Altmann, *Moses Mendelssohn*, 374-75).

41. Dubno, "Leaves for Healing," in Mendelssohn, *Jubilee Ausgabe*, 14:326, quoted in Altmann, *Moses Mendelssohn*, 369.

42. Ibid., 380.

43. Ibid.

44. Mendelssohn, Introduction, xxv.

45. Altmann, *Moses Mendelssohn*, 380.

46. *Nachlass Hennings,* no. 22, letter 8, fol. 11r-v, quoted in ibid., 344.

47. Weinberg devotes a large part of his article on Mendelssohn's translation to this question.

48. Abigail E. Gillman, "Between Religion and Culture: Mendelssohn, Buber, Rosenzweig and the Enterprise of Biblical Translation," in *Biblical Translation in Context,* ed. Frederick W. Knobloch (Bethesda: University Press of Maryland, 2002), 98.

49. Weinberg, "Mendelssohn's Pentateuch Translations," 210.

50. *Jubilee Ausgabe,* 7:279; *Gesammelte Schriften,* 5:605, quoted in Altmann, *Moses Mendelssohn,* 499.

51. Joshua Trachenberg, *The Devil and the Jews: The Medieval Conception of the Jew and Its Relation to Modern Anti-Semitism* (Cleveland: Meridian, 1943), 69-70.

52. Mendelssohn, commentary to Exodus 3:14, *Book of the Paths of Peace,* 13a-b.

53. Altmann, *Moses Mendelssohn,* 418. The reference is to Mendelssohn, *Jerusalem; or, On Religious Power and Judaism,* trans. Allan Arkush, introduction by Alexander Altmann (Hanover, N.H.: Brandeis University Press, 1983), 139.

54. Altmann, *Moses Mendelssohn,* 419.

55. Naftali Herz Wessely, "In Praise of a Friend" (Hebrew), in Mendelssohn, *Book of the Paths of Peace,* iv.

56. For a discussion of the sexual critiques of the Haskalah, see David Biale's chapter on "Eros and Enlightenment," in *Eros and the Jews: From Biblical Israel to Contemporary America* (New York: Basic Books, 1992), 149-75.

57. Cited in Steven M. Lowenstein, "The Readership of Mendelssohn's Bible Translation," *Hebrew Union College Annual* 53 (1982): 187.

58. Gillman, "Between Religion and Culture," 105.

59. Plaut, "German-Jewish Bible Translations," 8.

60. Homi Bhabha, *The Location of Culture* (London: Routledge, 1994), 4.

61. Ibid., 107.

62. Ibid., 89.

63. Ibid.

64. Daniel Boyarin, *Unheroic Conduct: The Rise of Heterosexuality and the Invention of the Jewish Man* (Berkeley and Los Angeles: University of California Press, 1997), 254.

65. Ezekiel Landau, in his approbation to Sussmann Glogau's "rather primitive" word-for-word German rendering, reproduced in *Hame'assef* (1786), 141ff., quoted in Altmann, *Moses Mendelssohn,* 383.

66. Peretz Smoleskin, *Ma'amarim,* 2:72, 83, 223, cited in Weinberg, "Mendelssohn's Pentateuch Translations," 201.

67. Sander Gilman, *Jewish Self-Hatred: Anti-Semitism and the Hidden Language of the Jews* (Baltimore: Johns Hopkins University Press, 1986), 2.

68. Leora Batnitzky, *Idolatry and Representation: The Philosophy of Franz Rosenzweig Reconsidered* (Princeton: Princeton University Press, 2000), 110.

69. Peter Eli Gordon, *Rosenzweig and Heidegger: Between Judaism and German Philosophy* (Berkeley and Los Angeles: University of California Press, 2003), 267.

70. Boyarin, *Unheroic Conduct,* 307.

71. Lawrence Rosenwald, "On the Reception of Buber and Rosenzweig's Bible," *Prooftexts* 14, no. 2 (May 1994): 153-60; Gillman, "Between Religion and Culture," 109.

72. Gordon, *Rosenzweig and Heidegger,* 5.

73. Kracauer, "Bible in German," 198.

74. Martin Buber and Franz Rosenzweig, "Die Bibel auf Deutsch," in *Die Schrift und Ihre Verdeutschung* (Berlin: Schocken, 1926), 291 (emphasis added). Rosenwald translates this sentence rather as "The word wants to speak—to every moment, into every moment, against every moment" ("The Bible in German," in *Scripture and Translation,* 159).

75. Plaut, *German-Jewish Bible Translations,* 18 (emphasis in the original).

76. Franz Rosenzweig, *Kleinere Schriften,* 534, quoted in Nahum N. Glatzer, *Franz Rosenzweig: His Life and Thought* (New York: Schocken, 1953), 170

77. Maurice Olender, *The Languages of Paradise: Race, Religion, and Philology in the Nineteenth Century*, trans. Arthur Goldhammer (Cambridge: Harvard University Press, 1992).

78. Baruch Spinoza, *Abrégé de grammaire hébraïque*, ed. J. Askenazi and J. Askenazi-Gerson (Paris: Vrin, 1968), 35-36, quoted in Olender, *Languages of Paradise*, 24.

79. Ernest Renan, *Histoire générale et système comparé des langues sémitiques* (Paris: Calmann-Lévy, 1947), 8:541.

80. Robert Lowth, *Lectures on the Sacred Poetry of the Hebrews*, trans. G. Gregory (Boston: Andover Press, 1829; Latin original, 1753), 33.

81. Ibid., 34.

82. Robert Lowth, "A Sermon Preached at the Visitation of the Honourable and Right Reverend Richard Lord Bishop of Durham" (London, 1758), quoted in Olender, *Languages of Paradise*, 31.

83. Ibid.

84. Franz Rosenzweig, "Scripture and Word," in Buber and Rosenzweig, *Scripture and Translation*, 44.

85. Ibid., 42-43.

86. Ibid., 45.

87. Rosenzweig, "Scripture and Luther," in Buber and Rosenzweig, *Scripture and Translation*, 67.

88. Martin Buber, "People Today and the Jewish Bible," in Buber and Rosenzweig, *Scripture and Translation*, 7.

89. Lawrence Rosenwald, "Reception," 145-46.

90. Buber, "People Today," 14.

91. Ibid., 16-17.

92. Ibid., 17.

93. *Genesis Rabbah* 18:4.

94. Martin Buber with Franz Rosenzweig, *Die fünf Bücher der Weisung* (Heidelberg: Lambert Scheider, 1987), 14.

95. Walter Benjamin, "The Task of the Translator," trans. Harry Zohn, *Illuminations: Essays and Reflections*, ed. Hannah Arendt (New York: Schocken, 1968), 78; "Die Aufgabe des Übersetzers," in *Illuminationen* (Frankfurt am Main: Suhrkamp, 1969), 65. I have altered Harry Zohn's translation in a number of places. Here, I translate *folgen* as "follow" rather than as "match," as does Carol Jacobs, to underscore Benjamin's rejection of any linguistic equivalence in meaning. For Jacobs's careful reading of the Benjamin essay and its retranslation of some of Zohn's renderings, see "The Monstrosity of Translation: The Task of the Translator," in *In the Language of Walter Benjamin* (Baltimore: John Hopkins University Press, 1999), 75-90.

96. Lurianic Kabbalah is the branch of Kabbalah developed by the sixteenth-century mystic Rabbi Isaac Luria, which posited a cosmic catastrophe at Creation that could be redeemed through mystical/ritual acts of *tiqqun*, the "fixing" of the vessels that were supposed to form the universe but which were shattered during the world-creating catastrophe. These acts of reparation return to the Godhead the divine sparks caught in the shards of these shattered vessels, the shards that comprise the world in its broken state.

97. Benjamin, "Task," 78.

98. Walter Benjamin, "Über die Sprache überhaupt und über die Sprache des Menschen," in *Gesammelte Schriften*, vol 2, part 1 (Frankfurt: Suhrkamp, 1977), 140-57. The essay was unpublished in Benjamin's lifetime. English trans., "On Language as Such and the Language of Man," trans. Edmund Jephcott, in *Walter Benjamin: Selected Writings*, vol. 1: *1913-1926*, ed. Marcus Bullock and Michael Jennings (Cambridge: Harvard University Press, 1996), 62-74.

99. Ibid., 74, 80; "Aufgabe," 60, 67. I have supplied the adjective "messianic" that Harry Zohn omits. Steven Rendall's notes to the translation in the *Translation Studies Reader*, 2nd ed., ed. Lawrence Venuti (New York: Routledge, 2004), 24, alerted me to this omission.

100. Paul de Man, "Conclusions: Benjamin's 'The Task of the Translator,'" in *The Resistance to Theory* (Minneapolis: University of Minnesota Press, 1986), 76.

101. Gershom Scholem, "The Name of God and the Linguistic Theory of the Kabbala," *Diogenes* 70 (fall 1972), 61.

102. Benjamin, "Task," 80; "Aufgabe," 67.

103. De Man, "Conclusions," 103.

104. The analogy is drawn in "Theses on the Philosophy of History," in *Illuminations*, 253.

105. Tejaswini Niranjana, *Siting Translation: History, Post-Structuralism, and the Colonial Context* (Berkeley and Los Angeles: University of California Press, 1992), 140.

106. Ibid., 115.

107. Benjamin, "Aufgabe," 69.

108. De Man, "Conclusions," 74.

109. Benjamin, "Task," 80; "Aufgabe," 67.

110. Benjamin, "Task," 79; "Aufgabe," 66. I have retained Benjamin's singular in "the word" that is the primary element of the translator as reflecting more clearly the theologically charged discourse Benjamin echoes here.

111. Walter Benjamin, "Some Reflections on Kafka," trans. Harry Zohn, in *Illuminations*, 144.

112. Robert Alter, *Necessary Angels: Tradition and Modernity in Kafka, Benjamin, and Scholem* (Cambridge: Harvard University Press, 1991), 46. The sentence I quoted continues, "and precisely that transposition is the source of the strain on credence." For Alter, Benjamin's is "not a very persuasive path." While I sympathize with Alter's skepticism in the face of the veneration of Benjamin's "most vatic pronouncements," I do find Benjamin's universalized literalism a coherent alternative to Western theory that is in some ways more persuasive (as well as less ethnocentric) than the Hebrew-based literalism of more traditional Jewish approaches to translation. It is part of the project of this chapter to make this case, and I will not repeat it here.

113. Benjamin, "Aufgabe," 68. The Rudolf Pannwitz citation is from *Krisis der europäischen Kultur* (Munich: H. Carl, 1921).

114. Benjamin, "Task," 76-77; "Aufgabe," 63-64.

115. Benjamin, "Task," 77; "Aufgabe," 64.

CHAPTER FIVE

1. Novick compares the Holocaust to other historical events that were publicly discussed largely in the first few years after they occurred. "With the Holocaust," he writes, "the rhythm has been very different: hardly talked about for the first twenty years or so after World War II; then, from the 1970s on, becoming ever more central in American public discourse—particularly, of course, among Jews, but also in the culture at large" (*The Holocaust in American Life* (Boston: Mariner Books, 1999), 1-2. Mintz writes, "For a brief moment immediately after the war, graphic newsreel footage taken by U.S. Signal Corps photographers when the army units liberated the camps was shown in American movie houses. But soon afterward, the murder of European Jewry was consigned to the category of evils that had been decisively crushed by the American victory" (*Popular Culture and the Shaping of Holocaust Memory in America* (Seattle: University of Washington Press, 2001), 5.

2. Annie Romein-Verschoor, *Omzien in verwondering. Herinneringen van Annie Romein-Verschoor*, Ger Harmsen (Amsterdam, 1971), 2:109, cited in Gerrold Van Der Stroom, "The Diaries, Het Achterhuis and the Translations," in *The Diary of Anne Frank: The Critical Edition*, ed. David Barnouw and Gerrold Van Der Stroom (New York: Doubleday, 1989), 67.

3. As Levi writes, "The manuscript was turned down by a number of important publishers; it was accepted in 1947 by a small publisher who printed only 2,500 copies and then folded. So this first book of mine fell into oblivion for many years: perhaps also because in all of Europe those were difficult times of mourning and reconstruction and the public did not want to return in memory to the painful years of the war that had just ended" ("Afterword: The Author's Answers to His Readers' Questions," in *If This Is a Man/The Truce*, trans. Stuart Woolf (London: Abacus Books, 1987), 381.

4. Eliezer Vizel [Elie Wiesel], *Un di velt hot geshvign* (And the world kept silent) (Buenos Aires: Central Organization of Polish Jews in Argentina, 1956), 245.

5. Gerd Korman, "The Holocaust in American Historical Writing," *Societas* 2 (summer 1972): 250-70.

6. Jeffrey Shandler, *While America Watches: Televising the Holocaust* (Oxford: Oxford University Press, 1999), 23.

7. The term was first popularized, to my knowledge, by Lawrence Langer, in an often-quoted essay entitled

"The Americanization of the Holocaust on Stage and Screen," in *From Hester Street to Hollywood: The Jewish-American Stage and Screen*, ed. Sarah Blacher Cohen (Bloomington: University of Indiana Press, 1983), 213-30.

8. In Sh[merke] Kaczerginski, *The Destruction of Jewish Vilna* (Yiddish) (New York: United Vilner Relief Committee, 1947), 56-57, cited in Ruth R. Wisse, *The Modern Jewish Canon: A Journey through Language and Culture* (New York: Free Press, 2000), 191.

9. David G. Roskies, *The Jewish Search for a Usable Past* (Bloomington: Indiana University Press, 1999), 39. According to Roskies, the last six issues of the *Oyneg Shabes* group were in Polish.

10. Walter Benjamin, "The Task of the Translator," trans. Harry Zohn, in *Illuminations: Essays and Reflections*, ed. Hannah Arendt (New York: Schocken, 1968), 71; "Die Aufgabe des Übersetzers," in *Illuminationen* (Frankfurt am Main: Suhrkamp, 1969), 58.

11. Primo Levi, *The Truce* (in *If This Is a Man/The Truce*), 226-227.

12. Millicent Marcus, *After Fellini: National Cinema in the Postmodern Age* (Baltimore: Johns Hopkins University Press, 2002), 256.

13. André Lefevere, *Translation, Rewriting and the Manipulation of Literary Fame* (New York: Routledge, 1992), 57.

14. Ibid., 8.

15. *The Diary of Anne Frank*, by Frances Goodrich and Albert Hackett (New York: Random House, 1956), 168.

16. Roskies, *Jewish Search*, 35.

17. See David Barnouw, "Attacks on the Authenticity of the Diary," in Barnouw and Van Der Stroom, *Critical Edition*, 87-88.

18. Elie Wiesel, "The Holocaust as Literary Inspiration," in *Dimensions of the Holocaust*, ed. Lacey Baldwin Smith (Chicago: Northwestern University Press, 1977), 9.

19. James Young, *Writing and Rewriting the Holocaust: Narrative and the Consequences of Interpretation* (Bloomington: University of Indiana Press, 1990), 21.

20. Mintz, *Popular Culture*, 39 (emphasis added).

21. Young, *Writing and Rewriting*, 89. Young's primary interlocutor in this section seems to be Alvin Rosenfeld, who writes that "There are no metaphors for Auschwitz, just as Auschwitz is not a metaphor for anything else. . . . Why is this the case? Because the flames were real flames, the ashes only ashes, the smoke always and only smoke. If one wants 'meaning' out of that, it can only be this: at Auschwitz, humanity incinerated its own heart" *A Double Dying: Reflections on Holocaust Literature* (Bloomington University of Indiana Press, 1980), 180.

22. Mintz, *Popular Culture*, 5.

23. Ibid., 51-52.

24. Elie Wiesel, *Night*, trans. Stella Rodway (New York: Hill and Wang, 1960); originally published as *La Nuit* (Paris: Minuit, 1958).

25. The term is from Juliane House, *Translation Quality Assessment: A Model Revisited* (Tübingen: Narr, 1997), 69.

26. For publication information on these pamphlets and other defamations of the diary, see Barnouw, "Attacks," 84-101.

27. Levi, *If This Is a Man/The Truce* (London: Publisher, 1979), 72, quoted in Young, *Writing and Rewriting*, 21.

28. Vizel, *Un di velt*, 7.

29. Young, *Writing and Rewriting*, 21.

30. Werner Schwarz, *Principles and Problems of Bible Translation: Some Reformation Controversies and their Background* (Cambridge: Cambridge University Press, 1955), 15.

31. Justin Martyr, *Dialogue with Trypho the Jew*, trans. A. Lukyn Williams (London: Society for the Promotion of Christian Knowledge, 1930), 73.

32. Willis Barnstone, *The Poetics of Translation: History, Theory, Practice* (New Haven: Yale University Press, 1993), 141 (emphasis original).

33. Douglas Robinson, *Translation and Taboo* (Dekalb: Northern Illinois University Press, 1996), 79.

34. These and other changes to the initial manuscript are discussed in Van Der Stroom, "The Diaries," 62-69.

35. Lawrence Graver, *An Obsession with Anne Frank: Meyer Levin and the Diary* (Berkeley and Los Angeles: University of California Press, 1995), 95.

36. Novick, *Holocaust in American Life,* 118 (emphasis added).

37. Philo, *On the Life of Moses* 2.6.36, in *The Works of Philo,* trans. C. D. Yonge (N.p.: Hendrickson, 1993), 494.

38. Novick, *Holocaust in American Life,* 115–16.

39. As an unnamed local American Jewish Congress leader said in a public speech, "Hitler felt that only by eradicating the Jews could he succeed in his campaign to destroy Judeo-Christian civilization and supplant it with primeval paganism" (radio broadcast for Rochester, New York, November 15, 1948, American Jewish Committee Papers, Box 49, quoted ibid., 116.

40. Levin's argument with the Hacketts and Otto Frank is discussed in Sander L. Gilman, "The Dead Child Speaks: Reading *The Diary of Anne Frank,*" in *A Scholarly Look at the Diary of Anne Frank,* ed. Harold Bloom (Philadelphia: Chelsea House, 1999), 46–50. The story of Levin's long struggle with Otto Frank and the Broadway producers of the Diary is also the subject of Lawrence Graver's full-length treatment, *An Obsession,* as well Levin's own aptly titled *The Obsession* (New York: Simon and Schuster, 1973).

41. Cynthia Ozick, "Who Owns Anne Frank?" *Quarrel and Quandary* (New York: Vintage, 2001), 102.

42. *Megillat Ta'anit Batra* 12.10; see n. 61 in the Introduction above for a discussion of its dating.

43. For a comprehensive analysis of this editing process, see Lefevere, *Translation,* 59–73.

44. Barnouw and Van Der Stroom, *Critical Edition; Anne Frank, The Diary of a Young Girl (the Definitive Edition),* ed. Otto H. Frank and Mirjam Pressler, trans. Susan Massotty (New York: Doubleday/Anchor, 1995).

45. Moreover, as in many of the controversies over Bible translation, arguments about the reworking of the memoirs of both Anne Frank and Elie Wiesel have come down to the difference between "word-for-word" and "sense-for-sense" translations—these slippery distinctions, for instance, played a part in the Stielau trial. The 1959 Schleswig-Holstein trial that prosecuted Lothar Stielau for libel, defamation, and slander against the Diary and Otto Frank, and which began with the confused, and malicious, accusation that Meyer Levin had written the Diary, led to the calling of expert witnesses to judge the authenticity of the German translation. While Dr. Annemarie Hübner testified that the Diary had been "faithfully translated," Stielau's lawyers drew on Hübner's finding that there were indeed some changes to argue that the translation was not an authentic "document," since "a document must be authentic word for word, or else it is not a document" (Noack and Noack to examining magistrate, July 29, 1960, Lübeck Landgericht, quoted in Barnouw, "Attacks," 88). The charge that Levin wrote *The Diary of Anne Frank* has a recent echo that strikes uncomfortably close: as part of an attempt to discredit Wiesel's Holocaust testimony, the Holocaust revisionist (or "minimizer") David O'Connell mangles my own research (which he seems not to have actually read) to argue that Mauriac had an "active role in the redaction of *La Nuit*" ("Elie Wiesel and the Catholics," *Culture Wars* 23, no. 11, November 2004, 27).

46. For "a (far from exhaustive) sampling" of recent accusations of the betrayal and mistreatment of Anne Frank's Diary, see Novick, *Holocaust,* 310 n. 56.

47. *Der Spiegel,* April 1, 1959, quoted in Van Der Stroom, "The Diaries," 73.

48. Zev Garber, "Why Do We Call the Holocaust 'The Holocaust'? An Inquiry into the Psychology of Labels," in *Shoah: The Paradigmatic Genocide; Essays in Exegesis and Eisegesis* (Lanham, Md.: University Press of America, 1994), 57.

49. Ibid., 61.

50. Elie Wiesel, "The First Survivor," Statement for the Niles Township Jewish Congregation, Skokie, Illinois, December 7, 1980, quoted ibid., 57. As Garber notes, similar statements have appeared in various other interviews, addresses, and essays.

51. David Roskies, *Against the Apocalypse: Responses to Catastrophe in Modern Jewish Culture* (Cambridge: Harvard University Press, 1984), 261.

52. Berel Lang, *Act and Idea in the Nazi Genocide* (Chicago: University of Chicago Press, 1990), xxi.

53. Garber, "Why?" 55. Garber continues, "Even more seriously, the sacrificial connotation of 'holocaust' also implies a third party to this 'ceremony,'—He to whom the sacrifice is offered: God, Himself."

54. Ibid., 62.

55. David Roskies, explaining the Israeli preference for the term *shoah* over *ḥurban,* writes that *shoah,* a biblical word "meaning ruin, calamity, desolation, was reintroduced into modern Hebrew by poets and politicians as early as 1940 to impress upon their audiences the enormity of the destruction of Europe; but after the war, *shoah* came to mean a unique transformational event that establishes a new relationship between God and his-

tory. Once Israelis, like English-speaking Jews, were caught up in a new historical era, they had no use for a term like *ḥurban/khurbm*, which harks back to a string of past catastrophes" (*Against the Apocalypse*, 261).

56. G. W. Bowersock, *Hellenism in Late Antiquity* (Ann Arbor: University of Michigan Press, 1990), 5.

57. Jan Assmann, "Translating Gods: Religion as a Factor of Cultural (Un)Translatability," in *The Translation of Cultures: Figurations of the Space Between*, ed. Sanford Budick and Wolfgang Iser (Stanford, Calif.: Stanford University Press, 1996), 33-34.

58. Paula Fredriksen, *From Jesus to Christ: The Origins of the New Testament Images of Christ*, 2nd ed. (New Haven: Yale University Press, 2000), 13.

59. Goodrich and Hackett, *Diary*, 48. For an analysis of *theokrasia* and its late antique variants, see Assmann, "Translating Gods," 34.

60. Ibid., 36.

61. Wiesel, *Night* (1960), 32.

62. A. M. Dalbray, "Les juifs des Silence," *Amif* (November 1967): 1771, quoted in Ellen Fine, *The Legacy of Night: The Literary Universe of Elie Wiesel* (Albany: SUNY Press, 1982), 30.

63. Elie Wiesel, "An Interview Unlike Any Other," in *A Jew Today*, trans. Marion Wiesel (New York: Vintage, 1979), 15.

64. Ibid., 19.

65. Wiesel, *Night* (1960), 109; *Nuit*, 127.

66. Elie Wiesel, *All Rivers Run to the Sea: Memoirs* (New York: Knopf, 1995), 239.

67. Many of these works can now be acquired through the National Yiddish Book Center in Amherst, Massachusetts, which is committed to "rescuing" Yiddish books and making them available again at reasonable prices.

68. Y. Palatitzky, review of Jonas Turkow's *Extinguished Stars* in *Dos Neye Vort* (Buenos Aires, 1955); reprinted in Eliezer Vizel, *Un di velt*, 253.

69. Wiesel writes in *All Rivers*, "I had cut down the original manuscript from 862 pages to the 245 of the published Yiddish edition. [French publisher Jérôme] Lindon edited *La Nuit* down to 178" (319). But his earlier description of writing the Yiddish manuscript implies that no revisions were made of the pages he had frantically scribbled "without rereading" (239) before handing them over to the publisher. Wiesel also complains that the original manuscipt of *Un di velt* was never returned to him. These confusing reports on the various versions of *Night* have generated a chain of similarly confusing critical comments. Thus, Ellen Fine reports (*Legacy of Night*, 7) that the Yiddish version of *Night* is more than 800 pages long, whereas David Roskies states (*Against the Apocalypse*, 301) that "the original Yiddish version is not only four times longer and less unified than its French (and later English) version, but has a different message." It is not clear to me whether Roskies is mistaken about the length or is speaking of the unpublished manuscript, which Wiesel implies was lost. Nor does the preface to the 2006 edition clarify matters. Wiesel writes that after numerous cuts, "The original Yiddish still was long" (Preface to *Night* [2006], x) and required further editing. Were these cuts to the published Yiddish version or to some never-published longer manuscript? And if they were cuts to the Yiddish book, why would that version, at 245 pages, have been too long for publication?

70. Vizel, *Un di velt*, 7. The critics faithfully echo this description, virtually always referring to Sighet as a "shtetl" (see Fine, *Legacy of Night*, 8). Mauriac also calls Sighet "a little Transvlvanian town" in his foreword to *Night* (1960), viii.

71. Vizel, *Un di velt*, 7. Wiesel describes his French publisher's objections to his documentary approach in *All Rivers* (319): "Lindon was unhappy with my probably too abstract manner of introducing the subject. Nor was he enamored of two pages which sought to describe the premises and early phases of the tragedy. Testimony from survivors tends to begin with these sorts of descriptions, evoking loved ones as well as one's hometown before the annihilation, as if breathing life into them one last time."

72. Vizel, *Un di velt*, [v].

73. Wiesel ascribes the choice of the title *La Nuit* to Lindon's editing (*All Rivers*, 319).

74. Vizel, *Un di velt*, 244. The French and English versions are very close.

75. Ibid.

76. Wiesel, *La Nuit*, 178.

77. Wiesel, *Night* (1960), 109.

78. Vizel, *Un di velt*, 244–45. This passage is also partially reproduced, in a somewhat different translation, in *All Rivers Run to the Sea*, 320.

79. Roskies, *Against the Apocalypse*, 301.

80. Mauriac, Foreword to *Night* (1960), ix.

81. Ibid., vi.

82. Ibid., vii–viii.

83. Ibid., viii.

84. Ibid., ix.

85. Mauriac's hierarchy of outrages, in which the loss of faith ranks as worse than the extinguishing of life, appears in similar form among other theologians of the Holocaust. As Amos Funkenstein points out, the privileging of religious-theological concerns over the importance of human life, any human life, historically has been both dangerous and unethical. Commenting on post-Holocaust theologians' Heideggerian interest in what he calls "a chimera of the authentic self," Funkenstein writes: "A commitment to higher values above the sanctity of the individual not only distracts from the study of man, but can and did lead to abuses and crimes of much greater extent than selfish self-interest ever perpetrated. Granted, this is not a necessary consequence of commitments to absolutes, but it has often enough been so. Now it matters little whether the higher values were transcendental or immanent, God, fatherland, race, or the ideal society of the future. In the name of all of them crusades were fought, genocides committed, persons murdered" ("Theological Responses to the Holocaust," in *Perceptions of Jewish History* [Berkeley and Los Angeles: University of California Press, 1993], 335).

86. Mauriac, Foreword, x–xi.

87. Ibid., viii.

88. Wiesel, "Interview Unlike," 16.

89. Ibid.

90. Ibid., 17.

91. Ibid., 18.

92. Ibid., 19.

93. For a fascinating discussion of post-Holocaust Jewish revenge (and its absence or sublimation), see Berel Lang, "Holocaust Memory and Revenge: The Presence of the Past," *Jewish Social Studies* 2, no. 2 (1996): 1–20.

94. Elie Wiesel, "To a Young Palestinian Arab," in *A Jew Today*, 126–27.

95. Edward Wyatt, "Oprah's Book Club Turns to Elie Wiesel's 'Night,'" *New York Times*, January 16, 2006; the correction appeared on January 19.

96. Wiesel, Preface to the New Translation, *Night*, trans. Marion Wiesel (New York: Hill and Wang, 2006), x.

97. Wiesel, "An Interview," 19.

98. Wiesel, Preface to the New Translation, xiii.

99. Edward Wyatt, "The Translation of Wiesel's 'Night' Is New, but Old Questions Are Raised," *New York Times*, January 19, 2006.

100. Wiesel, Preface to the New Translation, x.

101. Wyatt, "Translation." The relevant references are to *Night* (1960), 28, and *Night* (2006), 30.

102. Daniel R. Schwarz, *Imagining the Holocaust* (New York: St. Martin's Press, 1999), 50.

103. Wiesel, *Night* (1960), 28.

104. Wiesel, "Holocaust as Literary Inspiration," 5.

105. Mauriac, Foreword, *Night* (1960); references to "the child" or "the Jewish child" on viii, ix, x, and xi. Reference to the passivity of the Transylvanian Jews on viii.

106. This is apparent, as well, in the characteristics shared by the highly publicized retranslations of Holocaust narrative and the films rereleased in "Director's Cut," or the boxed CD sets of popular musicians, all of which both satisfy consumer desires for completeness and reenergize the market for otherwise too-familiar cultural products.

107. Vizel, *Un di velt*, 245; Wiesel, Preface to the New Translation, x.

108. Naomi Seidman, "Elie Wiesel and the Scandal of Jewish Rage," *Jewish Social Studies* 3, no. 1 (1996): 16.

109. Ron Rosenbaum, *Explaining Hitler* (New York: HarperCollins, 1998), 361 (emphasis original).

110. I adopt the term from Anita Norich's discussion of the Yiddish–English self-translations of Isaac Bashevis Singer as well as Singer's own reported usage of it. ("Isaac Bashevis Singer in America: The Translation Problem," in *Judaism* 44: 2 [spring 1995], 208). See also chapter 6 below, n. 18.

111. Eli Pfefferkorn and David H. Hirsch, "Shedding New Light on Wiesel's 'Night,'" Letter to the Editor, *Forward* (November 1, 1996).

112. Jean-François Lyotard, *Heidegger and "the jews,"* trans. Andreas Michel and Mark S. Roberts (Minneapolis: University of Minnesota Press, 1990), 27-28. Lyotard cites Wiesel, *Night* (1960), 19.

113. There are others that fit this description, particularly the 1999 Peter Kassevitz film *Jakob the Liar,* which explores remarkably similar terrain.

114. David Denby, *The New Yorker,* March 15, 1999, 99.

115. Hilene Flanzbaum, "But Wasn't It Terrific? A Defense of Liking *Life Is Beautiful,*" *Yale Journal of Criticism* 14, no. 1 (2001): 283.

116. Marcus, *After Fellini,* 269.

117. Sidra DeKoven Ezrahi, "After Such Knowledge, What Laughter?" *Yale Journal of Criticism* 14, no. 1 (2001): 293.

118. Ibid., 294.

119. Marcus, *After Fellini,* 271.

120. Roberto Benigni and Vincenzo Cerami, *Life Is Beautiful* [la vita è bella], trans. Lisa Taruschio (New York: Hyperion/Miramax, 1998), 109-10.

121. Ibid., 110.

122. Marcus, *After Fellini,* 277.

123. Franz Kafka, "On Parables," in *Parables and Paradoxes,* ed. Nahum N. Glatzer (New York: Schocken, 1958), 11.

CHAPTER SIX

1. Cynthia Ozick, "Envy; or, Yiddish in America," in *The Pagan Rabbi and Other Stories* (New York: E.P. Dutton, 1983), 51.

2. Ibid., 44.

3. Ibid., 75.

4. Ibid., 42.

5. Anita Norich, "Isaac Bashevis Singer in America: The Translation Problem," *Judaism* 44, no. 2 (spring 1995): 209.

6. David Roskies mentions Glatstein as the rival to Singer in a roundtable discussion of Isaac Bashevis Singer, perhaps because Glatstein was "one of Singer's fiercest critics" and Glatstein's name is so close to Edelshtein—*glat* means smooth, while *edl* means gentle or noble. See "The Achievement of Isaac Bashevis Singer: A Roundtable Discussion," in *Singer: An Album,* ed. Ilan Stavans (New York: Library of America, 2004), 70.

7. Yankev Glatshteyn, "Singer's Literary Reputation," *Congress Bi-Weekly* 32 (December 27, 1965): 17, repr. in *Recovering the Canon: Essays on Isaac Bashevis Singer,* ed. David Neal Miller (Leiden: Brill, 1986), 145.

8. Alana Newhouse, "Dissent Greets Isaac Bashevis Singer Centennial," the *New York Times,* June 17, 2004.

9. Irving Saposnik, "A Canticle for Isaac: A *Kaddish* for Bashevis," in *The Hidden Isaac Bashevis Singer,* ed. Seth Wolitz (Austin: University of Texas Press, 2001), 4-5.

10. Ozick, "Envy," 41.

11. David Roskies, Introduction to "Special Issue on Isaac Bashevis Singer," *Prooftexts* 9 (1989): 3.

12. Norich, "Singer in America," 209.

13. Gershom Scholem, "Zum Problem der Übersetzung aus dem Jidischen: Auch eine Buchbesprechung," *Jüdische Rundschau* 23, no. 2 (January 12, 1917): 16, repr. in Gershom Scholem, *Tagebücher* (Frankfurt am Main: Jüdischer Verlag, 2000), 1:495.

14. Ibid., 496.

15. Ozick, "Envy," 82.

16. Ibid., 74.

17. Norich, "Singer in America," 209.

18. In an interview with Irving Buchen, *Isaac Bashevis Singer and the Eternal Past* (New York: NYU Press, 1968), ix, quoted in Seth L. Wolitz, "*Satan in Goray* as Parable," *Prooftexts* 9 (1989), 14. Wolitz's disapproval of Singer's attitude toward the translation of his work into English is palpable: "Singer appears to downgrade the Yiddish or at least make the 'second original' coequal if not superior! . . . The 'new American' text instantly loses its Yiddish contextual setting, its original readership, its Yiddish literary tradition and is transmogrified into an American-language original devoid of almost any culturally privileged reader" (ibid.).

19. Timothy Brennan, *Salman Rushdie and the Third World: Myths of the Nation* (New York: St. Martin's, 1989), viii, 37, quoted in Anuradha Dingwaney, Introduction to *Between Languages and Cultures: Translation and Cross-Cultural Texts*, ed. Anuradha Dingwaney and Carol Maier (Pittsburgh: University of Pittsburgh Press, 1995), 5.

20. Edward W. Said, "Embargoed Literature," in Dingwaney and Maier, *Between Languages and Cultures*, 99.

21. Mahasweta Sengupta, "Translation, Colonialism and Poetics: Rabindranath Tagore in Two Worlds," in *Translation, History and Culture*, ed. Susan Bassnett and Andre Lefevere (London: Pinter, 1990), 58.

22. Isaac Bashevis Singer, "Problems of Yiddish Prose in America," trans. Robert H. Wolf, *Prooftexts* 9 (1989): 8. Yiddish original, 1943.

23. Ibid., 9-10.

24. Ibid., 12.

25. Glatshteyn, "Singer's Literary Reputation," 146.

26. Isaac Bashevis Singer, "Gimpel the Fool," trans. Saul Bellow, in *The Collected Stories* (New York: Farrar, Straus, Giroux, 1983), 3.

27. Singer, "Gimpl tam," in *Der shpigl un andere dertseylungen*, ed. Khone Shmeruk (Jerusalem: Hebrew University, 1974), 35.

28. Sidra DeKoven Ezrahi, "State and Real Estate: Territoriality and the Modern Jewish Imagination," in *A New Jewry? America since the Second World War*, ed. Peter Medding, Studies in Contemporary Jewry 8. (New York: Oxford University Press, 1992), 51.

29. Norich, "Singer in America," 213. See also Shmeruk, Introduction to *Der shpigl*, xxxv.

30. Strangely enough, critics with no access to Yiddish have mistakenly claimed that the ambiguity about Gimpel's status as both fool and sage is signaled in the title and first line of the story, "where the epithet used is '*chochem*' or 'sage,' which often has the ironic meaning of 'fool'" (Paul N. Siegel, "Gimpel and the Archetype of the Wise Fool," in *The Achievement of Isaac Bashevis Singer*, ed. Marcia Allentuck [Carbondale: Southern Illinois University Press, 1969], 160). This misstatement is duly repeated in Lawrence S. Friedman, *Understanding Isaac Bashevis Singer* (Columbia: University of South Carolina Press, 1988),189.

31. Norich, "Singer in America," 213.

32. For a discussion of the translation of "Gimpel the Fool" into German and its reception in Germany, see Leslie Morris, "1968: The Translation of Isaac Bashevis Singer's *Gimpel der Narr* Appears in the Federal Republic of Germany," in *Yale Companion to Jewish Writing and Thought in German Culture, 1096-1996*, ed. Sander L. Gilman and Jack Zipes (New Haven: Yale University Press, 1997), 742-48.

33. Janet Hadda, *Isaac Bashevis Singer: A Life* (New York: Oxford University Press, 1997), 130.

34. Singer, "Gimpel the Fool," 7.

35. Singer, "Gimpl tam," 38.

36. Sheldon Grebstein, "Singer's Shrewd Gimpel: Bread and Childbirth," in Miller, *Recovering the Canon*, 58-65. Nancy Tenfelde Clasby picks up on Grebstein's analysis, further suggesting that Gimpel's breadmaking be understood in the light of "the manna sent to the wanderers in the desert, the Passover bread, the miraculous widow's loaf that sustains Elijah and with other biblical images of bread as signs of divine providence" ("Gimpel's Wisdom: I. B. Singer's Vision of the 'True World,'" *Studies in American Jewish Literature* 15 [1996]: 91). Thomas Hennings, in "Singer's 'Gimpel the Fool' and The Book of Hosea," *Journal of Narrative Technique* 13, no. 1 (winter 1983), associates Gimpel—more interestingly, to my mind—with the prophet Hosea, who marries "a

woman of harlotry," is cuckolded, divorces his wife, and is reunited with her. By this analogy, Gimpel is not a parable for the Jewish people but rather for God, in His foolish love for undeserving Israel.

37. Paul Kresh, *Isaac Bashevis Singer: The Magician of West 86th Street* (New York: Dial Press, 1979), 204. Gimpel's credulity is viewed somewhat less sympathetically by Ruth R. Wisse, who suggests that it parallels the inability of Jews "to face reality" under the Nazi threat (*The Schlemiel as Modern Hero* [Chicago: University of Chicago Press, 1971], 66–67).

38. Grebstein, "Singer's Shrewd Gimpel," 65.

39. Ibid.

40. Singer, "Gimpel the Fool," 4; "Gimpl tam," 34.

41. Singer, "Gimpel the Fool," 14; "Gimpl tam," 46.

42. Kresh, *Singer,* 203.

43. Isaac Bashevis Singer, *Nobel Lecture* (New York: Farrar, Straus, Giroux, 1979), 29.

44. Roskies, "Achievement," 110.

45. Singer, "Gimpel the Fool," 3.

46. Yitskhok Bashevis, "Zaydlus der ershter," in *Der sotn in Goray un andere dertseylungen* (New York: Matones, 1943), 280; Isaac Bashevis Singer, "Zeidlus the Pope," trans. Joel Blocker and Elizabeth Pollet, in *The Collected Stories* (New York: Farrar, Strauss, Giroux, 1983), 175.

47. David Roskies, *A Bridge of Longing: The Lost Art of Jewish Storytelling* (Cambridge: Harvard University Press, 1995), 280.

48. Joseph Sherman, "Bashevis/Singer and the Jewish Pope," in Wolitz, *Hidden Singer,* 25.

49. Roskies, *Bridge of Longing,* 289.

50. Bashevis [Singer], "Zaydlus," 277; Singer, "Zeidlus," 172.

51. Bashevis [Singer], "Zaydlus," 279; Singer, "Zeidlus," 174.

52. Bashevis [Singer], "Zaydlus," 282; Singer, "Zeidlus," 175–76.

53. Bashevis [Singer], "Zaydlus," 286; Singer, "Zeidlus," 178.

54. Sherman mentions "Der yiddisher poypst," in *Mayse-bukh* (Basel, 1602); Ayzik-Meyer Dik, *R. Shimen Barbun der rabiner fun maynts; oder, der drayfakher troym* (Vilna: Rom Press, 1874); and "Der yiddisher poypst: a historishe dertseylung," in Yehiel Yeshaya Trunk, *Kvaln un beymer* (New York: Unzer Tsayt, 1958) (Sherman, "Bashevis/Singer"), 25.

55. Ibid., 13.

56. Roskies, *Bridge of Longing,* 289.

57. Ibid., 304–5.

58. Sherman, "Bashevis/Singer," 16.

59. Ibid.

60. Ibid.

61. Although Joel Blocker and Elizabeth Pollet have not, to my knowledge, published an account of their work with Singer, another of Singer's translators has; see Dvorah Telushkin, *Master of Dreams: A Memoir of Isaac Bashevis Singer* (New York: Morrow, 1997), esp. 44–50. See also Singer's statement:

> I have translated these stories with the assistance of collaborators, and I find that I do much revision in the process of translation. It is not an exaggeration to say that over the years English has become my "second" language. It is also a fact that the foreign-language editions of my novels and stories have been translated from the English.
>
> My translators, whose names appear at the end of each story in this book, are not only my first readers but also my first constructive (I hope) critics. . . . The "other" language in which the author's work must be rendered . . . is often the mirror in which we have a chance to see ourselves with all our imperfections and, if possible, to correct some of our mistakes.

Isaac Bashevis Singer, Author's note, *A Friend of Kafka and Other Stories* (New York: Farrar, Straus & Giroux, 1970), 3.

62. For a discussion of free indirect discourse, see Shlomith Rimmon-Kenan, *Narrative Fiction: Contemporary Poetics* (London: Methuen, 1983), 110–16.

63. Bashevis [Singer], "Zaydlus," 284.

64. Bashevis [Singer], "Zaydlus," 280; Singer, "Zeidlus," 175.

65. Bashevis [Singer], "Zaydlus," 281; Singer, "Zeidlus," 175.

66. Bashevis [Singer], "Zaydlus," 279.

67. Singer, "Zeidlus," 174.

68. Roskies, *Bridge of Longing*, 286. Roskies seems to be referring to Singer's manifesto on Yiddish writing in America, which called for a return to the traditional Yiddish of Eastern Europe over the deracinated American variety.

69. Bashevis [Singer], "Zaydlus," 286; Singer, "Zeidlus," 178.

70. Shalom Rosenberg, *Good and Evil in Jewish Thought* (Hebrew) (Jerusalem: Ministry of Defense, 1985), 100-101, quoted in David Levine Lerner, "The Enduring Legend of the Jewish Pope," *Judaism* 40, no. 2 (spring 1991): 168.

71. Singer, "Zeidlus," 178.

72. Ibid., 175.

73. Bashevis [Singer], "Zaydlus," 281 Because *kusi* (Samaritan) is a common rabbinic circumlocution for Gentile, the censorship of this phrase in the English actually represents a *doubling* of the censorship of the rabbinic text. I thank Saul Friedman for noting this point.

74. Sherman, "Bashevis/Singer," 25.

EPILOGUE

1. Johann Andreas Eisenmenger (1654-1704) completed *Entdecktes Judenthum* in 1700, but its publication was held up for eighteen years by a group of Jews who feared it would lead to violent unrest and lobbied the authorities to delay publication.

2. Scholem came close to saying this in print in a critique of the apologetic scholarship of *Wissenschaft des Judentums*, writing that the significance of the establishment of the state of Israel was that "the Jewish people can try to solve its problems without any squinting to the left or to the right; it can pose the question of confrontation of Jews and non-Jews; it can approach the clarification of all the historical and spiritual issues pending between Jews and Gentiles. Such problems can now be taken up and discussed, independent of what anyone else may have to say on the subject and without any regard for external considerations" ("The Science of Judaism—Then and Now," trans. Michael A. Meyer, in *The Messianic Idea in Judaism and Other Essays in Jewish Spirituality* (New York: Schocken, 1971), 311. Jacob Katz similarly discusses the censorship of the anti-Christian language in Jewish martyrologies by later German-Jewish scholars and translators in *Exclusiveness and Tolerance: Jewish-Gentile Relations in Medieval and Modern Times* (New York: Schocken, 1969), 89.

3. Sidra DeKoven Ezrahi, *Diaspora: Homelands in Exile*, with photographs by Frederic Brenner (San Francisco: Bloomsbury, 2004), 99.

Index